Multi-Tiered Systems of Support in Elementary Schools

Multi-Tiered Systems of Support in Elementary Schools is the leadership handbook and practitioner's field guide to implementation of Multi-Tiered Systems of Support (MTSS) in elementary schools, leading to improved student outcomes and school safety. Schools can creatively customize replicable best practices using this in-depth operations manual to guide MTSS teams in planning and delivering tiers of academic and integrated social-emotional and behavioral supports to meet the needs of all students. This text introduces *Healthy Minds, Safe Schools*, an evidence-based program that significantly improves student well-being, school safety, and teacher feelings of self-efficacy for delivering social-emotional and behavioral curriculum in the classroom.

Featuring team exercises and real perspectives from educators, this text shows how to make incremental yet manageable changes at elementary schools in accordance with public policy mandates and evidence-based practices by developing smart teams and programs, identifying roles and responsibilities, implementing layers of academic support and services, improving social-emotional and behavioral health of students, and creating an inclusive school culture. It details organizational psychology and socially just educational practices and is a handbook aligned with the U.S. Secret Service National Threat Assessment Center guidebook for preventing school violence and with the National Center for School Mental Health Curriculum.

Alison G. Clark, EdS, is a school psychologist in high-risk inner-city schools. She has expertise in mental health in schools, family wellness, positive behavioral instructional supports, Multi-Tiered Systems of Support, threat assessment, crisis response, and systems change.

Katherine A. Dockweiler, EdD, is a policy researcher and practicing school psychologist. Her particular interests include program design and evaluation as well as advocacy and education policy analysis.

Multi-Tiered Systems of Support in Elementary Schools

The Definitive Guide to Effective Implementation and Quality Control

Alison G. Clark and
Katherine A. Dockweiler

NEW YORK AND LONDON

First published 2020
by Routledge
52 Vanderbilt Avenue, New York, NY 10017

and by Routledge
2 Park Square, Milton Park, Abingdon, Oxon, OX14 4RN

Routledge is an imprint of the Taylor & Francis Group, an informa business

© 2020 Taylor & Francis

The right of Alison G. Clark and Katherine A. Dockweiler to be identified as authors of this work has been asserted by them in accordance with sections 77 and 78 of the Copyright, Designs and Patents Act 1988.

All rights reserved. No part of this book may be reprinted or reproduced or utilised in any form or by any electronic, mechanical, or other means, now known or hereafter invented, including photocopying and recording, or in any information storage or retrieval system, without permission in writing from the publishers.

Trademark notice: Product or corporate names may be trademarks or registered trademarks, and are used only for identification and explanation without intent to infringe.

Library of Congress Cataloging-in-Publication Data
A catalog record for this book has been requested

ISBN: 978-0-367-22590-2 (hbk)
ISBN: 978-0-367-22591-9 (pbk)
ISBN: 978-0-429-27579-1 (ebk)

Typeset in Bembo
by Apex CoVantage, LLC

In memory of my mother, Esther Reva Gresen, and Alisa Ann Ruch, after whom I was named.—AC

This book is dedicated to my aunt, Teresa A. Nuttelman. Always a leader ahead of her time, always a phenomenal woman.—KD

Contents

List of Illustrations   ix
Foreword   x
Acknowledgments   xiv

Introduction   1

1 New Foundations for Multi-Tiered Systems of Support   4

2 Evaluating Your School's Needs and Building Your Team   27

3 Invest in Resources at Your School   46

4 How to Build Your Program   78

5 How an Academic MTSS Team Works Together   95

6 It Is the Format, Not the Forms   117

7 Special Education Eligibility and Other Considerations   132

8 Early Childhood Recommendations   152

9 Family Engagement   172

10 School Safety and Student Well-Being   194

11 Social-Emotional-Behavioral MTSS   225

12 Program Evaluation and Feedback Looping   249

13 Advocacy and Policy Making   258

14	Troubleshooting Guide	269
15	Moving Forward Together	286
16	Resources and Glossary	300
	Index	310

Illustrations

Table

15.1 Examples of Tiered Components for Academic MTSS and
SEB MTSS 294

Figures

1.1 Multi-Tiered System of Support 7
1.2 Theoretical LIQUID Model 10
2.1 Multiple Layers of Support 32
2.2 School Risk Assessment Survey 40
6.1 Lead Decision Makers at Each Tier 120
11.1 *Healthy Minds, Safe Schools* Model 240
12.1 MTSS Evaluation Frequency and Intensity Framework 252

Foreword

> [I]f you are making mistakes, then you are making new things, trying new things, learning, living, pushing yourself, changing yourself, changing your world. You're doing things you've never done before, and more importantly, you're doing something.
>
> —Neil Gaiman

In 1647, the "Old Deluder Law" was enacted in Massachusetts to promote education among the common people. The first phase of the law revealed its real purpose to forestall Satan, the Old Deluder, from capturing the souls of the populace by depriving them of the opportunity to study the scriptures. By the close of the American Revolution, a growing nation demanded an educated populace. Formal education helped citizens attain material wealth and status in their communities. As the United States grew over the following 100 years, schooling became increasingly necessary for successful industrialization, business methods, scientific achievements, and government operations. In the early 1800s, many state boards of education were enacted. On July 3, 1839, three young women reported for the first formal, teacher training program. Today there are more than 250 colleges in the United States with more than 150,000 students preparing for public and private service teaching primary, secondary, graduate, and postgraduate students.

As America charged into the twentieth century, the United States assimilated more and more immigrants. Education served a paramount role in helping people from a wide diversity of cultures learn American customs. The role of formal education became increasingly important helping millions of immigrants integrate successfully into our society. Furthermore, mandatory education was used to prevent children from entering the workforce absent an education, being taken advantage of, and economically deprived.

As we have entered the twenty-first century, the role of education is again shifting. Rote, drill, memorization, repetition, and regurgitation of factual information have taken a backseat to thinking, reasoning, and executive functioning. Every member of our society has at his or her fingertips the knowledge of the world. Furthermore, this knowledge can be easily "googled." We must change our mindsets about education. We can no longer educate children as we have over the past 250 years and pretend that we are doing something new simply because we have introduced technology into the classroom. Education must find its way from a soft science filled with belief, unproven ideas, and misguided enthusiasm to a scientist-practitioner model in which educators develop, test, modify, and implement effective educational strategies to help today's students maximize their acquisition of knowledge while simultaneously developing their capacities for thinking, reasoning, problem solving, stress hardiness, and resilience.

As educators and school administrators continue to feel the pressure of high-stakes testing on educational practices and strategies, there is an accumulating awareness that the social-emotional dimension of students' lives is equal to if not more critical than academics. Unfortunately, rather than embracing the need to "educate the whole" student, a dichotomy has emerged prompting some educators to perceive that nurturing a student's emotional and social health is somehow exclusive from the task of academic instruction (Brooks, 2004). However, strengthening a student's self-esteem, resilience, stress hardiness, and emotional well-being is not an extra curriculum. A student's sense of belonging, security, and self-confidence provides the essential foundation for the enhanced learning, motivation, and self-discipline required for an educational atmosphere capable of instilling a resilient mind-set in every student. The healthy future of educational institutions is dependent upon their capability to provide social and emotional support hand in hand with academic education (Weist, 2003). A sustainable school environment must be capable of meeting the social, emotional, and academic needs of all students (Elias, Zins, Graczyk, & Weissberg, 2003).

Schools of the future must be capable of simultaneously evaluating and understanding the impact of causal attributions on beliefs about student behavior and required interventions, the manner in which direct and indirect services are combined, the impact of causative beliefs and academic standards on teachers' and administrators' perceptions of effective interventions, and the opportunity for ongoing support from the many consultants and resource personnel available in elementary and secondary schools. Educational interventions implemented with high integrity based on research-proven data are more likely to lead to successful outcomes. Increasingly behavioral, academic, and emotional challenges have an impact on a significant percentage of the school population. Yet only a small percentage of these are served through the Individuals with Disabilities Educational Improvement Act (2004).

Nearly 40 years ago, Kounin (1970) suggested that teachers in both well and poorly managed classrooms respond similarly to student behavior. However, teachers of well-managed classrooms are much more efficient in monitoring student attention and performance, structuring schoolwide activities, and implementing classroom rules and procedures (Gettinger, 1988). Classroom consultation has become an increasingly popular means of providing cost-effective assistance to teachers and students. Research in this area has steadily increased over the past 20 years. Recent trends in education to deal with problems as they occur rather than through a special education maze place an even greater emphasis on in vivo consultation and intervention. When consultants join consultees by framing interventions in a way that is in line with the consultees' mind-set and classroom system, effective change occurs. Consultation involves more than simply providing intervention strategies. Consultation is an ongoing process best implemented by knowledgeable and available support staff.

The body of existing science concerning effective practices and the important impact teachers have on students' acquisition of knowledge, capacity to think and problem solve, and stress hardiness is well demonstrated in the scientific, educational, and psychological research over the past 20 years. For example, teacher behaviors toward students have been found to create classroom conditions in which negative beliefs are minimized and students demonstrate higher math and science achievement (Griggs, Griggs, Rimm-Kaufman, Merritt, & Patton, 2013). Self-regulation in the classroom is enhanced when teachers deftly combine cognitive and affective behavioral/teaching strategies, provide a higher ratio of approving to disapproving comments toward students, utilize a positive emotional tone, and spend the greater proportion of their time guiding and teaching versus managing and supervising (Fuhs, Farran, & Nesbitt, 2013). Finally, high-quality classroom environments are created by teachers who provide students with effective organizational strategies and emotional and instructional support (Curby, Rudasill, & Perez-Edgar, 2011).

Our challenge is to create a viable and sustainable educational system building on the system we have shaped over the past 250 years with an appreciation of what the future holds for our citizens. A sustainable school environment must be capable of meeting the present social, emotional, and academic needs of all students while simultaneously setting goals for academic, citizenship, and life skills for the future. Daniel Siegel points out in his book, *The Developing Mind* (2015), "we are the architects of the way in which experience influences genetically pre-programmed but experienced, dependent, brain development" (p. 112). Our innate drive to help, to achieve mastery, to be connected to others, to treat others and be treated by others fairly, to be motivated by intrinsic rather than extrinsic consequences, and to be instinctually optimistic are all qualities of the human species that can and must be integrated in to the educational system we are building for the next 100 years.

With this foundation in place, it is my honor to author this Introduction of *Multi-Tiered Systems of Support in Elementary Schools*. This is the companion volume to the authors' first work focusing on secondary schools. With 40 years of combined experience, Alison G. Clark and Katherine A. Dockweiler have created a second valuable desk reference and resource for psychologists, educators, and allied health professionals working within elementary schools. These volumes arise from the increasing recognition that a significant group of elementary and secondary school students struggle as a result of mental illness, academic challenges, family conflicts, poverty, and illness. It is still the case that the most in need are often provided with inadequate or ineffective resources. This volume builds on Clark's and Dockweiler's experiences by providing a new theory of multi-tiered support as the foundation for schoolwide service implementation. LIQUID (Leadership, Implementation, Quality control, Universality, Implementation and feedback looping, and Data-based decision making) is designed to address the inequities that are rampant in elementary and secondary schools. This volume provides a nexus for leadership and inclusivity. It is increasingly recognized that multi-tiered systems of support must form the foundation of effective services for youth struggling in all walks of educational experience. As Clark and Dockweiler point out, it is their hope that this volume empowers educators' advocacy and guides them to make the critical changes necessary in our educational system. In doing so, we will prepare every student for their futures and ours.

Sam Goldstein, PhD

References

Brooks, R. (2004). To touch the hearts and minds of students with learning disabilities: The power of mindsets and expectations. *Learning Disabilities: A Contemporary Journal*, 2, 9–18.

Curby, T. W., Rudasill, K. M., & Perez-Edgar, K. (2011). The role of classroom quality in ameliorating the academic and social risks associated with difficult temperament. *School Psychology Quarterly*, 26(2). doi:10.1037/a0023042

Elias, M. J., Zins, J. E., Graczyk, P. A., & Weissberg, R. B. (2003). Implementation, sustainability and scaling up of social, emotional and academic innovations in public schools. *School Psychology Review*, *32*, 303–319.

Fuhs, M. W., Farran, D. C., & Nesbitt, K. T. (2013). Preschool classroom processes as predictors of children's cognitive self-regulation skills development. *APA PsychNet Direct*, 347–359. http://dx.doi.org/10.1037/spq0000031

Gettinger, M. (1988). Methods of proactive classroom management. *School Psychology Review*, *17*, 227–242.

Griggs, M. S., Rimm-Kaufman, S. E., Merritt, E. G., & Patton, C. L. (2013, July 29). The Responsive classroom approach and fifth grade students' math and science anxiety and self-efficacy. *School Psychology Quarterly*. Advance online publication. doi:10.1037/spq0000026

Individuals with Disabilities Education Act (IDEA) of 2004. Pub. L. No. 108–446, 20 U.S.C. § 1400 et seq.

Kounin, J. S. (1970). *Discipline and group management in the classroom*. Melbourne, FL: Krieger.

Neil Gaiman Quotes. (n.d.). BrainyQuote.com. Retrieved October 17, 2019, from BrainyQuote.com Web site: https://www.brainyquote.com/quotes/neil_gaiman_676237

Siegel, D. J. (2015). *The developing mind* (2nd ed.). New York, NY: Guilford Press.

Weist, M. D. (2003). Commentary: Promoting paradigmatic change in child and adolescent mental health and schools. *School Psychology Review*, *32*, 336–341.

Acknowledgments

Thank you, Gary, Noah, and Remi for supporting my work with love, encouragement, understanding, and lots of hugs. Special love to my whole family, including my father, Dr. Arthur Gresen, stepmother, Dorinda, my brilliant and incredible sister, Taylor, and my steadfast big brother, Solomon. I would also like to thank the entire Clark County School District Psychological Services staff, Robert Weires, and all my professional supervisors and mentors, including Ron Jordan (in memory), Melinda Hauret, Laurie Walz, Catherine C. Gardner, and Dr. Jo Velasquez. A special thank-you to the "B.F. Skinner of school psychology," James (Jim) M. Jones, for contributing to the field of school psychology with brilliant insights in student behavior–teacher interactions and discoveries in selective attention, school based social-emotional-behavioral modification techniques, and leadership excellence, while proving to be one of the greatest professional mentors of all time.—AC

This book would not have been made possible without the love of my entire family. Thank you, Audrey and Beau, for your patience and sharing of Mommy to help make schools safer for all children. Thank you to Paul, Ron, and Linda for all your help and support; to Mary for your expertise and listening ear; and to my parents, Greg and Vicki, for always giving all that you have, and more, with love.—KD

Our work would not exist without the support and experiences afforded to us over our many years of working in education. Thank you to the administrators, teachers, school psychologists, and other educators who contributed their voices from the field and offered connections to practice throughout the book. Your perspectives on the daily realities of our children and the systems that we must all navigate, lends authenticity to the work in which we endeavor. Thank you, Ryan Hofmann, Leslie Gallant, Kate Ferman, and their instructional assistants, Erica Buenrostro, Anait Akopyan, and Heather Atkin, for showcasing their inclusive and exceptional early childhood program targeting children living in poverty, modeling best practices, and marrying the strongest teaching elements of both general education and special education. Deep gratitude must be expressed to school principals: Melissa Gutierrez, who had the leadership and vision to take a data-based leap into implementing an integrated Social-Emotional-Behavioral Multi-Tiered Systems of Support (MTSS) model along with her team, Kimberly Conway, Jennifer Renville, Paula Kevish, Michael Abdessian, Shantee Cooper, and Sarah Barber; Dr. Christy K. Beaird, for vision and action in creating and sustaining academic MTSS practices from the early 2000s, which have become a blue-ribbon model of instruction in elementary schools today; and to Lisa Medina, for taking professional risks and a leap of faith to stand by her school psychologist through thick and thin to create a replicable, sustainable, and transferable model of integrated MTSS practices in secondary schools. The L in LIQUID remains the cornerstone of all MTSS efforts, and the individuals mentioned exemplify what it means to Lead.

We would also like to thank the following experts and researchers for their contributions to the field who have helped support, inform, and guide our own work: Dr. Sam Goldstein, Dr. Lindsay Diamond, Dr. Dave Shriberg, Dr. Clay Cook, James M. Jones, Dr. Todd Savage, Jacqueline Eddy, and Wynn Tashman. In addition, special appreciation to Dr. Sam Goldstein for writing our foreword, and Dr. Randy Sprick, Catherine Gardner, Dr. Tonia Holmes-Sutton, Dr. Katherine Lee, James M. Jones, and Meredith Smith for reviewing our original work and believing in us.

Introduction

Our groundbreaking book, *Multi-Tiered Systems of Support in Secondary Schools: The Definitive Guide to Effective Implementation and Quality Control* (Routledge, 2019), is a firsthand account of collective experiences in starting, growing, and sustaining integrated Multi-Tiered Systems of Support (MTSS) in secondary schools. The story continues with *Multi-Tiered Systems of Support in Elementary Schools: The Definitive Guide to Effective Implementation and Quality Control* (Routledge, 2020), and we are delighted to share our MTSS implementation guide for elementary school leaders and change agents, along with our latest advancements in the emerging science of school safety, with implementation requirements and outcome data from our Social-Emotional-Behavioral (SEB) MTSS model, *Healthy Minds, Safe Schools*. This elementary textbook combines best practices in education, organizational psychology, implementation science, school psychology, and educational leadership with practical lessons learned from experience, professional issues in the field, and reflections of culture in education and challenges of current times. It also provides evidence for educators to make advocacy and policy a personal and professional priority, as well as an ethical and moral responsibility. As we strive to improve the lives of all children through public schooling using a scientist-practitioner model, we hope to contribute our experiences and solutions in the implementation and maintenance of MTSS to the knowledge base of educational best practices, thereby promoting an equitable and socially just system that serves all, from elementary through secondary school.

Trying to prevent adverse outcomes for students sometimes feels like trying to hold back the ocean; challenges flow too deep and feel too vast for educators to make an impact. School violence, mental illness, and student failure are complex, multilayered problems that are compounded by poverty, inequitable services for the most needy, and a lack of civic education and responsibility. Education continues to be a key social justice issue in our lifetime. With zero-tolerance and mandatory retention policies that disproportionately impact students of color, English-language learners, and students living in poverty, the school-to-prison pipeline is bursting. Especially with fewer supports and funding, there are extreme pressures on public school systems to "figure it out" for every student to succeed in his or her education; because if they do not, many of our failing students are on the path to prison. Educators may not be able to hold back the entire ocean of adverse outcomes for children in society, although socially just practices in schools can help students from all backgrounds to not only keep their heads above water but also to learn how to ride the waves and be resilient in the face of tsunamis.

With nearly 40 years of combined observations, data collection, and experience working in the fifth-largest school district in the United States, we have developed a new theory, LIQUID (Leadership, Inclusivity, Quality control, Universality, Implementation and feedback looping, and Data-based decision making), to address the inequities that exist not only in large urban school districts but also small rural school districts and every kind in between. Integrating the constructs of leadership, inclusivity, quality control, universality, implementation and feedback looping, and data-based decision making, and applying it as a lens in which to provide multiple tiers of support for students, we can proactively provide racially and socially just educational services to our students.

MTSS is foundational for successful student outcomes, the equalizer to providing a socially just education for all students, and the framework for eradicating the school-to-prison pipeline. We intend to answer the question of *how* to successfully implement MTSS with fidelity so schools can begin addressing these inequities while building program capacity. Ideally, MTSS would be adopted into public policy, as it proves to be the most effective way to allocate resources and maintain services and supports for school children. School administrators need clear guidelines on implementation standards to improve effective program delivery and accountability. The organizational psychology principles required to operate functional MTSS at most schools are misunderstood, underestimated as necessary, underimplemented, and largely disregarded. MTSS is not a pathway to special education eligibility, although it can get there. MTSS is a resource allocation framework for stakeholders, especially school administrators, to map out school resources and build the systems and processes required to support those functions at each tier. It strives to support the needs of all schoolchildren and educators through climate and culture.

One of the best predictors of MTSS success on a school campus is the relationship between the school principal and the school psychologist. Clearly, school psychologists are some of the most knowledgeable experts in MTSS in schools. Talented individual practitioners of school psychology in addition to open-minded administrators and educators are the magic combination to unlocking MTSS potential on a school campus. If administrators actively buy into the MTSS framework, they seem more likely to value the expertise and input of the school psychologist, just as, if administrators do not buy into the framework, they may be less likely to value the input of their school psychologists. As mental and behavioral health needs in schools grow, school administrators and school psychologists need to work more closely together, as never before, because MTSS is an important part of the solution.

On October 1, 2017, our local community fell victim to the most deadly mass shooting in the United States at the Route 91 Harvest Music Festival in Las Vegas, Nevada. As mental health first responders reassigned from school district duties to the county in a state of emergency, we experienced crisis response firsthand on a grand scale. That devastating night caused trauma and despair across our hometown yet was mixed with countless acts of generosity to assist victims through donations, blood drives, food and water deliveries, and offers of mental health supports from trauma specialists calling from across the country. Our community united in facing the crisis with humanity and compassion, and we felt deeply honored to help our strong community through the dark hours and days that followed.

At the time, we struggled with the massive damage done to our community, the senselessness of the tragedy, and wondered what the signs of the shooter's path to attack were and who knew about it beforehand. We believed more than ever that MTSS implemented effectively in schools could help prevent future school shootings and school violence. As the horrors of the Parkland school shooting at Marjory Stoneman Douglas High School unfolded a few months later during the National Association of School Psychologists' national conference in Chicago on Valentine's Day 2018, we joined in solidarity with thousands of other school psychologists and the Florida community to share in grief while processing the devastation and trauma. That day we knew, without a doubt, that we have the individual and collective power to be a part of the solution, knowing that our work is more urgent than ever.

This textbook is intended to provide schools with guidelines on how to meet the leadership and organizational demands of implementing multiple tiers of support in elementary schools. It is intended as a companionship guide to all stages of MTSS implementation. Situational examples are shared based on field experiences with successes and failures of MTSS implementation science from real schools. Schools must become smart organizations. Our hope is to encourage and empower all educators to access their voice and engage in advocacy to influence policy and practices that impact schools, educators, students, and communities. If educators do not speak up, who will?

Chapter 1

New Foundations for Multi-Tiered Systems of Support

Key Terms

Social Justice
Multi-Tiered Systems of Support
Implementation Science
LIQUID Theory
Ecosystem
Counterintuitive Cultures

Chapter Concepts

In this chapter, readers will learn:

1. The intersection of MTSS and social justice.
2. How to use this practice guide to implement sustainable MTSS programming for academics, behavior, and mental health.
3. How to reframe organizational thinking and consider multiple perspectives.
4. The key tenets of a new theoretical model to ground MTSS implementation: LIQUID.
5. How to avoid counterintuitive practices.
6. Legal, perceptual, and value aspects of MTSS.

Working in schools has never been more challenging for educators than right now. Zeitgeist of the times is putting more pressure on public schools to perform miracles like never before with fewer resources and higher stakes when systems fail. Corporate interest campaigns have successfully damaged public perception of public schools, allowing for-profit schools to make significant dents in redirecting federal funding and general support away from public schools in state and national policies, without providing better outcomes. Schools are expected to provide greater service delivery to students, who have more needs than ever, while competing for funding that is inadequate to meet those needs. Civil rights in schools are precarious. Safety for students and staff at schools can no longer be taken for granted. Public education is on the verge of existential crisis, and time will tell whether the public education sector can figure out how to meet the evolving needs of children while making education more effective and relevant. The challenge will be for public education to effectively address these needs before the corporate world perfects the illusion that it can do it better, and in the process of convincing the public it is a good idea, they take away students' rights to a free appropriate public education.

Socially just practices in schools, at the individual and group levels, must include respect, equity, and access to all of a school's resources and benefits (Shriberg et al., 2008). This *social justice* occurs when all children, from all different backgrounds, regardless of socioeconomic background or demographic characteristics, are valued in a school community and have access to a relevant education. Current educational realities demand that teachers stop teaching a curriculum for the masses and start teaching a differentiated curriculum to real students with real challenges (Quintero, 2017; Rodriguez, Loman, & Borgmeier, 2016; Jimerson, Burns, & VanDerHeyden, 2016; Lane, Carter, Jenkins, Dwiggins, & Germer, 2015; Sprick, 2013). The *Multi-Tiered Systems of Support* (MTSS) framework is a socially just approach to providing equitable access and support to all students in the educational setting. Furthermore, it can be differentiated for real schools to address real student challenges; MTSS "is an evidence-based framework for effectively integrating multiple systems and services to simultaneously address students' academic achievement, behavior, and social-emotional well-being" (National Association of School Psychologists, 2017, para. 1). MTSS is an ideal framework for school systems because it relies on quality universal instruction and preventative proactive methods while providing increasingly strategic supports for students as their needs become more severe. This book demonstrates how MTSS is a recipe that can be replicated across schools with enough flexibility to adapt to the uniqueness of each school and their teams.

This unique approach to the implementation of MTSS in elementary schools is much like a bull's approach to organizing a china shop. Necessity is the mother of invention, so a system was devised through strategic data leverage points that crashed through much of the preestablished notions of what could and could not be accomplished. Through feedback looping and program evaluation, this approach to quality control of effective MTSS in elementary schools lends itself to reevaluation and refinement each school year (Yuen, Terao, & Schmidt, 2009; Hanson, 2003). This guide is intended as a road map for state departments of education, district superintendents, professors, administrators, principals, school psychologists, teachers, and other motivated educators who are attempting to implement real school change and ultimately increase achievement, promote student well-being, and improve promotion and graduation rates, especially for at-risk students. It requires confidence at the leadership level of decision making because change is not always welcome in the ranks. Change is hard to come by. The main questions for beginning this journey are, Where do you want to go, and where do you start?

Schools bear the brunt of responsibility for student outcomes, regardless of students' environmental challenges and the practical realities of adequately educating every student who has experiences beyond the control of educators. Many stakeholders understand *why* they need MTSS to expand supports for students, but most are unable to define *what* to implement or *how* to implement MTSS at the elementary level. This is especially true for SEB MTSS and using a data-based progress monitoring method to inform on its use at a variety of leverage points including student, staff, administration, and program level. Research is clear that MTSS models are a necessity for adequately addressing our students' needs on an individual level as well as a systems level

(Bamonto-Graney & Shinn, 2005; Shinn, 2007; Sprick, 2009; Shinn & Walker, 2010; Sprick, 2013; Sink, 2016; Rodriguez et al., 2016; Jimerson et al., 2016; Francis, Mills, & Lupton, 2017). However, at the elementary level, these practices are frequently reported to be implemented but rarely are evident, let alone implemented systematically and with fidelity.

This practical guide was developed to help educators make manageable changes at their elementary schools in accordance with public policy and best practices. It was also designed as a therapeutic guide to accompany educational leaders and professionals on the difficult journey of transforming their elementary campuses in multiple stages to allocate resources among the three tiers. Embedded throughout are Connection to Practice examples, Voices from the Field narratives from real educators, and Exercises to help guide teams through the MTSS process. The process required to instill new practices and systems, especially in large bureaucratic settings, is always fraught with barriers that require creative problem solving to address culture changes, implementation fidelity, and relationship issues among staff members that can be improved by consulting implementation science, which promotes the systematic application of data and research into practical use by professionals and into public policy. (Bryk, Gomez, Grunow, & LeMahieu, 2016). *Implementation science* incorporates the integration, application, and refinement of evidence-based practices in the field. Creating a climate to improve achievement, student well-being, and school safety is not easy on any campus, let alone in schools with significant risk factors. Creating and sustaining MTSS in elementary schools to systematically address the needs of all students is not for the faint of heart. Practitioners may be in the process of implementing tiered supports, or they may be starting on a new path because school outcomes are not what it could or should be. *Schools are complex organizations that are inherently resistant to change.* A wise master educator often emphasized with novices that one can lead a horse to water and *can* make it drink; however, if the horse does not drink, one cannot blame the horse.

From a managerial standpoint, if the sale is not made, it is not the customer's fault the salesman did not close the deal. It is the job of school administrators, the leadership team, and motivated educators to get staff and stakeholders on board and engaging with best practices through MTSS. It is up to schools to work more like smart organizations: using the skills of highly talented individuals in teams to operate efficiently and learn together to adaptively grow an organization and best practices by leveraging tools, information, knowledge, relationships, and collaborative experiences. Administrative leadership of smart teams must recognize that schools, like any other organization, are institutional in nature with political influences that impact change (Meijer & Bolívar, 2015).

What Is MTSS?

As mentioned earlier, MTSS is an ideal framework for school systems because it relies on quality universal instruction and preventative proactive methods, while providing increasingly strategic supports for students as their needs become more severe. Built on the familiar foundation of the tiered Academic MTSS framework, the Social-Emotional-Behavioral MTSS model is an extension of the same schema. There are numerous books and references as to why a multi-tiered support system is a best practice, and readers are directed to peruse explicit practitioners' texts, including the comprehensive list of more than 100 MTSS and related resources compiled by Shinn (2013), for further information. For practitioners who are already on board with intentions to implement a multi-tiered support system at a school but are not really sure how to put the processes in action, this is the right place to get inspired by practices that have been tried and were successful. Elementary multi-tiered support systems are an established practice and are generally more universally accepted than secondary multi-tiered support systems, but the evidence is clear that MTSS is best practice at all grade levels. Figure 1.1 is a visual representation of the multiple-tiered support system. This book will comprehensively review the components essential to both Academic MTSS, also commonly referred to as "Response to Intervention" (RTI), as well as Social-Emotional-Behavioral MTSS, also referred to as "behavioral and mental health" intervention. This includes a review of the tiered model, assessment, data-based decision making, and collaborative problem solving.

Not all schools require the same amount of intensity or the same scope of opportunities, depending on the student population. As described in the Safe and Civil Schools

Figure 1.1 Multi-Tiered System of Support

Note
Response to Intervention and Social-Emotional-Behavioral MTSS each have their own tiers of support and decision points. Systemic implementation includes evidence-based practices and procedures that must be followed with fidelity, at each tier, to ensure universally consistent instruction and behavior management.

(Sprick Booher, & Garrison, 2009; Sprick, 2009, 2013) approach, higher-needs classrooms' risk factors indicate the need for more intensive classroom structures, and higher-needs schools need a more intensive structure for tiers of support. The higher the needs of the student population, the higher the structure that is needed to support them. The lower the needs, the lower the structure needed. In reading this text, you will learn how to determine whether your school is low-, medium- or high-needs and then be guided through the steps to create a team to make the best decisions for students on your campus. Processes are outlined to help teams create levels of support that grow with a team's and school's needs, which have checks and balances based on a model of continuous improvement.

Organizational Framing

Bolman and Deal (2017) assert that there are four different perspectives from which organizations can be viewed in order to understand how they work: structural, human resource, political, and symbolic. Structural is rooted in sociology and is metaphorically represented as factories, human resource is rooted in psychology and is represented as extended families, political is rooted in political science and is represented as jungles, and symbolic is rooted in anthropology and is represented as temples. Viewing organizational operations through each distinct lens is a powerful tool in which to examine systems and practices from diverse angles simultaneously to understand the whole picture of how an organization operates. Each perspective may have an impact on leadership challenges, reframed as opportunities to grant authorship, love, power, or significance within the corresponding organizational ethics of excellence, caring, justice, and faith, respectively.

When schools are viewed through the structural frame with the goal of excellence, there is an expected hierarchy with rules, assigned roles, procedures, and systems. When schools are viewed through the lens of human resource with the goal of caring, unique individuals must be validated through interpersonal relationships and a shared sense that the collective health of the organization is a main priority. In schools viewed through the political frame with goals of justice and power, educators are motivated by leaders' power sharing and can be incentivized to concentrate efforts on shared purpose, with fairness as the currency. Last, in schools viewed through the symbolic lens, with the goal of faith and significance, culture is aligned with values and traditions rooted in stories, school spirit, and greater purpose. These leaders provide ceremony and promote faith in sacred shared beliefs within the organization.

When building MTSS at a school, all four leadership frames must be considered, beginning with structure. Bolman and Deal (2017) make a case that differentiation and integration are opposite sides of the same coin of structure, requiring individuals with specialized roles and responsibilities grouped into working units, to effectively coordinate efforts laterally (within and across teams) and vertically (up the hierarchy). The more complex the system, such as the implementation of MTSS, the clearer the roles, responsibilities, and procedures must be to meet the needs of individuals and the collective.

Theory

In addition to supporting MTSS as a practical framework that can be used to differentiate student needs and to provide interventions, this text also offers a theoretical approach in which to view MTSS. This new theoretical approach is referred to as LIQUID and consists of the conceptual notions of Leadership, Inclusiveness, Quality control, Universality, Implementation and feedback looping, and Data-based decision making.

Spanning more than 20 years, the researchers collected observations, staff interviews, student performance data, and MTSS artifacts and analyzed the data at iterative cycles using the qualitative procedure of emerging design grounded theory (Glaser, 1992) to hone and refine their theory until saturation was achieved (Bernard & Ryan, 2010). Grounded theory research "is a systematic, qualitative procedure used to generate a theory that explains, at a broad conceptual level, a process, an action, or an interaction about a substantive topic" (Creswell, 2008, p. 432). In this case, the substantive topic was the constructs necessary for successful MTSS implementation and sustainability. Structuring implementation and sustainability through the commonalities of a theory can enhance fidelity and ensure quality of the tiered program.

Glaser (1992) proposes a flexible approach to grounded theory research consisting of conceptual notions versus stringent codes or visual representations that must be forced into set categories. Moreover, he suggests grounded theory must align with four criteria: fit, work, relevance, and modifiability. The theory must fit the reality of those that it serves, and it must work to explain variations of participant (e.g., administrator, teacher, student) behavior. If both conditions of fit and work are met, then the theory has relevance. Finally, the theory must be modifiable and be malleable to change as new data become available. The *LIQUID Theory* meets these four conditions and is described in greater detail in the following section.

LIQUID Model

The LIQUID Model is a new theoretical construct to frame essential components in the implementation of MTSS to promote academic, mental, and behavioral health in elementary and secondary schools. The LIQUID Model was designed as a tool to assist in customizing MTSS for individual schools with unique needs and demographics; just as liquid fits the shape of any container. Across the three intervention tiers, the foundation of solid academic, mental, and behavioral health supports at a school rests on six micro and macro factors: leadership, inclusiveness, quality control, universality, implementation and feedback looping, and data-based decision making.

Borrowing from the configuration of an atom, Figure 1.2 illustrates how LIQUID components orbit and overlap to build and sustain the system. Each L–I–Q–U–I–D are "electrons" that orbit the MTSS "nucleus." As learned in chemistry, all physical matter is constructed of atoms, and electrons are essential components that balance the nucleus. The theoretical model of LIQUID must be present to balance MTSS. The MTSS chemical equation would not work without any of the six "electrons". H_2O requires two hydrogen atoms and one oxygen to be present in the right proportion to form water; the same is true for MTSS. MTSS cannot be formulated and implemented successfully if the six elements of leadership, inclusiveness, quality control, universality, implementation and feedback looping, and data-based decision making are not present in the requisite proportions for a particular school. These elements are woven together and continually influence one another.

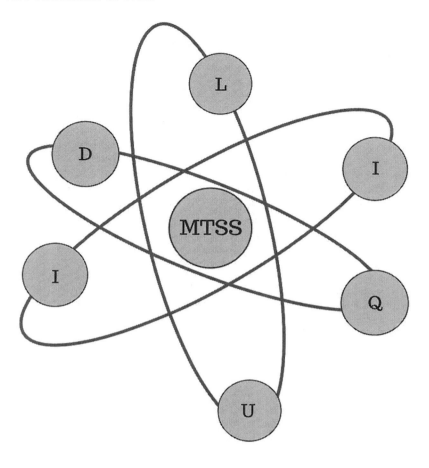

Figure 1.2 Theoretical LIQUID Model

Note
MTSS = Multi-Tiered System of Support, L = leadership, I = inclusiveness, Q = quality control, U = universality, I = implementation and feedback looping, and D = data-based decision making.

Leadership

This team-based approach to improving academic, mental, and behavioral health of students on a school campus begins with the leadership of the primary school administrator and a comprehensive vision for all three tiers. *Having a clear understanding of the relationships and differences between the tiers, how to effectively implement each tier of support, and how to allocate school resources to grow and sustain each tier is required.* If the primary school administrator makes the implementation of MTSS a priority and is willing to actively solve problems to overcome barriers, then MTSS can flourish in a school and systems issues can be resolved, while improvements are continually made and the integrity of the framework is sustained. Due to the complex systems and professional roles that are required to successfully execute MTSS, practices and procedures must be clear and monitored for fidelity, with corrective practices put into effect as necessary by the school leader. School principals must be willing to utilize the master calendar to drive MTSS scheduling requirements, select and endorse evidence-based supports and structures, monitor and enforce fidelity of evidence-based practices, and provide guidance and visible support for educator leaders on campus working in smart teams who are actively solving problems for students on campus.

Effective school leaders empower change agents and can redesign learning environments (VanWynsberghe & Herman, 2015). Ultimately, school leaders serve as role models, problem solvers, and decisive enforcers to publicly, visually, and materially support MTSS implementation at all phases, with issues large and small. Leaders should be willing to plan, prioritize, lead, and supervise all MTSS functions and processes. MTSS budgeting must be embedded in the school improvement plan, especially to invest in human capital and to symbolically lead the cultural shift on a school campus. Finally, school leaders must engage in ongoing reflection to evaluate and revise practices, continuously improve staff competencies with professional development experiences, and sustain the supports needed to implement functional programs. Leadership is the foundation of MTSS, and if this domain is not strong, anything built at any tier will be on shaky ground. If administrators are not leading, or at least actively supporting, an MTSS framework, practitioners must start here and try to get that horse to drink, to help principals solve their problems by connecting administrative priorities with effective solutions that align with MTSS.

Inclusiveness

Making school relevant for everyone at the micro- and macro-level is paramount. An inclusive school is welcoming and accessible to all staff, students, and families, not just those who are represented by the cultural majority. Culturally competent practices at schools are based on understanding, acceptance, respect for, and celebration of, diverse individual, group, and community values, languages, beliefs, principles, and customs (Jones, 2009; Pratt-Johnson, 2006). Cultural competence requires educators to be aware of their own biases and to include students' cultural diversity in a positive manner through all aspects of learning. Educators should have the disposition and skill to learn from other cultures and effectively include other individuals and groups from all backgrounds in all aspects of the school environment.

Teaching students where they are, validating where they are from, and having supports in place for all students at all levels to help them get where they need to go is the epitome of school inclusiveness. Schools demonstrate strength when working with diversity and viewing challenges as opportunities to improve service delivery to all students. There is a place for every person and group in an inclusive school because everyone fits in. Inclusiveness is the primary purpose of MTSS.

Quality Control

Fidelity, integrity, and accountability at the individual level of implementation of MTSS add up to fidelity, integrity, and accountability at the collective level. Micro-level assuredness that procedures and processes are being followed every time, for every student, as well as macro-level assuredness that practices are evidence-based and are shaped by data-based improvement measures, go hand in hand. Essential elements are required to meet the minimum standards of MTSS implementation that cannot be compromised and still considered to meet those same standards. Quality control means so much more than checking a box on a checklist to indicate whether a standard is present or not at a school. It embodies the spirit of the LIQUID Model to frame practices through different lenses to get multiple angles of the same problems leading to better solutions when systematically implementing tiers of support at a school to meet the needs of all students and staff, regardless of the population or risk factors of the school. Research demonstrates that large changes and school reforms *can* be implemented with fidelity, perhaps more so than small changes (Anderson, 2017).

Confidence in a product or service is achieved when the product or service has been repeatedly tested for effectiveness, and the consumer knows that any defect with the product or service will be replaced or corrected by guarantee. Quality control in MTSS is achieved when school leaders have a comprehensive vision and are willing to actively support implementation of MTSS, when educational practices are evidence-based and implemented with fidelity, and there is confidence that students are able to access instructional opportunities at the level of intensity they need, when they need it, by having processes in place to systematically address individual problems and systems problems within the organization. Quality control in MTSS relies on strong leadership, specific standards to which educators are held accountable, corrective practices embedded in school culture, and checks and balances built in the design of the systems to cyclically reflect on current practices then make revisions in response to data-based outcomes. School leaders are ultimately responsible for enforcing quality of school practices, even when there are policy issues that lie beyond the control of site-based administrators.

Universality

Universal means everyone. The universal tier, the foundation of high-quality instruction using evidence-based practices, is the most important tier in MTSS because it has an impact on *all* children on campus (National Association of School Psychologists (NASP), 2016). If every student gets quality instruction of developmentally appropriate academic, social, emotional, and behavioral curriculum, most students will positively respond, thus preventing undesirable outcomes most of the time. Expensive targeted solutions, added on top of poor universal instruction for underperformers without addressing root causes, including implementation fidelity issues in delivering curriculum, are much less effective than addressing the actual problem. If a higher number of students than reasonably expected are having difficulties, then evaluating and revising universal practices will have the greatest impact.

Universal practices are designed to maximize opportunities for all students to benefit from instruction, with a direct link to inclusive practices. All students are able to receive the intensity of support they require, starting with universal benchmarking, checking regularly for symptoms of underachievement and social-emotional-behavioral issues that may be indicative of greater overarching challenges that require timely treatment with more intensive targeted instructional experiences. Healthy lifestyle, getting regular health checkups, and getting timely treatment to address minor ailments and illness is sound preventative and maintenance health advice for everyone; as quality instruction, quarterly academic and social-emotional-behavioral screenings, and getting timely treatment to address underachievement and underperformance in school are sound preventative and maintenance health advice for all students in school. Multi-tiered support systems provide levels of care for students, beginning with healthy universal instructional practices and including built-in processes to examine practices at all three tiers. Systems that reinforce quality universal instruction and allow for increasingly intensive treatments, supports, and services available in a timely manner to every student who needs it, every time, captures universality in a school setting.

Implementation and Feedback Looping

Fidelity of implementation of evidence-based practices at the micro-level makes a huge impact at the point of service delivery and student outcomes. Macro-level fidelity is essential to impact the long-term capacity and sustainability of an initiative. The efficacy of a practice cannot be strategically evaluated if the practice is not being implemented with integrity and fidelity. The implementation of new practices requires leadership for close supervision and correction of implementation fidelity issues. *Macro-level review and the revision of the micro-level steps of quality control within a continuous improvement model are required.* Using a team-based approach will allow for collaborative responsibility in providing feedback and defining actionable steps to hone the effectiveness of MTSS on a school campus. The answers to almost all problems on a school campus are within the educators who work on that campus. Working collectively for shared purposes in smart teams, and accepting divisions of labor which are visibly and publicly reinforced to grow better practices by school leadership, will increase the probability of a successful implementation of new MTSS processes and procedures. Ultimately, practices that help make educators' jobs easier, such as providing structured opportunities for interventions, eliminating excessive documentation or paperwork, and increasing the automaticity of data collection, will increase motivation to sustain and improve future practices.

Feedback looping relies on examination of cause-and-effect processes, observing measurable outputs that lead to new input variables implemented in efforts to positively impact the system (Hanson, 2001, 2003; DiMaggio & Powell, 1991). A system is only as strong as its reflective practices and flexibility to respond adaptively to outcome data and new information in determining the continuing or changing current practices moving forward. A sustainable feedback loop includes many relevant sources of quantitative data, including achievement data, discipline data, and promotion rates, as well as qualitative data, including teacher and parent/caregiver surveys. MTSS by design is a layered network with procedures for appropriate application within each layer. Iterative reflection and evaluation can reduce barriers while streamlining processing and increasing efficiency and effectiveness. These iterative reflections can be formative as well as summative. Having systems in place to provide formative and summative feedback helps MTSS teams make better data-based decisions in continuous improvement practices of implement–review–revise cycles.

Data-Based Decision Making

Outcome data usually tell the truth about whether educational practices are working or not, although it may not tell the whole story; follow the data across multiple data sources to get the best understanding of trends and variables that impact trends. Triangulating data using a variety of sources to provide information to make decisions for students will only result in better decisions, including, but not limited to, improving the quality of implementation of instructional practices at the three tiers; successfully building and sustaining MTSS landmarks to support how systems acquire, process, and access data for decision making; having a positive impact on school culture; and crystallizing staff procedures and team processes systematically. Chapter 12 offers an MTSS Evaluation Frequency and Intensity Framework to guide teams through the data-analysis process. Data collection, repeated measurements, and documentation requirements must be automated as much as possible to sustain practices with any semblance of fidelity, regardless of the size of the campus. With feedback looping, MTSS teams use data to initiate targeted treatment in a case management model. Data are used to determine whether to intensify or reduce the intensity of interventions for students to successfully respond to instruction. Data may be formative or summative and may include, but are not limited to, observational, curriculum-based measurement; standardized tests; attendance history; enrollment history; grades; parent input; medical or developmental history; discipline reports; and universal screenings. School administration and MTSS team members must engage in reflective practices to review micro- and macro-trends, track systems issues, and make adjustments based on data-based outcomes.

Who Are Our Students?

There are many reasons why students do not achieve. Many of those factors are beyond the control of the school such as high rates of poverty, hunger, second-language and cultural factors, high rates of absenteeism, history of abuse and/or trauma, drug use, a lack of parent involvement, dysfunctional family systems, and other socioeconomic and psychosocial factors. School climate, diverse opportunities, and quality teaching practices are about the only factors schools have control over that lead to improved educational outcomes for individuals and groups of students.

Public schools are required to meet all the needs of all students. *Judging the success of an entire school population can be misleading because there are constantly successes and failures going on with every student, every day.* Some students are more difficult to help because of their complex, multiple layers of problems. Educators who have experienced success with hard-luck cases find those successes the crowning achievements of their careers in education. To save one child is noble and worthwhile, indeed. However, public schools are challenged with saving all children who cross the threshold of enrollment. Regardless of what challenges students have, the job of all educators in a public setting is to provide them with an appropriate education. However, the current definition of "appropriate" education in an ever-changing society, with global competition and rapidly evolving technology, is proving to require adaptation to struggle in its relevance.

Most caregivers can attest to the challenges of raising their children if they are being genuinely honest. To be responsible for the well-being and futures of hundreds, and even thousands, of other peoples' children can be a crushing responsibility, especially from an administrative standpoint. In the educational sense, *ecosystems* are the confluence and interaction of all persons on a campus who influence student growth and guide development and experiences. The federal ecosystem, the ecosystem of states, the local school district ecosystem, the school ecosystem, the family ecosystem, and the classroom ecosystem all contribute to educational outcomes for students. Administrators can never underestimate the power of the classroom ecosystem. Quality education really boils down to the skill of the educators working directly with children.

Teachers deserve true affection, respect, and admiration for their efforts and accomplishments in raising other people's children to be educated citizens. Most teachers are very well-meaning individuals doing the best they can. Elementary teachers have to be not only masters of curriculum but also masters of behavior management and often act as substitute parents. They need ninja warrior–like skills to manage up to 30 or more students at a time while keeping them engaged, on task, and productive. Especially in the lower grades, managing large numbers of young students is like herding cats. Students explore and interact in the environment independently, wandering off in different directions; just when teachers think they have wrangled students in a coordinated fashion in a designated area, inevitably, some escape the provided bounds. Teachers must teach students information they may or may not be prepared to learn for a variety of different reasons. Teaching is a *high-level skill*, which cannot be emphasized enough. Teachers have to think in terms of players on a chessboard, where their success in the classroom depends on the efficacy of the battle plan and flexibility to adapt, reorganize, and push through. They must understand rules of engagement enough to manipulate variables in the environment to elicit positive pro-academic behavior. Teaching requires constant creative problem solving.

Counterintuitive Cultures

Sometimes, practices in education are counterintuitive. *Counterintuitive cultures* arise when practices in the field are producing results opposite to that which is desired. Sometimes our solution to address a problem does not fix the problem; rather, it creates different problems or intensifies the existing one. For example, in order for teachers to increase the probability of students behaving correctly in class, there needs to be much more positive attention than negative attention given to students. Positive attention occurs during or directly after a student behaves in a prosocial or pro-academic way. Negative attention occurs during or directly after a student behaves in an antisocial or anti-academic way. Positive attention increases the probability of positive, prosocial behavior. Negative attention increases the probability of negative, antisocial behavior. Whichever type of behavior you pay more attention to is the type of behavior you are going to get more of (Jones & Kepner, 2007).

A common mistake that teachers make is when they move in proximity to a student who is off-task and talking. Depending on the function of the student's behavior, this teacher response may not be the best fit to correct the behavior. It would seem that standing next to the student would be a negative consequence for talking during a teacher-led activity and would reduce the probability of that student disrupting the class. However, when a student is repeatedly given attention for being off-task, rather than when he or she is on-task, that student (and every other student in the room) is taught that when a student disrupts teacher-led instruction, he or she gets more attention and power to disrupt (and controls the movement of the teacher). Repeated proximity, and other types of negative reinforcement, to an off-task student from the teacher actually increases the probability of that student disrupting the class again (Jones & Kepner, 2007). As mentioned, best practices can be counterintuitive.

The teacher has a better chance of improving behavior if he or she gives more *selective* attention to those seated around the disruptive student by praising the on-task peers for following classroom rules: listening respectfully when someone else is talking, raising their hands to speak, and waiting to be called on by the teacher before speaking

(Jones & Kepner, 2007). Not only does that draw attention to other students' on-task behavior, but it also shows other students who are off-task what they need to do to get more attention from the teacher. Most important, the target student must be given positive attention for following the rules as well, especially if she changed her behavior in response to the differential reinforcement given to others. Over time, through shaping, students in the classroom are more likely to use prosocial and pro-academic behaviors to get teacher attention (Jones & Kepner, 2007). Unfortunately, not all behavior problems are so simple, and this was an oversimplified example of one of the many principle components of an effective behavior management system that is found in the context of a positive, proactive classroom culture.

The classroom is a microcosm of schoolwide culture. Just as positive attention in the classroom grows more positive behavior from students, positive attention to schoolwide teacher competencies from the school administrator can draw attention to best practices in teaching, thus cultivating more effective teachers. There are always good and not-so-good practices going on in a school at any given time, like in any company or workplace. There are resisters and problem solvers. How do the problem solvers get rewarded, while retooling practices to address the resistance? Positive perceptions of school improvement may be achieved with positive reinforcement and success when using evidence-based practices.

Meaningful Change and the Law

When examining ways to grow best practices at a school to meet the most immediate needs, those processes directly and inadvertently generate solutions to address less immediate needs. Or in some schools, more pressing problems will reveal themselves that will lead to an even greater appreciation for, and validation of, effective processes being in place to tackle the issues. Change must occur from the top down as well as the bottom up, and that means there will be numerous moving parts at all times. Unlike many moving parts that do not work well together, and sometimes work counterproductively, implementing MTSS processes can work synchronously with adaptability to respond to the characteristics and unique needs at any school.

It is very challenging, and can be downright frustrating, to try to make meaningful changes at the school level. Schools are, by nature, bureaucratic institutions that have endless rules and regulations written and challenged by layers of federal and local government, advocacy groups, lawyers, court orders, Supreme Court rulings, and acts of Congress (Bolick, 2016; Robinson, 2015; Hallonsten & Hugander, 2014; Powell & DiMaggio, 1991). Changing rules and regulations requires tenacity and patience, and it is easy to give up. Making an impact at the top levels of bureaucracy takes strategy, perseverance, and many Ibuprofen. However, these are necessary evils in order to advance through numerous levels of bureaucratic decision making. Leaders must be convinced, as well as compelled to act, in which case buy-in must be had, if there is any chance that changes will actually occur at a school (Anyon, Nicotera, & Veeh, 2016).

Fortunately, the current education law passed by Congress in December 2015, the Every Student Succeeds Act (ESSA), entreats us to provide multi-tiers of support to students in a school setting. Disability education law requires that some eligibility categories for special education require interventions prior to eligibility determination, and ESSA recognizes MTSS supports as a viable use of federal funding to support programming for students (NASP, 2017). Interventions must be implemented with fidelity, with corresponding documentation of research-based methods and response to intervention data. However, the level of compliance with the spirit of the law is dependent on the knowledge and skill level of the building principal and the quality of the team of educational professionals on campus.

> **Box 1.1**
>
> **Voices From the Field**
>
> Throughout my career, intervention teams have reportedly become an expected part of elementary schools in our school district, with dramatic levels of variability in stages of implementation. After spending years developing MTSS processes for secondary schools, and assuming MTSS practices were finally accepted and occurring in elementary schools, coming back to work again in elementary schools was eye-opening.
>
> Out of the three elementary schools I was assigned to in the past two school years, only one earnestly tried to implement MTSS at their school. In my small sample, after roughly 20 years of state- and district-mandated protocol, implementation of MTSS, or approximation of it, only occurred at one-third of randomly assigned elementary schools, indicating that the implementation success of best practices of MTSS at the elementary level is highly exaggerated. Even more jarring, the school principals of the schools not implementing MTSS had little to no interest in understanding, building, or improving systems or processes of RTI and largely regarded it as a function of special education eligibility, not general education. There was, and still is, little concept or discussion of building any behavioral or mental health version of MTSS. The skill level of the building principal, including successful prior experience in one or more parts of implementation of MTSS, and the quality of educators empowered to be change agents in propelling MTSS forward by crafting supports based on the needs of the school, staff, and population, can be directly correlated to how well those teams implement MTSS, ranging from not at all to highly functional.

Comparing Practices

Even though some elementary schools understand and use intervention processes, many do not, despite best practice recommendations to train and support schools in doing so. On the other hand, many elementary schools do not provide systematic intervention opportunities at all, let alone documentation of teacher efforts to remediate skills deficits. There are mountains of obstacles to making changes in a bureaucratic system, especially school campuses. Many well-intentioned elementary educators give up on systemwide changes in the face of repeated failures to achieve implementation of MTSS processes without school leadership making MTSS implementation explicit, and they settle for personal efforts by individual teachers on a small scale. Small scale is valiant, but systemwide compliance with federal education law and state policy is better. Many educators do not understand the step-by-step mechanics of implementing the science of change in elementary schools that are necessary to support a multi-tiered support system, and they make the thinking error that it is too complicated and fraught with bureaucracy to systematically implement. *It is true that*

MTSS is a comprehensive system, which is why it is important to break it into bite-sized pieces that seem doable instead of impossible.

School psychologists have been supporting MTSS implementation and policy efforts for years (NASP, 2017). Professional shortages and logistical practicalities, among other factors, restrict school psychologists' practice to only testing students suspected for special education eligibility. This is problematic for many reasons, not the least of which that it is a colossal waste of qualified mental health support, child wellness advocacy, and mental and behavioral health leadership on school campuses. School psychologists may find their roles limited or perhaps allow themselves to be limited in their roles.

Some special education disabilities require documented, evidence-based interventions and the burden of proof for eligibility lies with the school psychologist. This is especially difficult when schools do not have systemic structures in place that promotes interventions and the collection of data. In turn, school psychologists often are faced with making data-based decisions without sufficient data or a guarantee of implementation fidelity of interventions. It is natural for school psychologists to be involved in leadership efforts in implementation of MTSS in a comprehensive framework of academic, social, emotional, and behavioral educational supports; they are highly specialized child advocates and mental health care providers already embedded in school systems, although oftentimes their expertise is underutilized by administrators. Many school psychologists spend much of their time completing clerical and repetitive paperwork that could be accomplished by an assistant at a fraction of the cost, freeing up these highly specialized children's advocates and mental health care providers in schools to focus on more direct student care and participation in roles and functions of overlapping smart teams of MTSS.

Having MTSS in place helps with other challenging problems, including reducing overidentification of minority students for special education programming and promoting restorative justice practices. Routine program evaluation may highlight issues that intersect and opportunities to remove barriers will become evident, such as how human capital can work more cohesively to work smarter, not harder, in repurposed roles. Preparing our children with the foundational skills to be successful in elementary school, middle school, high school, and life is at the core of elementary educators' missions. It is well established that children who do not have a high school diploma face considerable more financial difficulty and career limitations than those who have graduated (Tyler, 2004). It is paramount to teach students how to self-regulate, problem solve, and be independent so they can pursue their life goals with as much preparation as possible. Many require remedial skills, but all require the opportunity to graduate, regardless of risk factors.

It took an act of Congress to allow the use of research-based intervention as part of the eligibility determination process for some disabilities, such as specific learning disability, and to remove the severe discrepancy mandate (Assistance to States for the Education of Children with Disabilities, 2010). Public schools are required to provide opportunities for increasingly intensive levels of support to struggling students, depending on documented need and documented response to interventions. It is up to individual schools to figure out how to implement best practices with their schools' needs, population, and budget in mind; however, the framework of MTSS in schools is largely misunderstood, and necessary components underestimated, as a comprehensive model for academics *as well as* social-emotional-behavioral health. The LIQUID Model organizes the components that impact MTSS fruition: leadership, inclusiveness, quality control, universality, implementation and feedback looping, and data-based decision making. Every instructional practice, team operation, procedure, system, and decision should be evaluated through each lens of LIQUID to identify strengths and weaknesses and areas in need of improvement.

Change does not come easily whether that be in a low-, medium-, or high-risk school. The process for creating a decision-making model at a school is explained in the following chapters, and each administrator and educational leader will determine how much change can occur, how quickly those changes can be implemented, and what will be supported and enforced at any one time. Effective leadership in this process requires establishing clear expectations, providing ample professional learning opportunities, creating space and time for the tiers of support to develop, funding of resources, using highly positive reinforcement with staff and students, community involvement, and allowing for a lot of patience. In all cases, change will not occur as quickly as expected or exactly as envisioned.

Measuring a school's success based on aggregate student achievement data can be helpful, yet it can also be misleading. The hard-luck student who seemed to have no chance of promotion but then turned it around and was able to move up will always be considered a success for that school, regardless of the school aggregate indicators. But understanding the realities of the political climate, and the high expectation that every student will perform at the 50th percentile or above is a challenge indeed. In reading this book, rather than becoming discouraged by the apparent complexity of processes and procedures, readers are challenged to become more motivated. School leaders and educators will learn how to lead their horses to water and make them drink. And if the horses do not drink, the horses will not be to blame, nor will the stakeholders who do not understand the need to do anything differently, the educators who do not want to add more responsibilities to their jobs, or the students who choose to fail by putting in no effort and giving up on themselves. If the horses are not drinking, then the leadership team must reassess organizational frames, improve relationships with resistant stakeholders and validate their input, and systematically determine which opportunities must be developed to increase buy-in and, ultimately, output.

Perception and Value

Poverty and family culture have a significant impact on students' regard toward school. Students may not have good role models in the home, or in the community, and may have never learned appropriate school behavior, let alone a love of learning. Other students have beaten the odds and succeeded in spite of a lack of opportunities and resources. *School cultures that embrace cultural differences and provide appropriate learning experiences for all students, regardless of their needs, have the greatest chance for the best outcomes.* For example, high-achieving, high-risk schools share nine commonalities. These nine commonalities are (1) a culture that emphasizes high expectations; (2) supportive and respectful relationships between stakeholders; (3) a focused academic intent; (4) systematic formative and summative assessment of students; (5) team-based decision-making structures; (6) functions and processes; (7) a principal who supports equity; (8) strong staff motivation, perceived efficacy, and work ethic; and (9) the reallocation of staffing supports in a coordinated fashion (Kannapel, Clements, Taylor, & Hibpshman, 2005). There are numerous examples of what is needed to turn a low-achieving school into a better achieving school, but it is not always clear how to get started, build momentum, and sustain effective practices. The only way to eat is one bite at a time. Changing educational practices is no different and requires taking one small bite after another.

Start with perception. How is success defined? Are celebrations allowed if things are moving in the right direction toward the goal, or is celebration supposed to happen only after the goal is achieved? The number of students passing or failing is an indicator of a school's efficacy, although grade inflation and inconsistent grading policies across teachers and schools may make those numbers unreliable indicators of school success. Proficiency tests are also popular measures of a school's success, but what about students who are not good test takers, limited English proficient, or have disabilities and are unable to pass these tests? Are they all failures? When educators address one issue at a time, they need to find ways to celebrate small achievements, which lead to big achievements over time for individual students and whole schools. *Celebrations must occur at every opportunity and positive attention given when incremental improvements are attained.* There are no successes without failures, as any great inventor will tell you, so ultimate success goes back to building on what works and letting go of ineffective practices.

The value and emphasis must be on the process, not the outcome. The outcomes will then drive future changes to the process and additional areas of need can be addressed. Schools must constantly adapt to the growing needs of students and the realities of the school's teaching climate. Some of the factors that contribute to a school's teaching climate and fall largely under the control of school leadership include resource allocation, administrative support, corrective procedures for misbehaving students, and schoolwide expectations and procedures. Schools have no control over the raw materials, the students, in teachers' classrooms, which is why the business model of producing widgets does not compare. Factors such as attendance, grade-level preparedness, level of age-appropriate behavior, and family support fall into this nebulous uncontrollable realm. When working to produce widgets, inputs can be controlled; thus, there are quality control procedures in the input and output. When working with students, they come with their own unique sets of inputs and success cannot be measured in terms of uniform product development but in terms of individual growth, which depends on where they start. Educators impact the development of individual children every single day, and each child is precious and unique.

Once a school has been identified as requiring high, medium, or low structure, processes explained in this customizable guide can be expanded and adapted to meet the needs of individual school sites and populations. The recommendations herein may be challenged; however, be warned that a recipe will not come out the same if one picks and chooses which ingredients in the recipe to use, or not use. MTSS aims to ensure that all areas of student needs are systematically addressed, measures taken, and outcomes monitored. If the cake does not rise the way it was intended, then the recipe will have to be followed more closely. How do schools make the most meaningful changes most quickly? Does the school culture have to change first, or instructional practices? Understanding the cumulative variables that contribute to school outcomes will help teams better understand school needs and identify manageable steps moving forward. Any attempt to make change at the cultural level or the practical level is, most likely, better than no attempt. But again, the caution is that if the cake does not rise, and one did not follow the recipe, one cannot blame the recipe.

The Process

This book moves beyond traditional books that discuss what MTSS is and delves into the *how* of implementing changes at a school. It will serve as validation of the challenges that educators face on this transformational journey and may be of some solace during the difficult times when things do not seem to be going as planned. What happens so often in education is that when something does not work fast enough, the baby is thrown out with the bathwater. Then multiple new babies are adopted all at once, and when they do not produce change fast enough all the new initiatives are abandoned for something else. Change is always a constant in the field of education in terms of procedures, paperwork, assessment, and service delivery but oftentimes feels like nothing really ever changes. Before schools throw away any more babies, this guide can assist teams in systematically evaluating where they are in terms of MTSS implementation and development, both Academic and Social-Emotional-Behavioral MTSS: what they have, what they want and need, and where they are going in providing differential opportunities to learners with diverse needs that can be grown incrementally and systematically.

School-based teams must come up with the best solutions for their campuses with the resources that they have, and this book will guide teams through a series of exercises to evaluate their individual needs. Using the continuous improvement model, teams must be constantly reevaluating and reassessing what works and what does not work, continuing with what works, and trying new methods to address what is not working. Teams might find improvements in some areas but not in others, and then it may become evident that some structures and practices must be addressed first to impact growth in other targeted areas. For example, teams may strive to improve teachers' instructional practices in terms of content mastery and quality teaching, but if their classroom management skills are lacking, increased student achievement may not pan out. The type of interventions needed on a campus depends on whether a large number of students are struggling in a subject area or a smaller subgroup, with the intervention falling at the leadership, teacher, or student level or a combination of all three. Analyzing data systematically will help school leaders prioritize needs and implement practices that have the best chance of having an impact on the most students. Once basic instructional gaps are addressed at Tier 1, Tier 2, and Tier 3, intervention opportunities can be better designed and outcomes can be better evaluated, leading to better instructional practices.

Comprehensive Social-Emotional-Behavioral MTSS is perceived to be much more difficult to implement on school campuses than Academic MTSS instructional supports. Many elementary campuses implement some form of positive behavioral supports or social-emotional learning opportunities; however, they are rarely linked together or explicitly connected to the underlying impetus. Such supports should be linked and implemented intentionally to best improve student well-being, decrease self-harm, decrease acts of violence, and decrease the number of students entering the school-to-prison pipeline. A possible perception on elementary campuses regarding trauma and issues surrounding mental health is "not here, not *these* kids". Families in many communities feel that if they do not talk about mental and behavioral health, it eliminates the possibility of it happening in their backyard. The reality is that mental and behavioral health issues occur across all demographic groups and socioeconomic strata; not only will it occur in your backyard, but it also *already is occurring* in your backyard.

School leaders who turn their backs and do not implement strong Social-Emotional-Behavioral MTSS with intentionality are doing a disservice to their students and community. Overcoming fear of addressing the stigma, or offending parents' sensibilities, are realities that school leaders must be prepared to take on. The growth trajectory of a potential school shooter could be interrupted and realigned before the malformed seeds are even fertilized.

Several factors contribute to this underemphasis of systematic implementation of social-emotional-behavioral instructional opportunities for all students, especially access, confidence, and funding. To begin with, formal, universal Tier I social-emotional and behavioral instruction typically ends in the primary grades of elementary school. Also, targeted social-emotional and behavioral learning experiences are underprioritized, underfunded, underimplemented, and misunderstood which often leads to disruptive students being blamed and punished without the opportunity to correct their behavior. This pattern leads to a series of questions: Who is teaching students to do better? Who is teaching teachers to do better? How will these "problem students" ever learn how to be independent or contributing members of society without having multiple opportunities and consistent support to learn correct behavior? How can schools begin to interrupt the school to prison pipeline? They can start with a mandated, evidence-based social-emotional-behavioral curriculum that is implemented with fidelity from preschool through 12th grade.

Adding social-emotional learning and positive behavioral instructional supports is part of the multilayered recipe to making a multi-tiered support system wedding cake that marries best practices systematically. When does each ingredient get introduced on each level? Certain ingredients are added at Tier 1, Tier 2, and Tier 3 and must be customized based on the school's individual needs and resources. Just know that the ingredients must be in there, added at some point, or the cake will not rise and a comprehensive multi-tiered support system will not nourish all students and staff.

The journey to implementing best practices in schools, which requires systemwide change, is fraught with resistance to change. Most educators are not necessarily happy when change is presented. It requires a new way of thinking, a new way of acting, and an open attitude to make the effort. The trickle-down effect of negative attitude to change is often transparent in a school setting. If the administrator of the school is not excited about making required changes, the teachers will not be excited, nor will the students or the families. A bad attitude is contagious, as any classroom teacher can attest. If a school administrator is being directed to change without buying into the big picture, educators will be less likely to adopt those changes with integrity.

Sometimes, change is implemented on paper, but not in true practice, and is referred to as "the smoke and mirrors effect." Leaders on campus talk about systems changes as if they have occurred when, in fact, they have not. Principals may think that they have the MTSS framework in place, but in truth, they do not. Many of these schools have a remedial lesson plan, or two; a progressive discipline plan; and nothing more, with no foundation and team actively solving problems within a comprehensive system. When understanding of MTSS is unclear and access to academic and behavioral supports restricted, MTSS is an illusion.

On the other hand, if the system is too laborious and falls only on a few well-meaning teachers, the system becomes unfair. If only some of the educators have embraced change and others have not, the ones who are not working to implement real change can spread ill will like a bad rash. Those doing the hard work of adopting new ways of thinking and acting are going to feel punished because there is no consequence for those who are not doing their due diligence. Another problem arises when teachers and other professionals receive no overt rewards for working the program and are treated the same as the teachers and professionals who are *not* working the program. This creates a culture of resentment. And when the cake does not rise because the recipe is not being followed, the school staff members who did not follow the recipe are validated because the new processes did not work, and the teachers who were open to change are resentful because they did everything they could do and no one else was held accountable.

This guide will have a significant impact on readers' schools and will offer incremental steps toward meaningful changes. This is a process guide based on experiences in the field of administrative leadership, educational policy, and school psychology across a diverse range of school campuses. It is a process book that includes the content of established best practices and is designed to bridge the gap between best practices and actual practices with specific recommendations to lasting systemic change while increasing positive outcomes for students. Readers may not agree with all recommendations to the point that they may seriously disagree. Readers are encouraged to be mindful of emotional responses when reading through this guide to examine gut instincts and implicit bias, and address mind-set and thinking patterns that may interfere with solution-based activities. This book will not be therapeutic, or professionally encouraging, if readers are not monitoring and tracking their feelings. Leader and practitioner feelings about how things are going qualitatively are important, just as important as the quantitative outcomes.

This process is not a stagnant set of boundaries but a streaming river of opportunity. Some recommendations might be applicable or appealing and some not. The goals of this guide are to inspire, educate, and promote site-based problem solving. Feel free to disagree, just know that readers' thoughts and beliefs may be challenged so that they can make better decisions for their school growth, which ultimately leads to better results for their students. If readers have a strong reaction to a statement or recommendation, question why. Do some examples hit too close to home? Do readers feel like they need to defend their current practices? If the answer to either of these questions is yes, please consider recommendations in the nature in which they are intended, to assist schools and individual professionals in making the most of their multi-tiered support system.

Ultimately, it is school leaders, practitioners, and teams who are responsible for decision making on behalf of their students and making the process work with their school's needs in mind. Try to build on, modify, and create methods to meet the needs of unique school climates. To start, the focus is to determine the individual needs of your school and build your MTSS team, two of the biggest steps in the process. Then readers will establish their school supports in terms of basic resources, training, and scheduling. Examples of the evolution of practices at real schools will be illustrated, as well. Be aware that improving student and staff engagement, school culture, and addressing special needs populations require additional resources, training, and scheduling. Extra components added to the mix take additional time and patience to implement. Readers may not feel they need to address all components of the recipe based on the needs of their school, but those areas should be regularly evaluated and monitored nonetheless. Leaders and practitioners might not presently focus on a component, although they may find that they do indeed need to address it down the road based on outcome data. Patience is advised when working to implement this model and a phased rollout may be most practical as it allows time to build staff buy-in, to fully ingrain processes and practices into a school's culture, and to permit teachers to move on if they do not feel they can fully commit to the framework and service delivery.

Processes to make changes are offered and it is up to the reader to maximize their potential. Therapy is what individuals make of it. Readers are encouraged to consider these processes and take away what is needed to make sustainable improvements to student supports and services. For now, readers are encouraged to let go of defending what they have in place and start thinking about how to include more practices that work in a new or improved infrastructure. It takes courage and confidence for school leaders and educators to take schools to the next level by embracing the practice of a multi-tiered support system and applying it to their schools.

This is a guide to help administrators, and other motivated educators, with evaluating the needs of specific school sites and generating realistic recommendations that can be implemented to make positive school changes to impact schoolwide achievement. There are interactive exercises designed to strategically plan for school change. Every school is its own kingdom with its own ruler, its own citizens, and its own culture. Every school has its own personality, quality of teachers, resources, funding for resources, diverse student populations, and varying degrees of family engagement and support. There are commonalities between effective programs, but each school must find its own way. That said, there are questions to be asked that can lead to the right decisions at the right time for a school site.

Every school has access to the solutions to their own problems, and practitioners and their school teams have about ideas how to improve instructional quality and outcomes for their students. School leaders and administrators benefit from guidance on how to be their own best resource. If principals have already established a working MTSS model, they most likely have talented and experienced educators on their staff guiding their school and already implementing MTSS successfully because of their hard work, dedication, and reflective practices. If educators have not had the amount of success in implementing MTSS they wish for at their schools, want to fine-tune the MTSS process, or are just getting started, this book is the definitive guide to building and sustaining MTSS. Every school team has the solutions to their own problems. This guide will elicit those solutions.

Exercise 1.1

Reflection Journaling

Complete the following for both Academic MTSS and Social-Emotional-Behavioral MTSS:
- Take a moment and reflect on how you feel about this journey to build MTSS at your school.
- Write about any doubts or fears you may have.
- Write down the benefits of embarking on this path to ensure there are supports for all learners at your school.
  - What is your total student population?
  - What percentage, based on available data, do you estimate to fall within each tier?
  - What resources will you need to provide to meet the needs of the students at each tier?

- Imagine your school in a year and write about what that will be like in terms of improvements academically, behaviorally, and culturally.
- Now imagine your school in five years and what that might be like and write a few sentences about what outcomes you would expect.

References

Anderson, E. R. (2017). Accommodating change: Relating fidelity of implementation to program fit in educational reforms. *American Educational Research Journal, 54*(6), 1288–1315.

Anyon, Y., Nicotera, N., & Veeh, C. A. (2016). Contextual influences on the implementation of a schoolwide intervention to promote students' social, emotional, and academic learning. *Children & Schools, 38*(2), 81–88.

Assistance to States for the Education of Children with Disabilities, 34 CFR §300.307 (2010).

Bamonto-Graney, S., & Shinn, M. R. (2005). Effects of reading curriculum-based measurement (R-CBM) teacher feedback in general education classrooms. *School Psychology Review, 34*(2), 184–201.

Bernard, H. R., & Ryan, G. W. (2010). *Analyzing qualitative data: Systematic approaches.* Thousand Oaks, CA: Sage Publications.

Bolick, C. (2016). Jump starting K-12 education reform. *Harvard Journal of Law & Public Policy, 40*(1), 17–25.

Bolman, L. G., & Deal, T. E. (2017). *Reframing organizations: Artistry, choice, and leadership* (6th ed.). San Francisco, CA: Jossey Bass.

Bryk, A. S., Gomez, L. M., Grunow, A., & LeMahieu, P. G. (2016). *Learning to improve: How America's schools can get better at getting better.* Cambridge, MA: Harvard Education Press.

Creswell, J. W. (2008). *Educational research: Planning, conducting, and evaluating quantitative and qualitative research* (3rd ed.). Upper Saddle River, NJ: Pearson Education.

DiMaggio, P. J., & Powell, W. W. (1991). The iron cage revisited: Institutional isomorphism and collective rationality in organizational fields. In P. J. DiMaggio & W. W. Powell (Eds.), *The new institutionalism in organizational analysis* (pp. 63–82). Chicago, IL: University of Chicago Press.

Every Student Succeeds Act of 2015, 20 U.S.C. (2015).

Francis, B., Mills, M., & Lupton, R. (2017). Toward social justice in education: Contradictions and dilemmas. *Journal of Education Policy, 32*(4), 414–431.

Glaser, B. G. (1992). *Basics of grounded theory analysis: Emergence vs. forcing.* Mill Valley, CA: Sociology Press.

Hallonsten, O., & Hugander, O. (2014). Supporting 'future research leaders' in Sweden: Institutional isomorphism and inadvertent funding agglomeration. *Research Evaluation, 23*, 249–260.

Hanson, M. (2001). Institutional theory and educational change. *Educational Administration Quarterly, 37*(5), 637–661.

Hanson, M. (2003). *Educational administration and organizational behavior.* Boston, MA: Allyn & Bacon.

Jimerson, S. R., Burns, M. K., & VanDerHeyden, A. M. (Eds.). (2016). *The handbook of response to intervention: The science and practice of multi-tiered systems of support.* New York, NY: Springer.

Jones, J. (Ed.). (2009). *The psychology of multiculturalism in the schools: A primer for practice, training, and research.* Bethesda, MD: National Association of School Psychologists.

Jones, J. M., & Kepner, J. A. (2007). Learning to use selective attention: How and why. In R. P. Cantrell & M. L. Cantrell (Eds.), *Helping troubled children and youth* (pp. 265–279). Memphis, TN: American Re-Education Association.

Kannapel, P. J., Clements, S. K., Taylor, D., & Hibpshman, T. (2005). *Inside the black box of high-performing high-poverty schools.* Lexington, KY: Prichard Committee for Academic Excellence. Retrieved from www.prichardcommittee.org/wp-content/uploads/2013/02/Inside-the-Black-Box.pdf

Lane, K. L., Carter, E. W., Jenkins, A., Dwiggins, L., & Germer, K. (2015). Supporting comprehensive, integrated, three-tiered models of prevention in schools: Administrators' perspectives. *Journal of Positive Behavior Interventions, 17*(4), 209–222.

Meijer, A., & Bolívar, M. P. R. (2015). Governing the smart city: A review of the literature on smart urban governance. *International Review of Administrative Sciences, 82*(2), 392–408.

National Association of School Psychologists (2016). *Engaging school psychologists to improve multitiered systems of support*. Bethesda, MD: Author.

National Association of School Psychologists (2017). *ESSA and multitiered systems of support for school psychologists*. Bethesda, MD: Author. Retrieved from www.nasponline.org/research-and-policy/current-law-and-policy-priorities/policy-priorities/the-every-student-succeeds-act/essa-implementation-resources/essa-and-mtss-for-school-psychologists.

Powell, W. W., & DiMaggio, P. J. (1991). *The new institutionalism in organizational analysis*. Chicago, IL: University of Chicago Press.

Pratt-Johnson, Y. (2006). Communicating cross-culturally: What teachers should know. *The Internet TESL Journal, 12*(2). Retrieved from http://iteslj.org/Articles/Pratt-Johnson-CrossCultural.html.

Quintero, E. (Ed.). (2017). *Teaching in context: The social side of education reform*. Cambridge, MA: Harvard Education Press.

Robinson, S. (2015). Decentralisation, managerialism and accountability: Professional loss in an Australian education bureaucracy. *Journal of Education Policy, 30*(4), 468–482. doi:10.1080/02680939.2015.1025241

Rodriguez, B. J., Loman, S. L., & Borgmeier, C. (2016). Tier 2 interventions in positive behavior support: A survey of school implementation. *Preventing School Failure: Alternative Education for Children and Youth, 60*(2), 94–105. doi:10.1080/1045988X.2015.1025354

Shinn, M. R. (2007). Identifying students at risk, monitoring performance, and determining eligibility within RTI: Research on educational need and benefit from academic intervention. *School Psychology Review, 36*(4), 601–617.

Shinn, M. R. (2013). *Elementary version: References for professional development for multi-tiered system of services and supports*. Retrieved from www.tnspdg.com/pdf/RTItraining/2/Shinn%20Elementary%20Readings%20and%20Resources.pdf.

Shinn, M. R., & Walker, H. M. (Eds.). (2010). *Interventions for academic and behavior problems in a three-tier model, including Response-to-Intervention* (3rd ed.). Bethesda, MD: National Association of School Psychologists.

Shriberg, D., Bonner, M., Sarr, B. J., Walker, A. M., Hyland, M., & Chester, C. (2008). Social justice through a school psychology lens: Definition and applications. *School Psychology Review, 37*, 453–468.

Sink, C. A. (2016). Incorporating a multi-tiered system of supports into school counselor preparation. *The Professional Counselor, 6*(3), 203–219.

Sprick, R., Booher, M., & Garrison, M. (2009). *Behavioral response to intervention*. Eugene, OR: Pacific Northwest Publishing.

Sprick, R. A. (2009). *CHAMPS: A proactive and positive approach to classroom management* (2nd ed.). Eugene, OR: Pacific Northwest Publishing.

Sprick, R. A. (2013). *Discipline in the elementary classroom: A positive approach to behavior management* (3rd ed.). Hoboken, NJ: John Wiley & Sons.

Tyler, J. H. (2004). Does G.E.D. improve earnings? Estimates from a sample of both successful and unsuccessful G.E.D. candidates. *ILR Review, 57*(4), 579–598.

VanWynsberghe, R., & Herman, A. C. (2015). Education for social change and pragmatist theory: Five features of educative environments designed for social change. *International Journal of Lifelong Education, 34*(3), 268–283. doi:10.1080/02601370.2014.988189

Yuen, F. K. O., Terao, K. L., & Schmidt, A. M. (2009). *Effective grant writing and program evaluation: For human service professionals*. Hoboken, NJ: John Wiley & Sons.

Chapter 2

Evaluating Your School's Needs and Building Your Team

Key Terms

Cultural Change
Smart Teams
Human Capital
LIQUID Model
Neo-Institutional Theory
Universal Screening
Benchmarking
Progress Monitoring
Rate of Improvement
Strategic Opportunism

Chapter Concepts

In this chapter, readers will learn:

1. To engage in culture change at their schools through perception shifting.
2. To adopt a new MTSS leadership paradigm through the conceptual lens of the LIQUID Model.
3. The basic sociopolitical realities of our education system.
4. The basic components of a successful MTSS program.
5. Entry points to begin MTSS program implementation.

There Is No "No" in Yes

School change is a slow and laborious process. Many urban school campuses have large staff and student populations. When an elementary school has 60-plus teachers, with 20-plus support staff members, and 1,000 students, organized chaos is reliant on systems in place. Instantaneous incorporation of new practices in a large school setting is highly improbable. It takes time for practices to become accepted by school staff members, and it takes a high level of supervision and quality control to model professional standards, monitor professional performance, and provide corrective feedback to ensure implementation fidelity. Implementation outcome data indicate less than 5% of schoolteachers notified of new procedures implement those procedures with integrity initially

(Colter & Gibbons, 2018). Selling the value of evidence-based practices to educational professionals opens the door to improved compliance but does not necessarily ensure implementation or sustainment of the practices. Introducing changes incrementally within the framework, providing continuous follow-up training, and engaging in feedback looping is required to increase competence in new school practices. Making replicable and positive changes through Multi-Tiered Systems of Support (MTSS) in large urban and small rural school settings is possible, regardless of the obstacles.

Varying circumstances may impede the development of a multi-tiered support system in elementary schools. And yes, changing a school system is difficult. However, there is no "no" in yes. There's no "I" in team, and there's no "no" in yes. If the principal at a school decides to commit to growing a functional multi-tiered support system, commitment must be absolute, not partially, not a pilot study, not just for some students, but a total cultural change that impacts everyone. Culture is "the individually and socially constructed values, norms, and beliefs about an organization and how it should behave that can be measured only by observation of the setting using qualitative methods" (Hall & Hord, 2006, p. 20). Therefore, in a school setting, *cultural change* is the observable shift toward new standards, attitudes, and behavior.

In this chapter, readers will understand the premise behind this cultural change and will be introduced to actionable steps that will guide administrators and other motivated educators through the processes of evaluating school needs and building smart teams to grow MTSS (Cunliffe, 2017; Duffy, 2015; VanWynsberghe & Herman, 2015; Naraian & Oyler, 2014; Wilson, 2014). These smart teams are unique in their composition, emotional intelligence and task delegation that make them efficient and effective. *Smart teams* are comprised of individuals who contribute equally to the task at hand, are adept at reading the complex emotional states of others, and tend to have a greater number of female team members than males (Woolley, Chabris, Pentland, Hashmi, & Malone, 2010).

The MTSS framework can be represented by the overlapping nonnegotiable variables of **L**eadership, **I**nclusiveness, **Q**uality control, **U**niversality, **I**mplementation and feedback looping, and **D**ata-based decision making (LIQUID). *Each variable must be infused in all aspects of the framework to ensure the success of MTSS at a school.* The LIQUID Model is the standard in which to compare all phases of the MTSS process. If MTSS is spearheaded and actively supported by leadership, educational practices are inclusive; there are quality control measures to ensure that processes are set up to regularly monitor outcomes and correct practices that are not working; universal practices are in place to support the academic and social-emotional and behavioral health of all students, with universal screening measures to identify all underachievers for early intervention; the implementation of tiered supports are in place with fidelity checks and feedback looping processes embedded in automated systems; and data-based decisions are regularly made to improve student outcomes, then MTSS at a school may be running at peak efficiency. If one or more of these variables cannot be seen, heard, or experienced in one or more MTSS practices, then school teams will be able to identify the weak links to effectively match solutions to the right problems.

Taking the lead to implement MTSS requires changing perspectives of school staff by using an evidence-based best-practices cultural shift that will have an impact on everyone on a school campus. Most industries make decisions based on various sets of data, production data, efficiency data, or user data; education is one of the few fields where best practices are suggested but are largely optional (Ladd & Fiske, 2008). This lackadaisical approach is challenged in this textbook and removes the option of implementing poor policies and programs not backed by evidence-based practices.

The field of medicine also relies on standards and best practices that are critical. Not all medical professionals comply with updates to professional standards, even in the most obvious cases. In 1847, a Hungarian doctor, Ignaz Semmelweis, discovered the benefits of handwashing and disinfecting instruments in a chlorinated lime solution. By instituting these two simple practices in the hospital where he was working, he was able to reduce the mortality rate of his patients from approximately 16% to approximately 3% (World Health Organization, 2009). Even with overwhelming data to support the effectiveness of the new practices, physicians were largely opposed to such methods, as they took offense to a peer pointing out the errors of their ways. In 1867, a British doctor, Joseph Lister, contributed to the knowledge base of antiseptic science with his application of germ theory and his discoveries surrounding wound care, further reducing mortalities and improving surgical care (Pitt & Aubin, 2012). However, not until the mid-1870s did handwashing and disinfecting become best practices in medicine. And it was not until a century later, the 1980s, when national standards were set in the United States for hand hygiene in health care (World Health Organization, 2009). Presently, one would think that there are no valid arguments for a physician to not wash his or her hands before touching a patient because it has been best practice in medicine for almost 150 years; however, it is estimated that up to 50% of providers currently fail to do so (Goldmann, 2006). Educators can learn from medicine's lag in implementing best practices and recognize it as a call for transformational leadership and an opportunity to become a smart organization (Guerro, Fenwick, & Kong, 2017; Hanson, 2003). In education, when data exist to support a best practice that will benefit all students, it is worth investigating ways to implement it without extraneous delay. *All students have the capacity to learn, but not all have the resources to realize their potential.*

A key feature of evaluating the needs of a school and building a smart team rests with the human capital aspects of tier implementation. *Human capital* includes the competencies, value, and knowledge professionals on campus bring to the table. Hiring professionals with necessary capital who also buy into the administrator's vision for MTSS, including releasing those who resist it, is a foundational component of organizational change and building an MTSS team (Anyon, Nicotera, & Veeh, 2016; Foorman, 2016; Freeman, Miller, & Newcomer, 2015; McCarthy, Lambert, Lineback, Fitchett, & Baddouh, 2016; Meyer & Behar-Horenstein, 2015; Pinkelman, McIntosh, Rasplica, Berg, & Strickland-Cohen, 2015; Hall & Hord, 2006). In addition to competence and buy-in, staff motivation should never be underestimated as an essential ingredient of systems change. Implementation of new programs are most successful when administrators are inclusive and active in the change process, and all individuals on campus support the change efforts.

LIQUID Considerations

Following the new LIQUID Theory for MTSS, the *LIQUID Model* allows smart teams to analyze MTSS framework components and strategically evaluate how system processes are affected by each variable, which also reveals the effectiveness of structures that support functions and how well processes are organized, implemented, monitored, adapted, and supported. If each element is not adequately supporting the other elements, the system will not run synergistically and desired measurable student achievement outcomes will be less likely. Current and future educational practices must be appraised through each lens of LIQUID. *The LIQUID Model offers tangible milestones for critical exploration and problem solving to improve team building, operationalization of team functions, and growing site-based capacity of MTSS.* It synthesizes the core features of the most popular multi-tiered model that will result in positive outcomes for students. For every required landmark and systemic practice to grow, in efforts to build and refine tiers of support on a school campus, each component of the LIQUID Model must be considered and questions asked:

1. Leadership: How well will the school's administration lead and support each landmark or practice in MTSS, monitor fidelity of implementation, and correct ineffective practices? How visible is leadership and support of MTSS practices?
2. Inclusiveness: Is the implementation of a landmark or practice truly inclusive? What evidence is there to support that is true or not? Have implicit biases been taken into active consideration? What evidence is there that practices are socially just? How are socially just practices being measured?
3. Quality Control: How is the quality of a system or practice assured? How are processes monitored for efficacy? How often? How do improvements get made, who decides, and when? Are practices working? What evidence exists to support functional practices? Are all sources of information reliable? What evidence is there that practices are implemented with fidelity? Are the right things being measured?
4. Universality: How do school practices impact every student on campus, directly and indirectly? Has every student been counted? How do practices evolve to better meet the needs of all children? How do we teach critical thinking and provide social-emotional, and behavioral experiences that infuse instruction in communication, problem solving, and resilience as preventative medicine, such as immunizations and healthy nutrition? How are all students being actively monitored to check their educational health periodically to intervene at the earliest opportunity, if not by universal benchmarking? Is there universal access to instructional supports to all students who may benefit from them?
5. Implementation and Feedback Looping: Are practices being implemented as intended? Why or why not? How do we know? What are barriers to implementing supports that are needed at a school? Who is doing it well already? What actionable steps can be taken to improve the selection of research-based curriculum and implementation fidelity? How does the team get feedback, qualitative and quantitative, for discussion and decision making? How often? How responsive is the team to modifying supports and service delivery when data support the need to do so? How to select what are next steps based on feedback loop? Who ensures every school professional does his or her part?
6. Data-Based Decision Making: What do the data tell us? What are the trends? Is instructional service delivery working? Does it work in some instances and not others? Are qualitative and quantitative data consistent? Why or why not?

In shifting the leadership lens, we must also shift the practitioner lens. Students are challenging educators to create more relevant and holistic learning experiences personalized to meet individual abilities and needs, while policy makers are focused on other outcomes such as passing accountability standards based on high-stakes testing. The students in classes now are not the same students of the past, as technology has advanced the access to information sources a millionfold. Inexpensive electronic devices can store more information than could ever be memorized, yet even with immediate access to information and knowledge, our students think critically less and less. Our children have more "friends" on social media and fewer social skills and interpersonal relationships. They are unique individuals but are required to have identical studies and pass the same materials at the same rate, or they are deemed failures, regardless of their circumstances.

Thirty-five years ago, it was argued that bureaucratic structuralization had extended from the competitive marketplace to the professions (DiMaggio & Powell, 1983). Since then, schools, and the field of education, have continued to operate as bureaucratic structures and have become even more homogenous, not adapting to unique and diverse environmental demands. In other words, macro-level systems have been put in place without taking into consideration the diverse characteristics at the micro-level, such as individual schools, communities, and families. This *institutional isomorphism* may not be driven with a goal toward organizational efficiency or use of best practice, but rather, they may be driven by coercive, mimetic, and normative processes (DiMaggio & Powell, 1983). For example, schools are increasingly having demands placed on them from the outside, which hinders their ability and initiative to adapt and be reflexive. Conversely, districts repeatedly have mandates put on them from the state forcing them to align with some standard, thus making both districts and schools more homogenous. When these external sources have the power to dictate the narrative and the mandates, decision making at the lower levels is compromised. According to neo-institutional policy research, organizations may increasingly be concerned with goals of power rather than efficiency and, arguably, best practice (Dockweiler, Putney, & Jordan, 2015).

In the school setting, this isomorphism and lack of adaptive responsiveness pose new challenges for school leaders. The MTSS program is a valiant effort to teach a differentiated curriculum to real students, and administrators can promote this institutional shift through adopting MTSS practices that are designed and evaluated by the LIQUID Model standards, to have the most positive impact on a school's culture. *Neo-institutional theory* is a sociopolitical lens in which to view how organizations interact and how they impact society. Understanding that while schools may operate as bureaucratic structures, empowering school leaders to engage autonomously, shifts the paradigm away from homogenous decision making to individual decision making on behalf of students. One way to support responsiveness to environmental and individual student demands is through establishing an MTSS program.

Using a team-based model of decision making, four necessary components of MTSS programs will be reviewed in-depth: appraisal of the team's multiple tiers of support, human capital support, data-based decision making, and collaborative problem solving (Sprick, 2013, 2009; Shinn & Walker, 2010; Shinn, 2007). These four components must be underscored by administrative backing and are essential to maintaining efficacy and quality control of an MTSS program.

Multiple Tiers of Support Appraisal

Using a tiered support system can make it difficult for a team to determine where to focus its efforts. With Tier 1 universal instruction, Tier 2 targeted instruction, and Tier 3 intensive instruction, where does a team start? Many school teams begin with Tier 3 because this is where the most disruptive and most needy students reside. Teams may believe that it makes the most sense to start with Tier 3 because the neediest students who require the most intensive instructional and behavioral supports are interfering with instruction for the rest of the class. To reframe the issue, students usually do not learn maladaptive academic and social behavior overnight, and had Tier 1 and Tier 2 supports been in place to set a foundation of high-quality instruction for all, there would not have been as many students in Tier 3 requiring those intensive supports. Regardless of how established a school's tiers of support, it is always prudent to reevaluate and strengthen Tier 1, which is where the majority of teams will need to focus their efforts, at the base of the triangular framework.

Universal screening, benchmarking, progress monitoring, and rate of improvement are central tenants of a multi-tiered support system. *Universal screening* is administered to all students to determine their current level of performance in any given domain. *Benchmarking* is conducted at set intervals throughout the year to provide a snapshot of a student's performance. *Progress monitoring* is conducted at regular intervals, such as monthly or weekly, to build into the overall portfolio of student progress in response to the interventions provided. *Rate of improvement* is the student's actual rate of improvement and is contrasted against a goal rate of improvement to make decisions about the adequacy of progress. For more detailed explanations of each component and how to conduct them, it is encouraged that explicit practitioner texts be consulted.

Many assessments use a normal distribution to determine student performance with standard deviations representing how significant a student's deficits or strengths are. The greater the deviation below the mean, the greater the need for intensive interventions. The greater the deviation above the mean, the greater the need for enrichment opportunities. For representation purposes, the estimations presented within each tier are based on percentile performance along the normal curve. In doing so, students can easily be divided based on benchmark assessments to determine the requisite level of instructional intensity needed to accomplish core curriculum success and credit requirements. Depending on a student's performance (see Figure 2.1), they will fall within Tier 1, Tier 2, or Tier 3 (Shinn, 2007).

Data consistently support that students who fall above the 25th percentile will respond well to universal Tier 1 instruction. The majority of students respond to universal evidence-based classroom instruction provided within the general education

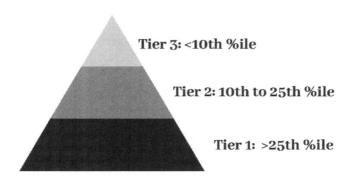

Figure 2.1 Multiple Layers of Support

setting and will not require more intensive supports. These students typically fall above the 25th percentile on benchmark assessments such as AIMSweb Plus (Pearson, 2017). Each tier represents a layer of instruction, and at Tier 1, students only receive one layer: high-quality universal core curriculum.

Some students require Tier 2 targeted instruction to ensure success in the general education setting. Students who fall below the 25th percentile on benchmark assessments may be appropriate for Tier 2 interventions based on team-decision criteria (Shinn, 2007). These students benefit from weekly intervention and monthly progress monitoring to measure the response to the interventions provided. These Tier 2 interventions should transpire for a specific number of minutes a week outside the core curriculum, for example, 180 minutes, and with a student-to-teacher ratio of approximately 6:1. At Tier 2, students receive two layers of instruction: high-quality universal core curriculum and small-group intervention.

A very small portion of students require Tier 3, intensive, individualized academic instruction provided in a specially designed intervention setting. These students fall below the 10th percentile on benchmark assessments such as AIMSweb Plus (Pearson, 2017). Students who fall within Tier 3 benefit from intensive instruction with a teacher *in addition to* Tier 2 interventions *and* the core curriculum, with progress monitoring occurring weekly. These Tier 3 interventions are recommended to occur for a specific number of minutes, for example, 90 minutes weekly, outside Tier 1 and Tier 2 with a student to teacher ratio of approximately 3:1. At Tier 3, students receive three layers of instruction: high-quality universal core curriculum, small-group intervention, and intensive instruction.

For Social-Emotional-Behavioral MTSS, the percentiles and structure are approximately similar. Tier 1 includes universal social-emotional-behavioral curriculum, Tier 2 includes students who require small-group counseling interventions or less intense behavioral support, and Tier 3 includes those students who require individualized behavior intervention plans and community-based supports. Additional guidance, screening procedures, and decision-making strategies are explored in Chapters 10 and 11.

Many urban or impoverished elementary schools are not going to start with the traditional 75% of students in Tier 1, 20% of students in Tier 2, and 5% of students in Tier 3. This 75–20–5 triangle model is more realistic for schools that have established MTSS programs or who have lower-risk student populations. For many high-risk schools starting out, it is not unrealistic to have more of a 25–50–25 diamond model. No matter what model a team is driving, they can still have a successful journey and reach their MTSS goal destination.

A shift in distribution from a 25–50–25 diamond model or a 10–40–50 upside-down triangle model to a 75–20–5 triangle model requires creative and persistent changes over time and will continue to require incremental growth. Depending on the needs of a school and the demographics of their student population, a traditional triangle model may be too high a goal. In these extreme high-risk schools, a 33–34–33 rectangle model may be more realistic and sustainable.

Through leadership fidelity checks (Chapter 4) and program assessment and feedback looping (Chapter 12), teams must continuously use formative and summative measures to evaluate the effectiveness of their MTSS implementation. The Voices From the Field boxes illustrate examples of schools that have made incremental changes to shift the weighted distribution of their model to increase student success at Tier 1 through ongoing reflection and analysis. Some of these examples include bolstering Tier 1 universal instruction through intensive teacher trainings in effective instructional practices, providing continuous subject-level collaboration opportunities for teachers, funding intervention resources and teaching positions, and investing in human capital.

For teams who are unsure of the functional aspects of how to set goals, how to deliver an intervention lesson, how to progress monitor, and how to record progress monitoring data, it is suggested that further resources be sought. While this book will provide teams with the macro-operational aspects of how to implement both Academic and Social-Emotional-Behavioral MTSS in elementary schools, it does not delve into the micro-functional aspects of pedagogy or how to deliver the specific interventions at each tier. Both the high-level operational components and the more minute functional components are essential to MTSS program success.

All things considered, progress monitoring data should demonstrate a growth trajectory that suggests a student is on track to closing his or her achievement gap. Students in Tier 1 who do not receive additional supports are typically able to achieve one year of academic growth per year. Students in Tier 2 and Tier 3 need incrementally more aggressive goals, and their target rate of improvement should be up to twice that of the typical growth rate of Tier 1 students. If a student does not respond adequately to Tier 3 supports (as demonstrated by a poor rate of learning and a low level of performance) over time, and the team suspects the presence of a disability, the MTSS team will submit the referral for special education testing to the Multidisciplinary Evaluation Team.

MTSS teams must ensure that they are diligent about their intervention implementation and documentation which ensures quality control, as special education law requires documentation of research-based interventions and response to instruction data prior to identification of some educational disabilities. Through the embodiment of the LIQUID Model, MTSS teams will not view Tier 3 as a track to special education eligibility but, rather, as a vehicle for meeting and managing the severe needs of students. Students in Tier 3 require substantial resources to be successful, and some of these students may eventually qualify for special education support. However, teams must also consider exclusionary factors as part of their decision making, so they are not contributing to the overidentification of students in special education. Teams should strive for quality control to avoid this overidentification of students, particularly minority students and English-language learners (Kincaid & Sullivan, 2017; Sullivan, 2011). Historically, these are two groups that are consistently overrepresented in special education.

In education, social justice is not just about validating cultural beliefs and acknowledging different holidays and traditions. Conceptual clarity for what a socially just education system looks like is needed and can lead to better policy making with fewer inequities for students (Francis, Mills, & Lupton, 2017). Education has the potential to be the true equalizer and to provide unlimited opportunity for all. Yet not all children have access to high-quality instruction or high-quality instructors who understand individualized differences and have the tools, resources, and systemic support to have inclusive classrooms. Justice is when all children, from all different backgrounds, regardless of socioeconomic background, belong in a school community and have access to a relevant education. *All* students would benefit from individualized growth plans, quite frankly, not just the ones who are low performers, who are from low socioeconomic backgrounds, or who have special needs.

> **Box 2.1**
>
> **Voices From the Field**
>
> My principal at Wong Elementary School implemented a successful MTSS program for reading and math. After our initial construction of structures, functions, and processes to support the model, our principal realized through data analysis that Tier 1 instruction was clearly not effective in our fourth grade in terms of English language arts (ELA) or math scores. A by-product of the lack of quality teaching at Tier 1 created stress on supports needed for a greater number of students in Tiers 2 and 3. Our principal knew that our fourth-grade students were suffering from a lack of quality basic instruction in ELA and math and would fall further behind without corrective action. After evaluating the curriculum, the principal took steps to replace outdated instructional tools with a newer research-based curriculum that supported best practices. Ultimately, the whole fourth-grade team of teachers did not respond adequately to training efforts to improve their instructional delivery and were transferred to other positions. More effective teachers replaced less effective teachers. Results the following school year supported the shakedown and buildup of the new fourth-grade team through outcome data, which demonstrated an administrative commitment to providing quality instruction universally to all students.

Human Capital Support

The second component of a successful MTSS program is human capital support. Sometimes school leaders must take drastic measures to impact outcomes and, most likely, those measures will have an impact on teachers' performance. If school leadership is strong, the curriculum is solid, and achievement is not improving as evidenced by evaluation data, then the scrutiny, and bulk of administrative support, must be placed on teaching practices. The important takeaway is that a school *must* evaluate Tier 1 instruction, curriculum tools, and efficacy of implementation before it can be determined whether a student is failing. *It may be that the established system is failing the student.*

Let's extrapolate the 75–20–5 triangle model to instructional supports for teachers. Teachers are similar to students in that they also require supports to varying degrees in order to be successful in the classroom (McCarthy et al., 2016; Meyer & Behar-Horenstein, 2015). Factors such as their background, education level, and innate ability to differentiate their instruction will all have an impact on the type and intensity of supports a teacher will require to teach successfully within a school with MTSS. The triangle ideal probably does not hold true for teachers-as-learners in many schools, especially in lower-income, high-risk schools that are harder to staff with highly qualified teachers, which typically have a high percentage of substitute teachers or teachers with limited experience. Depending on the composition of a school's teachers, the distribution of teacher supports may more closely resemble a 33–34–33 rectangle model or a 25–50–25 diamond model.

Box 2.2

Voices From the Field

When I first began working at Flor Gonzalez Elementary School (100% free and reduced-price lunch school with 85% English-language learners) as a school psychologist, a system did not exist for students to receive supports for anything outside what was happening in their classroom. Each grade level tended to consult within itself, and the teachers would offer, "Did you try this?" or "Did you try that?" However, if those things were tried and had failed, the teacher's only recourse was to refer the student for a special education evaluation or to the principal. Leadership at the school was weak, and there was a backup of 25 special education referrals because the school could not keep a school psychologist (and many of the referrals were poor ones to begin with). Having worked at schools with highly successful MTSS before, I introduced similar structures and functions to Flor Gonzalez Elementary. The principal was supportive in the sense that she permitted my attempts at instituting MTSS, but she assigned the assistant principal to sit in on the meetings and never once in three years attended an MTSS meeting. When significant issues arose (funding, resources, scheduling of interventions) and the assistant principal made a request of the principal for support, he was often denied. He was told that the team had to make do with what it had. This weak leadership had a profound impact on the staff. They were willing and ready to implement MTSS to its fullest, they liked and had the support of the assistant principal, but the principal stymied completed implementation due to lack of vision, interest (or knowledge), and support. I left that school soon after and found out that the principal also recently left. Now, with new vibrant leadership, the teachers are reporting the initial MTSS foundation that we attempted to lay is now flourishing and that the students are thriving.

In order to see change and success, the perception of educators as teaching the curriculum must shift to a paradigm of teaching curriculum to *real* students, with *real* challenges. Our schools are filled with students living with issues of poverty, food insecurity, homelessness, abuse, parental abandonment, addiction, trauma, and worse. One size does not fit all, in any scenario, and a differentiated model of support is essential. Teachers have taken over extended roles in society because of students' lack of access to basic needs, health care, mental health support, involved parenting, positive role models, and quality emotional support. Collectively, teachers are required to be more than teachers.

Teachers are learning to make data-based decisions to impact their quality of instruction on a daily basis. For many of our students, these decisions may include referrals to community-based agencies to support students in their homes in order to obtain basic needs such as food, housing, mental health, and medical care. *Basic needs are the true Tier 1 of appropriate instruction because if food, housing, and health security are not addressed, more intensive interventions will be much less effective.* In schools that have a large population of students without access to basic needs, a logical step would be for those schools to engage community partnerships to fill the void for those students and families (VanWynsberghe & Herman, 2015).

Changing adult behavior is not an easy task and school professionals are no different. Research on the psychology of organizational change in education repeatedly demonstrates that behavioral change of teachers is challenging, hard to enforce, and even more difficult to measure as successful (VanWynsberghe & Herman, 2015; Hanson, 2003). Some schools might have amazing talent and have all highly adept and adaptable teachers who will make the transition from maintaining few supports to actively working toward comprehensive supports without skipping a beat when directions change. Transitioning adult behavior collectively in a common cause of comprehensive supports for all students in an elementary school is not likely to happen without bumps in the road. In utilizing this book, and the exercises embedded within, teams will be well on their way to successfully gliding over the potholes on their journey ahead.

Data-Based Decision Making

The third component of a successful MTSS program is data-based decision making. In reviewing the tiered model, data-based decision making must start with Tier 1. Universal instruction at Tier 1 is the cornerstone of a tiered support model and is the place to begin laying a foundation. Otherwise, how can the efficacy of Tier 2 and Tier 3 instruction be evaluated when universal instruction is not being provided with fidelity? There are five imperative steps administrators must take to ensure the fidelity of Tier 1 practices:

1. Review the research regarding highly effective curricula to ensure that Tier 1 instruction is based on best practices.
2. Ensure that the curriculum is being implemented with integrity and fidelity. If a holistic program sequences lessons, ensure that the lessons are being delivered in order as prescribed.
3. Establish opportunities for staff to be engaged in continuous professional learning to keep teachers abreast of best practices and provide opportunities for guided practice and coaching.
4. Provide continuous collaborative opportunities for subject-level planning with a constant feedback loop to the school's leadership team.
5. Monitor teachers through observations (both scheduled and spontaneous) and administrative conferences to get feedback about curriculum, assessment, and instruction.

If the foundation of universal instruction is not solid, these five criteria will need to be reassessed and addressed to ensure they meet the standards of stable and quality Tier 1 instruction. If it has been determined that the established Tier 1 universal curriculum is evidence-based and is being implemented with fidelity, and students are still failing, what is next?

If the problems do not lie with administrative support, engagement, or reinforcement of teachers implementing Tier 1 instruction with fidelity, the next step is to examine processes and procedures. Are the wheels spinning but the car is not moving? How do students access the best opportunities to obtain targeted and intensive instruction through Tier 2 and Tier 3? The answers depend on the leadership, resources, and staffing available at individual schools. *Limitations must be viewed as opportunities, not challenges, to help shift the mind-set of the school.* Schools may face many opportunities including those of funding, team creativity, and minimizing staff resistance toward change. While a portion of the staff will be resistant, overcoming resistance provides the administrator with an opportunity to clearly outline the vision, set explicit expectations, establish open lines of communication with staff, and establish a system of continuous improvement.

Collaborative Problem Solving

The final component of a successful MTSS program is collaborative problem solving. *Effective MTSS programs rely on constant, iterative problem-solving cycles that involve the talents of a variety of team members and stakeholders.* These smart MTSS organizations share hard and soft knowledge school year to school year with new team members through "written record, organizational culture, socialization, in-service training, and imitation" (Hanson, 2003, p. 290). Hard knowledge is categorized by the processes, programs, and structures ingrained in an organization. Soft knowledge includes the values, perspectives, and attitudes of the organization's members. This evolving organizational memory is strengthened by constant reflection and review of how to improve both hard and soft knowledge.

Administrators must build relationships with their leadership team and staff for successful problem solving and collaboration. The speed and success in making inroads to achieve this often depend on the school climate, which is most often driven by the school principal. On a school campus, there are several established social systems, some formal and some informal (Hanson, 2003). The MTSS team operates as a formal social system while the group of teachers who walks together at lunch is an informal social system. Depending on the social system, the approach for obtaining buy-in and collaboration may differ. Regardless of the approach, this is a prime opportunity for the administrator to build the school climate around supportive MTSS practices. *Never overlook the impact informal social systems have on a campus, as they have just as much power to support or sabotage change efforts as formal social systems do.*

For an elementary school wishing to implement a multi-tiered support system, the first question to ask is, What are the bare essential elements of MTSS that can be established most quickly and effectively? The answer to that question depends on the administrator's commitment to implementation, the school's population, and various risk factors a school faces. It also depends on the status of the team with regard to the four required components of an MTSS program: multiple tiers of support appraisal, human capital support, data-based decision making, and collaborative problem solving.

When it is broached to school staff that it will be implementing an MTSS program, many questions arise. Common questions include the following:

- How can multiple layers of support be built in schools?
- What additional requirements will be put on me?
- How much time will it take from my already busy day?
- What new procedures will I need to learn?
- Which assessment tools do teams use to assess growth?
- How often are students assessed?

- How do students access the layers of support at the school?
- When do teams make data-based decisions?
- How do teams decide when there is enough intervention data to refer a student to the multidisciplinary team for special education evaluation and support?
- How does the collaborative problem-solving approach work?
  - Will we receive support and training?
  - Can we opt out of participating?

Patience is requested of teams as the problem-solving processes evolve. As the MTSS program is built, discussion points are brought up to administrators and their leadership teams to begin addressing the various opportunities on their campuses. There are several common steps in a classical decision-making process (Hanson, 2003, pp. 63–64):

1. Recognize, define, and situate the problem in relation to program goals.
2. Analyze and evaluate the problem.
3. Establish criteria and standards by which a solution will be evaluated or judged as acceptable and adequate to the need.
4. Define the alternatives.
5. Collect data on each alternative.
6. Apply evaluative criteria to each alternative.
7. Select the preferred choice.
8. Implement the choice.
9. Evaluate the results.

Starting Points

Before delving into meaty questions, some basics will be addressed to help drive solutions, which will depend on the risk level and needs of a school. The needs of each school and the student population will determine the level of support structure needed. Every school is unique, and each will require a differentiated approach within the tiered paradigm. Low socioeconomic schools experience challenges associated with poverty. Students in higher-socioeconomically advantaged schools most often have their basic needs met, but share the challenges faced by all students, such as learning problems, social and behavioral problems, mental health issues, trauma, and family issues that require supports and interventions. When generalizing risk factors, schools greatly require structures to be in place to systematically evaluate and monitor students' academic and behavioral achievement and support a decrease in the likelihood of recidivism (Taskiran, Mutluer, Tufan, & Semerci, 2017; McKee & Caldarella, 2016; Barrett & Katsiyannis, 2015). Effective instruction has to fit the needs of the community as well as the classroom population.

The School Risk Assessment Survey (SRAS) can be used by school teams to determine where their school falls along the risk continuum: high, medium, or low (see Figure 2.2). This informal survey is used as a reference to get an idea of the general need and risk-level of the school. At this time, school leaders will want to complete the SRAS.

School Risk Assessment Survey

Put a checkmark next to all the risk factors below evident in your school building and circle the corresponding risk level.

_____ Poverty	_____ Second Language Factors
_____ Hunger	_____ Low Funding for Education
_____ Transience	_____ Student Safety
_____ Absenteeism	_____ Teacher Burnout Rate
_____ Family Involvement	_____ Negative School Culture
_____ Family Issues	_____ Learning Problem
_____ Student Motivation	_____ Social/Behavioral Problems
_____ Overcrowded Classrooms	_____ Developmental Issues
_____ Teaching Quality	_____ Community Risk Factors

Low Risk	Medium Risk	High Risk
1–5 Factors	6–11 Factors	12+ Factors

Figure 2.2 School Risk Assessment Survey

The SRAS can be used by school teams to determine where their school falls along the risk continuum: high, medium, or low. In general, if the school community identifies with one to five of these challenges, the school is probably in the low-risk category. If the school community identifies with 6 to 11 of these factors, the school is probably in the medium-risk category. If the school community identifies with 12 or more of these risk factors, it is probably safe to say that the school can count itself in the high-risk category. Keep in mind that there are always high-risk students in low-risk and medium-risk schools and vice versa.

Why does it matter how many risk factors a school has when determining the needs of its students? *High-needs students need higher levels of support to succeed as a matter of equity.* Higher-needs schools require team processes that consist of more manpower, more resources, and more data to make better decisions. Higher-needs schools face more opportunities to remediate skill deficits. Lower-needs schools have fewer students in need, but make no mistake, they still require checks and balances to support low-achieving students and to provide enrichment to higher achieving students. With MTSS, teams have the opportunity to address the unique needs of all students, from the low performers to the high performers. Teachers should be able to access supports to help high-needs students, regardless of the socioeconomic status of the school. The more immediately school teams can identify student needs and put interventions in place, the better the chance the students have to improve and become successful learners and, ultimately, independent successful adults. Most teams already have a general idea about the implementation challenges they face. But, again, the barriers must be properly identified and be viewed as opportunities if there is any chance of overcoming them. It must also be made clear to staff that MTSS will not fix issues such as poverty, homelessness, or food scarcity. But it will help identify those students whose basic needs are not being met so that additional school-based and community supports can be offered and monitored.

Change from the bottom up has some advantages and may come in the form of increasing teacher leadership on a small scale or helping a targeted number of students. There are instances where grassroots efforts lead by teachers at the bottom have garnered attention from administration and resulted in lasting systemic change. These grassroots efforts lead to high levels of buy-in from staff that are essential to the change process (Pinkelman et al., 2015). However, lasting school change is most likely to occur from the top down through strategic opportunism (Isenberg, 1987). *Strategic opportunism* is a term borrowed from the business world that simply means the leader is able to adhere to the long-term vision, for example, higher student achievement, while remaining flexible enough in the short term to take advantage of opportunities that arise to support and help meet the long-term vision, for example, implementing a model of support consisting of multiple tiers.

The most significant change in the educational practices at a school will not occur through democracy, unfortunately. *Change will require the focused leadership of the school principal who can make decisions for the entire school staff and who can ensure change with guided enforcement and implementation of policies.* The administrator will make things happen through scaffolding, supervision, and evaluation of staff and programs. If a team would like to implement an MTSS framework but the school principal is not willing to take leadership, or at the very least support a team of leaders, there are two choices: wait until the principal is convinced and is on board or accept the fact that the team's best efforts may result in limited cultural change. In this case, teams can reframe the restricted support as an opportunity to collect data through a pilot study, by improving professional learning opportunities or helping a small number of students at a time.

Exercise 2.1

MTSS Team Development Mirror Exercise

At this point in the process, the individual or team of individuals driving the MTSS initiatives on a campus will want to complete the MTSS Team Development Mirror Exercise. This exercise is a recommendation for you to look in the mirror. You are the first step in your school's change by picking up this book and using it to guide your actions in regards to implementing a multi-tiered support system at your school. As you look in the mirror ask yourself if are you the only one in the picture that desires this change at your school and who else believes it is a good idea. If you are the leader at your school, and you are standing alone in that mirror, then know that you are going to have to cultivate and train a team of people that can help you attain your vision for your school. If you are a motivated educator, such as an assistant principal, a teacher, a specialist, or a school psychologist, and the primary administrator is not standing in that mirror next to you when you look at the reflection, then understand that your vision has a much smaller chance of obtaining fruition in a natural timeline. The more engaged and motivated the primary administrator, the greater the likelihood of MTSS programming success.

- Look in the mirror and describe what you see. Use kind words to describe yourself.
- Close your eyes and think about what your intentions are for your school. Set your intentions in simple sentences in your mind (i.e., I want to improve achievement or I want to

improve schoolwide behavior). Make it global in nature and decide what you want; planning action steps will come later. Now open your eyes and speak your intentions to yourself, as in a mirror. Write your intentions down.
- Be honest with yourself. Why do you want those things listed earlier? Do you have a passion for teaching? Helping children? Do you enjoy leading? Are you seeking experience for a promotion? Think about your own motives because self-awareness will help you keep your eyes on the big picture and help you understand how to motivate others to join your vision.
- List your motives now. Reflect on how your motives will benefit students and teachers.
- Think about who else shares your intentions at your school. List the names of personnel and staffing positions at your school who you are certain share your intent already and have the skill set to help you pull it off. This list will seed your decision-making team.
- Who is missing? List the people or staffing positions missing from the preceding list that you want or need to be on board your team.
- Why are those staff members not backing you? What do you think you can do to get the missing staff members to buy in? Other questions you may want to answer could include Who is the biggest obstacle to change in attitude and/or practice? Who has a strong voice on your campus who could help you win over others? and Who do you need to win over first?

After the MTSS Team Development Mirror Exercise Form has been completed, leaders will have a detailed vision of the intent for their school and they will know who shares, and does not share, that intent. Leaders may rejoice in knowing that their intentions are clear. Knowing where the train is going and who is on board is half the battle. The people who are not on board or yet convinced of leaders' intentions are going to know how much of a priority those intentions are as they are empowered and tasked with specific team functions and asked to delineate processes to meet the needs of all students. Leaders must continually reflect on their intentions and who will help them reach the goals by actively overcoming hurdles to the finish line.

Set this list aside for later reference.

Exercise 2.2

Evaluate Leadership Commitment to the Process

The first question administrators who are implementing, or who are considering implementing, a multi-tiered support system in their school should ask themselves is, How important is it to them? and Is this something they really believe will help their students?

On a scale of 1 to 10, how important is implementing a multi-tiered support system at your school?

Not Important	1	2	3	4	5	6	7	8	9	10	Very important

How can you increase your commitment, motivation, and dedication to implementing MTSS? Additional awareness to lend comfort? Diversifying the skill sets of educators on staff to enhance effectiveness? Increasing personal knowledge and professional development of MTSS?

Teacher Effectiveness

All professionals on a school campus have strengths and weaknesses. The leaders and experts in one subject may not be the ones selected to lead and guide practice in another. For this exercise, think about the strengths of the teachers on campus, with 1 being those teachers with the most opportunity to grow and 10 being the most accomplished teachers. Consider who needs to be on the MTSS leadership decision-making team, and think of at least two teachers, in addition to specialists, who can serve as leaders in decision making. The level of importance for implementing MTSS in a school should match with the level of teacher strength on the team. If a principal estimates the importance of MTSS at a high level, between 7 and 10, then he or she should match the skill level of teachers on the decision-making team with the importance level of the system. If the team is stacked with teachers in the 3 to 4 level range, that probably is the highest level of quality the team will get in results.

If school leaders believe they get what they pay for then why would they put less accomplished teachers on such an important committee that will shape instructional practices and culture at their school? While it is easy to burn out the best teachers with multiple functions, it is crucial to stack the MTSS team with competence from the start. Less accomplished teachers can get up to speed after MTSS is running well, but schools will need the best problem solvers on their MTSS team, especially at first. If administrators think that this committee has an importance level of 7 or above, they cannot afford to assign less accomplished teachers.

If the leadership team believes MTSS to have an importance level of 7 or above, then they need to assign committee members with a ranking of 7 and above to the team. *Pick your top performers, best thinkers, and best problem solvers on the team.* Go ahead, select the 9- and 10-level teachers for the team. They are role models and leaders for the whole school. They know how much work it is to do what they are asking other teachers to do, and they do exemplary work, going above and beyond with students, and with a positive attitude. The problem with picking the best teachers and problem solvers to be on this team is they are often overused and inundated with doing all the work on campus that others cannot or will not do (i.e., all the little pet projects that need to get done along with some quasi-administrative responsibilities), as well as all the other things they volunteer to do to make the school days run smoothly for students. This committee commitment really has to be the most important in terms of extra duties outside of the classroom that those teachers have because it is very time-consuming. In order to build capacity and sustainability of MTSS, all teachers on campus must feel supported and be given opportunities to improve their skills within the MTSS framework. Without this growth, the teacher leaders on campus will burn out and the entire system will falter. It is recommended that the school create a leadership position for this key individual(s) and have them serve in the capacity as a literacy coach or intervention specialist so that they can provide supports schoolwide as part of their daily duties, not on top of their regular classroom teaching duties.

Exercise 2.3

Build Your MTSS Team

- Who are your strongest (e.g., Levels 7, 8, 9, and 10) teachers by grade level and/or subject?
- Who are your specialists? What are their positions? Are they on board with MTSS?

- Are the people listed in this exercise many of the same listed on Exercise 1 that share your vision? Why or why not? How can relationships between stakeholders improve to get buy-in?

Combine your responses from Exercises 2.1 through 2.5. Review the SRAS results and begin problem solving. Organize the list by grade level, and try to have one representative per grade. Also try to incorporate specialists or other individuals on campus who can support MTSS efforts. These are staff members with particular expertise who can either help train staff or support the planning, structure, and function of MTSS at your school. Congratulations! You have an MTSS team. Now you have to convince them of their power to lead this endeavor and train them in the basic duties and responsibilities of leading this extremely important school improvement team. You have committed your best resources to the team in the form of human capital; now show your commitment to the team and the rest of the school community.

References

Anyon, Y., Nicotera, N., & Veeh, C. A. (2016). Contextual influences on the implementation of a schoolwide intervention to promote students' social, emotional, and academic learning. *Children & Schools, 38*(2), 81–88.

Barrett, D. E., & Katsiyannis, A. (2015). Juvenile delinquency recidivism: Are Black and White youth vulnerable to the same risk factors? *Behavioral Disorders, 40*(3), 184–195.

Colter, W. A., & Gibbons, K. A. (2018, February). *Creating thirsty horses: Three keys to increasing implementation fidelity*. Paper session presented at the National Association of School Psychologists Annual Conference, Chicago, IL.

Cunliffe, R. H. (2017). Conflict resolution classrooms to careers: An emergent theory of change with implications for a strategy in peace education. *Journal of Peace Education, 14*(2), 235–252. doi:10.1080/17400201.2016.1278165

DiMaggio, P. J., & Powell, W. W. (1983). The iron cage revisited: Institutional isomorphism and collective rationality in organizational fields. *American Sociological Review, 48*(2), 147–160.

Dockweiler, K. A., Putney, L. G., & Jordan, T. S. (2015). Enhancing the policy analysis process: Case studies using the layers of analysis framework. *Journal of Ethnographic and Qualitative Research, 10*(4), 87–103.

Duffy, M. (2015). Education, democracy and social change: Venezuela's education missions in theory and practice. *Journal of Education Policy, 30*(5), 650–670. doi:10.1080/02680939.2014.981868

Foorman, B. (2016). Introduction to the special issue: Challenges and solutions to implementing effective reading intervention in schools. In B. Foorman (Ed.), *Challenges to implementing effective reading intervention in schools: New directions for child and adolescent development, 154* (pp. 7–10). Malden, MA: Wiley Periodicals, Inc.

Francis, B., Mills, M., & Lupton, R. (2017). Towards social justice in education: Contradictions and dilemmas. *Journal of Education Policy, 32*(4), 414–431.

Freeman, R., Miller, D., & Newcomer, L. (2015). Integration of academic and behavioral MTSS at the district level using implementation science. *Learning Disabilities: A Contemporary Journal, 13*(1), 59–72.

Goldmann, D. (2006). System failure versus personal accountability: The case for clean hands. *The New England Journal of Medicine, 355*, 121–123. doi:10.1056/NEJMp068118

Guerro, E. G., Fenwick, K., & Kong, Y. (2017). Advancing theory development: Exploring the leadership-climate relationship as a mechanism of the implementation of cultural competence. *Implementation Science, 133*, 1–12. doi:10.1186/s13012-017-0666-9

Hall, G. E., & Hord, S. M. (2006). *Implementing change: Patterns, principals, and potholes* (2nd ed.). New York, NY: Pearson Education.

Hanson, M. (2003). *Educational administration and organizational behavior.* Boston, MA: Allyn & Bacon.

Isenberg, P. (1987, March). The tactics of strategic opportunism. *Harvard Business Review.* Retrieved from https://hbr.org/1987/03/the-tactics-of-strategic-opportunism.

Kincaid, A. P., & Sullivan, A. L. (2017). Parsing the relations of race and socioeconomic status in special education disproportionality. *Remedial and Special Education, 38*(3), 159–170.

Ladd, H. F., & Fiske, E. B. (Eds.). (2008). *Handbook of research in education finance and policy.* New York, NY: Routledge.

McCarthy, C. J., Lambert, R. G., Lineback, S., Fitchett, P., & Baddouh, P. G. (2016). Assessing teacher appraisals and stress in the classroom: Review of the classroom appraisal of resources and demands. *Education Psychology Review, 28,* 577–603.

McKee, M. T., & Caldarella, P. (2016). Middle school predictors of high school performance: A case study of dropout risk indicators. *Education, 136*(4), 515–529.

Meyer, M. M., & Behar-Horenstein, L. S. (2015). When leadership matters: Perspectives from a teacher team implementing response to intervention. *Education and Treatment of Children, 38*(3), 383–402.

Naraian, S., & Oyler, C. (2014). Professional development for special education reform: Rearticulating the experiences of urban educators. *Urban Education, 49*(5), 499–527.

Pearson. (2017). *AIMSweb plus introductory guide.* Retrieved from www.marshfieldschools.org/cms/lib/WI01919828/Centricity/Domain/82/aimsplus%20introductory%20guide.pdf

Pinkelman, S. E., McIntosh, K., Rasplica, C. K., Berg, T., & Strickland-Cohen, M. K. (2015). Perceived enablers and barriers related to sustainability of school-wide positive behavioral interventions and supports. *Behavioral Disorders, 40*(3), 171–183.

Pitt, D. P., & Aubin, J. M. (2012). Joseph Lister: Father of modern surgery. *Journal of Canadian Surgery, 55*(5), E8–E9. doi:10.1503/cjs.007112

Shinn, M. R. (2007). Identifying students at risk, monitoring performance, and determining eligibility within RTI: Research on educational need and benefit from academic intervention. *School Psychology Review, 36*(4), 601–617.

Shinn, M. R., & Walker, H. M. (Eds.). (2010). *Interventions for academic and behavior problems in a three-tier model, including Response-to-Intervention* (3rd ed.). Bethesda, MD: National Association of School Psychologists.

Sprick, R. A. (2009). *CHAMPS: A proactive and positive approach to classroom management* (2nd ed.). Eugene, OR: Pacific Northwest Publishing.

Sprick, R. A. (2013). *Discipline in the elementary classroom: A positive approach to behavior management* (3rd ed.). Hoboken, NJ: John Wiley & Sons.

Sullivan, A. L. (2011). Disproportionality in special education identification and placement of English language learners. *Exceptional Children, 77*(3), 317–334.

Taskiran, S., Mutluer, T., Tufan, A. E., & Semerci, B. (2017). Understanding the associations between psychosocial factors and severity of crime in juvenile delinquency: A cross-sectional study. *Neuropsychiatric Disease and Treatment, 13,* 1359–1366.

VanWynsberghe, R., & Herman, A. C. (2015). Education for social change and pragmatist theory: Five features of educative environments designed for social change. *International Journal of Lifelong Education, 34*(3), 268–283. doi:10.1080/02601370.2014.988189

Wilson, H. W. (2014). *The reference shelf: Embracing new paradigms in education.* Amenia, NY: Grey House Publishing.

Woolley, A. W., Chabris, C. F., Pentland, A., Hashmi, N., & Malone, T. W. (2010). Evidence for a collective intelligence factor in the performance of human groups. *Science, 330*(6004), 686–688.

World Health Organization (2009). *WHO guidelines on hand hygiene in health care: First global patient safety challenge clean care is safer care.* Geneva, Switzerland: Author.

Chapter 3

Invest in Resources at Your School

Key Terms

Education Malpractice
Controlled Chaos
Fidelity
Access
Overcorrection
Growth Model
Three-Pronged Motivation Approach
Triangulating

Chapter Concepts

In this chapter, readers will learn:

1. The current realities facing today's education field.
2. The need for a shift in the social perspective of an educator's value.
3. The critical need for proactive and adequate allocation of fiscal resources.
4. The benefit of evidence-based assessment tools for universal benchmarking and progress monitoring.
5. The importance of data-based decision making and how to triangulate data sources.
6. The demand for research-based interventions and fidelity of implementation.

In this chapter, the realities of today's education field are discussed as well as the need to shift the social perspective of educators' value. The critical resources of fiscal allocation, assessment tools, data-based decision making, and research-based interventions are also examined. This chapter "gets real" about current teaching conditions including socioeconomic challenges, outdated compensation and professional learning systems, and the unrealistic expectations and demands that are often placed on teachers' time (Preiss, 2015; Wilson, 2014; Odden & Picus, 2014; Odden, 2012; Ladd & Fiske, 2008). The demands placed on educators have increased over the past decade due to the continued growth of the accountability movement and the expanding needs of our students, but the infrastructure to support these professionals has remained stagnant.

Social perceptions of the teaching field are discussed and current shifts are presented that support the modernization and elevation of the teaching profession, led by the efforts of the 40 TeachStrong coalition partners, including, but not limited to, the Center for American Progress, Teach for America, The Education Trust, Association for Supervision and Curriculum Development (ASCD), Council of Chief State School Officers, Learning Forward, and the National Board for Professional Teaching Standards (Preiss, 2015). This coalition focuses on research and supports nine campaign principles to strengthen the entire teaching continuum, including the highest set of rigorous standards for accomplished teaching, National Board Certification, as developed by the National Board for Professional Teaching Standards (National Board for Professional Teaching Standards, 2016; Preiss, 2015; Layton, 2015; Martin, Partelow, & Brown, 2015; Sawchuk, 2015; Ladd & Fiske, 2008). Leveraging relationships with stakeholders is introduced with further discussion included in Chapter 12.

Realities of Today's Education Field

Working within the field of education is a noble endeavor. Whether serving as a teacher, a school psychologist, a school nurse, a teacher's aide, or in any other capacity, these professionals dedicate their lives to improving the quality of life for students, communities, and society. Educators invest in their own educational and professional learning throughout their careers costing them much of their hard-earned income. Many endure economic hardships themselves including paying back student loans, surviving student teaching and internship experiences for little to no pay, and existing at barely a living wage at the bottom of a school district's pay scale for years before reaching a minimum economic comfort level. Political climates impact teachers' daily functions depending on the emphasis of the day, whether that be high-stakes testing, mandatory Common Core State Standards (2010) instruction, or negative media bias regarding the education establishment in general or teachers' job security and benefits specifically. Teachers are often among the best role models in a child's life. Teachers help our children learn, guide them through critical thinking development, and nurture them through their formative years. Almost everyone can think of a teacher or caring adult at school who changed their lives for the better, one who deserves great praise.

Of course, there are also less effective educators. In all professions, there are individuals with uncertain intentions and lower expertise. In addition to less effective educators, there are ineffective practices that have a negative impact on children. There is no excuse for individual educators' apathy, malpractice, or outright abuse in the workplace: a case in point, states that allow legal corporal punishment in schools and allow adults in education to engage in abusive and harmful practices toward children. Institutionalized abuse has negative consequences that can last a lifetime for students. Some of these professionals can be rehabilitated with the appropriate training. Still, there are educators who will continue to engage in education malpractice and are not able to transfer from punitive to proactive practices. Such individuals should be monitored closely in the presence of children and be encouraged to leave the profession, in accordance with employee contracts and state laws. *Education malpractice* is the preventable adverse impact on a student through educator negligence or incompetence that goes against evidence-based practices.

Corporal punishment is a long-standing social construct used to physically command obedience and respect from children (Freeman, 2010; Foucault, 1995). Forms of physical abuse have historically provided parents with legal protections; however, children have not been afforded the same protections should they return the abuse to their parents (Freeman, 2010). As early as 1641, it was recognized in the Massachusetts *Body of Liberties* that parents should not use excessive severity in the punishment of their children (Pleck, 2004). This same law also provided children the right to report to authorities any instances of excessive punishment. While this early recognition of children's rights is encouraging, there is no documented evidence that any complaints were made or cases heard (Pleck, 2004).

In the centuries that ensued, and as education systems evolved in the United States, this allowance and social acceptance of corporal punishment have extended to its use in classrooms by teachers and administrators. Historically and presently, evidence does not support that corporal punishment is an effective way to model desired prosocial behavior (Straus, 2010; Foucault, 1995). Indeed, international research confirms that corporal punishment causes a high degree of emotional harm to children with the level of internalized behaviors, specifically anxiety and depression, directly correlated to the intensity of the abuse (Gershoff, 2010). The negative repercussions of harsh punishment include increased student behavioral problems, decreased academic achievement, clinical depression, and trauma and suicidal ideation, among other devastating impacts for children (Asghar, Munawar, Muhammad, 2015; Tong et al., 2015).

Minority students and those with disabilities are disproportionately targeted with the harshest forms of discipline (Sparks & Harwin, 2016). In a socially just school culture, adults never destroy children's trust by hurting them physically and emotionally; with certainty, *the opposite must occur by adults protecting children from hurt and guiding them during vulnerable years with care and purpose.* Concerned citizens should advocate against such practices by writing their congressional representatives and state legislators to have corporal punishment in schools outlawed in state policy. Educators practicing corporal punishment are not necessarily bad people but may be habituated to horrific abuses. In such cases, the abuse has become normalized, but that does not make it acceptable. Intentionally inflicting pain on children for teaching purposes will *never* be a valid teaching method or ethical practice.

Moving away from educational practices that do not work, at best, and are harmful to students, at worst, teachers are under a lot of pressure to demonstrate measurable growth in their students. In some school districts, resources are scarce, and their materials and technology are outdated due to budget constraints. In other districts, the constant mandating for updated curriculum, continual cycles of different types of testing, teacher documentation requirements, and school accountability reporting take up a staggering amount of teaching time that could be otherwise spent on meaningful learning activities. *Teachers must balance what they are mandated to do by state laws and district procedures with what they need to do to reach all students.* Teachers must have access to appropriate tools and continuing opportunities to improve their teaching methods in order to increase positive outcomes for students. Administrative support and leadership are critical for teachers' success with these endeavors.

Being an educator is hard work, arguably one of the hardest-working professions. Educators have a future of modest pay, which is just the beginning of the challenges they will face along their career paths. For example, teachers might be expected to teach a curriculum that may not be developmentally appropriate for their students; they may not have the preservice training, job support, or resources to adequately address student behavior difficulties; and they will have to accept varying levels of parent and community support. However, most educators are committed to improving the skills of their students. Some are more skilled than others at managing the demands for higher achievement in the classroom despite all the risk factors that have an impact on achievement. Some educators prefer to work with students who have knowledge gaps or learning problems. Working with children who do not learn the prescribed way, or at the expected speed, requires creative adaptation to engage those learners and fill in those gaps. Some educators find those same students difficult to reach and are taxed by the amount of time and energy that must be devoted to the higher-needs students. Overcrowded classrooms, a lack of adequate resources, and working over recommended ratios are also challenges to overcome. Educators are sometimes blamed and receive negative consequences as a result of poor student outcomes over which they had limited control over. Despite all the difficulties, many educators still consider being an educator the best job in the world.

However, educators are people too, and they fulfill many life roles including parent, spouse, and caregiver for an aging parent or parents, in addition to roles and responsibilities in community service. They have busy lives with personal interests, projects, family duties, and health issues. Educators have a lot of responsibility but not a lot of control over factors that have an impact on students. Educators must manage their time wisely in order to have a life of their own and a successful career concurrently, with a high percentage working multiple jobs to make ends meet. Many spouses and families will attest that their husband or wife, mom or dad, brings too much work home and spends too much time thinking about their students and work outside of work hours. Daily physical and emotional exhaustion and can have a negative impact on an entire family unit. Educational leaders must be very cognizant of the realities of educators when asking them to do anything more or differently.

Exercise 3.1

Educator Challenges and Opportunities Survey

- Take a moment and reflect on the broad challenges educators at your school are likely to experience in general. Write them down and be as specific as possible.
- Poll staff as to their perceptions about what broad challenges they face.
- Write some possible solutions and supports that may help educators with those challenges. In addition to writing solutions, craft several pathways for attaining the target. If X is the goal, devise pathways A, B, C, and D as a viable means to reach the goal. With multiple means to explore, the likelihood of one of them being viable increases.

Share these notes in discussion with the school's leadership team. Pick one issue at a time and address it with the school's staff. Try possible solutions and wait for feedback. Some issues are beyond quick fixes; however, if a listed problem has an obvious solution on your campus, make it happen as soon as feasible. *Positive results increase goodwill and trust, which go a long way toward educator morale.*

Social Perspectives and Educator Value

Budgets are tight and job security is scarce in many school districts across the nation due to unreliable funding. Compounded by issues of teacher shortages, school psychologist shortages, and staffing difficulties in all education-related professions, schools are grappling with how to adequately fill vacancies to meet the needs of its students. Nationwide, many of the large, at-risk school districts report significant shortage numbers. In the School District of Philadelphia, there were 190 teaching positions open in the 2016–2017 school year (Yaffe, 2016), and in Clark County School District (Las Vegas, Nevada), the number of open teaching positions pushed 1,000 during that same period (Gonser, 2016). In both districts, the shortages reported are a significant percentage of their local teaching force, which leave thousands of students without a licensed teacher. State departments and individual school districts are devising creative strategies to address this chronic shortage through incentive programs, partnerships with local teacher training programs at colleges and universities, and hiring substitute teachers and nonlicensed teachers (Gonser, 2016; Yaffe, 2016).

Teaching is a skill that cannot be approximated by only having knowledge of a subject matter. For example, just because someone knows how to read does not mean that the person knows how to effectively teach reading to someone else, let alone to classes of 30 to 40 children. State and national educational policies attacking the teaching profession and replacing qualified licensed teachers with untrained individuals will not produce good outcomes for vulnerable children who desperately need strong teachers. Students benefit the most from highly trained and accomplished teachers (National Board for Professional Teaching Standards, 2016).

Coast to coast there is also a shortage of school psychologists who can assist school teams and help implement evidence-based Multi-Tiered Systems of Support (MTSS) programs and support students' academic and mental-behavioral health needs (National Association of School Psychologists, 2017). Oftentimes, the ratio of school psychologist to students is as high as 1:3,500 (Nevada Association of School Psychologists, 2018), or five to seven times over the National Association of School Psychologists recommended ratio for comprehensive services of 1:500 to 1:700 (National Association of School Psychologists, 2010). A lack of sufficient training programs contributes to this shortage as does the inadequate compensation in some districts, which makes recruitment in these districts nearly impossible. Districts that have the greatest numbers of high-risk students would benefit most from the expertise and professional services of more school psychologists and greater access to mental health services in schools. Technology will have to be a vital element of psychological services and mental health supports in rural school districts, which can telecommute many of these services to their schools with proper funding.

In looking at the value of teachers in society, popular media glorifies some professions over others. The professional athlete is one such occupation, which sends a message to children that the athlete is far more valued than the educator. This is evidenced by pay and social status and the various methods that the media uses to influence the public (Smith & Sanderson, 2015; Hathorn, 2013). It also leads some students to the faulty conclusion that education is not a valuable profession, and education, in general, is not worthwhile.

Some struggling students believe they do not need an education because they plan to be professional athletes. Teachers may try to educate the student about the realities of this plan by asking them how they are going to get on a professional team, let alone stay on one, if they do not come to practice or games on time (because they do not get to class on time or at all). In addition, the students with star-studded dreams often do not practice (do their homework), are never prepared (bring required equipment), and tend to put in very little effort with a bad attitude (poor behavior toward teachers and peers). These students must be told with honesty that their professional coach would fire them before they got in the game, no matter how much natural talent they had, because they are not team players and have a poor work ethic. Teams count on each member of the team to do his or her part, and if a team member does not do his or her part, the coach will not let that person play on the team. Therefore, if past and current behavior are the best predictors of future behavior, how can students reasonably expect skill and discipline from themselves at a later date without putting effort into it now?

The same question could be asked about the future of education. If an investment in teachers is not made, in their training and ongoing professional learning and supports, how can they be expected to produce dividends in terms of successful teaching practices and positive educational outcomes for students? The short answer is that a plan that expects teachers to succeed without adequately preparing and supporting them will likely fail, just as the student expecting to become a professional athlete without putting in the discipline and teamwork will likely fail.

There must be a cultural shift to reject the ever-increasing burdens that educators are saddled with. Until the paradigm shifts away from requiring more work from teachers without adequate supports, teacher burnout will persist. Teachers principally leave the profession due to high emotional stress as a result of low supports. Society has perpetuated this injustice by accepting the present reality of increased work demands without increased support, at the expense of our teachers and students. Systemically, the field of education must rise in the esteem of the populace to break with the current model and replace it with one that justly supports the workers it employs. Adequate supports should be provided for all educators, and hard workers and strong performers in education should be rewarded. *School leaders can begin to shift the paradigm by fostering a culture of validation for quality work.*

Educators do a lot of extra work after school as it is. On most elementary school campuses, teachers are required to sign up for at least one school-based team or committee, such as the Sunshine Committee, the Campus Clean-Up Committee, or the Monthly Newsletter Committee. If school leadership is looking to build an Academic MTSS team or a Social-Emotional-Behavioral MTSS team, it must do so while providing time for the team members to meet during contract time. Initially, time outside contract hours may be required of some team members until the team is running smoothly and the team has a solid foundation. Until then, providing extra-duty pay to those teachers who are putting in extra time will go a long way.

If school leadership is looking to start up a committee, it must value the educators' time. Organizational demands and responsibilities of MTSS may not get done during the school day because of teaching duties and other job requirements. No one really wants to hear that. The public often thinks that educators should put in extra time out of the goodness of their hearts and that extra work is just part of the job; however, a lack of validation destroys educators' motivation and quality of effort over time. Either compensate educators' time after school, fit the work into their contract time and responsibilities, or decrease their teaching or workload during the day so they can work on their additional demands and responsibilities. Think of a scale; both sides must be in proportion in order for the scale to balance. If a salaried employee is compensated for eight hours on one side of the scale, the corresponding duties should balance on the other side. If the duties side becomes increasingly loaded, the compensation side should also have a proportionate quantity added to maintain the balance. A balance must be found between duties and compensation in order to maintain an appropriate and functional level of stress and to prevent teacher burnout.

Many, many educators suck it up and sacrifice their personal time for the greater good. Good bosses know that uncompensated work is not reasonable and leads to discontent and burnout, as does poor job training, poor organizational understanding, poor peer support, and limited forward career movement (Taormina & Law, 2000). A culture deprived of support and full of resentment must be avoided. Educators should be compensated for working additional hours on behalf of students past contract time. *Educators are trained professionals and should be compensated accordingly.* This point cannot be stressed enough. If there are grants to apply for or extra monies that can be (re)allocated for the MTSS team's additional work time, they should be paid for extra duty. Or find a way to compensate their time if additional funds cannot be found. Adjust the school budget to make the most out of schools' most valuable assets: its' educators. Schools must have basic supplies and technology; however, the adaptable, creative, and unlimited potential of educators can be more effective and a better investment than more computers or any other gadget. Bottom line, an educator actively solving problems for a student will always be that student's best resource.

It is extremely motivating for educators to earn more money or comped time for all the extra work that is required to make a multi-tiered support system model effective at a school. As important as it is to provide incentives and positive reinforcement to students, the same holds true for teachers and other educators who work with students. Educators frequently feel overburdened and many are not going to be thrilled to be on another committee, at least in the beginning. One-third of teachers leave the profession within the first five years because being a teacher is not easy (Farmer, 2017). Many of them will not be grateful for the extra burdens that go along with the team responsibilities of MTSS at first. It is important to remember that the workers experiencing the most emotional and occupational stress are going to burn out first (Farmer, 2017; Mérida-Lopez & Extremera, 2017). If administrators can somehow lighten educators' load in some way or give them extra duty pay, they must. It is the right thing to do and is a key element of the LIQUID (Leadership, Implementation, Quality control, Universality, Implementation, Data-based decision making) Model, starting with leadership. Effective leaders equitably support and compensate workers. Supported educators are more likely to work harder with a more positive attitude, which falls under quality control because they are more likely to take greater pride in doing a good job and implementing best practices with integrity. Taking care of staff members creates a culture of taking care of everyone in the school community. Actively supporting educators also addresses inclusiveness and social justice because educators have the tools and training to teach all learners and are motivated to teach all students, no matter how diverse their needs. Educators working in higher-needs schools should get paid more to work in communities with the most challenges to entice the strongest teachers to work in the most at-risk neighborhoods, giving students living in poverty access to the best educators and best chance to rise above their circumstances. Educators should also be compensated for required professional training that is mandated by state law or district policy and is not provided during contract time.

By adequately compensating educators, administrators will get what they pay for. Paying MTSS team members for their extra duties will increase the likelihood that they will give these important tasks the time, attention, and effort they require. If administrators expect educators to add more work to their day without compensation, the educators will squeeze it in somehow, but the quality of effort and the quality of outcomes will be pinched as well. Very few educators are not willing to work for extra pay. It is common sense. *As a society, removing the unrealistic expectation of more work for salaried employees without compensation must be part of the new paradigm shift.* Stop taking advantage of salaried educators. Educators deserve better, and so do students.

Another social shift that must happen in education is the negative perception that change equates to more work and could be a waste of time and effort. This thinking is not productive and is an opportunity for teacher-leaders to educate their peers about the positive impact of MTSS programs. While new learning and systematically making changes may require extra work the first year, it is not permanent and is a natural part of the growth process. The education leaders and change agents on campus are putting their necks on the line with their peers when asking them to make changes. Many educators do not like change, often perceive it as extra work, and may not be very appreciative or excited about the hard work to come. Planning and implementing instructional supports require a change of minds, hearts, and practice. Clearly explaining the process to change up front and how the demands on educators' time will gradually decrease as the system, structures, and process become more efficient, teachers will be more likely to buy-in.

Oftentimes, practice must change first, long before people change their minds about how much they value the new practice. And the value of the new practice must be felt to be beneficial over time to promote a change of heart. It is easier to change what you *do* than how you *feel*, and people do better when they feel better. If administrators wait for everyone to feel like changing before implementing changes, they will definitely be waiting a long time. The majority of educators might not be on board with the change at first. With school initiatives constantly coming and going, they might figure, "This too shall pass." The school's education leaders are going to be on the front lines defending challenges from colleagues who are not thrilled about new practices. Peers will have to be won over first in order to change their minds and hearts. It is imperative that school principals give clear directives and are willing to enforce the MTSS plan through follow-up supervision and support to the education leaders as they work to implement the administrator's vision, for this is the only real chance of consistent implementation of the new practice (Forman & Crystal, 2015; Meyer & Behar-Horenstein, 2015). When education leaders are valued and compensated, a powerful, symbolic message is sent to the entire school staff that the school principal supports educators with more than words and is willing to reward the most effective educators implementing best practices for best student outcomes.

Allocating Fiscal Resources

Fiscal allocation specifically addresses the two key domains of business plan development and compensation to educators. A common theme heard from colleagues on elementary campuses is that "I already differentiate instruction within my class," which leads to the misperception that remediation for students with delays should depend on special education support. Academic MTSS, or commonly referred to as Response to

Intervention, is perceived as too complicated and requires too much paperwork, leading to disappointment that teacher efforts did not lead to eligibility, and removal to an alternative setting, for underachieving students. Teachers may feel they are already asked to do too many things, and they cannot, or will not, implement Academic MTSS; which suggests that the infrastructure does not support teachers enough in those schools. If processes are not embedded to achieve automation of required functions then systems will fail to serve their intended purpose. The process will not work when educational leaders do not follow the recipe. Of course, in those instances, the recipe is blamed when the cake does not rise. And the cake will never rise as long as school leaders do not put the right ingredients in to make it work.

Shifting the perspective to view MTSS implementation through another lens, MTSS can be viewed from the angle of a business model for providing appropriate educational services to diverse students in diverse populations. The chief executive officer (CEO) of the school, the school principal, is in charge of all business in his or her school. The business of schools is to teach *every* child. The only flaw in the educational business model is that children are not widgets. Educators cannot return or disregard children when they arrive with gaps and do not function as the curriculum demands. If the business of school is to teach every child, and every child does not develop or learn uniformly, then there must be a systematic way to evaluate children's individual needs, provide timely remediation to address their deficits, and provide that support for as long as it is needed. MTSS is that business plan for education and will facilitate the delivery of quality instruction to every child and will guide data-based decisions to maximize school success.

In which business industry would a business plan unsupported by the CEO actually be successful? Probably none. How many successful business owners start a business without a plan? Probably none. MTSS is a research-based business plan, and like every other business plan, it probably will not be that effective without the CEO, the school principal, leading the vision of the plan and actively working to solve problems that may have an impact on the plan's fruition.

School administrators have an immense responsibility to an enormous number of people. School campuses are controlled chaos in which some level of disorderliness is expected and accepted. *Controlled chaos* is a term borrowed from the biology, engineering, and life sciences fields that recognizes some or whole segments may be disorganized yet can be controlled within given parameters (Uversky & Dunker, 2008). School principals have much on their plates and are responsible for everything on those plates. There are a lot of moving parts at any given moment in a large elementary school that require administrative attention. The MTSS process may feel overwhelming and undoable if principals do not feel like they have time to address issues comprehensively with their current workload or if they do not see the value in investing in the process with time, money, and active support. However, the benefits of an established MTSS will long outweigh the up-front inconvenience of extra work to lay the foundation. Once MTSS is up and running, it is like a well-oiled machine, and administrators will have to spend much less time reacting to problems because they are being addressed proactively with supports in place for every student on campus. *Like money in the bank, the bigger deposit you put down, the more interest you are going to earn.*

The leaders on a school's MTSS team are campus role models who work tirelessly to be the problem solvers for everyone, from the neediest students to the neediest educators, they help to identify practices that do not work and recommend fixes and work-arounds. They are ideally the strongest staff members in implementing effective instruction in the classroom for students. Depending on whether the leadership is for the Academic MTSS team or the Social-Emotional-Behavioral MTSS team, the need to adequately compensate remains. Help these educators feel like valued professionals. Value their expertise and time, and pay them extra for all the extra work and burdens they will have. In truth, administrators may not be able to fully compensate their MTSS team members for the extra hours of work they do, but they must make a good-faith effort. Pay them, and appreciate the value they bring to the school and community.

In the end, educators will want to be on this committee because they will have the power to make positive changes for students. Financially rewarding these educators for the extra work they do will empower them and will send a strong message to other staff members that these educators work to make the school principal's expectations come to fruition and have complete administrative backing. The MTSS team members are the leaders in implementing the boss's will to improve educational opportunities for all students, and all educators will be expected to change their instructional and professional practices accordingly.

Teachers are the best instructional resources on a school's campus. Invest in their learning, efficacy, and self-discovery and the school will reap invaluable rewards. There are several ways to promote such efforts on a campus. Promoting accomplished teaching practices, encouraging and supporting pursuit of National Board Certification (along with fiscal resources, if possible), and endorsing professional collaboration with colleagues are all ways to achieve this. Within the teaching profession, National Board Certification is the industry's highest designation of accomplished teaching: "Similar to medicine's Hippocratic Oath, the Five Core Propositions are held in common by teachers of all grade levels and disciplines and underscore the accomplished teacher's commitment to advancing student learning and achievement" (National Board for Professional Teaching Standards (NBPTS), 2019, para. 2). The Five Core Propositions transcend educational disciplines and grade levels and place an emphasis on knowing the whole child. The Five Core Propositions include the following:

1. Teachers are committed to students and their learning.
2. Teachers know the subjects they teach and how to teach those subjects to their students.
3. Teachers are responsible for managing and monitoring student learning.
4. Teachers think systematically about their practices and learn from experience.
5. Teachers are members of learning communities. (NBPTS, 2016b)

In pursuing National Board Certification, candidates learn how to learn more about their students. In turn, this deeper understanding helps them to better identify their students' individual needs, potential barriers to learning (both academic and social-emotional-behavioral), are reflective in their approach to service delivery, and use data to inform and guide their decision-making processes.

Lessons learned in pursuit of accomplished teaching help teachers see past the surface of their students and how they score on tests. They learn to see what students carry with them that is invisible and what factors are impacting them at home and in the community. One in five children present with mental illness (Merz, 2017; National Association of School Psychologists, 2017), and students with emotional and behavioral disorders are an underserved and underfunded population (Ennis, Blanton, & Katsiyannis,

2017). Many more than that will display symptoms of a mental illness depending on the risk factors and situational trauma they may be exposed to (Souers, 2017). No matter how many supports a school has in place, something will happen that exceeds what the school staff thought it was prepared for. When a problem-solving process is in place with effective teamwork, those teams will be able to handle any problems that come up. The team approach of both the business model and the health care model is well established and celebrated and must be implemented in education as well. Ideally, educators with varying perspectives and experiences can each contribute to the solutions of a team problem. Children's problems must be addressed systematically, as part of a team approach, in every school to teach every child. Teams learn to adapt and grow from experience. Once teams are trained to work together, they will be able to work more efficiently, which will give their administrators more time to attend to other pressing matters. MTSS is money in the bank with compound interest. Compensating educators validates them, which goes a long way toward that initial deposit, and those educators will be a greater asset in solving problems on their school campus.

Exercise 3.2

Administrator Challenges and Opportunities Survey

- Take a moment and reflect on some administrative challenges on your school campus that could be addressed by your team. Be as specific as possible. After you have generated your list of challenges, rank them by priority level. Save this list to discuss with your team.
- Brainstorm funding ideas to compensate your educators. Title I funding sources are flexible in terms of funding interventions for at-risk populations. Higher socioeconomic schools can consider fund-raisers and parent–teacher association donations. All should consider grants and reallocation of other resources.

Assessment Tools

Invest in a school's teachers, specialists, and support staff; human capital is a school's best asset. The investment does not stop there, naturally. Administrators must also invest in the tools required to get the job done. First, administrators must measure where they are and decide where their school is going. Then, they need to invest in intervention tools and training opportunities for staff in how to use the methods with *fidelity*, or accuracy and quality. Overall, an entire school needs to invest in MTSS development and processes to be able to make data-based decisions for its students.

To make the right decisions, an investment must be made in selecting the right tools. One tool, AIMSweb Plus, is popular and recommended for schools implementing Academic MTSS, as it screens all students using universal benchmarking to get a quick look at students' academic fluency skills at their given grade level (Pearson, 2017). Evidence-based progress monitoring and strategic monitoring tools are priceless when it comes to the data they generate, which help teams make decisions about the effectiveness of instructional practices and whether students are adequately responding to interventions (Shinn, 2007). In all schools, especially those with large populations, universal screening makes sense. Students often get lost in the shuffle if they depend on individual teacher referrals to support their needs.

For example, in an urban elementary school with approximately 1,000 students, it is not uncommon to have 250 students who require Tier 2 supports. With each classroom teacher serving as the case manager for the students in their class, they only need to manage five or so students. This then becomes more manageable and sustainable. It can become very burdensome to put the entire responsibility for the identification and remediation of failing students on teachers alone. There are some extremely resourceful, talented, and creative teachers who are responsive to students' academic needs and help students close their achievement gaps. However, students with Tier 2 and Tier 3 needs may fail repeatedly, over long periods, before someone intervenes. Oftentimes, it is one caring and persistent teacher who speaks up, a parent request, or a school counselor who advocates for additional supports for a student. This advocacy is often in the form of requesting special education testing because the school lacks systemic processes of tiered supports or parents do not really understand what they are asking for; they just know their child needs help. School counselors are often limited in helping students obtain remedial supports given the nature of their role and the availability of resources on the school campus and within the community.

If teachers and itinerant specialists perceive MTSS as more work than they feel it is worth, especially on top of their already busy schedules, they are not going to refer students very often, let alone systematically. Teachers may be providing some intervention supports, but if there are not functional MTSS teams in which students can be referred for further problem solving, they will not make the referral. There should be systematic procedures and general checkpoints for when a student should get referred to the MTSS teams for additional problem solving and Tier 2 and Tier 3 supports. Especially in elementary schools, teachers cannot be hesitant to refer students for interventions and monitoring. Low-performing children or students with behavioral and mental health issues in schools with limited resources and opportunities for remediation may be less likely to get intensive help and be referred for supports because the burden of proof falls solely on overburdened classroom teachers. These issues quickly become an issue of student *access* to remedial education and become another barrier to social justice. Access to, and benefits of, all a school's resources is one component of a socially just system, along with respect and fairness (North, 2006). Teachers expected to provide interventions during their "free time" are hard-pressed to implement quality interventions with fidelity and document accordingly.

Once a school has well-running MTSS teams, grade-level teams can review the benchmark scores and triangulate data to make decisions about students. This is especially true for Academic MTSS. For example, if fall benchmarking occurs during the fourth week of school, grade-level teams can review academic data from benchmarking and additional data sources such as diagnostic measures (e.g., CORE Phonics) to devise the necessary Tier 2 and enrichment classes necessary. If a grade-level team is composed of five teachers, one teacher can take the students who performed the highest and create an enrichment group. The other four teachers can divide the rest of the students up and provide learning opportunities at their instructional levels. Students who receive the universal Tier 1 instruction, as well as the small-group Tier 2 interventions, and still do not make adequate growth, would be good candidates to be referred to the Academic MTSS team for further problem solving and potential Tier 3 supports.

Universal benchmarking allows administrators to take a snapshot of the student population and quickly identify students who may be at risk for school failure (Freeman, Miller, & Newcomer, 2015; Gill, Borden, & Hallgren, 2014; Shinn, 2007).

There are other indicators that must be cross-referenced, or triangulated, because snapshots are not always accurate. Other indicators could include grades, behavioral history, diagnostic assessments, parent and teacher reports, attendance history, criterion-referenced tests, English-language fluency assessments, and enrollment history. When data across sources consistently identify a student as requiring interventions, then the student can be quickly placed in remedial programs. Students with conflicting data would be discussed by the team, and other factors could be addressed.

At the elementary level, many of the risk factors students experience are beyond educators' control. For example, many students in the early grades who underperform suffer from poor attendance or their caregivers bring them late to school every day. For a young student, they often do not have an alarm, know how to tell time, or have an alternative way to get to school if their family does not bring them. Expecting young children to attend to their own attendance and tardiness issues is not effective. In these cases, the intervention must be implemented with the caregiver, not the student. Many families suffer from issues with transportation, drug or alcohol abuse, or work schedules that are not conducive to getting their children to school in the morning. In such cases, the MTSS teams can connect the families to outside resources and supports to promote the well-being of their child(ren). Again, the school must have functional MTSS teams in which to take the referral to.

Universal benchmark scores also come in handy when students arrive at a school with little to no history of their data. Whether your school is high risk or low risk, benchmarking at regular intervals, and when a new student enrolls, is strongly recommended because it helps the school team identify low-performing students as soon as possible and allows the team to schedule them into the needed intervention groups immediately, not a semester later wasting time and opportunity for those students. With regular benchmarking, low-performing students are also picked up throughout the year, which is critical as many school populations have a high transiency rate and the students beginning the year will not necessarily be the same ones at the end of the school year. Ideally, if a district can purchase a benchmarking tool, such as AIMSweb Plus for all its schools, the data can travel seamlessly with the student if he or she transfers schools within the district. These data would also stay with the students as they are promoted from elementary school to middle school and middle school to high school. Providing continuity for transient students is another example of why MTSS should be strategically allocated for and financed at the state and district levels.

As mentioned earlier, one such universal benchmarking tool that has shown repeatedly to be a favorite among practitioners is AIMSweb Plus for its ease of use and practicality (Pearson, 2017). There is up-and-coming competition to this product, but for years there has been no comparison. Do-it-yourself (DIY) benchmarking and progress monitoring might be on readers' minds. Beware of setting up for failure; DIY documentation and intervention logging are highly labor-intensive and fraught with fidelity issues, especially on a large campus. Some teachers just "know" a student has a learning problem but do not have documentation of high-quality interventions or valid data to reflect student response over time. Perhaps those teachers were unable to keep up with the organization and details required to systematically deliver interventions with fidelity and document faithfully. *Fidelity at all levels of the tiered model is of utmost importance.* Lacking quantitative data, specialists such as school psychologists often find themselves graphing a teacher's qualitative data because the teacher lacks the resources to collect quantitative data and input it into graph form to demonstrate trajectory and rate of progress. Throughout the data design, implementation, and collection process, there are many steps to monitor for efficacy. It really takes a team to support teachers with documentation, and it takes the best tools for the job to methodically monitor students. AIMSweb Plus has been an especially convenient managerial tool because the data can be input by teachers systematically and there are local area managers who can monitor which teachers are complying and assist those who may need additional support.

Another useful and much less expensive alternative for finding and using grade-level fluency levels and probes is easyCBM. Star 360 and i-Ready as also viable alternatives. The more complicated and labor-intensive the tool is, the less likely educators will use it with fidelity or at all. If your school chooses to forgo an established method of benchmarking and progress monitoring, in lieu of a DIY method, go ahead and try. However, be warned, teams will be faced with pervasive labor and fidelity issues.

Box 3.1

Connection to Practice

Weigh Yourself

Behavioral change is not easy. For example, the behavioral changes required for losing weight are difficult. Making healthy food choices and exercising every day is not easy to do, as is evidenced by the obesity epidemic in Western civilization. Most consumers already know that a healthy weight is based on access to healthy foods, portion control, and daily exercise, but how many diet books are there on the market selling a different way to get thin fast?

As public consumers, success is desired to happen quickly, with efforts materialized in positive results instantly. How long will it take an individual to lose enough weight to wear a size 4? Of course, it depends on how large the person is to begin with. If she went from a size 22 to a size 16 in one year, most people would consider her diet a success even though she did not reach her goal of a size 4 by that time. Data would support continuing with the successful behavioral changes made. A data-based decision could be to continue with the plan as is, or parts of it could be reviewed and revised to try for quicker results.

Conversely, if a man started at a size 40 pant size and went up to a size 52, most people would tell him to go on a different diet because the data do not indicate that his behavioral practices were leading to a smaller clothing size or ultimate weight loss. He might even need more intensive support to help keep him on track, such as Weight Watchers or Jenny Craig, with weekly weigh-ins, nutritional advice, premade food, and counseling to guide him through the emotional and behavioral challenges of overeating. If he cannot achieve success with what interventions he has implemented, he might require working with a team of specialists. Such an approach may consist of meeting with a doctor specializing in weight loss, planning with a nutritionist, hiring a chef to make healthy foods, and getting a personal trainer to motivate him daily to engage in cardio and weightlifting exercises. If he were morbidly obese, he might even consider gastric bypass surgery when other efforts have failed.

Most people cognitively understand "best practices" in weight loss (i.e., eat healthy foods, limit portion size, exercise daily), but what works for one person may not work for another. The intensity of intervention required depends on how overweight one is to begin with, genetic and health issues, emotional and cognitive-behavioral issues, motivation, willpower, and how that person will be supported in daily behavioral changes in his or her environment. The intensity of interventions should increase when lesser intensity interventions have failed. The same is true for educational practices.

Educational progress is like weight loss in more ways than one. Educators want spectacular improvement with quick results. However, expecting instant success by getting students at or above grade level in a week, or even one year, is just as unrealistic as expecting a woman to go from a size 22 to a size 4 in the same amount of time. It could happen, but dramatic results are not the realistic norm. There are many methods to reach success academically but the basics remain the same. Using Maslow's research (1943) as a baseline, students must have a sense of belonging, and they require consistent, engaging, quality instruction led by qualified teachers.

Each education leader has their own ideas about what good teaching is and is not. Most educators have experience with students who do not respond to quality instruction as planned. Like weight loss, some need more help than others to follow a diet and exercise plan, or the problem is so severe it may require bariatric surgery. Before performing "surgery" on students, or cutting them out of the general curriculum to go to a special education class, less intense interventions should be tried first to see if they work.

Struggling students should have the opportunity to learn the skills they do not possess in order to gain the necessary building blocks to stabilize their educational foundations. Skill development helps them gain confidence, even if those skills are not at the expected grade level. They may need help to make better choices (i.e., going to class, getting to school on time, paying attention to instruction, completing classwork and homework) and require the necessary supports in order to do so. Every success increases students' academic and emotional stability.

The goal of interventions is to make incremental gains. It is highly improbable that an individual would lose six dress sizes after a week of dieting. It is more realistic to make incremental changes to behavior and is more motivating to celebrate incremental successes instead of brooding over failure to reach more ambitious longer-term goals. Losing 1 pound per week does not sound like much success, but losing 52 pounds in a year is a smashing success. Even if the individual only achieved "minimally" adequate results, a half-pound weight loss per week, losing 26 pounds in a year would also be considered a significant success. Same with educational growth. Increasing academic growth incrementally is a cause for celebration. And if the incremental growth is not occurring the team needs to improve its approach, and perhaps intensify its efforts. It should not wait a whole year before deciding its approach is unsuccessful.

Like using a scale or dress size to measure weight loss success, data should be used to make instructional decisions for teaching hard-to-teach students. Instructional strategies must be differentiated when needed, according to formative assessment and outcome measures. In doing so, opportunities will arise to celebrate incremental growth for students who would not otherwise be celebrating their achievements.

Data-Based Decision Making

Some administrators do not have the appetite or constitution for dramatic and intensive changes at their schools, and those administrators may want to implement changes more slowly. Some schools do not need to have such intensive overcorrection because educational practices are currently effective or have a lower risk of student failure due to socioeconomic and community factors. *Overcorrection* is the explicit repeated practice of a desired behavior. In all cases, quarterly grade-level benchmarking is an effective way to quickly and easily identify at-risk students and get them into support services as soon as possible. Lower-risk schools may elect not to benchmark the entire school quarterly and may benchmark smaller subpopulations on a quarterly basis, subpopulations such as English-language learners, special education students, or students with unstable enrollment histories. While this is not recommended, since best practice would be to benchmark the entire school, it is the administrator's prerogative. Should subpopulations be targeted initially, it is never too late to implement a phased rollout to increasingly include grade levels to build up to whole-school universal screenings.

Higher-risk schools are going to identify far more at-risk students than lower-risk schools, and the process must be structured in such a way as to support every student identified. In this sense, the MTSS must be ultra-efficient if it is going to be sustainable. Every teacher on a school campus is involved in MTSS and is required to take a group of students for intervention or enrichment. When the intervention block is scheduled into the master schedule, this process becomes ingrained and second nature, no teacher is left out, and no student is left out.

Universal benchmarking will capture grade-level academic fluency of your school population. Progress monitoring at grade level and strategic monitoring on the instructional level will occur at regular intervals for students identified as needing interventions. Oftentimes, if the student is two or more grade levels below his or her instructional level, progress monitoring at grade level will not be sensitive enough to pick up on growth trends. In this case, the student receives the intervention that he or she needs, based on triangulated assessment and diagnostic measures, and is progress monitored using weekly or biweekly probes at his or her grade level, as well as at his or her instructional level. For students with significant gaps in their attendance and instructional histories, this dual progress monitoring will allow teams to determine if growth is being made and gaps are closing in a student's academic repertoire.

Repeated measures of these same skills are absolutely necessary for progress monitoring Tier 2 and Tier 3 intervention outcomes. The trajectory of student performance over time will help teams determine whether the intervention is effective, whether an intervention change is required, and whether each student requires more intensive or less intensive support. If a student is flat-lining after six to eight weeks with a particular intervention, as demonstrated by the graphed data points from the progress monitoring probes, then the team will want to consider a change of intervention for an additional six to eight weeks. If intervention intensity has been maximized for a significant time, as evidenced by documentation and progress monitoring, and students are not making an adequate rate of improvement, then the decision-making point may be to refer to the multidisciplinary evaluation team for further consideration. AIMSweb Plus has an efficient online system to monitor student growth that uniquely contributes to ease of administration, scoring, input, and remote access of data (Pearson, 2017). The graphs it produces help support instructional decisions in the classroom, as well as provide reliable indicators of student needs. Finally, it can also provide data to support special education eligibility in severe cases of underachievement.

Box 3.2

Voices From the Field

When we started a comprehensive multi-tiered support system at my elementary school the first thing we decided to do was "weigh" ourselves regularly with quarterly benchmarking for all students. Students who were identified with skills' deficits were given further diagnostic tests such as CORE Phonics (or another appropriate diagnostic tool) in addition to administration of monthly grade-level math and reading fluency probes to assist with determining Tier 2 and Tier 3 interventions. In addition, students requiring Tier 3 supports had weekly monitoring at the instructional level in reading and math fluency. Weighing ourselves at regular intervals helped us be accountable for student growth at all tiers. Our school principal knew that changing teacher attitude and beliefs would require small steps in the right direction. Just like dieting, we had to have the courage to step on the scale regularly. Even though we were not on a consistent sensible diet at first, we weighed ourselves anyway. The whole school participated, every grade level, every quarter.

One of the tools used over the years was AIMSweb 1.0 (Pearson, 2015) for benchmarking, progress monitoring, and strategic monitoring of reading, writing, and math fluency. It had fluency measures in grade-level reading, writing, math calculation, and math application skills, among other measures. Administration, scoring, and inputting scores were fairly easy to learn. The best part is that the scores were normed for comparisons to average grade-level achievement and the data could be accessed remotely by any authorized user. Our school district even generated English-language-learner norms for use within the district. As our school budget had less money to allocate for resources, we transitioned to another fluency tool, EasyCBM, which allows users to go online and download math and reading CBM probes and compare grade-level growth to national norms. Being able to access fluency probes and norms online makes it easy for educators to access appropriate grade leveled tools quickly, which improves ease of implementation. Benchmarking data and progress monitoring data, no matter the tool preferred, can be input into Google Sheets for shared input and access to data (if the screening tool does not have a built-in database component), which allows administrators to monitor for adherence to procedures.

Data collection and reporting should be made as easy as possible for educators. Make it easy to access information to guide instructional decision making. Make it easy for administrators to monitor teacher input. The monetary cost of using an effective online program is worth it for the ease of use and the value of information it captures. That data can be captured other ways, but fidelity issues will suffer. Invest in quality benchmarking and progress monitoring tools in order to provide targeted support to MTSS processes. I have heard arguments about fluency measures not being the best way to measure growth over time, my answer to that is if you can find a quicker, easier, legally defensible way to benchmark students or capture academic strategic progress monitoring data then do it. Remember, benchmark data should only be one piece of evidence to support student growth.

The Voices From the Field box illustrates a win–win situation for educators and students. The easy access to appropriate fluency probes and the shared Academic universal screening warehouse improves the fidelity of benchmarking and progress monitoring. The school learned to weigh itself regularly, which allowed it to make adaptations to its intervention plans for students without having to wait until the grading period to know if a student failed (or that it had failed a student). Teachers who did not buy in to the new practices ultimately moved on because the school culture was changing and they did not want to change with it. There is no *I* in team, remember? But there is an *I* in investment. Invest in your team. Invest in appropriate tools to measure baseline and monitor growth, and invest in high-quality research-based instructional practices, curriculum, and interventions.

As with all tests administered to students throughout the year, students' eyes often glaze over when they hear they have to take another test. Students may not care about testing on a given day for various reasons, and they do not give their best effort. Some school districts are using high-stakes test data as part of teachers' evaluations, and in some cases, school funding processes (Lavy, 2007). Basing teachers' professional ratings and school funding decisions on test data puts a lot of power in students' hands. Systemically, is it wise for teachers' job security to depend on the effort and motivation of young students or the responsibility of their parents to ensure that they are well rested and fed on any given test day?

With progress monitoring and strategic monitoring, over time and with multiple data points, schools can get a better idea of student growth than a onetime, high-stakes, one-and-done, test score; especially with higher-needs students. This growth model is composed of rich data points that measure student growth, or lack thereof, over time. The *growth model* is well documented as more effective at determining a student's performance than high-stakes tests in high-risk schools (Freeman et al., 2016).

Testing is like taking a picture. Even the best students can have "bad-hair days," and their yearbook picture is not their best. If an adult has their picture taken right now, and they are having a "bad-hair moment," that does not mean their hair is going to look that way in 20 minutes if they decide to style it with some brushing and gel. But if a student does not care what he looks like that morning, leaves the house without brushing his hair, and does not do it when he gets to school, is the teacher responsible for the outcome of the picture? That might be like asking if an adult's hairdresser should be poorly rated on Yelp by whether the client styles his or her hair. Someone might judge how it looked this morning when she woke up late and put no effort into grooming, instead of judging the cut and color received at the salon. Is the client's maturity, effort, and motivation to perform really a fair evaluation of a hairdresser's skills and quality of the salon? Of course not. Is the maturity, effort, and motivation of a student to perform a fair evaluation of a teacher's quality and the quality of a school? The truthful answer is yes, whether that is fair or not is a matter of opinion. Fair or not, we have to lead those horses to water and make them drink. Not all people find tests to be motivating or engaging in any way. How do we get students more motivated to take tests seriously?

One method that has proven successful to increase student buy-in and motivation is the *Three-Pronged Motivation Approach*. The three prongs consist of including students in the data collection and analysis process, increasing student buy-in through teacher motivation, and incentivizing achievement at all levels. These underlying processes are incredibly powerful in increasing the intrinsic motivation of students and increasing the likelihood that they will engage in the learning process willingly and with purposeful intent. The more motivated students perceive their teacher to be for teaching their given subject matter, the more intrinsically motivated students will become to learn (Radel, Sarrazin, Legrain, & Wild, 2010).

The first prong, *including students in the data collection and analysis process*, is especially beneficial with students in the upper grades of an elementary campus, Grades 3 through 5. Having students be ambassadors of their own learning, setting goals, evaluating progress toward those goals, and determining their own needs can be incredibly empowering. Their engagement can also contribute to Student Centered Academic Sessions discussed in Chapter 9.

The second piece of the Three-Pronged Motivation Approach is to *leverage teacher engagement with students* to earn student buy-in for testing efforts. Encouragement and positive relationships go a long way with children, many of whom may not have much positive attention in their worlds. The motivation for learning is contagious. Students who historically may not have valued education, who were not invested in their own growth, or who thought they could not succeed can be motivated by their teachers' motivation and excitement for teaching (Radel et al., 2010).

Incentives can be earned by students through a schoolwide positive behavior reinforcement system for solid attendance, completing assignments or homework on time, or progressing from one intervention group to the next. For example, students who graduate from needing Tier 2 and Tier 3 interventions get principal recognition resulting in a private congratulation from the school principal, a choice of something in the "treasure box" and/or a preferred activity or campus privilege, such as earning game time, pizza with the principal, or donuts with caregivers at a family–teacher breakfast. Students should be celebrated at all levels.

Exercise 3.3

Benchmarking Reflection

Take a few minutes and process how you feel about benchmarking your entire student population. Some things to think about:

- What are the challenges?
- What are your feelings in response to those challenges?
- Are you able to benchmark all students, and if not, which subpopulations might benefit?
- What tool might you use?
- What do you currently use to monitor student progress in response to interventions?
- What will you do with benchmark data?
- How can you improve the effectiveness and usability of your data-based decision making?

Research-Based Interventions

Research-based interventions that have been validated by evidence-based practices are ideal. Universal benchmarking is an ideal way of determining students' academic fluency, which is highly correlated with achievement (Jimerson, Burns, & VanDer-Heyden, 2016). Results can be sorted quickly and can be used as a starting point to prioritize which students require more intensive academic supports. However, fluency alone cannot be used to determine a student's needs. It is best used as an indicator to quickly identify underachievement to assist in prioritizing which students may require additional supports and assisting in monitoring response to interventions. Other sources must be cross-referenced and considered, such as CORE Phonics results, to identify target skill deficits to ensure that the correct remedy is applied to the correct problem. For example, if a student performs below average on fluency measures but scores high on comprehension measures, it is likely that the student requires an accommodation, such as extended time to read a passage, not a reading intervention, because the student understands the material and can answer questions about what was read. If another student performs low on fluency measures and low on comprehension measures and other sources of triangulated historical data support learning gaps and under-achievement, then that student's data indicate a need for more intensive reading interventions and investigation of other areas of need to support the whole student. Getting the right solution matched to the right problem is one of the primary goals of Academic MTSS team data analysis, and using fluency data may not always be the best indicator. For example, teams must take a student's language proficiency into account with fluency measures. Students who are learning a second language will not perform as well as native English speakers just by virtue of their language status and often require vocabulary enrichment, extended processing time, and frequent opportunities to listen and speak to other English speakers as part of their Tier 1 curriculum, not as a special-needs population necessarily. It is important to emphasize the need for rich data sources to be triangulated in the context of whole student functioning, which will lead to effective data-based decision making, leading to the most appropriate interventions based on a student's unique needs.

A school's Academic MTSS team must consider multiple sources of data when considering students for placement in Tier 2 or Tier 3 intervention blocks, including grades, attendance, language proficiency, criterion-referenced test scores, AIMSweb Plus scores, other standards-based or formative assessments, all progress monitoring data, counselor input, discipline data, teacher observations, parent report, and health records. A health screening, including vision and hearing, is required for all Tier 2 and Tier 3 students. Students who are below the 25th percentile achievement on grade-level benchmark scores are all considered for interventions and receiving Tier 2 supports in addition to the Tier 1 curriculum. Teams can triangulate data from multiple data sources and types to find the convergence of information (Creswell, 2008). *Triangulating* data sources for consistency helps teams identify which students need interventions and accommodations versus those who had a "bad-hair day" or did not care when testing. Teams can evaluate whether students have consistent difficulties across data sources and which areas of need are not being met. Interventions can range from intensive supports to a proverbial kick in the pants for motivation.

Once students have been identified as requiring help, what next? In the elementary grades, classroom teachers are expected to know how to differentiate instruction and to be inclusive of all types of learners, but that is not necessarily the case. Teachers are expected to keep pace with a fast-moving curriculum that may not contain developmentally appropriate rigor for all children. The strenuous pace may stress students and teachers alike, making both sides feel like failures when achievement rates do not meet expectations. Depending on how many at-risk learners there are in each class per grade level will have an impact on how resources are allocated to support students requiring more intensive instructional opportunities. In higher-risk schools, there are simply too many students with achievement gaps to refer out to intervention specialists for remediation, and Tier 1 teaching supports must be the primary target of resource allocation to avoid overwhelming Tier 2 and Tier 3 supports. As is often the case, with 25% of students or more performing below average, Tier 1 needs to be flexible enough with supplemental supports to teach a majority of below-average students. However, there must be systemic support to students who cannot achieve adequately without Tier 2 and Tier 3 and may have difficulty even with those intensified supports. Every school year, it is a new challenge to have enough supports for students and teachers in all three tiers. School supports must be planned prior to the school year due to basic logistics and budgeting. Based on successful Academic MTSS programs, it is better to start with a few high-quality intervention blocks that follow highly scripted intervention lesson plans, implemented with integrity than to attempt too many remedies at once and have them poorly executed.

An example of a good strategy with poor implementation in practice includes the actual practice of academic computerized programs. There are many good programs; however, the curriculum is often very specific and includes mandatory instruction hours, including direct instruction for certain content components. Computer time is usually highly desirable to students, and the lessons are often perceived as higher interest tasks than typical lectures. Oftentimes, school teams choose to purchase computerized or online guided practice as a supplement to teaching because they allow teachers to differentiate instruction without each student constantly demanding individualized attention from the teacher. When teachers follow curricula as prescribed and engage students with direct instructional supplementation, they are going to reap the benefits of these tools with achievement gains.

However, when teachers do not follow the curricula as prescribed, these gains are not realized. There is a high rate of abuse and misuse of putting students on computers during core curriculum instruction, not during supplemental instruction times. Some students with academic difficulties are going to present with behavioral problems, due to work avoidance or poor social and behavioral regulation, which will be disruptive to other students. This is especially true in elementary schools where young students are struggling with the basics of reading, associating letters and sounds, and anything above this will be far too difficult for them. Individualized support is essential and a computer program can walk students through their difficulties one-on-one without detracting from the teacher's time while still meeting the student's needs. However, teachers with the intent of engaging disruptive students, while being allowed to teach the rest of the class with fewer distractions, tend to overly rely on computerized programs. Sometimes, lower-performing students are expected to work independently without the required teacher supports or direct instruction, and they get further behind because they miss what is happening during class while they are on the computer. Other times, teachers have limited independent work time for the whole class and they use that "extra 15 minutes at the end of class" to let lower-performing students practice skills. But again, the students are typically not on the program for as long as they need to be, or the teacher did not fully implement the direct instruction piece. In either scenario, the computerized intervention would not be considered implemented with fidelity as prescribed and cannot be considered a valid intervention (Marino & Beecher, 2010).

Computer programs are alluring as a first choice of intervention investment for schools because they are often strong programs backed by research, when used as directed, and they are more likely to be higher interest to students, thus increasing student motivation to work independently (Marino & Beecher, 2010). The reality is that teachers must be highly trained in these programs and must adhere to the curriculum as directed, which many do not because of all the competing demands on their time and attention. Last, computerized programs are usually expensive. License purchase prices for these programs have climbed steadily over the past 10 years to the point of being cost-prohibitive. It is even more cost-prohibitive if teachers are not implementing the program with integrity and are much less likely to get successful results generalizing to gains of achievement.

The decision to purchase computerized intervention programs is a personal decision by every school administrator. There are pros and cons that must be weighed. The importance of using these tools as directed cannot be emphasized enough; otherwise, teams are simply wasting time and money. Time and space will need to be carved out, above and beyond core instruction, as the best chance of implementing these programs correctly is not during core class time. As frequently must be explained and shared with teams, especially those with a principal who is not willing to invest in time or resources for intervention opportunities for at-risk students, there is no such thing as Tier 1 interventions. *Tier 1 is the core curriculum.* Intensive instructional opportunities outside of Tier 1 must be implemented systematically and at the student's instructional level (not grade level) for the prescribed amount of time for it to be considered Tier 2 or Tier 3.

Many teachers are not accustomed to teaching skills two or more grade levels below their assigned grade level and often ask, "What is the difference between Tier 2 and Tier 3 level of interventions?" The simple answer is that Tier 3 students are much further behind than Tier 2 students and require even more individualized supports. Tier 2 students may need a little boost, such as remedial skills practice, to get more out of Tier 1, such as improved reading, writing, or math fluency skills. This increased practice makes learning new material easier for students as they are better able to perform basic skills with automaticity and read with greater prosody (Calet, Gutierrez-Palma, & Defior, 2017; Kuhn & Stahl, 2003). Students in Tier 2 are often referred to as the "bubble kids" and are the students that schools tend to focus on as they are the closest to nearly passing high-stakes standardized tests. Oftentimes, this focus is to the exclusion of lower-performing students who are less likely to perform over the threshold for adequate performance on high-stakes tests. Administrators are concerned about the number of students who pass high-stakes tests for a variety of reasons, such as maintaining funding levels for schools or to reduce punitive damages for underperforming programs (Lewis & Hardy, 2015; Bogin & Nguyen-Hoang, 2014).

Students who are in Tier 3 have a larger learning gap, oftentimes are performing two or more grade levels below expectation, and require intensive remedial instruction and reteaching of lower-level skills. Students in Tier 3 often have a history that supports their learning deficits, such as coming from higher risk environments, being victims of poverty, experiencing chronic trauma, or having breaks in their school history including attendance problems, transience, and issues associated with family risk factors. Especially in the elementary grades, second-language factors have a significant impact on early student performance. Many English-language learners are born in the United States but are not exposed to formal English until kindergarten. These students start out with a five-year language deficit compared to most English-language speakers.

This language deficit impacts their rate of learning because they are not understanding the instruction that is being presented to them. While the majority do not have true learning disabilities or learning deficits, they present as such and are often difficult for teachers to teach. These students also tend to memorize rote information such as letter names or letter sounds due to sheer repetition in the classroom; however, their skills will break down on higher-order tasks or abstract reasoning demands because they are processing in a language other than English. Important to keep in mind, second-language elementary school students most likely are not receptively understanding all that is being taught to them, and they are not expressively able to convey responses at a level or manner typical for their age- or grade-level peers.

These students need opportunities to close their achievement gaps with high-quality instruction and evidence-based practices. Bottom line is that nothing replaces direct instruction for low-performing students, and it is critical that an evidence-based curriculum be available for teachers to use. There are many tools available in different styles, and new tools come along all the time. Like any CEO, administrators should be asking which tools are most effective at the most reasonable cost to target the needs of most students on their campus. *The end of the school year is a perfect time for curriculum and teaching practices to be evaluated and retooled for a fresh start the next school year.*

One example is the case of Wilson Elementary School. Wilson Elementary School had tried multiple evidence-based curriculum brands over a six-year span in reading, writing, and math subjects. Some curriculum tools were mandated by the school district, some were tried based on popularity in educational circles, some were suggestions made by staff members, and some were random choices to fill a particular need. Some were more effective than others. Why was that? What makes a product pass the test of fit and effectiveness? Keep in mind that curriculum tools alone cannot be deemed effective or ineffective. Implementation factors have an impact on the validity and fidelity of the interventions provided, and some evidence-based curriculum tools and remedial products are better than others. Every student population and staff needs are different and thus will require a differentiated approach. It is up to your administrator and MTSS teams to evaluate the quality of a product, monitor the integrity of implementation, and weigh the costs of the programs in terms of the opportunity cost of other options and return on investment. Does the brand name program give the greatest bang for the buck? Which programs work best? The answers will vary by school but can be systematically addressed.

As the saying goes, Rome was not built in a day; MTSS will also take time to grow. The process may take years to get into place and realize positive outcomes. Academic MTSS may be realized before Social-Emotional-Behavior MTSS. Documenting growth over time is ideal, just remember that teams may not get miraculous results immediately. If teams do see a large leap in growth, they should take it with a grain of salt, because they most likely will not have skyrocketing development every year. There may even be declines the first year before that aggregate group data moves in the right direction. Disappointment in outcome data can happen. It feels incredibly unfair when a school team goes to heroic efforts to rescue underachievers and its test scores do not reflect its efforts. The issue of aggregate group data that do not correspond to a positive trajectory is especially true at schools with a high student transiency rate. In many urban high-risk schools, there may be a 50% transience rate or more, and many of the students starting the school year move away before the high-stakes exams in the spring. In such schools, students who began the school year and received Tier 2 or Tier

3 interventions have since moved and have been replaced by "new" students on high-stakes testing days who have not received such interventions. The "new" students frequently have large numbers of absences, behavioral problems on other campuses, and have all the high-risk factors with little history of school support or remediation. If school leadership wants to demonstrate growth outside what the school district requires, especially in schools of high transiency, they may want to consider conducting growth analyses on the students who remained at the school for the entire year to refute any charges that "that school is not making any progress." Regardless of a school's challenges when it comes to outcome data, the important message is to stick with good strategies and replace ineffective practices. The obvious first place to start with effective instruction is Tier 1.

The first thing the school principal and MTSS teams should consider when evaluating effective instruction is Tier 1, core curriculum implementation. At-risk students need high-quality Tier 1 instruction as well as opportunities for filling in gaps through remedial instruction. How many students are struggling per grade level, per teacher? The intervention model would depend on how many students are underachieving. Going back to the ideal intervention triangle introduced in Chapter 2, 75% of students will ideally be successful with Tier 1 instruction alone. In many urban at-risk schools, both elementary and secondary, the idea of the triangle is a myth.

Many schools have a distribution of Tiers 1, 2 and 3 like an inverted triangle. There are more students struggling in a major way, indicating a need for more Tier 3 supports, than there are students successful at Tier 1. With those kinds of numbers, a gigantic red flag is raised indicating a need to revamp Tier 1 instruction, improve teaching practices, and select the highest quality curriculum possible, engage and support families, and build community supports. Over time, the distribution of tiered students will more closely resemble a rectangle as the MTSS team pushes more Tier 2 students down to Tier 1 and more Tier 3 students down to Tier 2.

Go where the data take you. If a whole subject level is floundering, it is more effective to address it as a whole, whether that be curriculum, teacher support, or teaching practices, than try to fix things piece by piece. If the curriculum is not working, replace it. If a teacher is not getting results using strong curriculum and tools, look at available teacher supports, peer coaching, or teaching practices. If a student is not achieving in the context of solid curriculum and excellent teaching practices, look to more intensive supports to help that student overcome learning challenges. *Never overlook the importance of Tier 1, in fact, look there first.*

Once a team is confident that Tier 1 is stable and teaching, academic, and social-emotional-behavioral practices are effective, it can begin looking into building up Tier 2 and Tier 3 resources. Teams can start asking themselves, what resources should be used? As long as high-quality teaching practices are occurring, the product brand of the intervention is less important than the fact that it is research-based. Teams may find that certain interventions work better for their population of students over other brands. It is essential to ensure that the teachers are implementing interventions with fidelity and are not picking and choosing the parts of a program they want to implement. When the process of effective implementation becomes cyclical, with constant reflection and refinement, teams will have a continuous improvement cycle with feedback loops to address the trifecta of curriculum quality, teaching practices, and growing resources. The limit to a school's investment in remedial tiers depends on its budget and the creativity and quality of its educators and leaders.

One of the best diagnostic tools is CORE Phonics Survey (Scholastic Red, 2002) and can be used to assist in triangulating data and grouping students after a universal Tier 1 academic screener has been administered. *When addressing the whole child, one assessment measure should not be used to determine a student's programming.* With the CORE Phonics Survey, depending on how the students perform, teams can devise Tier 2 groups according to short vowel sounds, long vowel sounds, r- or l-controlled vowels, or multisyllabic words. Words their Way (Pearson, 2019) is another outstanding diagnostic tool that leads to the identification of root causes of reading difficulties and identifies the strategic opportunities for target skill remediation. Regardless of tools selected, teachers must be specifically trained and given the opportunity for supervisory feedback on the implementation integrity of skills-based assessment and remediation.

It is not easy to be an educator. A hostile political climate, education budget cuts, and high-stakes testing are a few of the challenges faced. Teachers have all the responsibility for student outcomes with no control over what happens to students outside of class. Getting systems in place to help school leaders support students *and* educators alike will improve educational outcomes. Universal benchmarking and triangulating student data to identify at-risk students are the surest ways to effectively target underachievers to be directed into high-quality remedial programming. Ensuring high-quality instruction at Tier 1 is the place to start.

Investing in high-quality benchmarking tools and evidence-based curriculum at all levels is paramount. Paying educators for their overtime and expertise is also critical as they are the mice in the wheel of the school's engine. Validate educators' efforts and grow best practices by rewarding those who help grow the best practices through extra work and effort. Leaders also need to increase socially just practices on campus. One way to do so is by improving school culture and giving students a voice; have them invested in their own learning and teach them to advocate for themselves. Also, make school relevant for all students and provide multiple layers of support to help students achieve their goals in school and beyond. Selecting the highest-quality curriculum and looking for evidence of implementation fidelity in the classroom are key. Evaluate Tier 1 and scale out into Tier 2 and Tier 3 with effective evidence-based practices. Finally, it is essential to engage in continuous improvement cycles using feedback looping and reflection to determine whether practices are working and how to improve.

Exercise 3.4

Review Your Resources

Use the following worksheet to document which programs you are currently using across the tiers. Also list the pros and cons of what you are using and discuss whether the outcomes are going in the right direction. In those same columns, generate a wish list of things you would like to add or programs you would like to learn more about (see Chapter 16 for resources). Encourage team members to research new programs to discuss. Choose a small number of new resources or practices to add to your "intervention bank" of research-based interventions. Examine your school's curriculum quality–teaching practices–growing resources trifecta and refer to this worksheet at least annually to review and revise.

List the names of programs, tools, and curriculum you currently have along with their pros and cons.

- Tier 1
  - Reading
  - Mathematics
  - Writing
  - Social-Emotional
  - Positive Behavior Supports
- Tier 2
  - Reading
  - Mathematics
  - Writing
  - Social-Emotional
  - Positive Behavior Supports
- Tier 3
  - Reading
  - Mathematics
  - Writing
  - Social-Emotional
  - Positive Behavior Supports

Now list the names of programs, tools, and curriculum you want to incorporate or wish you had at each of the three tiers, and consider ways to work toward obtaining them in terms of budgeting and resource reallocation.

Exercise 3.5

Review Your Staff Needs

Before providing any professional learning opportunities to your staff, it is essential that a needs assessment be conducted. This assessment can be informal (self-made through Survey Monkey or Google Forms) or formal (existing assessments with preestablished questions). Various needs assessments will need to be conducted over the life of your MTSS programs, and they are especially essential at the very beginning. As a school leader, why would professional learning be provided in an area where the staff already had high efficacy? That would be a waste of time and resources. For example, poll your staff ahead of time to gauge their strengths and weaknesses for data-based decision making and delivery of a social-emotional-behavioral curriculum. Do not overlook the support staff on campus as well. They are also essential to the culture, vision, and success of a school and the reinforcement of its overarching mission and goals. Conduct surveys with them as well in order to gather information about how to best provide targeted training and what valuable insight they may have to offer. Examples of possible surveys to administer to staff include the Data-Driven Decision-Making Efficacy and Anxiety Inventory (Dunn, Airola, Lo, & Garrison, 2013) and the Social and Emotional Learning Beliefs Scale (Brackett, Reyes, Rivers, Elbertson, & Salovey, 2012).

Box 3.3

Voices From the Field

A blue-ribbon principal, Dr. Walker, has turned low-performing elementary schools into high-performing schools and has perfected the art of academic MTSS in at-risk schools over the span of her career. She is a highly organized and focused leader who targets teacher competencies and creates systems to support students at all levels. Dr. Walker has an unwavering vision of effective instructional practices and provides teachers with ongoing professional development using evidence-based programs. She considers "training teachers to be better" a labor of love. Teaching adults to improve their teaching practices is time-intensive and requires patience and communication skills. No growth is *not* an option in Dr. Walker's school. Something has to change if there is no growth, so she asks her staff about what needs to change. Student engagement, a book level, *something* needs to happen differently if students are not demonstrating growth. Problem solving for students on her school campus is deliberate and systemic. Dr. Walker is clearly at the helm of her ship and strongly believes that a school administrator, preferably the principal, has to chair and lead MTSS at a school. She believes a coordinator could lead the Academic MTSS team in some circumstances, through a distributed leadership model, as long as the coordinator was in close communications with the administration.

Tier 1 instruction is a main priority. In reading, the Kathleen Brown model is used, which comes from the University of Utah Reading Clinic. It is very systematic in terms of leveled reading lessons and books, templates, observations, and manual operations. In training her school staff in this reading model, she focused first on training her leadership team in coaching and how to give feedback to teachers. Dr. Walker feels strongly that the only way to ensure valid and reliable teaching methods at a school is to frequently observe teachers teaching and provide feedback to them for continuous improvement opportunities. "Inspect what you expect" is her motto. A random observation schedule is required because the unpredictability increases the probability that teachers are sticking to the curriculum and delivering it well, whether that be at Tier 1, 2, or 3. If the program is implemented as prescribed, reading improvement should occur. If improvement has not occurred then something has to change, and the Academic MTSS team can help the classroom teacher make changes to target students' skills deficits.

Resources are strategically allocated across grade levels. Universal benchmarking, team functions, interventions, and supports are carefully planned and executed. Human capital investments include an MTSS coordinator funded by Title monies, two intervention specialists, one off-ratio teacher, and three special education teachers who help teach Tier 3–level instruction to students regardless of the eligibility status of students. Students with disabilities receive all individualized education program (IEP) services through intervention blocks that may or may not be co-taught by general education teachers. After complaining, a new special education teacher who felt strongly in only servicing her 18 special-needs students was accommodated with a typical resource room schedule. However, she soon learned to regret it due to the lack of maneuverability and the decrease in shared responsibility for student achievement that were transpiring throughout the rest of the school culture. It did not take long for that special education teacher to request integration back to being a Tier 3 interventionist. The intersection of interventions and special education has never been more eloquently maneuvered, as the range of supports and services on a campus with a highly functional MTSS can be reflected in a student's IEP, taking into consideration the greater options of getting appropriate instruction in a less restrictive environment.

Coordinating tiers of support through the master schedule has become a fine art for Dr. Walker. The number of students in intervention groups must not exceed seven students in Tier 2 or five students in Tier 3. In the event that there are too many targeted students for small groups, new groups can be added by adapting the schedule for the highest Tier 2 students to attend intervention blocks on alternating days, with direct instruction one day and independent practice the next. When there are not enough students to fill intervention block seats at the Tier 2 level, they target the students on the watch list for Tier 2 in an even more proactive manner. All teachers are trained to have "A" and "B" groups, with independent practice at students' instructional levels on odd days. There is a 45-minute block for reading interventions at Tier 2 and Tier 3 at the end of the reading block, with math and writing intervention blocks of 30 minutes occurring at the end of the math and writing blocks in the master schedule and in lesson plans. Grade levels are paired to share resources, including the use of instructional assistants and computers. The scheduling of intervention groups is also flexible to ensure they do not overlap with specialist classes, such as art, music, and physical education. Some students have to give up their specialist period to attend the most appropriate intervention group and add highly intensive minutes of instruction into their day. Dr. Walker reports that she can sleep at night if students can read as a result of those intensive instructional opportunities but miss out on specials classes. Scheduling is always a moving puzzle to assemble.

Dr. Walker grew better teaching practices through continuous staff engagement and professional development. She started holding voluntary grade-level professional learning communities to address Academic MTSS during teachers' prep periods. The meetings were not mandatory, but the teachers responded well to the high frequency of support from the administration and other teachers at these meetings, and all attended. She was able to buy out their prep period some years, but not others, as funding is never guaranteed. Teachers found these meetings highly valuable and voted to continue. Grade-level collaboration at the meetings includes analyzing data, instructional planning, gleaning what unit data instruction reveals, and making data-based decisions. The first year of the rollout, they had two Academic MTSS meetings a week, one dedicated to math and one to reading. The next year, they had one Academic MTSS meeting a week, alternating math one week, with reading the next. These days they hold one grade-level Academic MTSS meeting every three weeks to review the response-to-instruction data and make decisions whether to intensify instruction or move students into higher groups as warranted. As teacher competencies improved, they needed less direct support from administration. According to Dr. Walker, teachers have a human need to contribute, much like gang mentality. She describes having Academic MTSS gangs on campus actively solving problems and overcoming barriers for students. The staff stays motivated by successes.

Celebrations for students are big at Dr. Walker's school. They have many incentives and engagement opportunities for the children. Every month, students earn rewards for reaching academic, behavioral, and attendance goals. Students earn "brag tags" for attendance and can earn special privileges. They can earn VIP passes so they get to go to the front of every line while they hold the pass. Students have the opportunity to earn treats and treasures often. A big event is the monthly dance club at recess for students with perfect attendance for the month, the "Attend Dance." A "dance floor" is roped off during recess with a party inside the ropes for students reaching their attendance goals. Students at the party can dance with friends to blaring music, eat treats, and socialize like superstars. Anything that gets children wanting to be at school is fair game. Through leveraging community relationships, Dr. Walker has an agreement with a local corporation who donates four bikes every month to deserving students who earn raffle tickets based on progress. Four winners are chosen monthly for new bikes. Using Title I monies, donations, and other funding sources, numerous after-school activities are available including sports, robotics, drama, and gardening. Enrichment and fun increase student engagement, effort, and attendance.

Growing better teaching practices, building capacity, and developing and sustaining leadership at all grade levels is the name of the game for this blue-ribbon principal. Every teacher is responsible for presenting their own data at Academic MTSS team meetings because when they have to present to their peers, they feel more accountable. If teachers feel that high expectations are too high, there will be push back. When teachers are accountable to each other, it helps them feel more connected to other teachers, which leads to better morale. There are Academic MTSS grade-level representatives at each grade level and the MTSS coordinator who write plans, support grade-level teachers, and help with data organization. Team chemistry is a highly underrated variable that has an impact on school culture and is not something that can be counted on or replicated. At the end of the day, Dr. Walker would rather take a mediocre teacher over a rockstar teacher if the mediocre teacher is willing to work the program. Rock-star teachers are often high maintenance, and if one school has too many rock stars, they clash. Mediocre teachers can turn into solid teachers and teachers who work hard for kids are the educators Dr. Walker can work with.

References

Asghar, A., Munawar, S., & Muhammad, R. (2015). The impact of positive and negative attitude of teachers towards corporal punishment on students' achievement in mathematics. *Dialogue, 10*(2), 182–188.

Bogin, A., & Nguyen-Hoang, P. (2014). Property left behind: An unintended consequence of a no child left behind "failing" school designation. *Journal of Regional Science, 54*(5), 788–805.

Brackett, M. A., Reyes, M. R., Rivers, S. E., Elbertson, N. A., & Salovey, P. (2012). Assessing teachers' beliefs about social and emotional learning. *Journal of Psychoeducational Assessment, 30*(3), 219–236.

Calet, N., Gutierrez-Palma, N., & Defior, S. (2017). Effects of fluency training on reading competence in primary school children: The role of prosody. *Learning and Instruction, 52*, 59–68.

Common Core State Standards Initiative (2010). *Common core state standards for mathematics.* Retrieved from www.corestandards.org/wp-content/uploads/Math_Standards1.pdf

Creswell, J. W. (2008). *Educational research: Planning, conducting, and evaluating quantitative and qualitative research*. Upper Saddle River, NJ: Pearson Education, Inc.

Dunn, K. E., Airola, D. T., Lo, W., & Garrison, M. (2013). What teachers think about what they can do with data: Development and validation of the data driven decision-making efficacy and anxiety inventory. *Contemporary Educational Psychology, 38*, 87–98.

Ennis, R. P., Blanton, K., & Katsiyannis, A. (2017). Child find activities under the individuals with disabilities education act: Recent case law. *Teaching Exceptional Children, 49*(5), 301–308.

Farmer, L. (2017). How to beat teacher burnout: With more education. *Education Digest, 83*(2), 13–16.

Forman, S. G., & Crystal, C. D. (2015). Systems consultation for multitiered systems of supports (MTSS): Implementation issues. *Journal of Educational and Psychological Consultation, 25*, 276–285.

Foucault, M. (1995). *Discipline and punish: The birth of the prison* (2nd ed.). New York, NY: Random House.

Freeman, J., Simonsen, B., McCoach, D. B., Sugai, G., Lombardi, A., & Horner, R. (2016). Relationship between school-wide positive behavior interventions and supports and academic, attendance, and behavior outcomes in high schools. *Journal of Positive Behavior Interventions, 18*(1), 41–51.

Freeman, M. D. A. (2010). Upholding the dignity and best interests of children: International law and the corporal punishment of children. *Law & Contemporary Problems, 73*(2), 211–251.

Freeman, R., Miller, D., & Newcomer, L. (2015). Integration of academic and behavioral MTSS at the district level using implementation science. *Learning Disabilities: A Contemporary Journal, 13*(1), 59–72.

Gershoff, E. T. (2010). More harm than good: A summary of scientific research on the intended and unintended effects of corporal punishment on children. *Law & Contemporary Problems, 73*, 31–56.

Gill, B., Borden, B. C., & Hallgren, K. (2014). *Final report: A conceptual framework for data-driven decision making*. Princeton, NJ: Mathematica Policy Research.

Gonser, S. (2016, November). Why Las Vegas is recruiting uncertified teachers. *The Atlantic*. Retrieved from www.theatlantic.com/education/archive/2016/11/are-uncertified-teachers-better-than-substitutes/509099/

Hathorn, T. (2013, November). *The glorification of athletes, not just a media thing*. Retrieved from https://taylorhathorn.wordpress.com/2013/11/04/the-glorification-of-athletes-not-just-a-media-thing/

Jimerson, S. R., Burns, M. K., & VanDerHeyden, A. M. (Eds.). (2016). *The handbook of response to intervention: The science and practice of multi-tiered systems of support*. New York, NY: Springer.

Kuhn, M. R., & Stahl, S. A. (2003). Fluency: A review of developmental and remedial practices. *Journal of Educational Psychology, 95*(1), 3–21.

Ladd, H. F., & Fiske, E. B. (Eds.). (2008). *Handbook of research in education finance and policy*. New York, NY: Routledge.

Lavy, V. (2007). Using performance-based pay to improve the quality of teachers. *The Future of Children, 17*(1), 87–109.

Layton, L. (2015, November). How to build a better teacher: Groups push a 9-point plan called TeachStrong. *The Washington Post*. Retrieved from www.washingtonpost.com/local/education/how-to-build-a-better-teacher-groups-push-a-9-point-plan-called-teachstrong/2015/11/08/2b28b824–84c8–11e5–8ba6cec48b74b2a7_story.html?utm_term= .5483e0629e6f

Lewis, S., & Hardy, I. (2015). Funding, reputation and targets: The discursive logics of high-stakes testing. *Cambridge Journal of Education, 45*(2), 245–264.

Marino, M. T., & Beecher, C. C. (2010). Conceptualizing RTI in 21st-centruy secondary science classrooms: Video games' potential to provide tiered support and progress monitoring for students with learning disabilities. *Learning Disability Quarterly, 33*, 299–311.

Martin, C., Partelow, L., & Brown, C. (2015). *Smart, skilled, and striving: Transforming and elevating the teaching profession*. The Center for American Progress. Retrieved from www.americanprogress.org/issues/education/reports/2015/11/03/123747/smart-skilled-and-striving/

Maslow, A. (1943). A theory of human motivation. *Psychological Review, 50*, 370–396.

Mérida-Lopez, S., & Extremera, N. (2017). Emotional intelligence and teacher burnout: A systemic review. *International Journal of Educational Research, 85*, 121–130.

Merz, S. (2017). Who in your class needs help? *Educational Leadership, 75*(4), 12–17.

Meyer, M. M., & Behar-Horenstein, L. S. (2015). When leadership matters: Perspectives from a teacher team implementing response to intervention. *Education and Treatment of Children, 38*(3), 383–402.

National Association of School Psychologists (2010). *Model for comprehensive and integrated school psychological services.* Retrieved from www.nasponline.org/standards-and-certification/nasp-practice-model/nasp-practice-model-implementation-guide/section-i-nasp-practice-model-overview/nasp-practice-model-overview

National Association of School Psychologists (2017). *Shortages in school psychology: Challenges to meeting the growing needs of U.S. students and schools [Research summary].* Bethesda, MD: Author.

National Board for Professional Teaching Standards (2016a). *The proven impact of board-certified teachers on student impact.* Retrieved from www.nbpts.org/wp-content/uploads/impact_brief_final.pdf

National Board for Professional Teaching Standards (2016b). *What teachers should know and be able to do.* Arlington, VA: Author.

National Board for Professional Teaching Standards (2019). *Introduction: By teachers, for teachers.* Retrieved from http://accomplishedteacher.org/introduction

Nevada Association of School Psychologists (2018). *Shortage of school psychologists in Nevada: Challenges in meeting the growing needs of our students' academic, social-emotional, and mental-behavioral health [Research summary].* Las Vegas, NV: Author.

North, C. E. (2006). More than words? Delving in the substantive meaning(s) of "social justice" in education. *Review of Educational Research, 76*, 507–536.

Odden, A. R. (2012). *Improving student learning when budgets are tight.* Thousand Oaks, CA: Corwin.

Odden, A. R., & Picus, L. O. (2014) *School finance: A policy perspective* (5th ed.). New York, NY: McGraw Hill.

Pearson (2015). *AIMSweb software guide version 2.5.10.* Retrieved from https://aimsweb2 pearson.com/aimsweb-frontoffice/helpsupport/help/aimsweb_software_guide2510.pdf

Pearson (2017). *AIMSweb Plus introductory guide.* Retrieved from www.marshfieldschools.org/cms/lib/WI01919828/Centricity/Domain/82/aimsplus%20introductory%20guide.pdf

Pearson (2019). *Words their way.* Retrieved from www.pearson.com/us/higher-education/series/Words-Their-Way-Series/2281883.html.

Pleck, E. (2004). *Domestic tyranny: The making of American social policy against family violence from colonial times to the present.* Champaign, IL: University of Illinois Press.

Preiss, A. (2015, November). *Release: 40 education organizations unite to launch TeachStrong, a campaign to modernize and elevate the teaching profession.* Retrieved from www.americanprogress.org/press/release/2015/11/10/125052/release-40-education-organizations-unite-to-launch-teachstrong-a-campaign-to-modernize-and-elevate-the-teaching-profession/

Radel, R., Sarrazin, P., Legrain, P., & Wild, T. C. (2010). Social contagion of motivation between teacher and student: Analyzing underlying processes. *Journal of Educational Psychology, 102*(3), 577–587.

Sawchuk, A. (2015, November). Can a new political campaign to 'modernize' teaching succeed? *Ed Week.* Retrieved from http://blogs.edweek.org/edweek/teacherbeat/2015/11/can-new-campaign-to-modernize-teaching-succeed.html

Scholastic Red. (2002). *CORE Phonics Survey.* Retrieved from http://www.scholastic.com/dodea/module_2/resources/dodea_m2_tr_core.pdf

Shinn, M. R. (2007). Identifying students at risk, monitoring performance, and determining eligibility within RTI: Research on educational need and benefit from academic intervention. *School Psychology Review, 36*(4), 601–617.

Smith, L. R., & Sanderson, J. (2015). I'm going to Instagram it! An analysis of athlete self-presentation on Instagram. *Journal of Broadcasting & Electronic Media, 59*(2), 342–358.

Souers, K. (2017). Responding with care to students facing trauma. *Educational Leadership*, 75(4), 32–36.

Sparks, S. D., & Harwin, A. (2016, August). Students still face paddling in U.S. schools: Punishment rates for Blacks nearly double those for Whites. *Education Week*, 36(1), 1, 16–18.

Straus, M. A. (2010). Prevalence, societal causes, and trends in corporal punishment by parents in world perspective. *Law & Contemporary Problems*, 73(2), 1–30.

Taormina, R. J., & Law, C. M. (2000). Approaches to preventing burnout: The effects of personal stress management and organizational socialization. *Journal of Nursing Management*, 8, 89–99.

Tong, L., Shinohara, R., Sugisawa, Y., Tanaka, E., Watanabe, T., Koeda, T., & Anme, T. (2015). Buffering effect of parental engagement on the relationship between corporal punishment and children's emotional/behavioral problems. *Pediatrics International*, 57, 385–392.

Uversky, V. N., & Dunker, A. K. (2008). Controlled chaos. *Science*, 322(5906), 1340–1341.

Wilson, H. W. (2014). *The reference shelf: Embracing new paradigms in education*. Amenia, NY: Grey House Publishing, Inc.

Yaffe, D. (2016). Tackling the teacher shortage: School leaders turn to bonuses, affordable housing, outreach to college students, and other solutions. *Education Digest*, 81(8), 11–15.

Chapter 4

How to Build Your Program

Key Terms

Infrastructure
Physical Capital
Strategic Resource Allocation
Master Schedule
Fidelity
Reliability
Validity
Leadership Fidelity Checks
Unintended Consequences
Positive Class Culture
MTSS Extension Opportunities

Chapter Concepts

In this chapter, readers will learn:

1. The importance of the MTSS program infrastructure.
2. The need for responsible fiscal management and strategic resource allocation.
3. The critical role of the master schedule to MTSS program success.
4. The necessity of leadership fidelity checks to ensure accurate MTSS program implementation.
5. The demand for MTSS extension opportunities: what they are and why they are important.
6. The reason for MTSS team meetings and their role in making timely decisions about students.

You Are Here. Ever look at a map in a large amusement park to try to find how to get to a specific location? The first crucial piece of information the group needs is to figure out where they are. They have to orient themselves to their location on the map if the map is going to be useful. Determining where they are going is obviously the second crucial piece of information needed to get to their destination. People can usually pinpoint their desired destination before knowing their actual location on the map;

however, how do they get where they are going if they do not know where they are? They might look for major landmarks like large signs or rides to orient themselves to their location. They can then follow other landmarks to ensure they are going in the right direction.

The same principle could hold true for the direction and movement of a multi-tiered support system and team. Through information provided in the previous chapters, teams now have the necessary supports and skills to begin building their Multi-Tiered Systems of Support (MTSS) programs. With guidance and support from administrators, the structure in the MTSS framework has been engineered to empower, motivate, and compensate members for their efforts. They have evaluated their current curriculum and invested in additional researched-based methods to support Tiers 1, 2, and 3. MTSS teams have selected high-quality members to work together to systematically monitor at-risk students on campus to make data-based decisions. Teams have selected a method of universal screening for each domain and trained teachers on its administration to help identify underachievers or those in need of social-emotional-behavioral supports and cross-referenced data from multiple sources to identify at-risk students. Now, the goal is to orient the team to where they are and then map where it seeks to go. What are the landmarks that are going to guide the MTSS team? Who is going to lead the way? That all depends on where the team starts and the unique qualities of each team member.

Landmarks that will guide the process of MTSS growth and implementation of MTSS include leadership, human capital, professional compensation, material resources, team building, teacher and staff training, inclusive practices, quality universal instruction and benchmarking, systematic monitoring of student data, intervention implementation and documentation, progress monitoring, data-based decision making, program evaluation through feedback looping and problem solving, and professional communication. Each landmark is an essential element for a school to achieve in order for it to reach the ultimate goal of an MTSS program with a solid foundation poised for sustainability. The following four components will help guide the journey: infrastructure, budgeting, the master schedule, and intervention block class scheduling.

Infrastructure

Kevin Costner's character in the motion picture *Field of Dreams* espoused the philosophy "build it and they will come" (Gordon & Robinson, 1989). However, when the masses are already "there" before the infrastructure is adequately built, remodeling can get a little tricky. An MTSS *infrastructure* is the foundational framework that supports data-based decisions about students on campus. It is easier to build school programs and culture from the ground up and to have the requisite infrastructure in place before students ever set foot in class. Like any well-constructed building, it is important to have a solid foundation (Foorman, 2016).

The base of the foundation of effective MTSS is at Tier 1. *Tier 1 must be evaluated for structural integrity before anything else can be reliably built on top of it.* Tier 1 instruction must be effectively delivered using evidence-based practices. Then more intense and more comprehensive tiers of support can grow from a healthy baseline of effective practices. Tiers 2 and 3 have a greater chance of being implemented with fidelity if Tier 1 is solid. It is very difficult to reliably make inferences about Tier 2 and Tier 3 practices or evaluate outcomes through feedback looping, otherwise. Examination of educational practices, whether starting a new school or reforming an existing one, must begin at Tier 1.

Whether or not Tier 1 is strong, students will require supports at Tier 2 and Tier 3. The quality of additional layers of support will always be correlated to the quality of the bottom layer at the base of the structure. In reality, *all three tiers must grow structurally together*. Tier 1 has to support Tiers 2 and 3, but Tiers 2 and 3 must, in turn, make Tier 1 stronger by supporting all students in an inclusive culture. For schools that are "remodeling" existing structures of educational practices, it is important to examine outcome measures from previous years and make changes incrementally every new school year to solidify practices that are working and grow new layers of MTSS infrastructure. The foundational quality of a school's MTSS rests in the construction details. For schools that are "remodeling" existing structures of educational practices, it is important to remember that schools can make changes incrementally to solidify their foundation each school year. The best time to implement new practices in a school setting is always at the beginning of the school year. Sometimes tweaks are necessary throughout the year and a new practice emerges from necessity. However, big-picture initiatives must begin implementation at the beginning of the academic year with most of the planning conducted at the end of the prior school year and through the summer for administrators.

Construction, or reconstruction, of MTSS on a school campus depends on existing structures and where the team is at in the building process. The infrastructure needed for staff and student success should be in place before children ever set foot in a classroom (Odden & Picus, 2014; Sprick, 2013; Shinn & Walker, 2010; Sprick, 2009; Shinn, 2007). Without a clear blueprint, educators find themselves responding to student needs and school problems reactively, rather than proactively, which is time-consuming and exhausting to have to constantly reinvent solutions to problems rather than having a problem-solving framework already in place. *The importance of a well-constructed MTSS with a solid foundation cannot be overemphasized.* Whether a team is building a new program or remodeling existing structures of educational practice, the school should start conservatively to ensure compliance with, and integrity of, new practices. Additions and improvements can be made incrementally each school year to expand the dimensions of the tiered support system.

Budgeting

Before a comprehensive MTSS program can be implemented, a budget must first be devised. Given the chronic shortage of monies at both the federal and state levels that are allocated for education, a school must adopt a strategic approach to using its funds (Odden, 2012). At the state and district levels, budgetary decisions may be made that have an impact on salary freezes, class size, or decentralizing structures and programming. These decisions will certainly have an impact on individual schools, but each school will need to devise a strategic plan to best use its resources. *Responsible fiscal management and strategic resource allocation are about directly aligning each initiative on campus to the overall school improvement plan to maximize efficiency and enhance student outcomes.* Schools will review the effectiveness of their school improvement plan annually, including their fiscal management and resource allocation strategy, on a formative basis, as well using a structured format, such as through use of a logic model (Forman & Crystal, 2015;

Epstein & Klerman, 2013; Mirabella, 2013; Carman, 2010; Frechtling, 2007; Trevisian, 2007; McDavid & Hawthorn, 2006). More about using logic models, program evaluation, and feedback looping is discussed in Chapter 12.

Teams must know their budget long before the start of the school year. School funding varies depending on numerous student factors, including, but not limited to, the number of total students as well as those with special education eligibilities, limited language proficiencies, and free or reduced-price lunch status (Odden & Picus, 2014). Some federal funds are available to states under the Individuals with Disabilities Education Act (IDEA, 2006) to assist states in providing a free and appropriate education to qualified special education students (20 U.S.C. §1411[a][1]). Funds are allocated from two primary funding sources, state education agency, and local education agency, and depending on the health of each, a school may be better funded some years over others. School administrators must make a long-term financial commitment to fund physical capital as well as human capital. *Physical capital* includes the tangible tools necessary to implement an MTSS program and includes materials needed to execute the research-based interventions as well as the computerized assessment tools necessary for benchmarking and progress monitoring. *Human capital* includes the competencies, value, and knowledge the professionals on campus bring to the table. These costs are also extended to staffing highly qualified educators, training for highly qualified educators (including substitute teachers and support staff to cover for educators in trainings during school hours or sending school leaders off campus for training), retaining these accomplished staff members, and providing compensation for MTSS team members who work extra duty.

Strategic resource allocation is part of the school's overall school improvement plan linked to fiscal management and is a puzzle to be assembled by administrators in school settings. Weighing the benefits and costs of allocating time, money, and manpower for any given initiative is important to the decision-making process (Forman & Crystal, 2015). Ideally, schools prefer to target the greatest number of students with any new initiative to obtain the greatest return on their investment (Jimerson, Burns, & VanDerHeyden, 2016; Sailor, 2015). The more students an initiative targets successfully, the better schools can celebrate those successes and build on what works. Implementation of new systems in school organization takes investment not only in appropriate researched-based methods but also in training staff in how to use those methods (Lane, Carter, Jenkins, Dwiggins, & Germer, 2015). Effective staff training cannot be overlooked, and if not done thoroughly and with efficacy, it can undermine the entire initiative. The interaction between the infrastructure and the ability of individuals to act on initiatives is complicated by the bureaucratic structures in which schools must operate, the needs of various stakeholders, and the continuous push for greater accountability and outcomes (Rigby, Woulfin, & Marz, 2016; Robinson, 2015). Building successful and sustainable MTSS infrastructure requires material resources and clearly established procedures, as well as staff buy-in and skill development. The directions of many simultaneously moving parts must be anticipated, accounted for, measured, and corrected within the framework. Getting people to row in the same direction is a leadership skill that is made possible when everyone has the tool(s) they need to paddle and they have received clearly communicated procedures. Teachers must be given a place to practice and use newly adopted methods, and the school administration must allocate time for these activities to take place in order for them to be successful. Planning goes back to the basics of who, what, where, when, and how.

Master Schedule

On an elementary campus, the master schedule provides organizational support and the definitive answers to all administrators' questions about what is happening on campus (Forman & Crystal, 2015; Weisz, Ugueto, Cheron, & Herren, 2013). The *master schedule* provides the calendar and timetable to support the hourly, daily, weekly, monthly, and annual activities on a campus and is essential for successful program implementation. By calendaring MTSS activities at the beginning of the school year, team members can plan for meeting times, students will have a differentiated MTSS block or two built into their school day, and teachers can prepare to teach their differentiated MTSS block classes. Some schools refer to these differentiated MTSS block classes as intervention blocks, or just "Intervention." This terminology is a bit misleading and does not represent inclusive practices. Even if the use of the phrase "intervention block" started off as a well-meaning description of addressing individual student needs, it may serve to further highlight certain groups of students. Since entire grade levels are divided up during this block of time and receive instruction at their individual level, whether it be regarded to be an intervention (for students performing below grade level) or an enrichment (for students performing at or above grade level), *all* students are receiving the level of support that they need. As such, a more inclusive term, differentiated MTSS blocks, is used.

As previously mentioned, MTSS has almost no chance of being comprehensively successful for students without the school principal actively supporting the process and leading the direction of infrastructure growth (Marston, Lau, Muyskens, & Wilson, 2016; Muhartono, Supriyono, Muluk, & Tjahjanulin, 2016). *The master schedule is the administrative commitment to providing time and space for MTSS team functions.* The master schedule must reflect several MTSS priorities: the allocation of staff and resources to the MTSS team, scheduled differentiated MTSS block classes with use of evidence-based curriculum, established MTSS team meeting dates and reserved locations, and calendaring of MTSS team functions, including scheduled universal benchmarking assessments, assessment reporting dates, and other staff development activities and duties. The master schedule must also have family and community engagement opportunities intertwined with all stakeholders in a child's life; these are critical components to a successful MTSS.

Why do the MTSS teams need the master schedule? The answer rests in the very fabric of a school's culture; MTSS must be woven throughout all aspects of a school, and the master schedule is the way to achieve this. The infrastructure and organizational components may look different on each campus, as it is important to customize MTSS according to each school's individual needs, but each piece must be present. As previously mentioned, there are landmarks to the process of implementation: leadership, human capital, professional compensation, material resources, team building, teacher and staff training, inclusive practices, quality universal instruction and benchmarking, systematic monitoring of student data, intervention implementation and documentation, progress monitoring, data-based decision making, program evaluation through feedback looping and problem solving, and professional communication. Decisions regarding these activities and processes impact every educator and child on campus either directly or indirectly.

Creating scheduled blocks on the master calendar and staffing them with highly effective teachers provides the most reliable way to ensure the implementation of interventions using a research-based curriculum (Goldharber, 2008). *Using attendance records makes documentation of interventions with large numbers of students simple by using teacher lesson plans as evidence of targeted skills practice without the need for laborious note-taking for individual students on a teacher's part.* Expecting students and teachers to meet as needed, without a required commitment or systematic curriculum to improve academic outcomes, are not interventions that are sustainable, reliable, or valid (Freeman, Miller, & Newcomer, 2015).

Regular meeting times and locations for MTSS team meetings must be in the master schedule to ensure that team meetings are certain to occur. The MTSS meeting schedule will reflect the needs of a school, as higher-risk schools will need to meet more often than lower-risk schools (Taskiran, Mutluer, Tufan, & Semerci, 2017; McKee & Caldarella, 2016; Barrett & Katsiyannis, 2015; Shinn, 2007). However, regularly scheduled sessions to systematically review student data and engage in problem solving for students is mandatory regardless of a school's risk level. These mandatory meetings can occur weekly or twice a month depending on the school's needs. It is recommended that MTSS teams meet weekly to best keep informed of student needs and prioritize which students need closer attention. Meeting monthly is not effective for most schools, as the less frequent data analysis schedule is too limited to sensitively respond in a timely manner to difficulties students are experiencing (McKee & Caldarella, 2016; Killeen & Schafft, 2008). Monthly meetings are much less effective in impacting changes to at-risk students' academic, or emotional-behavioral, trajectory in a timely manner. Teams at higher-risk schools and those with larger campuses need to meet weekly due to the volume of students who require attention. How often the team meets, when, where, and who is required to attend is memorialized in the master schedule to ensure accountability and that all stakeholders have sufficient notice and opportunity to be present (Forman & Crystal, 2015; Freeman et al., 2015; Averill & Rinaldi, 2011; Shinn & Walker, 2010).

Differentiated MTSS Block Scheduling

Scheduling blocks of time for meeting students' differentiated needs is the most systematic way to hold teachers and students accountable for attending differentiated MTSS block sessions and for tracking outcomes in an elementary setting. Valid interventions will not occur during class "free time," independently at home, or occasionally after school. Block scheduling allots time for differentiated instruction to occur and allows for leadership to ensure curriculum implementation fidelity. Expecting teachers to fit remedial instruction or enrichment opportunities into the day without a dedicated time in the lesson plans to conduct those lessons will create an intervention schedule that is done at whim, which is not sustainable or reliable in large school systems, and ultimately will not meet the intervention requirements in the Every Student Succeeds Act (2015) and most state education laws. Intervention outcomes must be systematically monitored by the MTSS team to ensure *fidelity*, or trust in the accuracy and quality of the overall implementation process. The first step is to ensure that the intervention is being delivered with *reliability*, or the intervention procedures are being implemented consistently as a treatment each time the intervention groups meet. The second step to measuring outcomes is to systematically evaluate the *validity* of the intervention data; in other words, the MTSS team must determine if the data collected can be used meaningfully to create inferences and make decisions about the students from the scores collected.

The following two scenarios detail cases of reliability and validity. At Summit Elementary School, the MTSS team was concerned when it realized some students on their caseload were not responding adequately to the interventions provided. However, on closer inspection, many of those students were not attending school regularly. In this case, the team was experiencing an issue with the reliability of the intervention implemented. The problem-solving step for these particular students was to address their poor attendance instead of deeming the intervention unsuccessful. Intervention effectiveness cannot be determined if students are not in class to receive the intensive instruction. If the team had not considered attendance and found it to be the culprit, the team may have recommended other solutions that would not have accurately addressed the underlying problem. Students must reliably receive interventions in order for them to be effective.

In a second scenario, at Lake Elementary School, a differentiated MTSS group was meeting reliably; however, the teacher was lackadaisical in collecting the intervention data, resulting in issues of validity. Due to feedback looping and school *leadership fidelity checks*, this teacher's lack of commitment to collecting intervention data with integrity came to light. Leadership fidelity checks are a review of all aspects of the implementation procedures conducted by the administration or a member of the leadership team that occurs on both a regular and a random basis, as needed. These leadership fidelity checks should occur at least twice a year. In this particular case, the teacher was using AIMSweb R-CBM as a strategic monitoring tool to assess basic reading fluency. Administered correctly, this is a valid tool to measure student growth in reading speed and accuracy, which highly correlates with reading achievement and reading comprehension; however, any tool administered incorrectly produces questionable data. Per the administration rules, the students are not allowed to see the teacher's computer screen as he or she is marking off incorrect student responses in real time (Pearson, 2015). If students are allowed to see their errors as they read, it creates issues of *internal validity* as the data collected will be compromised due to teacher error and participant experience (Creswell, 2008). As a result, a causal relationship between the interventions provided and the outcomes obtained cannot be determined.

Several questions arose from the situation that the MTSS team at Lake Elementary School had to consider. Most immediately, was the student truly capable of reading more words per minute fluently? This was an easy problem to address by administering a second, similar probe correctly with the student to get a true snapshot of their current skills and to begin determining a causal relationship between interventions and outcomes. At a higher level, if the teacher compromised the integrity of the data because of how he or she administered the fluency probe, were the other students' progress monitoring probes being administered incorrectly as well? Had the teacher also been compromising the integrity of the interventions that were provided to the students? This would then require a systemic review of the teacher's performance, and all student data from this particular teacher's intervention group would need to be reexamined for validity.

As a general rule, problem solving is less effective, not to mention a waste of time and resources, if the implementation of interventions is not systematically monitored for reliability and validity. Appropriate scheduling of differentiated MTSS blocks on the master schedule, tracking attendance, and school leadership fidelity checks help to solve issues of reliability and validity.

Which academic content areas do most students at school struggle in? How many students require interventions and in which content areas, will determine how differentiated MTSS groups are scheduled and when. A low-risk school may not require as many intervention groups as a high-risk school and may have more enrichment groups offered during the differentiated MTSS block. Higher-risk schools will require high-quality Tier 1 instruction with scaffolding and flexibility to allow for targeted reteaching of gap skills if a majority, or significant number, of students lack those skills. Whether block scheduling, adding additional minutes in the school day, or reallocating instructional class time to allow for it, targeted, differentiated instruction must be on the master calendar, with approved instructional lesson plans and curriculum in place to allow for leadership fidelity checks. Schools will want to start with as many intervention opportunities as possible while keeping the student-to-teacher ratio low. Certain conditions must accompany the smaller student-to-teacher ratio, such as increasing the intensity of the individualized intervention to remediate skills and the accuracy of the differentiated, targeted instruction (National Center on Response to Intervention, 2013). The greater the duration of data collection, the greater the validity of the data for making data-based decisions for students (Van Norman & Christ, 2016). If a school can only reasonably implement one intervention group per grade level, for example, in reading, while they work up to building differentiated MTSS blocks into the master calendar, start there. The goal is to address students' needs without compromising fidelity. When the differentiated MTSS block can be calendared, teams may also have the capacity to consider adding sections to address math and written language as well.

The differentiated MTSS block must be built into the master schedule by grade level. Grade-level teams must meet to triangulate data sources on their students and place them into academic groups based on skill levels. For example, in a first-grade team, there may be six teachers. Each teacher is going to teach during the differentiated MTSS block; however, they will not be teaching their own students, and the instruction will be at the instructional level based on the results of a diagnostic assessment. There may be three groups of letter sounds, one group of blending, one group of fluency, and one large group of enrichment for those students who are at or above grade level. These differentiated MTSS blocks are especially beneficial for students who are highly transient or do not speak English as their first language. Such students often have gaps in their learning due to exposure or comprehension, not an underlying disability, and providing learning opportunities to fill these gaps are critical. As such, it is not uncommon for schools to offer more literacy and reading remediation intervention than mathematics. Some schools code the groups based on animal names, flowers, or some other method to promote inclusivity and decrease any negative bias for being part of a particular intervention group. That is not to say that students, especially those in higher elementary grades, will not decode what the groupings mean, but at least the school has done what it can to promote inclusive practices.

Communities with a high population of second-language students, or language-deprived students, will need a greater number of intervention opportunities in the areas of reading and vocabulary development than English only communities. This population will also require extended periods of guided language exposure to help fill in missing language and academic learning gaps, in addition to inclusion in schoolwide universal learning designs (Sailor, 2015). Populations with students and families living in chronic states of crisis may also require more remedial groups and wraparound supports. One of the goals of MTSS implementation is to increase supports over time, and schools should only begin with the number of differentiated MTSS blocks they can offer while maintaining the integrity of the supports while still addressing the critical needs of the students. Schools will need to prioritize their intervention offerings and should strive to establish as many supports as possible while maintaining integrity and accuracy of intervention implementation. Such classes may target mathematics interventions, behavioral interventions, written language interventions, and any other documented area of need at a school.

Scheduling differentiated MTSS blocks to address all areas of need could take years to build up. The sooner teams start building supports in schools, the sooner they will have the requisite number of intervention classes to sufficiently serve the entire school population. Providing MTSS to students can be a voluntary process that each school principal or district can elect to implement. At the state level, or in very large school districts, the fidelity of implementation can become difficult as the interpretation of the law may vary greatly district to district, or even building to building. Many factors including leadership variability, implementation ambiguity, or policy misalignment can lead to *unintended consequences*, or outcomes that are realized without purposefully working toward them.

Box 4.1

Voices From the Field

In 2015, the Nevada legislature passed Senate Bill 391 aimed at improving student literacy through early intervention supports in grades kindergarten through third grade and was dubbed Read by Grade 3. The bill also included language that would mandatorily retain students if they did not meet a predetermined cut score on their third-grade high-stakes reading assessment. While the intent of the law was well meaning, unintended consequences occurred as a result. For example, while the intent of the law was to emphasize and implement tiered student supports for reading, the reporting mechanism written into the law was not the number of students identified as needing interventions, the number who received interventions, and the number who met or did not meet their interventions goals, but rather the reporting mechanism was number of students retained. Therefore, one of the unintended consequences of the law included schools that were not held accountable for providing the intervention services with fidelity; schools were only held accountable for reporting on the number of third-grade students they retained. Students did not receive the interventions they so greatly needed due to a variety of factors including poor systems to identify student needs and provide supports, high numbers of substitute teachers, a lack of understanding as to the intent of the law, insufficient curriculum, and a lack of progress monitoring tools.

On the bright side, under the exemplary leadership of the late Assemblyman Tyrone Thompson, in 2019 the Nevada legislature passed Assembly Bill 289 that amended the original Read by Grade 3 law. Aligning with the original intent of the law, the amended version of the law bolstered literacy supports by expanding them to include *all* elementary grades and aligned the reporting mechanism to require schools to report on the number of students identified as needing interventions, the number who received interventions, and the number of students who were and were not on track to meeting their individualized goals. It also repealed the mandatory retention component of the law, thus avoiding even more unintended consequences that retaining students can bring about such as increased social-emotional issues, decreased rates of high school graduation, and increased financial burdens to the state.

Schools can never overestimate how many students on their campuses will require interventions, especially on at-risk campuses. Given many of the aforementioned risk factors, such as poverty and language acquisition status, and the high correlation between reading proficiency and long-term student success, many schools elect to start their intervention supports with an emphasis on reading. For any differentiated MTSS block, it is important to begin with choosing the evidence-based curriculum and tools that best fit your student population. In most elementary schools, explicit repetition and reteaching of deficit skills do not require expensive materials or programming. Teaching CVC (consonant–vowel–consonant) patterns can be taught through repeated practice during the differentiated MTSS block using a mix of manipulatives and pattern blocks. Additionally, having students read repeated reading passages may improve sight word vocabulary, reading fluency, and prosody. Ease of use, expense, and training requirements all have an impact on a school's choice of purchased or self-made curriculum, but the efficacy of the selected method must be supported by positive and valid research-based outcome measures.

The next step is for leaders to ensure that teachers deliver the evidence-based curriculum with fidelity. The most effective teachers will be those who are willing to get to know their students and differentiate their teaching based on students' needs, not just students' onetime performance on a test. According to the National Board for Professional Teaching Standards (2016) there are five core tenets, or propositions, that teachers should adhere to and be able to demonstrate in their teaching. Commitment to students and their learning is Proposition One of accomplished teaching (National Board for Professional Teaching Standards, 2016) and getting to know the challenges students face outside the classroom is another way teachers must learn to differentiate instruction based on need, not just performance.

Accomplished teachers are going to inspire students the most, creating a positive class culture of celebrating progress. *Positive class culture* is defined as a learning environment based on trust in which the students are encouraged and empowered to make and learn from mistakes. Once a student has reached their intervention goal and is consistently able to perform at a level typical for their grade, the student is exited from intervention class or advances to the next level. When students are exited from monitoring at Tier 3, after consistently demonstrating success in accomplishing academic expectations without intense supports, they are publicly recognized with rewards and celebrated. For example, the MTSS team might nominate students for Principal's Recognition after they have achieved their way off the MTSS team monitoring list. The honor could include a personal visit with the school principal, a letter of commendation, and choices from the treasure box, which might contain store gift cards and fast food certificates.

Ultimately, differentiated MTSS blocks with leveled groupings need to be memorialized in the master calendar for the entire school year so students can get scheduled in, and out, as necessary. On an elementary school campus, grade-level teams are responsible for making Tier 2 changes regarding students' intervention groupings and Tier 3 changes after the MTSS team makes recommendations. Students can move between differentiated MTSS groups, and new students can be moved in, depending on data analysis across multiple sources of response to instruction documentation. Remember, at-risk student data are reviewed *at least every two weeks* so decisions can be made whether to enter, remain, or graduate a student from the intervention group(s). Students who have consistently met their intervention goal and are to be transitioned to the next higher-level group would make that change at any time. Conversely, students new to the school can be placed at their appropriate level group after initial diagnostic assessment. While all students receive instruction through the differentiated MTSS block, only those below grade level, or who are receiving interventions, are progress monitored.

The bottom line is that students need opportunities to remediate skill deficits in addition to, and outside of, core curriculum classes (Cavendish, Harry, Menda, Espinosa, & Mahotiere, 2016; Forman & Crystal, 2015; Shinn, 2007). Teachers are best able to implement interventions with integrity with scheduled block periods built into the master schedule where they can dedicate time and energy to quality instruction. These differentiated MTSS blocks are essential to closing student gaps between expected progress and actual achievement. When school administration can celebrate teachers and students for positive outcomes, everyone wins.

How to fit it all in:

- Begin with fewer targeted content areas and build layers.
- Establish dedicated differentiated MTSS block(s) into each grade's master schedule.
- Allow flexible teaching groups and student grouping.
- Fund after-school tutoring opportunities.
- Provide supplemental online resources and supports.
- Offer supplemental class supports.
- Add an evidence-based curriculum designed for Tier 2 and Tier 3 incrementally.
- Establish a routine program evaluation.
- Review, revise, and implement using feedback looping and continuous improvement model.

Grade-Level and MTSS Meetings

Students are initially placed into their leveled Tier 2 MTSS groups during grade-level team meetings immediately following the first benchmark. While teachers probably will have a cursory idea of which students may be in need of more intensive supports, they need to have the benchmark data and subsequent diagnostic scores before they can group students during the grade-level meetings. It will be several weeks before teachers will have sufficient data to bring referrals to the Academic MTSS team for discussion about possible Tier 3 supports. In general, grade-level teams determine which students require targeted, intensive Tier 2 supports. Based on student response to the interventions provided, or lack thereof, the grade-level teams may choose to refer certain less responsive students to the MTSS teams. At the MTSS team meetings, members can decide what additional Tier 2 supports the student may benefit from and how those services can be provided to the student or accessed by the family.

MTSS team meetings help facilitate the movement of students from Tier 2 to Tier 3 for all grades. Regular MTSS meeting times and locations must be built into the master schedule to ensure that team meetings occur. The MTSS meeting schedule reflects the needs of a school with higher-risk school teams needing to meet more often than lower-risk school teams. Regardless of the frequency of the meeting schedule, they must be held at regular intervals to systematically review student data and engage in problem solving for students. Keep in mind, these meeting can occur once a week or every two weeks but not as infrequently as monthly. Meeting monthly or less is not effective for most schools because a sporadic meeting schedule is much too limited to respond to the difficulties students may be experiencing. There is a constant need for ongoing revisions to adjust the academic and social-emotional-behavioral trajectories of individual students in a timely manner. Students are not widgets that stay stable over time, and they require vigilant care to address their needs. Many can be put back on track in a timely manner with minor adjustments, and others are going to require routine maintenance. *The key element is that decisions are made in a timely manner.* The highest-needs students, with the most severe behavioral deficits, require teams to discuss them on a more frequent basis than other at-risk students, and they may be selected for further monitoring by other school-based teams, such as the social-emotional-behavioral team.

MTSS Extension Opportunities

Offering structured learning opportunities outside the school day is an excellent way to expand services to students. MTSS can be extended to individualized supports such as homework clubs, Saturday school programs, and summer school programs with students allowed to participate in intervention programming, as long as the intervention is provided consistently, with fidelity, and the student's progress is being monitored. The opportunity to benefit from intervention should include MTSS extension opportunities, as students benefit from intervention throughout the year. *MTSS extension opportunities are programming options or incentives for students outside of traditional school offerings.*

If funding permits, Saturday school and extending the school year throughout summer are options for schools to consider when scheduling additional time and space for interventions within the master calendar. These supports could be offered on a voluntary school-by-school basis or part of a larger, systemic approach to educating students up through a high-risk school (Fleming, 2013). Research has long demonstrated that students, especially those from high-risk environments, tend to lose content knowledge after large breaks from structured academic settings (Cooper, 2003; Copple, Kane, Levin, & Cohen, 1992). Summer school is one way to remediate this loss and, ideally, would be redesigned as a positive learning opportunity, like camp, rather than a penalty of hard labor for slacking off during the school year.

As a matter of equity, students living in impoverished socioeconomic areas should be funded higher to provide year-round schooling and intervention opportunities for children to thrive in continuity of exposure and practice to academic concepts. Students who are not native English speakers or who are from impoverished backgrounds will require more deliberate practice and support in order to achieve mastery in reading. Mastery of a skill requires extensive and continuous practice over time.

In many high-risk schools, academically underexposed, underachieving students are the majority on campus. *It is important to remember that the Common Core State Standards Initiative (2010a, 2010b) and traditional education structures target the aggregate majority, not the actual majority of students on many campuses.* Summer school helps close the language and academic gaps of students who do not have access to books over the summer or are not motivated to read independently to master reading.

Other opportunities for MTSS extension at the state and local levels is through investments in schools, libraries, and parks to provide free learning experiences for children. These investments could also help support students to get in additional hours of reading, engaging learning activities, and ultimately increasing the probability of becoming master readers. Families with socioeconomic disadvantages are less likely to have access to books to motivate children to read and develop skills throughout their summers off from school, thus getting in fewer hours of reading compared to their more socioeconomically advantaged peers. More affluent communities would also benefit from summer school programs; however, the fees to attend, hours of operation, and curriculum may differ. Allocating resources for summer school and intervention programs is a matter of equity, not equality, for students who may be victims of social injustices (Francis, Mills, & Lupton, 2017).

Schools are often the first place where students' needs are identified because it is guaranteed that students will bring their problems to school. It is much more effective to have structures and functions in place with prepared school professionals actively monitoring and responding to constantly evolving student difficulties, rather than winging responses haphazardly when problems arise. Reactive practices, rather than proactive practices, lead to multiple missed opportunities to have a positive impact on students. A higher frequency of planned MTSS meetings, carving out time and space for the MTSS team to engage in timely problem solving, is always better than not having enough time to address the needs of students. *Weekly meetings should be the gold standard.* Remember, with the exception of a few members, not all the same team members have to be at every meeting. Scheduling weekly MTSS meetings on the master calendar will weave MTSS tighter into the fabric of the school culture and will help teams to reach MTSS landmarks and their ultimate destination of comprehensive supports by addressing student needs in a timely and efficient manner.

Box 4.2

Connection to Practice

MTSS Planning and Implementation Timetable

Note: this is not meant to be an exhaustive timetable of events and may vary based on the unique needs of the school.

Spring of the year before implementation:

- Select MTSS team chairs.
- Inquire about which current educators would be a good fit for case managers.
- Evaluate the current academic curriculum and select an evidence-based curriculum and interventions to be used in Tiers 1, 2, and 3.
- Evaluate the current social-emotional-behavioral learning curriculum and supports, and select an evidence-based curriculum and resources to be used in Tiers 1, 2, and 3.
- Look at the master calendar and schedule MTSS meeting dates, times, and locations.
- Schedule academic and social-emotional-behavioral benchmark periods.
- An administrator must start identifying teaching practices to grow schoolwide.
- Consider school culture and climate and any changes that could be made.
- Build differentiated the MTSS blocks, structure, and processes into the master calendar and teacher resource guides.

- Explore community resources to share with staff and families.
- Investigate ways to incorporate family engagement throughout the upcoming school year.
- Poll families on what type of family engagement opportunities they would like.

Summer before implementation:

- Train MTSS chair(s), case managers, and specialists in universal benchmarking and use of progress monitoring tools.
- Ensure master calendar reflects MTSS priorities, benchmark windows, differentiated MTSS blocks, meetings, and so on.
- Ensure all resources are available to support implementation at all three tiers for Academic and Social-Emotional-Behavioral MTSS.
- Establish schoolwide expectations and positive behavioral supports.
- Work out any glitches in funding for resources and staff allocations.
- Train MTSS team to ensure orientation to framework and responsibilities.
- Train at best, or orient at minimal, the entire staff on MTSS framework, procedures, and structure.
- Work through any scheduling and meeting logistics.
- Contact and establish pathways for community engagement and support.
- Establish family engagement opportunities and calendar them to occur at least every other month.

Beginning of the school year:

- If the MTSS team members have not been selected and oriented in summer, do so within the first week of school.
- If team members have not been trained in universal benchmarking and use of progress monitoring tools, do so within the first week of school.
- If the entire staff has not been oriented to MTSS, do so within the first week of school.
- The first whole-team MTSS meeting should be held as close to the beginning of the year as possible, after which grade-level MTSS meetings rotate thereafter
- Team expectations are reviewed, the master calendar is reviewed, meeting etiquette rules are reviewed, caseloads are disseminated, and problem solving begins.
- Entire staff must be trained with guided practice in universal benchmarking and progress monitoring.
- Establish and provide training on schoolwide expectations, positive behavioral supports, and use of the incremental correction system.
- Fall benchmarking

Throughout the school year:

- Follow continuous improvement model.
- Follow MTSS Evaluation Frequency and Intensity Framework.
- Conduct benchmark assessments during fall, winter, and spring benchmark windows.

End of the school year:

- Convene the leadership team to review, revise, and revamp processes.
- Use feedback looping to use data collected as inputs for future planning and decision making.
- Consult with outside agencies or partners to bolster any identified gaps in programming.
- Determine where advocacy opportunities may lie.

References

Assembly Bill 289, Nevada 2019.

Averill, O. H., & Rinaldi, C. (2011). Multi-tier systems of support. *District Administration, 9*, 91–94.

Barrett, D. E., & Katsiyannis, A. (2015). Juvenile delinquency recidivism: Are Black and White youth vulnerable to the same risk factors? *Behavioral Disorders, 40*(3), 184–195.

Carman, J. G. (2010). The accountability movement: What's wrong with this theory of change? *Nonprofit and Voluntary Sector Quarterly, 39*(2), 256–274.

Cavendish, W., Harry, B., Menda, A. M., Espinosa, A., & Mahotiere, M. (2016). Implementing response to intervention: Challenges of diversity and system change in a high-stakes environment. *Teachers College Record, 118*, 1–36.

Common Core State Standards Initiative (2010a). *Common core state standards for English language arts and literacy in history/social studies, science, and technical subjects.* Retrieved from www.corestandards.org/wp-content/uploads/ELA_Standards1.pdf

Common Core State Standards Initiative (2010b). *Common core state standards for mathematics.* Retrieved from www.corestandards.org/wp-content/uploads/Math_Standards1.pdf

Cooper, H. (2003). Summer learning loss: The problem and some solutions. *ERIC Digest*, 1–7.

Copple, C., Kane, M., Levin, D., & Cohen, S. (1992, April). *The national education commission on time and learning: Briefing paper* (Issue Brief No. 372–482). Washington, DC: The National Commission on Time and Learning.

Creswell, J. W. (2008). *Educational research: Planning, conducting, and evaluating quantitative and qualitative research.* Upper Saddle River, NJ: Pearson Education.

Epstein, D., & Klerman, J. A. (2013). When is a program ready for rigorous impact evaluation? The role of a falsifiable logic model. *Evaluation Review, 36*(5), 375–401.

Every Student Succeeds Act of 2015, 20 U.S.C. (2015).

Fleming, N. (2013, June). Districts turning summer school into learning labs: Goal is to engage and teach students. *Education Week, 32*(35). Retrieved from www.edweek.org/ew/articles/2013/06/12/35summer.h32.html

Foorman, B. (2016). Introduction to the special issue: Challenges and solutions to implementing effective reading intervention in schools. In B. Foorman (Ed.), *Challenges to implementing effective reading intervention in schools: New directions for child and adolescent development, 154* (pp. 7–10). Malden, MA: Wiley Periodicals, Inc.

Forman, S. G., & Crystal, C. D. (2015). Systems consultation for multitiered systems of supports (MTSS): Implementation issues. *Journal of Educational and Psychological Consultation, 25*, 276–285.

Francis, B., Mills, M., & Lupton, R. (2017). Toward social justice in education: Contradictions and dilemmas. *Journal of Education Policy, 32*(4), 414–431.

Frechtling, J. A. (2007). *Logic modeling methods in program evaluation.* San Francisco, CA: Wiley, Jossey-Bass.

Freeman, R., Miller, D., & Newcomer, L. (2015). Integration of academic and behavioral MTSS at the district level using implementation science. *Learning Disabilities: A Contemporary Journal, 13*(1), 59–72.

Goldharber, D. (2008). The value of teacher quality. In H. F. Ladd & E. B. Fiske (Eds.), *Handbook of research in education finance and policy* (pp. 146–165). New York, NY: Routledge.

Gordon, L. (Producer), & Robinson, P. A. (Director). (1989). *Field of dreams* [Motion picture]. United States: Universal Studios.

Individuals with Disabilities Education Act, 20 U.S.C. § 1400 et seq. (2006 & Supp. V. 2011).

Jimerson, S. R., Burns, M. K., & VanDerHeyden, A. M. (Eds.). (2016). *The handbook of response to intervention: The science and practice of multi-tiered systems of support*. New York, NY: Springer.

Killeen, K. M., & Schafft, K. (2008). The organizational and fiscal implications of transient student populations. In H. F. Ladd & E. B. Fiske (Eds.), *Handbook of research in education finance and policy* (pp. 146–165). New York, NY: Routledge.

Lane, K. L., Carter, E. W., Jenkins, A., Dwiggins, L., & Germer, K. (2015). Supporting comprehensive, integrated, three-tiered models of prevention in schools: Administrators' perspectives. *Journal of Positive Behavior Interventions, 17*(4), 209–222.

Marston, D., Lau, M., Muyskens, P., & Wilson, J. (2016). Data-based decision-making, the problem-solving model, and response to intervention in the Minneapolis Public Schools. In S. Jimerson, M. Burns, & A. VanDerHeyden (Eds.), *The handbook of response to intervention: The science and practice of multi-tiered systems of support* (pp. 677–692). New York, NY: Springer.

McDavid, J. C., & Hawthorn, L. R. L. (2006). *Program evaluation and performance measurement: An introduction to practice*. Thousand Oaks, CA: Sage Publications.

McKee, M. T., & Caldarella, P. (2016). Middle school predictors of high school performance: A case study of dropout risk indicators. *Education, 136*(4), 515–529.

Mirabella, R. M. (2013). Toward a more perfect nonprofit: The performance mindset and the "Gift." *Administrative Theory and Praxis, 35*(1), 81–105.

Muhartono, D. S., Supriyono, B., Muluk, M. R. K., & Tjahjanulin. (2016). Implementation of education services in sound governance perspective. *International Journal of Multidisciplinary Approach & Studies, 3*(4), 101–118.

National Board for Professional Teaching Standards (2016). *What teachers should know and be able to do*. Arlington, VA: Author.

National Center on Response to Intervention (2013). *RTI in middle schools: The essential components* (Publication No. 2313–10/12). Retrieved from https://rti4success.org/sites/default/files/RTI%20in%20Middle%20Schools-The%20Essential%20Components.pdf.

Odden, A. R. (2012). *Improving student learning when budgets are tight*. Thousand Oaks, CA: Corwin.

Odden, A. R., & Picus, L. O. (2014). *School finance: A policy perspective* (5th ed.). New York, NY: McGraw Hill.

Pearson (2015). *AIMSweb software guide version 2.5.10*. Retrieved from https://aimsweb2.pearson.com/aimsweb-frontoffice/helpsupport/help/aimsweb_software_guide2510.pdf.

Rigby, J. G., Woulfin, S. L., & Marz, V. (2016). Understanding how structure and agency influence education policy implementation and organizational change. *American Journal of Education, 122*, 295–302.

Robinson, S. (2015). Decentralisation, managerialism and accountability: Professional loss in an Australian education bureaucracy. *Journal of Education Policy, 30*(4), 468–482. doi:10.1080/02680939.2015.1025241

Sailor, W. (2015). Advances in schoolwide inclusive school reform. *Remedial and Special Education, 36*(2), 94–99.

Senate Bill 391, Nevada 2015.

Shinn, M. R. (2007). Identifying students at risk, monitoring performance, and determining eligibility within RTI: Research on educational need and benefit from academic intervention. *School Psychology Review, 36*(4), 601–617.

Shinn, M. R., & Walker, H. M. (Eds.). (2010). *Interventions for academic and behavior problems in a three-tier model, including Response-to-Intervention* (3rd ed.). Bethesda, MD: National Association of School Psychologists.

Sprick, R. A. (2009). *CHAMPS: A proactive and positive approach to classroom management* (2nd ed.). Eugene, OR: Pacific Northwest Publishing.

Sprick, R. A. (2013). *Discipline in the secondary classroom: A positive approach to behavior management* (3rd ed.). Hoboken, NJ: John Wiley & Sons.

Taskiran, S., Mutluer, T., Tufan, A. E., & Semerci, B. (2017). Understanding the associations between psychosocial factors and severity of crime in juvenile delinquency: A cross-sectional study. *Neuropsychiatric Disease and Treatment, 13*, 1359–1366.

Trevisian, M. S. (2007). Evaluability assessment from 1986–2006. *American Journal of Evaluation, 28*, 290–303.

Van Norman, E. R., & Christ, T. J. (2016). How accurate are interpretations of curriculum-based measurement progress monitoring data? Visual analysis versus decision rules. *Journal of School Psychology, 58*, 41–55.

Weisz, J. R., Ugueto, A. M., Cheron, D. M., & Herren, J. (2013). Evidence-based youth psychotherapy in the mental health ecosystem. *Journal of Clinical Child & Adolescent Psychopathology, 42*(2), 274–286.

Chapter 5

How an Academic MTSS Team Works Together

Key Terms

Hybrid Committee Selection Model
Role
MTSS Chairs
MTSS Grade-Level Representatives
Distributed Presentation Style
Case Manager Model
Developmental MTSS Schools
Transitional MTSS Schools
Adept MTSS Schools
Responsive Adaptability
Academic MTSS Student Database
Case Notes
Legitimization
School Counselors
School Psychologists
Specialists

Chapter Concepts

In this chapter, readers will learn:

1. How to incorporate valuable professional roles into one cohesive MTSS team.
2. Who organizes student cases and presents their information at MTSS team meetings.
3. The organization and flow of an MTSS team meeting.
4. The necessity for responsive adaptability in today's education climate.
5. The importance of legitimizing processes into the culture of the MTSS program.
6. The need to uphold certain meeting etiquette from all MTSS team members.

With the infrastructure of a solid Multi-Tiered System of Support (MTSS) program in place, it is time to train the Academic MTSS team on how to support the students on campus. Chapter 5 delves into how your selected team members work together to form a cohesive unit to target students' needs and skills deficits and define the roles and responsibilities of each member. Chapters 10 and 11 address similar team processes and responsibilities for the Social-Emotional-Behavioral (SEB) MTSS team. Specifically, in Chapters 5, 10, and 11 the roles of staff members are discussed, including, but not limited to, MTSS grade-level representatives, classroom teachers, school counselors, school psychologists, speech and language pathologists, school social workers, and specialists. Leading up to this chapter several foundational supports have been discussed, including strong leadership, a budget prioritizing MTSS funding, and the selection of research-supported Tier 1, Tier 2, and Tier 3 curriculum, teaching, and intervention materials. Also, factors such as scheduled intervention blocks; highly qualified teachers working with at-risk students; meetings and functions of MTSS, both Academic and SEB, memorialized in the master calendar; and the most effective educators positioned in leadership roles have been reviewed.

Before the start of the school year, MTSS team members should be selected based on the processes and discussion points from Chapter 2. Most teachers volunteer for which committees to serve on in elementary schools as they are usually required to participate in a specific number of them. However, school leaders should consider a *hybrid committee selection process* in which the administrator assigns each teacher to one committee based on the individual's strengths and then lets them volunteer for the other one or two committees that they would like to serve on. This process should be recognized and can serve as a work-around when the team is composed of volunteers who may not be the strongest academic instructors. A hybrid model ensures that the teachers with the strongest academic intervention skills sit on the Academic MTSS team, the teachers with the strongest behavior intervention skills sit on the SEB MTSS team, and the other committees are composed of teachers of similarly strong skills. If a school is newly implementing MTSS, it is strongly encouraged to schedule initial training for the Academic and SEB MTSS team members prior to the beginning of the school year because once the students arrive on campus the proverbial train will be in motion and gaining speed as the weeks pass. It is much more difficult to board a moving train than one docked at the station. If training cannot be scheduled for team members prior to the start of the year, the team should meet within the first two weeks of school.

On a school campus, the schedule is the axis around which everything rotates. Team members need a schedule to conduct duties, and organizational timelines are established from before the first day of the school year through the last day of the school year (Forman & Crystal, 2015; Freeman, Miller, & Newcomer, 2015; Averill & Rinaldi, 2011). Organizing MTSS teams, defining roles, and establishing a calendar are no different. *It is important to understand that each MTSS role is not bound to one person or position on the team.* A *role* is a function assumed by a particular person; it is duty- or skill-specific, not title-specific. When building a solid MTSS foundation it is essential to define each role clearly before deciding the best professional on campus to fill that role. A school will typically fill a role based on a profession. It is important to define the roles in a traditional sense before making substitutions based on the realities of the campus. School administrators can then make allowances if necessary to fill the positions based on personnel available on their campus.

Academic MTSS

While effective school Academic and SEB MTSS teams both share the burden of duties and decision making, each operates just a little differently. Each educator is uniquely qualified to provide a separate, but important, perspective that other professional roles cannot fulfill. Role responsibilities can be shared and may be interchangeable, but each perspective should be considered in the decision-making model. Relying solely on one or two teachers or specialists to be the workhorses of the entire team is unrealistic and cannot be sustained over time. It burns out passionate educators who are trying to make a difference because others are less willing to contribute to the team's success. For Academic MTSS, teams will need to define the responsibilities for the following professionals to ensure quality control: administrators, teachers, school psychologists, special education teachers, specialists, school counselors, school nurses, school social workers, and other licensed professionals. The MTSS chair position will also need to be defined and responsibilities made explicit. This type of distributed leadership model increases the buy-in of staff and prevents a burdensome load from falling on any one person's shoulders. A typical core Academic MTSS team is composed of the MTSS chair, six grade-level representatives from kindergarten through fifth grade (often selected by the administration through the hybrid committee selection model), and when available an administrator, school psychologist, school counselor, and school social worker.

Each Academic MTSS team member has specific responsibilities that contribute to the team's success, and these unique roles each complement one another. Every person on the team contributes a piece to the puzzle of student success, which is why it is so important to assemble the big picture together. That is not to say that roles could not be combined into fewer positions, such as specialists trained to bear more of the brunt of organizational tasks, but more hands make the workload lighter and more sustainable. The best practice would be for every team member to attend every meeting. On an elementary school campus, it is incredibly helpful to have all members present for the first few months of school. This is when the Academic MTSS team meets to review students' progress for those who have been placed in intervention groups and discusses the status of students who appear to not be making adequate progress in response to the interventions provided. Multiple perspectives are needed and valued, especially when discussing some of the older students because the earlier grade teachers offer valuable background and insight as to the student's performance and family history in previous years. When meeting on younger students, the same is true as younger students may have older siblings and that family and environmental history is helpful in forming context. Toward the end of the year when the Academic MTSS team conversations shift to evaluating longitudinal progress in response to the interventions and changes to interventions provided at Tier 2 and Tier 3, this insight is less necessary as the team has already discussed and considered it earlier in the year.

MTSS teams operate along a continuum depending on student population, the number of students requiring intensive interventions, staff experience, administrative leadership, and the length of time implementing and refining MTSS practices. *Developmental MTSS schools* are on one end of the continuum and require significant and continuous technical support and leadership in getting their MTSS processes up and running, while on the other end of the continuum are *Adept MTSS schools* that have built capacity over time and have fully functional and sustainable MTSS practices.

Schools are constantly in a mode of transition along this continuum and MTSS is meant to meet teams where they are. Systems and structures can still be built and honed regardless of which end of the continuum the school falls.

MTSS is structured so that meetings can proceed whether or not all team members are available, which is likely to occur due to the many demands and responsibilities of school professionals. For example, if an Academic MTSS grade-level representative knows they are to be absent one day, it is best to have another teacher from their same grade level attend to present student data and bring back the information discussed to the grade-level representative and relate the decisions that were made. In doing so, students in need are not pushed back on the Academic MTSS calendar because the lead teacher on the team was not available and they can still receive support in a timely manner.

Team members who should plan to be at every meeting weekly include the designated administrator, Academic MTSS chair, grade-level representatives, school counselors, school psychologists, and school social workers. The aforementioned group has professional responsibilities to students across grade levels and subject levels. It is unlikely that everyone can attend every meeting every week, but the more who attend, the better the team can function. *This well-rounded panel of professionals expands the breadth of decision making for at-risk students.* The MTSS chair or co-chair must be present to run the weekly meeting and in the absence of the chair, an administrator or administrative liaison must be present to chair the meeting.

The following sections outline the roles and responsibilities of the Academic MTSS chair, MTSS grade-level representatives, and classroom teachers depending on whether the school best identifies as being an MTSS Developmental school, Transitional school, or Adept school. In the broadest sense, the classroom teachers facilitate the collection of student data, the *MTSS grade-level representative* liaises between the grade-level team and the MTSS team, and the *MTSS chair* organizes MTSS meetings and maintains the digital record of cumulative student data. Specialists, school counselors, school psychologists, speech and language pathologists, and special education teachers are then discussed regarding the specific value and perspective each brings to the Academic MTSS team.

Classroom Teachers

Each classroom teacher on an elementary school campus is a case manager. They manage and advocate for each student in their classroom. While the classroom teacher may not always be the teacher providing the interventions, they are still in charge of making sure data-based decisions are made about their students and that intervention folders are complete. Each teacher manages their own classroom of students and only comes to the Academic MTSS team meetings when discussing their own student(s). This differs from the role of grade-level representatives who are required to come to each MTSS meeting. Some MTSS teams choose a *distributed presentation style* where the grade-level representatives come to MTSS meetings and present data on students pertaining to their grade level on behalf of all teachers in that grade level. All grade-level teachers would organize the data and provide to the grade-level representatives prior to meetings, as well as follow recommendations from the MTSS team shared at grade-level meetings. Developmental schools may start here or may try for the more ambitious case manager model with a *direct presentation style* in which all grade-level teachers attend and participate in their grade-level MTSS meetings with all the MTSS grade-level representatives and extended team members.

Regardless of data team meeting configuration or presentation style, the case manager model is an effective way to share responsibility for students with other teachers and school professionals, which provides built-in accountability and expands the network of supports available (Stearns, 2017). The *case manager model* is student-centered and assigns a specific educator to advocate for the students they are assigned to represent. On the elementary school campus, this is the classroom teacher. Classroom teachers are case managers and are responsible for researching and documenting student history, collecting data from multiple sources, presenting data, and communicating changes to student instructional interventions at grade-level and Academic MTSS team meetings (when necessary), and getting feedback and progress monitoring data from the intervention teacher on the efficacy of interventions and progress made. Student data discussed at grade-level team meetings include student grades, standards-based test scores, curriculum-based test scores, formative assessment results, summative assessment results, benchmark and progress monitoring data, behavioral data, discipline data, health information, attendance history, teacher observations, and parent/guardian report to make decisions for students (Sprick, 2013; Dishon, 2011; Shinn & Walker, 2010; Sprick, 2009; Shinn, 2007). Grade-level meetings are where this data is discussed and depending on the student's progress during the intervention process, the grade-level team may refer the student to the Academic MTSS team. Depending on the school's proficiency with this process and whether they operate more as a Developmental school or an Adept school, school A may refer more students to the Academic MTSS team than school B.

In summary, classroom teachers' duties include the following:

- Review records including the following considerations: attendance, summative and formative test scores, report cards, discipline data, behavior data, health status, and benchmark and progress monitoring data
- Facilitate communication with the school nurse, ensure vision and hearing screenings completed, and consider health history
- Correspond with parents and caregivers, as needed, and make attempts to obtain student family and health history forms from caregivers
- Communicate with intervention teacher by requesting feedback and providing feedback
- Organize data in folders, discard old data, and ensure current data are available for decision making at grade-level meetings
- Prepare data and present student information to team members at grade-level meetings
- Maintain constant communication with a grade-level representative regarding any persistent student concerns, procedural concerns, or implementation barriers
- Attend all grade-level meetings
- Complete the Academic MTSS Team Referral Form (if and when deemed necessary by the grade-level team)
- Attend Academic MTSS team meeting when their student(s) are being discussed (or this responsibility may be deferred to the MTSS grade-level representative depending on the team's structure)

MTSS Grade-Level Representative

Grade-level representatives do just that, they represent the grade levels they are reporting on. Therefore, on a traditional K–5 campus, there would be six grade-level representatives on the schoolwide Academic MTSS team. This structure facilitates the opportunity for grade-level representatives to work with the classroom teachers in grade-level team meetings and increases the probability that grade-level representatives already have a working knowledge of the students they are discussing when responsibility to report to the Academic MTSS team is deferred to the grade-level representative. The reason the classroom teacher–as–case manager model works so well in elementary schools is because it creates a focal point in the storm of fast-moving information for student data, observations, and recommendations to be gathered, discussed, and disseminated. With large numbers of students, individual needs may get overlooked due to the sheer volume of information teachers must manage for high numbers of students.

Educators are more likely to buy into processes that are driven by their peers, that they feel have high efficacy, and that are endorsed by school leadership (Anyon, Nicotera, & Veeh, 2016; Pinkelman, McIntosh, Rasplica, Berg, & Strickland-Cohen, 2015). The strongest teachers should be recruited through the hybrid committee selection model, and financially rewarded (especially when establishing an MTSS program), to be on the Academic MTSS team to help grow better practices schoolwide. Accomplished educators actively supporting the effectiveness of other educators who have challenging students breeds better teaching on campus. Using grade-level representatives increases the "street credibility" of the MTSS process. Other school professionals may be successful in the role, of course, but teachers are mandatory members of a successful MTSS team and optimally in leadership positions. Extenuating circumstances may precipitate that an experienced literacy coach or off-grade-level teacher serve as a grade-level chair for a particular grade if it is composed predominately of substitute or novice teachers. For purposes of discussing this model, there is one grade-level representative who is aligned with the grade level they teach.

The classroom teacher–as–case manager model allows for the rotation of classroom teachers to be present at Academic MTSS meetings. Three popular continuum models exist, one for Developmental schools with a high number of students performing in the highest tiers, one for Transitional schools, and one for Adept schools with fewer students performing in the highest tiers. For Developmental schools with a high number of students receiving Tier 2 and Tier 3 interventions, it may work best to have a six-week rotation schedule in which each grade level comes to the Academic MTSS team to discuss their students who are the most resistant to intensive interventions. Under this model, the only students discussed at each Academic MTSS team meeting would come from a single grade, such as second grade. In this example, the Academic MTSS chair, the six grade-level representatives, and all second-grade teachers with students to discuss would need to attend the meeting, along with administration and related team members based on their availability. In some cases, such as this one, the second-grade-level representative may elect to present the information to be discussed on behalf of all second-grade teachers, which frees up time for the second-grade classroom teachers and excuses them from attending the meeting. This type of distributed presentation style can work; however, since the grade-level representative is not usually the classroom teacher who manages the case, he or she may not have as much insight or be able to answer any ad hoc questions that arise.

Transitional MTSS schools are beginning to master some of the foundational components of the Academic MTSS model and are growing beyond a Developmental school. Ideally, as the capacity for intervention implementation and decision making increases, fewer students will need to be brought to the schoolwide Academic MTSS team as more decisions can be made at the grade-level team meetings. In doing so, the school could transition to combining two grades at a time for the Academic MTSS team meetings, which would put each grade on a three-week rotation on the master calendar. Eventually, as grade-level capacity continues to grow, teams could evolve to the Adept schools model as they will have fewer and fewer students needing the highest levels of intervention support. For Adept schools with a fewer number of students receiving Tier 2 and Tier 3 interventions, it may work best to calendar students for the Academic MTSS team as their individual grade-level teams refer them. Under this model, it would be possible for the Academic MTSS team to meet on one third-grade student, one kindergartener, and one fourth grader all in one meeting. In this example, the Academic MTSS chair, the six grade-level representatives, and the three classroom teachers of the students being discussed would need to attend the meeting along with administration and related team members based on their availability.

The time between meetings allows for interventions to be implemented, progress monitoring data to be collected, and classroom teachers to get feedback on their students from the intervention teachers.

Academic MTSS Chair

The Academic MTSS chair is the conductor of the Academic MTSS train and ensures that the meetings stay on track for the duration of the scheduled time. The *chair* communicates Academic MTSS meeting dates, schedules students to be discussed, records meeting discussions, tracks students reviewed and next steps determined, leads meetings, problem solves Academic MTSS functions and processes and liaises with stakeholder groups. Additional responsibilities of the chair can be negotiated, but they should be clearly defined prior to the start of the school year. At the elementary school level, the school principal or a trusted appointee may be the MTSS chair; MTSS must be a systems, as well as a cultural, priority with leadership actively and visibly supporting all team functions. In Developmental schools, it is more common for an administrator to be the MTSS chair, whereas in more Adept schools the MTSS chair is often a skilled classroom teacher or specialist. If the Academic MTSS chair is not the primary administrator, then all planning of supports and training should be decided in partnership with the administration *before* the first Academic MTSS training to ensure there are no gaps in coverage of responsibilities and to make explicit the understanding of the role by both parties. This shared understanding and recognized value that the educators bring to the team is key in the integrated delivery of intervention services (Rainey & Gifford, 2016).

The need for supplementary duties may also arise via iterative feedback throughout the year, especially during the first year of implementation. The chair of an Academic MTSS team is most often an administrator or specialist on an elementary campus, especially until the school has built capacity and the processes, roles, and functions are structurally sound and operate with automaticity. Classroom teachers are certainly able to chair Academic MTSS; however, until processes become automated and honed, they may encounter challenges due to the amount of work required during the school day, such as follow-up meetings and data research, that could potentially have an impact on their time in the classroom. Teachers with special assignments may be considered to chair or co-chair the Academic MTSS team with preference given to school professionals with the most flexibility during the day to enable timely response to issues that may arise. There are six broad and explicit roles of the Academic MTSS chair:

- Communicate meeting dates and times with the team and reschedule meetings as necessary
- Calendar students to be discussed at the Academic MTSS team meetings
- Record meeting discussions, data, and next steps in the Academic MTSS Student Database
- Lead Academic MTSS team meetings
- Problem solve team functions and processes
- Liaise with administrators and stakeholder groups

The first and second roles of the Academic MTSS chair is that of *communicator* to ensure that messaging of dates and times of Academic MTSS meetings are shared among all school personnel through the master calendar, schoolwide memos, and emails or other established communication tools with staff. *Clear and consistent communication is nonnegotiable and an essential component to the success of an Academic MTSS team.* The MTSS chair must take full responsibility for communicating and scheduling meetings, scheduling students to be discussed, and they must hold themselves accountable for sharing meeting dates and times. Any number of school problems may arise that interfere with scheduling; "expect the unexpected" is a healthy mind-set for the Academic MTSS chair. There will always be school events, staff responsibilities, and student or school issues that compete with meeting times for team members. The key to success over time is to adapt quickly to interruptions of meeting times and dates to ensure that the meeting(s) are rescheduled as quickly as possible, in any way possible, to guarantee that student needs are addressed in a timely manner. Efficiently scheduling, or rescheduling, meetings to discuss particular students also demonstrates respect and the value of colleagues' time. Giving team members sufficient time to prepare materials and not requiring them to unnecessarily show up at a meeting that has been rescheduled are respectful shows of appreciation for their time and the value they bring to the table.

The Academic MTSS chair will be in charge of effectively communicating and liaising with administrators, teachers, and other stakeholders to find the most reasonable time to reschedule meetings. *Sometimes the MTSS chair has to be creative, and creativity in scheduling on an elementary campus always requires administrative support.* This support may come in the form of finding a suitable location for the meeting or finding coverage for a teacher's duties while attending an off-schedule meeting and then obtaining administrative support to make it happen. Sometimes rescheduling meetings causes more problems than can be compensated for, and meetings simply must be shifted forward a week in the rotation. In such instances, all future meetings are also shifted forward a week. The Academic MTSS chair, with administrative oversight, must balance the pros and cons of rescheduling or postponing meetings that have an impact on Academic MTSS team members and possibly other teachers and staff members.

The specific responsibility of the Academic MTSS chair to ensure meetings consistently take place is a seemingly simple task that can also become the most challenging.

Elementary schools are like beehives in that "worker bees" are trained to support the hive and to follow signals from the queen. Unlike bees who can collectively change their behavior instantaneously, school systems are not as automated or efficient due to their bureaucratic nature. A bureaucratic system is unlikely to change quickly, but an effective school must be adaptable and make timely changes to respond to community and district requirements. The constantly changing demands in an elementary school environment require responsive adaptability from workers in the system to succeed. *Responsive adaptability* is the ability to quickly and seamlessly adjust to ever-changing environmental demands. Like beehives, sometimes the "worker bees" in schools can be resistant to change and become highly aggressive if order is not followed. Staff members may not be receptive to altering their schedules, or covering for others, on short notice. *A school culture built on responsive adaptability is more likely to succeed in implementing MTSS than schools with rigid cultures and staff members.* All functions of MTSS team members are made easier with active administrative backing and problem-solving engagement, starting with hands-on administrative leadership or visible support for the Academic MTSS chair. The administrative expectation of responsive adaptability and cooperation among all staff members in supporting functions of MTSS must follow.

The third crucial responsibility of Academic MTSS team chairs is to *record* MTSS team meetings in the digital Academic MTSS Student Database of case notes. The *Academic MTSS Student Database* is the storehouse that archives all data for students who are discussed at Academic MTSS team meetings, and is achieved by creating and maintaining a running record of at-risk student history, interventions implemented, school performance, current needs, and recommendations for school success. *Case notes* are supplemental data that are entered into the Academic MTSS Student Database that are not otherwise captured in one of the predetermined columns. There are many different formats and styles of documentation and presentation of information team members may prefer. Some teams want more information; some want less. There is a bare minimum of content areas that must be recorded for the team to process together at meetings. Extraneous student information may be included in the Academic MTSS Student Database as long as the information is relevant to student decision making and the information during the discussion does not become a distraction, wasting precious time during team meetings.

A visual representation of critical student information should be used to facilitate discussions at meetings. Excel spreadsheets and Google Sheets are an excellent way to summarize large amounts of information on students into one document, boiling down data on numerous students to one or two pages. This is one way to lend legitimization to the Academic MTSS program itself and provides artifacts that serve as a running record of team engagement (Guéguen, Pascual, Silone, & David, 2015). *Legitimization* occurs within an organization when an act or process becomes entrenched in its values and norms. When discussing individual students, the MTSS chair can verbally review a student's history or progress with the core team because it has been recorded and the process formalized within the meeting notes. Only the core Academic MTSS team should have access to the information, or those with a *legitimate educational interest* in the student per the Family Educational Rights and Privacy Act (FERPA; 1974). On campuses with an Academic MTSS team and an SEB MTSS team, there will usually be two separate MTSS Student Databases. Or, the chairs of the two teams may have dual access to an integrated spreadsheet that they each update. To maintain protections under FERPA, the school administration will want to set clear definitions and standards on what the guidelines of *legitimate education interest* are and which team members have access to what information.

The Academic MTSS chair, or designee, updates team decisions on the spreadsheet at *each meeting* so that there is a dated digital record of recommendations made and who made the recommendations. Note-taking must not be onerous or extensive; however, enough detailed information must be provided so the team does not "go backward" in recommending efforts that have already been tried. The Academic MTSS Student Database of case notes on every student in the school identified as at-risk academically, social-emotionally, or behaviorally is one of the most valuable tools professional educators have in keeping track of large numbers of individual student needs and tracking evidence-based outcomes. Remember, the Academic MTSS team only meets on those students requiring the greatest academic supports, such as Tier 2 or Tier 3, and other individuals on campus may be supporting or tracking the lower-risk academic or high-risk social-emotional-behavioral status of students. For example, in Adept schools each grade level may have a spreadsheet tracking student intervention grouping and outcomes that they discuss at grade-level meetings, or the school psychologist may maintain a schoolwide database of student social-emotional-behavioral benchmark scores and interventions. The Academic MTSS Student Database is only for those requiring the most intensive academic supports.

The style and format of the Academic MTSS Student Database and case notes can, and should, be personalized for user preferences. The database must be user-friendly, easy to read, and designed to reflect student priorities monitored by the team. Some teams use one data sheet per student, while others use a combined spreadsheet for the grade or school. In paper-free schools, some teams prefer to use technology with SMART Boards, televisions, or computers and projectors during their meetings and do not print out case notes for team members; team members write notes in their own notebooks or electronic devices. What format of documentation and which style of visual presentation works for a school and its team are fair game. As long as relevant student history, programming, current functioning, and rate of progress over time is captured in the MTSS case notes, any format and style that works for the team is the one that should be used.

The Academic MTSS Student Database should be the gold standard for tracking at-risk students by a multidisciplinary team of educators. With the appropriate credentials and training, almost any member of the Academic MTSS team can be substituted. The information passes on from generation to generation of Academic MTSS team members instead of being lost forever when educators with specific knowledge of students move on or a new school year starts. All reports of a student's needs over time have been documented, and the next educational professional can pick up where the last educator in that position left off. This ensures that there are paths forward for each student and that they are each supported and monitored by the Academic MTSS team. Likewise, if a student moves or changes schools, case notes could be released to parents and the new school of enrollment. The data should be sent to forwarding schools within the same school district, or out of the district, in an attempt to provide students with continued supports at their next school. Families should be provided this documentation at the time of withdrawal so that they can advocate for the child's needs at the next school.

Information on each student monitored by the Academic MTSS team and recorded in the Academic MTSS Student Database should include name, student identification number, name of intervention teacher(s), name of intervention group(s), attendance history (from kindergarten on up if possible), pertinent health information, criterion-referenced or summative test scores, language proficiency levels (if English is a second language), enrollment history, discipline history, and benchmark academic scores. If benchmark social-emotional-behavioral scores are available and teams decide to combine the Academic and SEB MTSS Student Databases they may choose to do so into a combined Integrated Student Database. A spreadsheet is effective and easy to use, as it can be customized any number of ways to allow for documentation to be completed with checkmarks, dates, and numbers in corresponding boxes and columns, saving time and effort. In addition to student-level reporting, aggregate reports can also be run at the grade and school level, with proper spreadsheet formatting.

Some of the information in the Academic MTSS Student Database will remain static while some will be constantly transitional. Static information is relevant to decision making and is all but impossible for team members to remember when discussing large numbers of students, for example, student names and student numbers. Some information changes over time and has to be regularly updated, such as attendance or progress monitoring scores. One of the most important columns on the spreadsheet is "Comments and Case Notes," which qualitatively reflects current student issues that cannot be captured by a checkmark or score in a column. The best Academic MTSS Student Databases capture input from team members actively solving problems for students, which leads to the next steps.

The fourth priority for the Academic MTSS chair is to *lead* Academic MTSS team meetings. Predetermined meeting etiquette protocols should be observed to ensure professional and on-topic discussions. All team members should be trained in the established Academic MTSS meeting format, including preparation and presentation of data, at the beginning of the school year so that team meetings will run efficiently (Van Norman & Christ, 2016). If organized and well executed, teams can expect to discuss many more students per hour, situation dependent. If a student's issues are too severe or require more attention than a quick status check allows, the MTSS chair must table further discussion and direct the specific team members needed to get together and problem solve after the meeting. *Overspending meeting time on one student results in less time to discuss the other students on the monitoring list.* It is not uncommon for classroom teachers who are presenting about their student(s) to be emotionally attached to the child and to go off on a tangent about some minor variable that they feel strongly may be a huge contributing factor. Or they may reminisce about a former student who had a similar issue and digress in discussing what happened to that student. The Academic MTSS chair must intervene and put a stop to distracting dialogue. Some teams prefer to set a timer for each student up for discussion so they get in the habit of short and focused power conversations to make informed swift decisions. When the timer goes off, decisions are made and documented, and team members agree to discuss the student's case more in-depth outside the Academic MTSS meeting or at a future Academic MTSS meeting date. All decisions and recommendations are reported in the digital database case notes.

Greater organization on behalf of the classroom teachers results in more efficient discussions and meetings. The more organized classroom teachers are, the faster discussions go. Some students' information can be reviewed more quickly than others because there are no unexpected changes or there is an obvious overarching issue, such as attendance. In these instances, the overarching issue must be addressed first. Other times, positive changes are reported to case managers and less discussion time is needed. For example, a student may be demonstrating improved effort and performance in their classes, their attendance and/or grades are improving, or their growth is documented to be promising across sources and class environments. Interventions for students who are making adequate progress in response to the interventions provided are typically short conversations. In such cases, the intervention would be deemed effective, so the decision to continue progress monitoring should be easy with minimal discussion.

The Academic MTSS chair provides input to decisions during discussions and keeps the discussions moving when team members get off-topic or get held up on irrelevant gossip about the student, which eats up valuable meeting time. Typically, in more Adept schools, the students who are making expected progress and do not require more intensive interventions or supports will not need to be discussed at the Academic MTSS team meetings because they will be monitored and discussed at their grade-level meetings. For Developmental schools, still navigating the process and becoming familiar with data-based decision making, they will have more students to discuss at Academic MTSS team meetings until they build capacity and efficacy of team members. The Academic MTSS chair can provide guidance on when Developmental teams are ready to transition to Transitional teams, and when Transitional teams are ready to transition to more Adept team configurations.

The fifth priority of the Academic MTSS chair involves *problem-solving* with the administration. The Academic MTSS chair must take notes of trouble spots in team functions and processes, and communicate any issues with relevant administrators and stakeholders in an effort to get solutions. *Solving problems with MTSS processes relies on collaborative communication with staff members.* The Academic MTSS chair serves as the liaison between the grade-level representatives and school administrators regarding the efficacy and efficiency of Academic MTSS processes. Grade-level representatives can obtain feedback from classroom teachers during their grade-level meetings, professional learning communities, or a Google Form survey that only takes them two minutes to click through and complete. Teachers who consistently shirk their duty to collect or provide grade-level representatives with student performance data must ultimately be addressed by administration, and liaising through the grade-level representative is the way to achieve this. Grade-level representatives are responsible for getting feedback from teachers to enable the Academic MTSS team to make instructional support decisions. With regular grade-level meetings set aside in which to review students' progress monitoring data and related indicators of student performance, much of these difficulties can be proactively eliminated. Without the crucial outcome evidence of current performance in the classroom, Academic MTSS team decisions are not guaranteed to be timely or effective, and in most cases, the classroom teacher will not be allowed to get on the Academic MTSS team calendar without these data. When reasonable efforts have failed to get feedback from a teacher, the next step must include administrative supervisors in professional conversations.

As part of the problem-solving process, Academic MTSS chairs must build collegial relations with all educators on campus. As an educational leader, it is imperative that the Academic MTSS chair be seen as a critical resource for staff and not as an adversary out to impose discipline. Some educators need a gentle nudge to organize their time and prioritize the needs of their highest-risk students. Others require more direct administrative directives. Grade-level representatives, as well as the classroom teachers, are the ones who look unprepared at Academic MTSS meetings when their colleagues do not do their part in providing classroom performance feedback, and they must let the Academic MTSS chair know when they are having problems getting reports from individual teachers. The Academic MTSS chair communicates with the school administrator in seeking support with the teachers. If direct conversation and offers to assist prove ineffective, electronic communications to the unresponsive teacher are a good way to provide documentation when feedback requests are being made and ignored. In such cases, the Academic MTSS chair should always copy the direct administrator on the email to improve the probability of a response. Administrators supporting the success of Academic MTSS must actively promote the participation of all staff members in schoolwide practices.

Last, the Academic MTSS chair is the *liaison* between this important school improvement team and the rest of the staff on behalf of the school's neediest and most vulnerable students. The Academic MTSS chair must be able to work collaboratively, professionally, and effectively with all relevant stakeholders in their school. The chair of this committee will need to communicate with others regarding the urgency of intense needs of struggling students that require systematic schoolwide supports, as well as monitor the process itself for improvements that can be made to better serve those students. The Academic MTSS chair must be a master of all trades and know when and how to elicit input from administrators, school counselors, speech and language pathologists, school psychologists and other staff to support students and improve educational practices and outcomes for at-risk students.

Investing in personnel, resources, and intervention processes without enforcing best practices is like building an expensive ship and leaving holes in the bottom. Assuming that the school administration has invested in evidence-based practices and supports scheduling, the Academic MTSS chairs can see where holes are in the ship. They do this by monitoring the quality of case manager functioning, teacher engagement and timeliness of feedback, the robustness of progress monitoring data, and administrative backing.

Specialists

Specialists are often teachers on special assignment and are one of the most adaptable resources on campus. They may have the official title of literacy specialist, intervention specialist, or behavior specialist; however, they are jacks-of-all-trades and help fill in teaching gaps for target students. They serve as substitute teachers, quasi-administrators, disciplinarians, and lunch-duty supervisors, basically, any role or function that is required to support administrators looking to fulfill miscellaneous responsibilities for students on campus. They often work with special populations of at-risk students as intervention teachers. They also support the functions of educators and other intervention specialists overseeing data collection, providing testing supports for high-stakes testing, and filling in where needed as determined by the administration. Specialists should be selected for participation on the MTSS leadership team as they are an excellent source of information. They are often inside classrooms and around campus and are positioned perfectly to have insights into what is working and what is not working for students and staff. Specialists are encouraged to use their unique skill sets to view student problems through different lenses, leading to supports with wider breadth and as supplements to other teachers on campus. In addition to teachers, other specialists who may participate and contribute to the MTSS team are itinerant professionals including school nurses, speech and language pathologists, school social workers, and other related or wraparound service professionals with specific talents and training who support students. The more people with diverse backgrounds who engage in decision making for students, the better the recommendations and prospects are for struggling children.

School Counselors

Elementary school counselors are invaluable in supporting struggling students for a variety of academic, social-emotional-behavioral, and personal reasons. *School counselors* provide academic, personal, social, and career support to students (American School Counseling Association, 2017). Besides being a lifeline for students with emotional difficulties, social problems, and life challenges, elementary school counselors are responsible for character development, teaching coping skills, and helping teach students how to make good life choices. School counselors provide interventions for students regularly and help them plan for the future, facilitate peer mediation, offer focused problem solving, run counseling groups, and advocate for students with caregivers and teachers. School counselors support students through crises, emotional challenges, and personal issues in addition to academic planning and advocacy with teachers.

School counselors are an essential part of the MTSS team. Best practice would be for the school counselor to attend every Academic and SEB MTSS team meeting. The school counselor should be on the leadership team to actively solve problems with students, offer relevant services, and follow through with outreach and other team recommendations to benefit student growth and development. Elementary schools that have sacrificed counseling positions for other teaching or administrative positions are missing out on the social, emotional, and behavioral support school counselors bring to the table. They are usually a lifeline to students and families: helping with community health referrals, food, and clothing; noticing signs of neglect and abuse; hearing about the emotional lives of young children; and guiding them through insecurities, anger, depression, and trauma. They have training to teach emotional competencies and are skilled at intervening to teach and protect students.

Elementary school counselors also provide classroom lessons that are often character-based and focused on conflict resolution and resilience. Counselors are instrumental in social-emotional and behavioral development and add value to the classroom and school culture at Tier 1 through schoolwide positive behavior initiatives and classroom social-emotional lessons. At Tier 2, they are regularly engaged in running counseling groups (e.g., coping skills, anger management, friendship skills) and short-term individual counseling to address issues in depth. School counselors often attempt to motivate students and use every opportunity as a teaching moment. Additionally, they provide important background information that may impact achievement or have insights into student behavior and affect, or offer follow-up counseling services to students, which may include incentive planning, checking in/out, and supporting behavior plans. At Tier 3, school counselors engage in crisis counseling, behavioral interventions, mental health school-to-community liaison, and offer teacher support. During the Academic and SEB MTSS team meetings, school counselors report on topics such as referrals to the office, lunchroom behavior, and issues with other students. School social workers, school counselors, and school psychologists should work together to address students' emotional needs that may require counseling services, community resources for basic needs, and referrals for community medical and mental health services.

School Psychologists

School psychologists must be actively involved in the Academic and SEB MTSS teams on a school campus. They have much to offer these problem-solving teams when not pigeonholed into solely testing and qualifying students for special education. *School psychologists* are uniquely trained individuals on a school campus who provide mental and behavioral health supports to students, assist teams with intervention planning, analyze intervention outcomes, and help school administration implement evidence-based policies and programs. It is difficult for school psychologists to be MTSS chairs because of their competing responsibilities, but they are champions of interventions, social-emotional and behavioral supports, and data-based decision making. School psychologists should be involved in leadership decisions in forming the MTSS teams, training the MTSS members, and monitoring efficacy and functions of the team with the MTSS chair. According to the National Association of School Psychologists (2014),

> [s]chool psychologists provide direct support and interventions to students; consult with teachers, families, and other school-employed mental health professionals (i.e., school counselors, school social workers) to improve support strategies; work with school administrators to improve school-wide practices and policies; and collaborate with community providers to coordinate needed services.
>
> (p. 1)

Integrating the unique perspective of the school psychologist on the MTSS teams is a win–win for students, families, staff, and administration. School psychologists should not be perceived as gatekeepers to special education because, in reality, they endeavor to keep the gates open to appropriate instruction for everyone. Having a school psychologist actively participate in the MTSS teams makes the framework stronger at a school. It is not a conflict of interest for school psychologists to be on the MTSS teams and the special education multidisciplinary team. It is a conflict of interest when qualified professionals do not support struggling students for artificial reasons. Using a social justice framework, school psychologists strive not only to protect the rights and opportunities for all (Shriberg et al., 2008) but also to create those opportunities as well.

School psychologists are adepts in analyzing formative and summative evaluation information, academic functioning, and psychological processes, as well as advocating for students and families in countless ways. School psychologists are teachers in the truest sense, educating adults in children's environments about how to best work with students with unique needs. The skill set of school psychologists is comprehensive and includes not only assessment abilities but also administrative skills, counseling skills, knowledge of mental health foundations and positive behavioral supports, an understanding of growth and development as it relates to learning and behavior, and an understanding of barriers to organizational changes. *An active school psychologist working on the front end of proactive practices on an elementary campus can only add to the quality of supports in a school dedicated to educating every student.* They must also form relationships with families and community service providers to serve students whose needs exceed the scope of traditional school interventions. Communication with mental health providers and referrals to community services is shared by school psychologists, school nurses, school counselors, and school social workers.

One important role of school psychologists is the assessment of students for special education eligibility and programming. School psychologists must be diligent in not only helping school teams implement MTSS (both academic and social-emotional-behavioral) but also following through with MTSS teams' recommendations when assessment is recommended. When quality control conditions are met with interventions that have been provided reliably and with fidelity, and the MTSS team recommends testing for special education eligibility due to poor rate of progress and inadequate level of performance; the school psychologist must honor the referral. The biggest frustration and disappointment for teachers who follow through with due diligence of intervention implementation and documentation for students suspected of having an educational disability is when the MTSS team referral for special education testing does not result in a completed psychoeducational evaluation. Students who have no clear path forward with general education initiatives and MTSS remediation alone are the students who must be considered for special education eligibility and special programming. The school psychologist must honor these referrals and respond with good faith in a timely manner to avoid the perception that teachers went through the intervention process for nothing.

As an active participant on the MTSS teams, the school psychologist can offer insights and recommendations *along the way*, so as to avoid being the gatekeeper at crucial decision-making points. Even though MTSS functions should support a majority of students coming through interventions *without* needing special education supports, the most severe underachievers or atypically behaved students will require special education. The school psychologist, as part of a multidisciplinary team, must ensure that students whose functioning meets the criteria of an educational disability get appropriate services as described in the Individuals with Disabilities Education Act (IDEA, 2006). Special education eligibility is never the goal of MTSS, but when there is sufficient evidence to support a suspicion of a disability, it is important for the school psychologist to address the potential special education needs of a student, starting with a timely evaluation for special education eligibility.

It is a matter of fairness, checks, and balances that keeps MTSS going. Teachers must believe that the MTSS teams actively support their students. Most teachers are willing to do extra work and go the extra mile to help struggling students. *In a multi-tiered system that supports underachievers, trust is built because all school professionals do their part.* If educators are doing their part on the front end, within the infrastructure administration has provided, then all school professionals must do their part in good faith. After all, good faith is what keeps organizational practices going and allows better practices to emerge. If team members do not do their part, and there is no accountability built in, resentment rears its ugly head and professionals give up before they start because they do not trust the system to respond adequately to the needs of students or staff. In such cases, teachers expect that extra efforts are a waste of time, and their compliance with prescribed best practices is certain to diminish over time.

School psychologists should be a strong resource for counseling and mental health interventions. Depending on the flexibility of their position at their school(s), they may offer parenting classes and family support, train administration and staff on school-wide positive behavioral intervention strategies, and offer a continuum of other staff, student, and community supports. School psychologists may contribute insight to help caregivers and teachers better understand students by conducting short-term support services that involve limited amounts of counseling or testing of academic and social-emotional-behavioral functioning to obtain more information outside of eligibility determination. The purpose of these short-term supports is to gather more individualized information on the student, not necessarily to gather information to use in a special education evaluation.

School psychologists may lead and assist in schoolwide social-emotional-behavioral universal screenings, intervention design and implementation, and facilitation of the disbursement and collection of clinical rating scales between physicians, teachers, and families to help physicians make diagnoses and medication recommendations for students. The expertise that school psychologists can offer for suicide prevention, threat assessment and evaluation, crisis response, and community mental health needs should not be overlooked by school teams seeking to provide supports and services to students in a socially just context. School psychologists can be the linchpin for helping to assure that all students' needs are met. They are particularly effective when given regular opportunities to participate in actively solving problems within smart teams. School psychologists' training, talents, experiences, and analytical skills make them necessary MTSS team participants.

Special Education Teachers

Special education teachers have the unique perspective of being adepts in differentiated instruction and behavior modification. Similar to school psychologists, the perception may be that it is a conflict of interest to have special education teachers on an MTSS team whether it be academic or behavioral. As previously discussed, all talent on a school campus must be leveraged and special education teachers are no different. The biggest barrier to special education teacher participation is the fact that they must hold individual education program (IEP) meetings, and these IEP meetings often take place before school, which also frequently is the same time that committee meetings such as MTSS take place.

Having a special education teacher participate in decision making during MTSS meetings is important because that person can bring another perspective on individual differences to the table. Because special education teachers already know how to write academic and behavior plans, the special education teacher is a natural fit for writing MTSS plans, specifically individualized behavior intervention plans (BIPs). School counselors can be helpful in writing these plans as well (depending on the issue requiring remediation) and in writing less formal incentive plans, as MTSS requires many hands to make the workload lighter.

Special education teachers often appreciate the opportunity to make extra duty pay and to participate in meaningful processes to improve educational outcomes for students with challenges. Plan writing is an opportunity for the professionals with the most knowledge of special needs to work on behalf of at-risk students without identified disabilities, and only a fraction of students monitored by MTSS will even require formalized MTSS academic or behavior plans. Depending on the state or school district, such plans are often legal documents, and in many cases, may become educational records used to build evidence for special education disability criteria, including specific learning disabilities and emotional disturbance. Writing MTSS plans for the highest-needs students who receive the most intensive supports must be completed and implemented with integrity, and special education teachers are highly qualified to support MTSS this way. Oftentimes, classroom teachers do not feel comfortable implementing a behavior plan and may not have experience using a behavior reinforcement schedule, tracking data, and analyzing the data. This is also where a special education teacher can excel. They can work with classroom teachers who have students with BIPs as data coaches, leading and building the capacity of the classroom teacher so that they can begin implementing and collecting data with confidence and efficacy.

Broadly, special education teachers are highly trained Tier 3 instructors trained in documentation and adaptation for special populations and diverse learners. Creative scheduling and resource allocation can take special education teachers out behind closed doors and integrated into the school culture. Students with IEPs can still get their minutes with specialized instruction by specialized instructors, but students without IEPs also can benefit from this expertise and Tier 3 groupings. Flexible grouping and scheduling are the keys to getting opportunities that allow for systemic scheduling of more intensive supports, whether academic or behavioral. Special education teachers can report observations succinctly to the MTSS teams and are often one of the first to suspect that a student may have special needs based on direct observations and interactions with the student. Special education teachers are often in constant communication with the school psychologist and school counselor and can help problem solve and follow-up on student issues that expand beyond the scope of meeting time.

Meeting Etiquette

Participation in Academic MTSS meetings is required of Academic MTSS team members and certain meeting etiquette should be followed. The extent of preparation for each team member depends on position and role. Grade-level representatives and classroom teachers bear the brunt of preparation for meetings, but Academic MTSS chairs and other meeting participants also need to have their ducks in a row to make the distributed leadership model of Academic MTSS meetings run effectively and within a specific amount of time. A week or so before the meeting, it can be helpful for the Academic MTSS chair to reach out to the grade-level representatives, reminding them of required preparation and to extend an offer to assist with logistical aspects of artifact gathering. The grade-level representatives, in turn, can then reach out to remind the classroom teachers when necessary. As stated earlier, it is crucial for team discussions to be orderly and to remain on-topic. The Academic MTSS chair, or designee, must take leadership of the meetings to guarantee brief, data-based professional discussions ensue. A process for meetings should be established, and all Academic MTSS team members should be trained in meeting rules at the earliest Academic MTSS team training of the school year.

Team accountability is extremely important so that all professionals on the team are doing their part. *Guidelines explaining expectations for preparation and presentation at MTSS meetings should be designed to enable teams to thoroughly discuss large numbers of students in short periods.* Every year, these norms must be revisited and revised if necessary as team members may transition on or off the team. Even when there are no new team members, it is good to review the norms of preferred meeting etiquette. Academic MTSS chairs are responsible for running meetings, making executive decisions, redirecting team members who have gotten off track, and keeping the momentum going during conversations. Information presented at Academic MTSS meetings should follow a general formula with established decision rules to ensure speed and accuracy of student updates and efficient problem solving (Van Norman & Christ, 2016). The Academic MTSS chair may choose not to schedule unprepared classroom teachers or bypass classroom teacher reports on students if they are disorganized or incomplete, which is a natural consequence for poor preparation. Waiting on classroom teachers to rummage through files and work samples to dig up information during meetings wastes valuable meeting time. This is especially true for Developmental schools with direct presentation style during whole grade-level Academic MTSS meetings. Teachers may take for granted that their students will be discussed so they are not always prepared with organized data to present at meetings. They may bring work samples, and little else, as documentation. This is less the case with more Adept schools with grade-level teams who have built capacity and have discussed and filtered student referrals to the Academic MTSS team.

There are always reasons why grade-level representatives or classroom teachers are unprepared for one or more student reports to the Academic MTSS team, such as a lack of intervention teacher feedback or fluency updates, but the Academic MTSS chair must make executive decisions for the good of the order. Student files that are not prepared to be discussed in an efficient fashion may be postponed until the next regularly scheduled meeting for that grade level, even though current information would have to be provided to the Academic MTSS chair by an arranged time. A student's case should not be postponed more than once as it may be detrimental to the long-term outcomes for a student. Repeated violations of the meeting preparation expectation may be an individual grade-level representative problem, a classroom teacher problem, or an Academic MTSS systems issue. Regardless of the barrier to preparation, Academic MTSS chairs and school administrators must be dedicated to addressing the weak links so that students have the best opportunities for data-based decisions to be made on their behalf, and they are not inadvertently penalized for their teachers' poor preparation.

The first three rules of meeting etiquette are preparation, preparation, and preparation. Grade-level representatives or classroom teachers must be prepared to present case notes on each student in a fluid fashion so that multiple students can be discussed thoroughly and recommendations can be made quickly. Whether it is the grade-level representative or the classroom teacher presenting, he or she will need historical information, attendance, grades, teacher feedback on classroom performance and progress, behavior, and health updates if any, and current fluency or response to instruction data if they are presenting on behalf of a classroom teacher. Classroom teachers should try to organize individual student folders and stay organized by throwing away old data (much of it is logged in the digital database anyway) and keeping documentation current. Because classroom teachers are the focal points for information on at-risk students, all MTSS team members and staff are encouraged to keep lines of communication open with them in regards to events and issues that have an impact on students on their caseloads.

School counselors should bring their databases and records to meetings as well so that information can be easily accessed during meetings and they can answer any questions team members may have. In addition, school counselors are a rich source of qualitative information regarding a student's personal and family history, social life on campus, discipline referrals, counseling referrals, and chronic visits to the school counselor's office or health office. School counselors provide valuable information that grade-level representatives and classroom teachers may not have access to. School counselors must be prepared qualitatively and quantitatively to discuss current student performance in the context of school problems during the meeting. Other itinerant specialists may also contribute reports and provide them to the school counselor or Academic MTSS chair so their information can be presented to the team if they cannot attend a meeting.

As the Academic MTSS chair leads team meetings, classroom teachers are asked to review student data with the team. All team members should bring pertinent information and documentation regarding student functioning to meetings. After the Academic MTSS chair calls the meeting to begin, grade-level representatives immediately take over if whole grade levels are being discussed. Otherwise, the Academic MTSS chair will prioritize the students to be discussed and provide an ordered list of classroom teachers to present. It may save time to organize student case folders by grade or alphabetically in the order they are listed on the Academic MTSS Student Database to reduce paper shuffling and lost time during meetings. The following presentation example will help case managers most efficiently present information at meetings.

The following is the recommended presentation process at meetings:

1. State reason for referral
2. Brief history of pertinent history including, but not limited to attendance, transience, criterion-referenced scores, benchmark history, discipline, health, language proficiency, grades
3. Baseline progress monitoring score(s)
4. Present intervention plan(s) and goal(s) if students have them
5. Review teacher progress reports:
    a. Updated progress reports are *required* at every meeting. If there is difficulty getting feedback, begin including administrators on communication attempts with teachers.
    b. If there is repeated failure to engage teacher response, then administrative follow up is required.
6. Present *current* graph (throw away old; print or present new)
7. Review interventions currently in place and discuss suggestions for future steps, such as progress monitoring schedule, add or change interventions, refer to the school counselor, or schedule a parent–teacher conference
8. When possible, plan in advance for any absences by choosing a backup presenter and forward caseload data and folders for the students who are to be presented at the meeting

If grade-level representatives and classroom teachers are organized, the above structure provides the information needed to make informed decisions with team input. Old information can be reviewed quickly to bring the Academic MTSS team up to speed and provide a background of student needs. New information can be presented succinctly, providing team members with a comprehensive perspective of past and current needs to make decisions. Team members with additional knowledge and documentation who are invited to provide input include special education teachers who may be assisting with academic or behavioral observations and plans, the school nurse (or designee) reporting health updates, and the school psychologist providing leadership, guidance, and feedback. Recommendations for next steps, depending on available resources at school and in the community, are then determined together. The Academic MTSS chair should update new information in the Academic MTSS Student Database and grade-level representatives should follow through to ensure action steps are carried out.

Action steps may include a community-based referral to the student's family for basic needs or counseling. The school social worker or school counselor will usually volunteer to be the lead person to contact the family for such community-based requests. Follow-up by the nurse may be required including rechecking vision status, contacting caregivers about medication schedule, or getting a release of information to talk with student's prescribing doctor or psychiatrist for insights into the medical or psychological impact on behavior and performance. A recommendation to the classroom teacher to change a student's intervention would also fall under the category of action steps.

The goals of the Academic MTSS team are to identify areas of student need, determine baseline status, systematically provide interventions, revise student interventions based on documented response, and to max out the available resources on campus to respond adequately to intensity of student need, resulting in access to community resources if student needs exceed scope of the school. This systematic process to monitor outcomes for students who struggle despite the provision of high-quality instruction will provide more than adequate documentation for prior intervention criteria to fuel special education eligibility team processes, if needed. The decision for a comprehensive evaluation referral for special education programming could be recommended, in which case the school psychologist would bring evidence of student need and response to interventions to the Multidisciplinary Team to address potential identification of an educational disability.

The Academic MTSS team now has a cohesive membership that can work together efficiently and effectively to support student success. Through the diverse roles and contributions of administrators, teachers, specialists, school counselors, school social workers, and school psychologists, the problem-solving process can be maximized.

References

American School Counseling Association. (2017). *Role of the school counselor*. Retrieved from www.schoolcounselor.org/administrators/role-of-the-school-counselor

Anyon, Y., Nicotera, N., & Veeh, C. A. (2016). Contextual influences on the implementation of a schoolwide intervention to promote students social, emotional, and academic learning. *Children & Schools, 38*(2), 81–88.

Averill, O. H., & Rinaldi, C. (2011). Multi-tier systems of support. *District Administration, 9*, 91–94.

Dishon, T. (2011). Promoting academic competence and behavioral health in public schools: A strategy of systemic concatenation of empirically based intervention principals. *School Psychology Review, 40*(4), 590–597.

Family Educational Rights and Privacy Act of 1974, 20 U.S.C. § 1232g. (1974).

Forman, S. G., & Crystal, C. D. (2015). Systems consultation for multitiered systems of supports (MTSS): Implementation issues. *Journal of Educational and Psychological Consultation, 25*, 276–285.

Freeman, R., Miller, D., & Newcomer, L. (2015). Integration of academic and behavioral MTSS at the district level using implementation science. *Learning Disabilities: A Contemporary Journal, 13*(1), 59–72.

Guéguen, N., Pascual, A., Silone, F., & David, M. (2015). When legitimizing a request increases compliance: The legitimizing object technique. *The Journal of Social Psychology, 155*, 541–544.

Individuals with Disabilities Education Act, 20 U.S.C. § 1400 et seq. (2006 & Supp. V. 2011).

National Association of School Psychologists. (2014). *Who are school psychologists?* Bethesda, MD: Author.

Pinkelman, S. E., McIntosh, K., Rasplica, C. K., Berg, T., & Strickland-Cohen, M. K. (2015). Perceived enablers and barriers related to sustainability of school-wide positive behavioral interventions and supports. *Behavioral Disorders, 40*(3), 171–183.

Rainey, H., & Gifford, E. (2016). Working together: Asset based communities of learning in Higher Education. *International Journal of Integrated Care, 16*(6), 1–8.

Shinn, M. R. (2007). Identifying students at risk, monitoring performance, and determining eligibility within RTI: Research on educational need and benefit from academic intervention. *School Psychology Review, 36*(4), 601–617.

Shinn, M. R., & Walker, H. M. (Eds.). (2010). *Interventions for academic and behavior problems in a three-tier model, including Response-to-Intervention* (3rd ed.). Bethesda, MD: National Association of School Psychologists.

Shriberg, D., Bonner, M., Sarr, B. J., Walker, A. M., Hyland, M., & Chester, C. (2008). Social justice through a school psychology lens: Definition and applications. *School Psychology Review, 37*, 453–468.

Sprick, R. A. (2009). *CHAMPS: A proactive and positive approach to classroom management* (2nd ed.). Eugene, OR: Pacific Northwest Publishing.

Sprick, R. A. (2013). *Discipline in the secondary classroom: A positive approach to behavior management* (3rd ed.). Hoboken, NJ: John Wiley & Sons, Inc.

Stearns, E. M. (2017). Effective collaboration between physical therapists and teachers of students with visual impairments who are working with students with multiple disabilities and visual impairments. *Journal of Visual Impairment and Blindness*, 166–169.

Van Norman, E. R., & Christ, T, J. (2016). How accurate are interpretations of curriculum-based measurement progress monitoring data? Visual analysis versus decision rules. *Journal of School Psychology, 58*, 41–55.

Chapter 6

It Is the Format, Not the Forms

Key Terms

Automatization
Teacher Efficacy
MTSS Student Portfolios
Intervention Plan
Intervention Log
Intervention Graphs
MTSS Meeting Logs

Chapter Concepts

In this chapter, readers will learn:

1. To successfully format and sequence an MTSS program for optimal implementation.
2. To structure automatization and stable procedures into the MTSS organization.
3. The special considerations for behavioral documentation.
4. The responsibilities of the team at each phase of intervention.
5. How to track and maintain records in a student database.
6. How to address common questions with school-based solutions.

The success in building the foundation of Multi-Tiered Systems of Support (MTSS) instructional practices and growing effective approaches to have a positive impact on all learners relies on three key elements: fidelity, supports, and oversight. More specifically, teachers must use an evidence-based curriculum with fidelity, teams must implement proactive and positive academic and behavioral supports, and the administration must provide support and oversight to ensure that quality instruction takes place. If the MTSS team is certain that these anchors are in place, documentation can be streamlined because each educational practice will not need to be thoroughly vetted each time a student requires additional supports. MTSS teams will not waste their time chasing forms and documentation and can focus on problem solving for students to close the gap between actual and expected achievement.

While the flexibility of documentation is extended to programs built on a solid foundation of MTSS principles, a minimum level of expectation remains for documenting student need and performance. The format of MTSS programming is still key, and the following minimally recommended forms will help teams streamline their paperwork. At the minimum, it is recommended that schoolwide MTSS teams maintain an MTSS Student Database for Academics and Social-Emotional-Behavioral (SEB) each, typically organized by grade level, and MTSS Meeting Logs and sign-in sheets for accountability purposes. Grade-level teams are recommended to maintain MTSS Student Portfolios for each student at Tier 2 or Tier 3.

Automatization

In general, educators are very attached to forms and checklists on paper. Forms help to track events and provide a level of accountability that something is happening. We rely on forms to communicate professionally with others to ensure all stakeholders do their part and know that others are doing their part. Forms and checklists help busy, creative, driven, fast-paced teachers keep track of important concepts and duties and communicate information to others on the school team. However, separate forms and documentation procedures can also slow down processes resulting in decreased efficiency. Automate as many parts of your MTSS as possible to ensure the sustainability of the support tiers in your school (Forman & Crystal, 2015; Freeman, Miller, & Newcomer, 2015; Averill & Rinaldi, 2011). *Automatization* is the result of processes that have been converted from loose implementation to automatic implementation.

There are important processes that depend on documentation, and having an easy-to-implement format with simple forms to capture time-stamped data is essential. Having systems in place to automate MTSS saves much time and effort. Organization is key to maintain the flow of MTSS implementation and sustainability, and more forms are not the solution. Forms can be one of the most common counterproductive practices in education and are not the answer to automating MTSS. *Getting organized and staying organized are the secrets to staying on top of MTSS documentation; overdocumenting is not.* Teachers who are required to individually document interventions often struggle to do so and are less likely to complete the forms with integrity (Freeman et al., 2017; Freeman et al., 2016). Intense, individual documentation occurs for a very small percentage of students and most likely happens at Tier 3.

Overwhelmed teachers might experience feelings of burnout and, in extreme cases, impairment of emotional capacity and regulation (Mérida-Lopez & Extremera, 2017). Educators affected by Burnout Syndrome may experience the following three symptoms: emotional exhaustion, depersonalization, and a loss of self-confidence or lack of "Personal Accomplishment" (Maslach & Jackson, 1986). Teachers who are feeling insurmountably hopeless to meet the demands of the classroom will be much less likely to document with fidelity or at all. Sometimes, busy, time-pressed teachers deem accurate intervention logs a low priority. Burnout and time management challenges result in inaccurate intervention logs, which lead to less effective MTSS teams and program evaluation decisions. Logs are the school's documented guarantee that an evidence-based intervention was implemented as directed on a given day, how long the intervention session lasted, which target skill was addressed, and any relevant outcome notes. Intervention logs are primary artifacts in quality control of MTSS and may become legal documents when used for special education evaluation and eligibility purposes.

Documentation of valid interventions is often one of the most challenging tasks for teachers who already have too many responsibilities and too little time to fit them all in. When teachers' time–compensation–responsibilities scale does not balance, emotional well-being and professional productivity suffer. Even the most detail-oriented teachers are unable to keep up with individualized documentation for students on a daily basis, and they should not have to. A conservative number of forms and online communication tools can be useful to help teachers and MTSS team members collect, report, and review relevant data sources.

To run a well-oiled MTSS machine, many parts of MTSS need to operate with a high level of automaticity and institutionalizing effective processes and procedures is key. Investing in an evidenced-based curriculum for teachers to use with students in differentiated MTSS blocks takes out all the extra steps teachers typically have to take to vet intervention materials or create themselves. Intervention logs are accountability logs and record that evidence-based interventions took place and students were in attendance. *Using attendance logs in combination with lesson plans reduces duplicative work and simultaneously automatizes MTSS intervention logs* (Freeman et al., 2017; Freeman et al., 2016; Forman & Crystal, 2015; Freeman et al., 2015; Averill & Rinaldi, 2011).

Leadership plays a critical role in automating schoolwide MTSS. When administrators are certain that teachers are implementing the curriculum with integrity, as supported by classroom observations and administrative monitoring, these lesson plans and attendance logs can be used as documentation of participation in valid interventions. If the student requires Tier 3 supports, the level of documentation can be more detailed and will need to be reviewed more frequently. There is almost never a need to document individually academic-based interventions unless the student is receiving a very specific and unique intervention one-on-one, such as writing fluency. It is more common to document individually behavior-based interventions, such as those detailed in an individualized behavior intervention plan. The limited need for additional documentation would depend on individual characteristics of the student's response to instruction. For the most part, the number of students requiring additional individualized documentation would be few and would typically be reserved for students with individualized behavior plans.

If patterns of student data from a particular class consistently indicate a poor rate of progress across students, then the teaching practices and use of the curriculum with fidelity should be called into question. As a system of quality control, MTSS identifies problems, implements time-sensitive solutions, and monitors all aspects of the evidence-based outcomes leading to next steps in a continuous improvement model (Bryk, Gomez, Grunow, & LeMahieu, 2016; Freeman et al., 2016). It is up to the MTSS chair and leadership team, after collaboration and discussion, to bring any systemic or procedural concerns to the administration's attention for troubleshooting.

Academic MTSS Documentation

Tier 1 is the heart of a solid MTSS framework and begins with the critical work of classroom teachers. Classroom teachers are case managers and compile relevant information on student performance for all students receiving Tier 2 intervention services. When a student consistently is not responsive to the interventions provided, and after the classroom teacher has problem solved and consulted with their grade-level team, they can make a request to bring the student to the Academic MTSS team for further brainstorming and request for Tier 3 assistance (see Figure 6.1 for a visual representation for the lead decision makers at each tier). When this happens, they must

Figure 6.1 Lead Decision Makers at Each Tier

bring the Academic MTSS Student Portfolio(s) for each student of concern. These Academic MTSS Student Portfolios are required for all students referred to Academic MTSS meetings. The Academic MTSS team will then make decisions about Tier 3 supports and facilitate access to additional resources as needed.

Academic MTSS Student Portfolios are composed of the artifacts to present to the Academic MTSS team when making decisions about a student and to help support the Academic MTSS Student Database. Even though the information in case files are reported in abbreviated fashion on the Academic MTSS Student Database, classroom teachers, as case managers are encouraged to have copies of important artifacts should questions arise that require checking the information source for accuracy and additional information. Annually, classroom teachers discard outdated information in the Academic MTSS Student Portfolios for every student on their caseload, after first ensuring that the Academic MTSS chair has recorded the data in the Academic MTSS Student Database. Important impressions, observations, or recommendations moving forward should be inputted to the Case Notes section of the Academic MTSS Student Database. Case managers should add the following artifacts in their Academic MTSS Student Portfolios:

- Completed Request for Assistance form
- Family history and student's health-developmental questionnaire completed by a parent or guardian
- Cumulative folder review: "Student records typically contain students' attendance, discipline records, health screenings, grades and performance on standardized testing over the years. It can also contain a range of documents including custody arrangements, legal documents, and school photographs" (Florell, 2014).
- Current vision and hearing screening results
- Intervention plans (academic and/or behavioral)

- Intervention logs (if not tracked by lesson planning and attendance)
- Intervention graphs (most recent)
- Semester and quarter grades, real-time class grades as of meeting dates
- Updated discipline history, if relevant

Much of this information can be garnered from school database systems or student enrollment folders held in the registrar's office. The intervention data will be less static, and teams will need to be aware of its ever-changing nature. The *Intervention Plan* defines the student's area of difficulty and targets a discrete skill for a baseline to enable goal setting. The *Intervention Log* tracks the date, type, and duration of intervention provided. The *Intervention Graph* is the visual representation of scores obtained during progress monitoring data collection cycles. From these data, the rate of improvement over time is monitored, and instructional supports are intensified as deemed necessary by the team.

Academic MTSS Student Database

As discussed in the previous chapter, the Academic MTSS Student Database is the storehouse that archives all data for students who are discussed at Academic MTSS team meetings. This database is achieved by creating and maintaining a running record of at-risk student history, interventions implemented, school performance, current needs, and recommendations for school success. There are a variety of options for structuring an Academic MTSS Student Database; however, the most common would be the use of a database program such as Google Sheets or Microsoft Excel. Individual, hard-copy data sheets may also be used and stored in a binder marked by year. It is up to each team to decide what organizational structure will work best for them.

Regardless of the tool used, the following headings should be staples of all Academic MTSS Student Databases:

- Student name
- Student identification number
- Intervention teacher or block
- Classroom teacher (case manager)
- Intervention subject(s)
- English-language placement scores and level of language proficiency (if applicable)
- Attendance or tardiness issues
- Discipline or behavioral history (if applicable)
- Health issues
- Fluency benchmark scores
- Instructional level of fluency
- Most recent progress monitoring or strategic monitoring score
- Case notes

With assured implementation of an evidence-based curriculum and teaching practices, intervention documentation is briefly captured in the Academic MTSS Student Database and Case Notes. Intervention plan(s), logs, and graphs are nonnegotiables of a strong MTSS program. Beginning and ending date range(s) indicating implementation of each type of intervention provided can be captured in the column of intervention type along with the intervention teacher's name, which can be cross-referenced with attendance logs. Intervention group attendance logs can be used for documentation.

SEB MTSS Documentation

Behavioral interventions are some of the most challenging for school professionals to document succinctly. Sometimes, these behaviors occur naturally in the classroom without a seemingly specific antecedent, or an antecedent that was unseen. Teachers manage student behavior all day long, and there is a wide berth of typical behavior in a classroom, which is often predicated on teacher tolerance for noise and movement. From an early age, externalized behaviors and negative student mood within a classroom have been documented to have a negative impact on student learning (Scrimin, Mason, Moscardino, & Altoe, 2015). These externalized behaviors, including conduct problems, attention problems, and hyperactivity, are the most common disruptive behaviors that interfere with teaching and can lead to coercive relationships with teachers (Reinke et al., 2014). The most challenging students, with disruptive or defiant behavior, usually end up in the administrator's office because teachers often lack the skills or experience to foster positive relationships with students who do not demonstrate appropriate coping skills. These reactive practices will never be as effective as proactive practices. Students with behavioral challenges will require more positive interactions with adults, more opportunities for guided practice in social-emotional learning experiences, and many more opportunities for nonpunitive behavioral feedback (Dugas, 2017; Reinke, et al., 2014).

The majority of students will respond well to Tier 1 classroom management and problem-solving structures within the classroom. Those students requiring additional supports and Tier 2 level interventions may come to the attention of the grade-level teams in one of two ways, or both: benchmarking scores and direct referral from a teacher or caregiver. Similar to the layers of academic problem solving, social-emotional and behavioral supports are layered in much the same fashion. Students may be identified for Tier 2 supports through the use of a universal screener during benchmark windows, or for students with more extreme behavior problems, they may be identified through direct teacher referral outside the benchmark windows. If the behavior is severe, the student may be referred for Tier 2 and Tier 3 supports simultaneously. This is usually at the discretion of the school administrator, school counselor, school psychologist, or school social worker. Remember, classroom teachers are primarily responsible for decision making within Tier 1, grade-level teams (that can include the school counselor or any other key resources teams want to bring in) are responsible for decisions about who may require Tier 2 supports, and the SEB MTSS Team is primarily responsible for making decisions and providing access to Tier 3 supports.

When making a referral for Tier 3 supports, similar documentation is needed to present a student to the SEB MTSS Team as is required to discuss a student during an Academic MTSS Team meeting. The following are the required documentation needed for SEB MTSS Student Portfolios:

- Completed Request for Assistance form
- Family history and student's health-developmental questionnaire completed by a parent
- Cumulative folder review: "Student records typically contain students' attendance, discipline records, health screenings, grades and performance on standardized

testing over the years. It can also contain a range of documents including custody arrangements, legal documents, and school photographs" (Florell, 2014).
- Current vision and hearing screening results
- Universal SEB Screener scores for Internalizing and Externalizing
- Information regarding adverse childhood experiences (if known)
- Token economy response data and Tier 2 modifications or accommodations provided
- Frequency and use of a pressure pass and/or check-in, check-out system
- Semester and quarter grades, real-time class grades as of meeting dates
- Individualize behavioral intervention plan (if already in use)
- Behavioral intervention tracking documentation (measures of student response to the intervention provided, frequency of goal attainment, etc.)
- Behavioral graphs (most recent)
- Updated discipline history

In the classroom, there are countless methods to record behavioral data and the tool used will depend on the positive behavioral instructional supports (PBIS) in place. Positive reinforcement systems such as token economies can be in the form of a reward board, a token game system, or a sticker chart. These behavior management systems, or PBIS, should be positive in nature, focus on a specific task or goal, and not punitive. Clip systems in which students "clip up" or "clip down" are a public display of punitive shaming and do not teach critical social-emotional learning skills such as self-awareness and self-regulation (Jung & Smith, 2018). Students are not only publicly called out for engaging in nondesired or "bad" behavior; they are also often disciplined again when they get home as teachers often use clip movement as a daily communication log with families. So, if a student is "on red" at school and the daily log reports that home to the family, the student is dually penalized, often for behavior that is not always significant and may be developmentally appropriate. This type of classroom behavior management system could be likened to a staff meeting. What if the principal called out teachers every time they were late, looked at their phone, or talked to their neighbor? The teachers would begin to loath staff meetings and resent their administer(s), and the culture among the staff would decline. So, for the sake of students, ditch the clip.

Positive behavioral instructional supports should focus on a high ratio of positive attention given, preferably five times more positive attention than negative attention, to target students. Practicing self-regulation skills, breaking tasks into manageable lengths to increase opportunities for positive reinforcement, and responding unemotionally to behavior problems are highly successful strategies for teachers intervening proactively in student behavior. Different tools can be used across the three tiers, and the method selected will depend on the behavior to be modified and monitored (PBIS World, 2017). These collections methods will vary by team and may be digital or manual using pencil and paper with data collected privately, not publicly for the whole class to see. The tool selected will depend on the behavior under investigation as well as the teacher's efficacy in collecting the data (Petty, Good, & Handler, 2016; Tshannen-Moran & Hoy, 2011; Goddard, Hoy, & Hoy, 2010). *Teacher efficacy* is a teacher's perceived level of ability to have an impact on student learning through their instruction, data analysis, motivation, and organization. A master educator asserted that student celebrations should be made in public and corrections made in private.

A common tool that teachers feel comfortable using is a frequency chart, which targets a specific behavior during a specific period. A frequency chart can also include a place for documenting the intensity and duration of target behaviors and accompanying notes of antecedents or peculiarities describing specific situations. SEB MTSS teams are cautioned to only recommend formal behavior intervention plans in the most severe cases of chronic misbehavior, up to 2%, within Tier 3. For example, in a recent elementary school that conducted universal SEB screening, approximately 4.5%of students were identified as having significant behavior issues. After meeting individually with the teachers, triangulating data, and getting to the heart of the students' issues, only 1.5% of the students ended up needing individualized behavior intervention plans (Dockweiler & Diamond, 2019). Furthermore, in most cases, there will not be multiple students with an individualized behavior plan in a single class. If there are, the teacher may require additional supports to design and implement the plans, tapping into the expertise of the SEB MTSS team.

Tier 1 classroom management strategies for the whole class are key and, with consistent implementation, can decrease the number of students requiring Tier 2 and Tier 3 supports. Programs such as SLANT (Buffum, Mattos, & Weber, 2012) or CHAMPS (Sprick, 2009) are effective at the Tier 1 level for implementation with whole classes and campuses. Oftentimes, students with challenging behaviors are more rigid in class and let teachers know if discipline is fair. If rewards and consequences are not fairly applied to all students in a class, behavioral strategies will be less effective over time. Personal relationships with students and families are an educator's first line of defense with misbehaving students requiring a higher level of positive interactions (Dugas, 2017; Reinke et al., 2014). Well-executed incentives, along with natural consequences, combined with genuine positive regard for students, work with most students. Students whose behavior or circumstances are extreme outliers for expected behavior in a school population should be tracked closely for mental health issues, family systems issues, and emotional disturbance or other educational disabilities.

Student behavioral issues lead to emotional and physical exhaustion for teachers (Mérida-Lopez & Extremera, 2017; Maslach & Jackson, 1986). Upset teachers must be validated. Students who misbehave are challenging and take much of a teacher's time and energy to ensure classroom integrity, at best, and personal and student safety, at least. Oftentimes, teachers want to discuss Tier 3 behavioral problems during Academic MTSS team meeting times; however, this is not the purpose of the Academic MTSS team and can chew through their entire meeting time. This is why an overlapping SEB MTSS team, with separate team meeting times and overlapping professionals, is recommended to give students' problems the attention, support, and oversight they require for best chances of positive outcomes (see Chapters 10 and 11). Teachers are more likely to implement behavioral interventions and document outcomes with integrity if they feel actively supported by administration and a team of school-based mental health professionals.

Behavioral documentation need not be time-consuming, even in the most severe cases. There is no need to replicate data captured in school discipline data, nurse's reports, or counselor's logs, and the data should be available to the SEB MTSS team, school-based mental health professionals, and administrators to examine when relevant. In doing so, teams are better able to identify individual patterns over time and holistically are able to reflect, revise, and revamp their intervention processes. Referrals to the school counselor's office and health office are often tracked by systems already in place at schools. If not, those incidences can be easily tracked by the school counselor and health office staff in simple daily logs with names and dates, which can be accessed by school counselors and nurses to report back to the SEB MTSS team when needed.

The goal of social-emotional and behavioral documentation is to make sure that all sources of relevant data are current in real time at SEB MTSS meetings so that teachers, administrators, and SEB MTSS team members can determine the trends of student progress quickly, and informed and timely decisions can be made. Teams that follow a format for data collection and reporting spend significantly less time digging for relevant information, pulling teeth of colleagues who do not respond to requests for documentation, figuring out which solutions have been tried and failed, and searching for outcome data written on sticky notes lost in piles of papers on teachers' desks. Any forms required as tools to accomplish these feats should be brief, condensed, and easy to use. Shared Google Drives and other technology can help simplify processes and create accountability methods for service providers. The format drives what needs to be on the forms, and the forms should never duplicate sources of data that are readily available.

SEB MTSS Student Database Structure

The SEB MTSS Student Database can be drafted in Excel with tabs for special programs (self-contained special education programs), each grade level, and the whole school. In a kindergarten–fifth-grade elementary school, this might result in a database spreadsheet with eight separate tabs. Given the sensitive nature of the SEB data collected, it is advised, according to Family Educational Rights and Privacy Act, that only those with a genuine educational interest in a student have access to a student's information. This does not mean that only the classroom teacher be made aware of a student's SEB status. Social-emotional learning strategies and individualized behavior intervention plans should occur across all education settings, and oftentimes, teachers within a grade departmentalize and divvy up students during the day. As such, grade-level teams who meet to discuss student needs within grade-level professional learning communities are encouraged and should not have restricted access to information pertaining to students within their grade.

Data to be included in the SEB MTSS Student Database will vary school by school and should be updated on a rolling basis, at the most, and at benchmark periods, at the least. In general, the SEB MTSS Student Database should include the following:

- Student name
- Student identification number
- Results of the SEB screener
- ACEs (adverse childhood experiences) information (if known)
- Discipline history
- Academic risk(s)
- Identified internalized needs, interventions, and outcomes with notations
- Identified externalized needs, interventions, and outcomes with notations
- English language placement scores and level of language proficiency (if applicable)
- Attendance or tardiness issues
- Health issues

Some schools prefer to document every student in the school whether they pop up as at-risk during one of the benchmark periods or not. In tracking *all* students on a campus, the SEB MTSS team can identify trends in student SEB functioning.

Current grades, attendance, discipline and behavior problems, medical issues, personal issues, and any academic issues are required to be tracked. For students receiving Tier 3 support, monitoring and updating information become more simplified within an established reporting format. Other relevant information captured on the SEB MTSS Student Database for Tier 3 students may include which intervention(s) the student is receiving (or did receive with dates of implementation and outcomes), any intervention changes made, the name of intervention teachers and specialists, and other formative and summative assessment scores that can be considered to determine whether interventions need to be more intense or less intense for students. The SEB MTSS team must then decide where the problems lie, whether that be within the student's environmental and family ecosystem, mental health problems, language and communication problems, classroom teacher qualities, curriculum and assessment implementation issues, documentation issues, MTSS chair issues, comprehensive system issues including adequate number of intervention opportunities, or any other number of problems that pop up in team functions.

MTSS Meeting Logs

MTSS Meeting Logs are the official dated documentation of the students and case notes discussed at MTSS team meetings and who attended and is updated during or after each meeting. The MTSS Meeting Logs are recommended to be maintained by the MTSS chair or designee.

MTSS Team Meeting Decision Making Model—Questions and Solutions

Does the student have a significant developmental history or been identified with a developmental issue?
Students with developmental issues, especially those from low socioeconomic homes, are at a greater risk for school problems (Williams, Landry, Anthony, Swank, & Crawford, 2012). Students with a history of developmental delays (and environmental disadvantages) need more high-quality school and community-based supports, which require closer monitoring of academic growth, social and emotional difficulties, behavioral problems, independent living skills, health issues, and communication skills.

Does the student have a significant family history and/or socioeconomic or ecological factors that influence school attendance or functioning? What are the known adverse childhood experiences? In what ways does the student's family support the student's education?
School problems tend to run in families as children from the same homes often experience the same social-demographic risk factors and, to some extent, academic risk factors. Individuals who experience multiple forms of ACEs, social trauma and academic failure are the most likely to be impacted. In a nationally representative study of 14,736 students, researchers have demonstrated an inverse relationship between the number, not necessarily the severity, of risk factors and academic success (Lucio, Hunt, & Bornovalova, 2012). When students experience 2 or more of these 12 predictors

(academic engagement, academic expectations, academic self-efficacy, attendance, school misbehaviors, educational support, grade retention, homework, school mobility, school relevance, school safety, and teacher relationships), they are significantly more likely to suffer from academic failure (Lucio et al., 2012). Furthermore, contact with the juvenile justice system (delinquency) and school expulsions (discipline) are high predictors of negative school outcomes (Robison, Jaggers, Rhodes, Blackmon, & Church, 2016; Henry, Knight, & Thornberry, 2012).

Solutions depend on what the families' needs are. Are the students' and families' basic needs being met? If not, the school social worker or school counselor can often coordinate food and medical assistance as well as referrals to community agencies for shelter, food, clothing, and job assistance to help reduce transience. Are there multiple family members with the same problems such as mental illness, behavioral problems, drug or alcohol problems, learning problems, and attendance problems? If yes, students should be monitored more closely for school issues and interventions should be implemented accordingly. If the family does not support the child's education, family outreach efforts to provide positive school experiences and relationships between teachers and caregivers/guardians are encouraged. Attendance contracts and incentives may be helpful.

Is the student's primary language English?
Second-language acquisition factors should be taken into account when determining the amount or intensity of English learner supports necessary for student success. Students who are newer English speakers, and those with lower language proficiency scores, will require greater vocabulary/language exposure and rehearsal, adapted materials, and adapted grading criteria to ensure an equitable system for their unique language needs.

Does the student have significant environmental trauma or mental health history?
Students with mental health problems, ACEs, and trauma histories have a greater risk for academic and behavioral difficulties and are more likely to engage in delinquent activities (Mallett, 2015). Students demonstrating signs of psychiatric disorders should be monitored closely for school issues and interventions should be implemented accordingly. A family history including incarceration, trauma, and having one or more comorbid psychiatric condition increases instances of criminal engagement (Taskiran, Mutluer, Tufan, & Semerci, 2017; Mallett, 2015). Juvenile youth with Attention Deficit Hyperactivity Disorder and Conduct Disorder were found to be engaged in more severe crimes than those with internalized behaviors, such as anxiety, who engaged in less severe crimes (Taskiran et al., 2017).

Frequency and intensity of problem behaviors in the school setting will need to be tracked and lines of communication between school staff and medical/mental health service providers and caregivers must be open to ensure transparency between home and school. In addition, daily emotional and physical health information should be monitored including hygiene, affect, social living skills, emotional stability, explosive anger, and aggression toward self and others. Students with poor self-regulation may end up in the justice system when laws are broken or injuries occur. The school psychologist, school counselor, school nurse, school social worker, and other behavior mentors on a school campus should be working together, and with the family and community health providers, to actively solve problems and provide supports for these students (Lucio et al., 2012). Students can be paired with a teacher mentor or other supportive adult they already know on campus, and students' teachers should be given positive behavioral strategies to implement (Moore-Partin, Robertson, Maggin, Oliver, & Wehby, 2010). Checking in/out, incentives for students, pressure passes, and formal behavior plans are all options for teams to consider.

Are formative and summative assessment results consistent with other indicators of student success? Do results indicate underachievement?
Does the student have a history of performing on grade level? If no, underachievement may be a chronically severe problem and more intense interventions should be implemented at the soonest opportunity. If yes, then explore possible reasons for the newly presenting academic difficulties, any lack of consistency in programming and instructional delivery, difficulties at home, and other explanations for where things possibly got off track. This will help focus solutions on the key problem areas and the associated manifest difficulties. The triangulation of information should be considered from multiple sources, including grades, classroom performance reports, environmental or home reports, and current fluency graphs at an instructional level.

If performance is not consistent across sources then further discussion at MTSS team meetings must ensue to narrow down to the real issues having an impact on the student's lack of performance. On occasion, fluency graphs do not capture student performance or growth. For example, some students read at a slow pace, but reading comprehension is not negatively impacted. In such cases, grades, other test scores, and classroom performance reports would be better indicators of success. More likely than not, most sources of data for underachievers are consistent across the board. After establishing a baseline, students should be put on a strategic or progress monitoring schedule with interventions implemented accordingly.

The most important question to answer at MTSS team meetings is whether the student is responding to treatment or not.
If the student is getting better, according to a preponderance of evidence, then continue the intervention and continue to progress monitor. If there is no change, the team may continue to monitor for another monitoring period, change the intervention, or add another intervention. If a student's problem is getting worse over time, then current interventions are not successful, and the team should recommend changing the intervention or implementing a more intensive intervention. If the student is getting maximum levels of Tier 2 and Tier 3 support and demonstrates resistance to instruction over time, across interventions implemented and across data sources, then the student should most likely be referred to the Multidisciplinary Team for an evaluation for special education for a suspected disability.

Does the student require an intervention group or a more intensive model of instruction or support in one or more areas?
The MTSS teams should have a menu of supports in Tier 2 and Tier 3 with a continuum of services for struggling students. Teams may devise their own interventions, or there are several options available to teams to purchase (Macklem, 2011). Schools that have limited options for intervention groups or those who lack a research-based curriculum and opportunities for academic or behavioral remediation must actively work on growing supports over time for students. If a struggling student is not getting the inter-

ventions, he or she requires then efforts must be made to remediate deficits. Teams must ensure that students are getting interventions in their area(s) of need and the identified problem area(s) are being monitored systematically for growth over time. Outcome data will dictate whether students continue to require that level of intensive instruction or if supports can be faded with less intensive instruction to maintain success.

How do teams prioritize student problems with complex issues?
Several factors contribute to a student's success on a school campus. Students' basic needs and school attendance must be addressed first before any other school intervention is implemented. Behavioral problems also interfere with the success of interventions, so if behavior is a problem, environmental variables and mental health issues must be addressed simultaneously with academic interventions. Sometimes students' maladaptive behavior precludes them from being successful in an academic intervention group and their needs are better addressed, at least initially, in a social-emotional and behavioral learning intervention group. Underperforming students often have multiple layers of deficits. When students have problems in both reading and math, reading is often typically addressed first if teams have to choose which area to focus on. In a perfect world, treatment plans for the whole child could be put in place for all areas of need, but in reality problems must be prioritized and addressed systematically within the limitations of the system. Students may not receive interventions in all areas of need simultaneously, nor do they necessarily demonstrate improvements in all areas simultaneously even if they have comprehensive support.

How often should fluency measures be administered to students?
Teachers should aim to administer fluency measures either weekly (at most) or bimonthly (at least) for the students in their intervention groups. When teachers administer fluency tests weekly, student absences and outlying scores average out. When fluency testing occurs monthly, if the student is absent on the testing day or is not feeling well, then no data (or skewed data) are recorded, and the valuable opportunity for curriculum-based measurement is lost for timely MTSS team decisions. It is the responsibility of the intervention teacher to ensure that at least two monthly data points of current instructional-level fluency are accessible to case managers prior to MTSS team meetings.

Does the student struggle in class? Are things going better for the student?
Qualitative teacher progress reports capture information that grades and test scores cannot. Classroom teachers must provide monthly feedback on student academic and behavioral improvements to the MTSS teams. Good progress reports measure attitude, effort, participation in class activities and verbal discussions, work quality, organizational skills, work completion rates, behavior, conflict with peers or adults, and grades. This information is invaluable to team decisions regarding the necessity of increasing or decreasing the intensity of instructional supports for a student.

Is the student on target for meeting his or her individual goals?
If no, continued Tier 2 and Tier 3 supports are warranted. If multiple domains have been identified as deficit areas, the MTSS teams should strive to meet as many of the student's needs in as many of the domains as possible. Communications with students, caregivers, and teachers should be required to address reasons for deficiency. Efforts to

improve incentives for performance or push opportunities for summer school, online, or weekend programs should be explored. More intervention opportunities or wraparound services may be required.

As MTSS team members habituate themselves to discussing students systematically, the aforementioned questions and answers get reviewed quickly, and appropriate next steps come more easily. The idea of valuing format over forms in the documentation of MTSS team functions is that *team processes* become engrained in the school fabric and can then become automated. If the format is in place, abbreviated documentation is possible. Teachers will have less paperwork and more opportunities for direct professional communication with other staff on students' behalf. Status updates can be completed on a Google Doc or Google Sheets in minutes for ease of use and accountability among multiple school professionals. Each educator must do his or her part.

In a well-run MTSS, the outcome data always points to the weakest links.
The weak links may be a lack of intervention opportunities, a lack of funding for evidence-based resources, poor communication between staff members, a lack of appropriate progress monitoring processes, a need for greater supports for teachers or itinerant staff, and resistance by stakeholders to MTSS itself. All issues can be addressed systematically by the MTSS teams to identify problems and school-based solutions. Ultimately, the school principal is responsible for actively providing solutions to barriers in the implementation of MTSS and reinforcing the desired change. If the school principal's leadership is not strong at a school and that principal is resistant to change or does not have the skills to reinforce the change, the necessary change will not happen. There is no intervention, short of a new principal, that will fix consistently weak leadership.

Effective systems require many moving parts to work together cohesively. Unfortunately, automation of functions, processes, and professional competencies in a school setting cannot be managed with a disseminated form or checklist. Changing educators' behavior to engage in more effective practices must be shaped. B. F Skinner (1953), arguably the father of modern behavioral modification techniques, described the concept of shaping using his learning model of operant conditioning, where the association between a new behavior and the resulting consequence is learned in repetitive trials. Shaping new behavior is established through reinforcement of successive approximations toward the desired behavior, and new responses are progressively reinforced until the desired behavior is achieved. School leaders must not only have a clear vision of MTSS to be able to put all the structures, functions, and processes in place, but they must also be actively involved in shaping the entire staff in better practices and reinforcing those changes; growing and sustaining a culture that nurtures and supports students and educators.

References

Averill, O. H., & Rinaldi, C. (2011). Multi-tier systems of support. *District Administration, 9*, 91–94.
Bryk, A. S., Gomez, L. M., Grunow, A., & LeMahieu, P. G. (2016). *Learning to improve: How America's schools can get better at getting better*. Cambridge, MA: Harvard Education Press.
Buffum, A., Mattos, M., & Weber, C. (2012). *Simplifying response to intervention: Four essential guiding principles*. Bloomington, IN: Solution Tree Press.
Dockweiler, K. A., & Diamond, L. L. (2019). *Student risk significance level after data triangulation chats*. Unpublished raw data.
Dugas, D. (2017). Group dynamics and individual roles: A differentiated approach to social-emotional learning. *The Clearing House: A Journal of Educational Strategies, Issues and Ideas, 90*(2), 41–47.

Florell, D. (2014, September 28). Right to see student cumulative record. *Richmond Register*. Retrieved from http://mindpsi.net/blog/right-to-see-student-cumulative-record/

Forman, S. G., & Crystal, C. D. (2015). Systems consultation for multitiered systems of supports (MTSS): Implementation issues. *Journal of Educational and Psychological Consultation*, 25, 276–285.

Freeman, F., Sugai, G., Simonsen, B., & Everett, S. (2017). MTSS coaching: Bridging knowing to doing. *Theory into Practice*, 56(1), 29–37.

Freeman, J., Simonsen, B., McCoach, D. B., Sugai, G., Lombardi, A., & Horner, R. (2016). Relationship between school-wide positive behavior interventions and supports and academic, attendance, and behavior outcomes in high schools. *Journal of Positive Behavior Interventions*, 18(1), 41–51.

Freeman, R., Miller, D., & Newcomer, L. (2015). Integration of academic and behavioral MTSS at the district level using implementation science. *Learning Disabilities: A Contemporary Journal*, 13(1), 59–72.

Goddard, R., Hoy, W. K., & Hoy, A. W. (2010). Collective teacher efficacy: Its meaning, measure, and impact on student achievement. *American Educational Research Journal*, 37(2), 479–507.

Henry, K. L., Knight, K. E., & Thornberry, T. P. (2012). School disengagement as a predictor of dropout, delinquency, and problem substance use during adolescence and early adulthood. *Journal of Youth and Adolescence*, 41(2), 156–166.

Jung, L. A., & Smith, D. (2018). Tear down your behavior chart! *Association for Supervision and Curriculum Development*, 76(1), 12–18.

Lucio, R., Hunt, E., & Bornovalova, M. (2012). Identifying the necessary and sufficient number of risk factors for predicting academic failure. *Developmental Psychology*, 48(2), 422–428.

Macklem, G. L. (2011). *Evidence-based school mental health services: Affect education, emotion regulation training, and cognitive behavioral therapy*. New York, NY: Springer-Verlag.

Mallett, C. A. (2015). The incarceration of seriously traumatised adolescents in the USA: Limited progress and significant harm. *Criminal Behaviour and Mental Health*, 25, 1–9.

Maslach, C., & Jackson, S. E. (1986). *Maslach burnout inventory manual* (2nd ed.). Palo Alto, CA: Consulting Psychologists Press.

Mérida-Lopez, S., & Extremera, N. (2017). Emotional intelligence and teacher burnout: A systemic review. *International Journal of Educational Research*, 85, 121–130.

Moore-Partin, T. C., Robertson, R. E., Maggin, D. M., Oliver, R. M., & Wehby, J. H. (2010). Using teacher praise and opportunities to respond to promote appropriate student behavior. *Preventing School Failure*, 54(3), 172–178.

PBIS World. (2017). *Data tracking*. Retrieved from www.pbisworld.com/data-tracking/

Petty, T. M., Good, A. J., & Handler, L. K. (2016). Impact on student learning: National board certified teachers' perspectives. *Education Policy Analysis Archives*, 24(49), 1–16.

Reinke, W. M., Stormont, M., Herman, K. C., Wang, Z., Newcomer, L., & King, K. (2014). Use of coaching and behavior support planning for students with disruptive behavior within a universal classroom management program. *Journal of Emotional and Behavioral Rob Disorders*, 22(2), 74–82.

Robison, S., Jaggers, J., Rhodes, J., Blackmon, B. J., & Church, W. (2016). Correlates of educational success: Predictors of school dropout and graduation for urban students in the deep south. *Children and Youth Services Review*, 73, 37–46.

Scrimin, S., Mason, L., Moscardino, U., & Altoe, G. (2015). Externalizing behaviors and learning from text in primary school students: The role of mood. *Learning and Individual Differences*, 43, 106–110.

Skinner, B. F. (1953). *Science and human behavior*. New York, NY: The Free Press.

Sprick, R. A. (2009). *CHAMPS: A proactive and positive approach to classroom management* (2nd ed.). Eugene, OR: Pacific Northwest Publishing.

Taskiran, S., Mutluer, T., Tufan, A. E., & Semerci, B. (2017). Understanding the associations between psychosocial factors and severity of crime in juvenile delinquency: A cross-sectional study. *Neuropsychiatric Disease and Treatment*, 13, 1359–1366.

Tshannen-Moran, M., & Hoy, A. W. (2011). Teacher efficacy: Capturing an elusive construct. *Teaching and Techer Education*, 17, 783–805.

Williams, J. M., Landry, S. H., Anthony, J. L., Swank, P. R., & Crawford, A. D. (2012). An empirically-based statewide system for identifying quality pre-kindergarten programs. *Education Policy Analysis Archives*, 20(17). Retrieved from http://epaa.asu.edu/ojs/article/view/1014

Chapter 7

Special Education Eligibility and Other Considerations

Key Terms

Discipline
Social-Emotional Regulation
Protective Factors
Implicit Bias
LGBTQ+
Alingual
Linchpins
Unicorns
Three As

Chapter Concepts

In this chapter, readers will learn:

1. How MTSS and special education intersect and complement each other.
2. To reinforce intervention systems from an asset-based approach.
3. To understand the unique needs of gifted students, language-deprived students, and English-language learners.
4. How to shift perspectives to think inclusively and to acknowledge that injustices and inequities exist in our schools.
5. How to better understand and support the role of school psychologists and other specialized staff on campus.

Multi-tiered support systems, response to instruction, response to interventions, student study teams, student intervention teams and the like are nothing new in educational circles (Dishon, 2011). Historically, these terms have most often been used to fuel the special education eligibility determination machine at schools. The definition of certain eligibility criteria has required intervention implementation and documentation of outcomes since the 1980s, but school communities are still struggling to standardize the intervention process (Ladd & Fiske, 2008). Some schools do very little in terms of differentiated instruction and systematically implementing remedial opportunities, while others are very responsive to the academic and behavioral needs of students (Forman & Crystal, 2015).

The MTSS and Special Education Intersection

School-based intervention plans have been, and continue to be, perceived as stepping-stones to special education eligibility in many schools and school districts. While some teachers may perceive it as the route to get their students "into" special education, specialists on campus can help inform on the process to help balance the eligibility scales (Nellis, Sickman, Newman, & Harman, 2014). Beware when eligibility considerations depend more on service providers' judgment than actual data, as it may contribute to the misidentification of students eligible for special education. As general education teachers feel overwhelmed, or underprepared, to handle the needs of at-risk students, these children tend to get pushed out of their classes with the misguided belief that special education is going to be a magical cure.

Any students who do not fit neatly into the general curriculum may not receive the support they need. These students tend to be disciplined more often and are more frequently singled out by teachers "so the students can get the help he or she needs." *Discipline* is the training of adherence to codes or behavior and may include punishments to correct noncompliance. *It is important for educators to keep in mind that students who struggle academically are more likely to act out behaviorally.* At best, when regular education teachers push struggling students out those children become another teacher's responsibility. Hopefully, the educators who end up with the children who require additional supports know how to inclusively cultivate an engaging learning environment and demonstrate mastery of content knowledge and delivery. At worst, and more predictably, those children get "managed" somewhere on campus with other struggling students and have the least qualified teachers with the most militaristic supervision.

The management of school children is nothing new. The current education system we have, including its bureaucratic structures, time schedules, grade-level divisions, student rankings, and behavioral expectations are rooted in the disciplinary methods of monasteries, armies, and workshops from the seventeenth and eighteenth centuries (Foucault, 1995). A description of such a space in 1762 is described:

> [T]he educational space unfolds; the class becomes homogenous . . . 'rank' begins to define the great form of distribution of individuals in the educational order: rows or ranks of pupils in the class, corridors, courtyards; rank attributed to each pupil at the end of each task and each examination; the rank he obtains from week to week, month to month, year to year; an alignment of age groups, one after another; . . . in this ensemble of compulsory alignments, each pupil, according to his age, his performance, his behavior, occupies sometimes one rank, sometimes another.
>
> (Foucault, 1995, pp. 146–147)

Students who conformed silently and did not require individualized attention were praised as model pupils. Those with individual needs or those with behaviors that fell outside the desired norm were sent to reformatories, or, worse, sent to prison. Thus, emerged the very beginnings of the modern school-to-prison pipeline.

While these rankings and structures of education uniformity have changed little in nearly 300 years, social attitudes toward discipline have. Under the leadership of Le

Peletier (1791), radical laws were enacted in eighteenth-century France to ensure that "the punishment fit the crime" for those who violated the laws of society. This was a radical departure from then existing discipline structures that predominately included death by hanging, even for trivial crimes. The goal of such disciplinary power was to imprison the offender in an attempt to retrain his behavior and to discourage repeat behavior. However, to rely on a punishment model creates the counterproductive error of expecting different behavioral results without providing an appropriate intervention to teach and reinforce expected behavior. Two hundred years later, behavioral psychologists such as Maslow, Bruner, Piaget, and Skinner began exploring the motivations of human actions and sought to find more positive ways in which to understand and change behavior.

While work still needs to be done to address the school-to-prison pipeline, society has come a long way in how it treats students with special needs and those who require social-emotional and behavioral interventions. Through an Multi-Tiered Systems of Support (MTSS) program, students are able to receive the supports they need, at the level of intensity best needed to address their unique problems. Successful MTSS programs also consider the individual environmental and cultural influences on students, view these factors through an asset-based social justice lens, and use restorative practices.

A culturally inclusive MTSS does not push students out; it surrounds students with a proverbial hug of relevant supports and provides them with an opportunity to access the general curriculum to the greatest extent. Cultivating positive teacher–student relationships along with student motivation, perseverance, and reward systems can be used to bolster student feelings of belonging at school (Dueck, 2014; Moore-Partin, Robertson, Maggin, Oliver, & Wehby, 2010). A well-integrated MTSS embraces flexibility and responsive supports to groups of students, as well as individual students. This may include groups of students who have like deficits in specific subject areas or individual students who are not adequately responding to increasingly intensive interventions.

Setting high expectations for all learners is paramount, and students with behavioral difficulties require behavioral instruction as well as academic instruction (Sprick, 2013; Dishon, 2011; Shinn & Walker, 2010; Moore-Partin et al., 2010; Shinn, 2007). In order for all students to reach their personal best, schools must create a culture of safety and inclusiveness that is socially just (Francis, Mills, & Lupton, 2017; Sink, 2016; Shriberg & Clinton, 2016; Shriberg, Song, Miranda, & Radliff, 2013). Ideally, a high-quality education system for students who do not fit standard grade-level expectations would include opportunities to obtain specialized supports without having to jump through hoops of special education eligibility first.

Expectations should be high for *all* learners to reach their personal best. This is especially true for students who receive special education supports and in instances where education laws only specify a "minimal" level of support rather than a maximum level to support comprehensive student learning (Abou-Rjaily & Stoddard, 2017). Students with behavioral problems require behavioral instruction *and* guided social-emotional learning (SEL) experiences, in addition to high-quality academic instruction. Learning is a braided experience consisting of social, emotional, and academic components (The Aspen Institute: National Commission on Social, Emotional, and Academic Development, 2018). Students who are exposed to an SEL curriculum demonstrate long-term benefits. In a recent meta-analysis of 82 studies and nearly 100,000 students, researchers with the Collaborative for Academic, Social and Emotional Learning and partner universities found that "[p]articipants fared significantly better than controls in social-emotional skills, attitudes, and indicators of well-being. Benefits were similar regardless of students' race, socioeconomic background, or school location. Post-intervention social-emotional skill development was the strongest predictor of well-being at follow-up" (Taylor, Oberle, Durlak, & Weissberg, 2017, p. 1). These benefits continued to be realized up to 18 years after being exposed to the SEL curriculum. Additional findings suggest that participants demonstrated long-term benefits of increased empathy and teamwork and decreased rates of conduct problems, emotional distress, and drug use.

Students who struggle with social-emotional regulation and behavior require emotional safety to ask questions they believe everyone else seems to know the answers to, and they need a safe space with a teacher with whom they can form a caring relationship (Schonert-Reichl, 2017). *Social-emotional regulation* is the ability to control and negotiate emotions, thoughts, and behaviors effectively and efficiently. Many of the most problematic students have never had social-emotional regulation modeled or taught to them; have not developed a strong, quality relationship with a caregiver; and lack the protective factors needed to establish emotional trust and stability (Robison, Jaggers, Rhodes, Blackmon, & Church, 2016). "Trust between a child and adult is essential, the foundation on which all other principles rest, the glue that holds teaching and learning together, the beginning point for re-education" (Hobbs, 1982, pp. 22–23.).

Protective factors are conditions that positively contribute to student well-being and include factors such as having their basic needs met as well as having resilience skills, strong social connections, and social-emotional skills. Students without sufficient protective factors or who lack a strong, caring relationship with a caregiver often do not believe in themselves, nor do they believe in the adults around them, oftentimes with good reason. The adults in the students' lives have always let them down, so they do not believe that a teacher could care about them, let alone help them. It stands to reason that angry, resentful, discarded students are going to try to make teachers feel more miserable than they feel themselves by acting out and disrupting the learning environment. Sometimes, children act out to test the adults at a school to see if and when they are going to be punished or discarded by another adult who says they care; other times, students are disruptive simply because it is more fun than remaining confused and feeling incompetent and unsuccessful.

Establishing a continuum of shared governance between families and educators is one way to maximize outcomes for students and reinforce school–family engagement (Garbacz et al., 2016). This shared responsibility is encouraged and reinforces to students that their teachers and family are working together. Academically and behaviorally deficient students must be able to access opportunities to be retaught basic academic and behavioral skills they are lacking without destroying their fragile egos and sense of self-worth. Schools must step up efforts to make school relevant and unbiased for everyone. For school psychologists, social justice can be promoted by making connections between "promoting best practices in school psychology, conducting culturally fair assessments, and advocating for the rights of children and families" (Shriberg, Wynne, Briggs, Bartucci, & Lombardo, 2011, p. 49).

> **Box 7.1**
>
> **Voices From the Field**
>
> Some students remain with you and their stories stay vividly clear even as the years pass. Willie is one such student. I knew Willie for the duration of his educational career at my elementary school, kindergarten through fifth grade. He was, and still is, incredibly sweet; his good-natured disposition has yet to be taken from him regardless of all the challenges he faces. Aside from his academic challenges, he resides in a home with a single parent who works evenings and weekends and his two older brothers, one who was taken into custody and no longer resides in the home and one who is a high school student. Willie essentially has raised himself and is occasionally looked after by his one older brother when he is around. Willie consistently misses school or is late. His first two years of school he had an absence rate of approximately 25% each year.
>
> As a kindergartener, he began school not knowing any pre-academic skills, such as colors, numbers, or letters. He consistently got lost and did not ask for help; he would sit compliantly at his assigned seat, happy as could be. Through the MTSS process, he was provided with academic interventions and made little progress. Tier 2 and Tier 3 interventions continued into first grade, and by the end of first grade, he could finally write his first name. By then, the team had enough information that they were suspecting a disability and had ruled out absences as the primary source of the student's difficulties. Initially, the team suspected a specific learning disability; however, after observing the student a few times and reviewing his educational history, I suggested to the team that what we were really suspecting was an intellectual disability. As far as the school referral process was concerned, the team had followed the procedures to a "T" and were spot on with the referral.
>
> Since kindergarten, Willie's classroom teachers have been in constant communication with the parent regarding Willie's absences and academic progress. The parent claimed that the student would eventually catch up and was not concerned. When approached about the referral for special education assessment, the parent was adamant that Willie was fine and that "there is nothing wrong with him." Without informed parent consent, the referral stalled, and Willie went into second grade with his Tier 2 and Tier 3 supports.
>
> Wraparound and community supports were offered to the parent and were denied. Increased parental contact was made with the parent to help demonstrate to the parent the intensity and need for the services provided to the student. Eventually, at the end of second grade, the parent provided informed written consent to conduct the special education evaluation to explore an intellectual disability but still insisted that Willie was "fine." At the end of the evaluation, Willie did indeed meet the criteria as a student with an intellectual disability, and the team found him eligible for services. The parent still maintained that he was "fine" but did consent to the special education services. One of the additional services written into Willie's individualized education program (IEP) was for transportation, which significantly helped increase his attendance.
>
> Several takeaways that stick with me include the tenacity of the teachers to continuously communicate and engage the parent to understand where Willie was performing in relation to his same-age peers and to share everything they were doing to support Willie. Also, what sticks with me is the strength of the MTSS structures in place at

the school so that supporting Willie at Tier 2 and Tier 3 for years was not a problem. While not ideal, because the team clearly suspected a disability, strong structures are necessary as there will always be parents and families who for a variety of reasons do not want their child assessed or found eligible for special education. And finally, the collaboration of the teachers and MTSS team at the school to work in concert with me and the speech and language pathologist and to shift the suspected disability from specific learning disability to intellectual disability. It was truly a team decision based on all available data and helped to further hone interventions implemented with Willie and the overall approach we took to address his unique educational needs.

Special Considerations

Gifted students are especially prone to unique social-emotional and behavioral challenges due to their giftedness (Peterson, 2006). Many highly gifted students never reach their full potential due to the emotional toll of being smarter than those around them and not having the social skills or problem-solving processes to allow them to adequately work with others or build self-discipline and patience to persevere when things get difficult (Kaplan & Geoffroy, 1993). Gifted students are some of the most undersupported special needs students in the educational system in the United States, and students from culturally, linguistically, and ethnically diverse backgrounds are especially underrepresented (Siegle et al., 2016; Michael-Chadwell, 2010). SEL curricula targeting the needs of this population are strongly encouraged, as are opportunities for additional academic enrichments. Gifted and highly gifted students have unique challenges and differences that should be supported and nurtured. The bottom line is that all students must be given equal opportunities to learn the skills needed to maximize their potential to be successful citizens.

African American students are targets for severe punishment in schools and are significantly more likely to be harshly disciplined than White students or other minority groups for similar offenses, including disproportionately receiving consequences of corporal punishment, out-of-school suspension, and expulsion. According to a recent study, African American students are seven times more likely to experience exclusionary discipline while Latino and Native American children are two times as likely (Bal, Betters-Bubon, & Fish, 2017). Data do not support that African American children have higher organic rates of antisocial behavior or engage in more deviant behavior than any other child (Gershoff, 2010).

Research on implicit bias indicates a systemic problem in school culture, which disproportionately punishes African American students in comparison to White counterparts (Staats, Capatosto, Wright, & Contractor, 2015). *Implicit bias* is the underlying beliefs, stereotypes, and attitudes that unconsciously have an impact on a person's decision making. This bias, also sometimes referred to as social implicit cognition, is pervasive, is not mutually exclusive to explicit bias, and does not always align with declared beliefs. This is based, in part, on biased stereotypical beliefs that African American students are more aggressive, disruptive, dangerous, less respectful, less honest, and less hardworking than peers from other racial backgrounds (Staats et al., 2015). Negative stereotypes and implicit bias hurt students in school communities by disengaging children from their education, embracing a culture of failure with irrational blame focused at children for matters beyond their control, and creating a school-to-prison pipeline for children of color. Understanding implicit bias through a cultural lens may be the best way to begin shifting and changing perspectives (Payne & Vuletich, 2017). In this sense, addressing the underlying and explicit social contexts in which our school and communities exist can help decrease the underlying implicit bias. This perspective is essential when working with policy makers and drafting policies that impact society (Payne & Vuletich, 2017).

Problems of injustice in school systems, including disproportionality of punishment for children of color and overidentification of eligibility for special education in minority populations, must be addressed as an issue of social justice. School teams must acknowledge that White privilege exists, listen and learn from others, think and reflect, and, finally, take data-based action to rectify the perpetual racial and social injustice that transpires in our schools (Shriberg, 2016). As part of this process, educating school staff and providing cultural sensitivity training in working with students from diverse racial and ethnic backgrounds must take place. In addition to better understanding students from racial and ethnic diverse backgrounds, educators must also be able to attend to the needs of *LGBTQ+* youth. This population of students, regardless of their racial or ethnic background are "at risk for negative mental health outcomes and reduced academic success" (National Association of School Psychologists, 2016, p. 1).

Educators may believe that awareness of and having the skills to address the needs of LGBTQ+ are not necessary in elementary schools; however, LGBTQ+ students are requiring earlier and earlier supports, and elementary schools are the perfect place to provide them. Many young children with nonconforming gender identities or sexual orientation are not able to verbalize why or how they feel different than other kids, nor are many able to express their confusion regarding their gender identity, societal expectations, and how they fit in. The National School Climate Survey conducted biennially by the Gay, Lesbian, & Straight Education Network on the experiences of LGBTQ youth in our nation's schools has documented the unique challenges LGBTQ students face and the prevalence of these negative experiences. The most recent version of this survey examined indicators of negative school climate experienced by LGBTQ students in the areas of hearing biased remarks in school, feeling unsafe in school because of personal characteristics, missing school because of safety reasons, and experiencing harassment and assault in school, as well as experiencing discriminatory policies and practices at school (Kosciw, Greytak, Zongrone, Clark, & Truong, 2018). Some students have families that do not look like families represented in pictures, books, and imagery on school campus, with a male father and female mother; they may have LGBTQ+ caregivers and siblings and unique family configurations (Moorhead, 2018). Schools can use an environmental scan tool to evaluate and improve inclusive practices, such as a school readiness assessment for gender-diverse students that investigates educator cultural competencies, education materials, language and imagery around campus and on websites, building-level policies and communications, equitable practices for students, safe spaces, and access to inclusive materials in libraries (Savage, Springborg, & Lagerstrom, 2017). In addition, schools must evaluate and provide appropriate structures and procedures to promote the safety of LBGTQ+ students (Sadowski, 2016). They must also ensure that school-based mental health professionals are trained to handle the unique needs of LGBTQ+ students and are following the recommendations put forth in their professional association position statements and ethical standards guidelines (GLSEN, ASCA, ACSSW, & SSWAA, 2019). There is a demonstrable need for school psychologists to learn how to identify heteronormativity within the materials and discourse used throughout their professional practice in schools, as well as in private settings (Tashman & Song, 2018). These client materials may take many forms, including, but not limited to, the text and images contained within brochures, fliers placed at front desks or given to students and their caregivers, policies, as well as regulations, wall décor in waiting rooms and offices, and school websites. The expression of heteronormativity through these materials and related discourse can be perceived as microaggressions by LGBTQ+ students but will typically go unnoticed by the school psychologists who enact them, despite good intentions to prevent discrimination (Tashman & Song, 2018). Based on the aforementioned research, some questions to consider when building an inclusive elementary campus should include Are inclusive images present, such as library books displayed with LGBTQ+ individuals represented in a positive way? Does the librarian read books to children with LGBTQ+ characters represented in the stories? and Do staff members have adequate professional development to bring awareness to inclusionary opportunities for students? Culturally sensitive social-emotional-behavioral supports can be grown to support all student needs, starting with Tier 1, by using an inclusive curriculum that is representative of all students. As a leader in the movement California passed Senate Bill 48 (2011), the FAIR (Fair, Accurate, Inclusive, and Respectful) Education Act, mandating LGBTQ+ achievements be taught in history and social studies. New Jersey was the second state to add a mandate for such a curriculum, and most recently, Illinois became the third state by passing House Bill 246 (2019) to include the roles and contributions of the LGBTQ+ leaders in the civil rights movement. In the event that a child identifies as other than assigned birth gender, or as nonbinary, the school must make accommodations and those accommodations may be captured in a Gender Support Plan, including using gender-neutral pronouns, as well as providing alternatives to gender-based bathrooms. Students with more intensive needs may require more targeted interventions to address social-emotional-behavioral issues through Tier 2 and Tier 3 supports. According to The Trevor Project, rates of attempts and completions of suicide are high among LGBTQ+ students. In one study LGB children attempt suicide at a rate of almost five times their heterosexual counterparts (Center for Disease Control, 2016), and an astonishing 40% of transgender adults reported attempting suicide, with 92% of them reporting they had tried to commit suicide before the age of 25 (James et al., 2016). It is evident that supporting LGBTQ+ students early in their development with culturally competent practices is an urgent mental health crisis.

All teachers must consider whether their Tier I classroom behavior management skills are effective for regulating behavior in the learning environment and do not penalize or shame students for poor behavioral choices. Developing positive teacher-student relationships is one of the best ways to remedy misunderstandings with students regarding their behavior in the classroom (Moore-Partin et al., 2010). The very same student who struggles behaviorally in one teacher's class may be perfect a citizen in another teacher's class. Schools that embrace the framework of MTSS train their staff to have higher ratios of positive interactions with students and less emotionally charged negative interactions. These positive interactions and relationships support an increased probability of positive outcomes for students (Sprick, 2013, 2009). When misbehavior is punished, without opportunity for remediation or restitution, students are much less likely to learn from their actions, especially when discipline does not seem fairly applied to all (Moore-Partin et al., 2010). In addition, zero-tolerance policies need to be reconsidered so that students are not kicked out of school arbitrarily or disproportionally applied to racial and ethnic minority students (Verdugo, 2002). Also, progressive discipline plans cannot be coined as MTSS; they are punitive in nature and do not offer incremental opportunities for self-correction and intervention assistance. Such plans may also be termed restorative discipline, but *it does not matter what pronoun is placed in front of the word* discipline *as they are all just various forms of disciplinary procedures for schools to follow, not a restorative justice approach under an MTSS framework.*

MTSS creates a problem-solving culture among school staff, families, and the community, which improves communication and understanding among all stakeholders. The team approach allows a struggling child to have numerous adult advocates on campus to have a positive impact on individual school success and, ultimately, success in life. Too often, students are denied remedial opportunities because schools do not fund interventions; however, they do have federal funding for special education (Kincaid & Sullivan, 2017). As a result, there are many cracks in the school's foundation and alternative supports may be overlooked. Instead of evaluating program delivery, teaching competencies, culturally sensitive instructional practices, and positive behavioral supports, schools take shortcuts and overidentify students, frequently minority students, for special education.

Conversely, in many school districts, second language students may fall victim to underidentification of disabilities because of the opposite assumption: that any learning difficulties are due to second-language acquisition factors, not an underlying disability (Kincaid & Sullivan, 2017; Sullivan, 2011; Cummins, 2008; Krashen, 1988; Krashen, 1987). Second-language students with unidentified disabilities tend to get passed from grade to grade without receiving the supports they need. This pattern continues until they hit a brick wall in middle school or high school and can get no further in their education due to failure to pass mandated assessments and an inability to earn credits toward graduation. Some elementary school systems help students skate along without adequate supports until the student reaches fifth grade, and then the teacher makes a referral for special education evaluation "so the student can get the support he or she needs in middle school."

Just passing students along in elementary school without providing the requisite interventions, including not proceeding with special education evaluation and supports when warranted, puts unnecessary pressure on middle schools to figure things out for the underperforming students who move up to sixth grade. This sets students up to fail: Oftentimes, data from the elementary school do not exist or do not transfer to the middle school, many middle schools do not have functional MTSS and do not process referrals for supports quickly, and incoming sixth-grade students may not be a priority for middle school MTSS teams who have students with even more urgent needs. Elementary school MTSS teams are encouraged to prioritize fifth graders who have received significant interventions over the course of their elementary careers to determine if those intensive interventions are required to continue in middle school. If so, teams may want to consider whether the student requires a plan that captures those intensive supports and, depending on the data, could result in a 504 Plan, special education eligibility with an IEP, or an academic intervention plan that can be forwarded to the next school for consideration at the beginning of sixth grade. Determining adequate rate of progress depends on numerous factors, and the teachers who know the student and have been working with them for years are better equipped to plan ahead for their student's transition to middle school; it also better prepares middle school educators to support the unique student needs from the very first day of school.

MTSS teams must have team members who understand second language acquisition theory, including typical rates of development for basic informal communication skills (BICS) and cognitive academic language proficiency (CALP; Cummins, 2008). It is imperative that the team has at least one team member who can serve as the expert in second-language acquisition and inform the team as to whether a student is making adequate progress in relation to their exposure and language history. Factors that go into determining adequate progress include, but are not limited to, student's time of exposure to the second language, proficiency in their native language (BICS and CALP), proficiency in the second language (BICS and CALP), and home language usage. Typically, a student's academic and language proficiencies in English are expected to progress at a commensurate rate, with writing literacy skills to be one of the last academic skills mastered. If a student's academic proficiency does not progress at a relatively commensurate rate within a specific time frame (relative to the length of exposure and the various factors mentioned), this lack of progress could be due to an underlying disability.

Providing interventions early on and monitoring language status are essential so that teams can target underlying deficits not otherwise explained by language acquisition factors (O'Connor, Bocian, Sanchez, & Beach, 2012). Especially in high-poverty areas, struggling second-language students may not adequately develop skills in their primary language, which, in turn, has an impact on the acquisition of a second language. The same holds true for English-speaking language deprived students. Students who are, in essence, *alingual* (not proficient in any language) enter school at a significant disadvantage academically and socially. Students with expressive language deficits at the age of 2 are predictive of higher rates of anxiety, depression, and withdrawal at the age of 3 (Carson, Klee, Lee, Williams, & Perry, 1998). Without remediation, these deficits become compounded and lead to further social-emotional difficulties. Beyond language status, socioeconomic status also has a significant impact on students' vocabulary and language processing. According to key research conducted at Stanford University, the language gap between students from high- and low-socioeconomic families are evident as early as 18 months of age for vocabulary and language processing efficacy (Fernald, Marchman, & Weisleder, 2013). Furthermore, by 24 months of age, this gap widens to six months with regard to language-processing skills.

Second-language and language-deprived students are also a group misidentified for speech and language special education services (Pieretti & Roseberry-McKibbin, 2015). Those in the first group often are misidentified because teams oftentimes lack qualified individuals with knowledge of second-language acquisition, or they lack a bilingual speech and language pathologist to conduct the communication evaluation, and the team chalks any language difficulties up to second-language acquisition status. Language-deprived students are often underidentified as they tend to be quieter, less confident speaking, or speak using predominately slang and poor grammar, which breeds preconceived and stereotypical beliefs about students' intelligence. Without a rich vocabulary and semantic knowledge, students often are less likely to verbalize and speak out as much in class as their typical peers. Their deficits often go unidentified because teachers have not heard the student talk enough to suspect the presence of a problem or they suspect lower intellectual skills. The earlier the communication team can provide supports and services for those individuals who qualify, the better the long-term educational outcomes for students. Training and preparing MTSS team members to strategically assess student needs and prioritize relevant interventions at the intensity level students require are paramount to support all types of learners. *Regardless of a student's unique characteristics, special education eligibility should not be the goal of interventions; positive educational outcomes should be.*

Attention School Psychologists

Informal surveys of school principals across a large urban area overwhelmingly indicated that the efficacy and success of a school's MTSS and the intervention team processes depend more on the skill level of the school psychologist than any other factor. School psychologists should no longer be thought of as gatekeepers to special education services but as *linchpins* holding various elements of complicated structures in place to keep students from sliding off into an abyss of school failure. *If students fail and no one is watching, did the students fail, or did the system fail the students?* School psychologists have the ability, education, and training to socially engineer positive educational practices in schools for students (National Association of School Psychologists, 2016). As they are often the most knowledgeable on campus about SEL, psychology of learning, behavior modification, and special education law, school psychologists can be engaged as leaders who are empowered to contribute to decision making that has an impact on students directly and indirectly, proactively and reactively.

Schools that maintain school psychologists in a special education testing-only role are missing out on all the benefits of having true psychological services on campus, as well as all the academic benefits. School psychologists are uniquely qualified to lead and participate in selecting and overseeing implementation of Tiers 1, 2, and 3 behavioral and SEL infrastructures at a school in cooperation with school counselors, school social workers, teachers, and administrators (NASP, 2016a). In addition, school psychologists invest in professional development activities and research effective schoolwide academic and behavioral practices, as well as evidence-based methods, to remediate target behaviors and academic delays. School psychologists have a wealth of skills and knowledge and are often underutilized as the goldmine of resources for children that they are. However, their time is often filled with paperwork, begging individual teachers to try something extra for struggling students, chasing forms and documentation, and appeasing endless parent requests for special education eligibility assessments. Without empowerment to be on the proactive end of instructional practices, school psychologists find themselves reacting to variables in the environment with little control of outcomes for students, like a pinball flying across the game board bouncing off barriers, intermittently scoring, and finding themselves in a dark hole when the game is over.

School psychologists are the unicorns on a school campus. Unicorns are mythological creatures with unique talents and characteristics and have been critically likened to human rights: imaginary constructs that do not exist (McIntyre, 1984). School psychologists are like *unicorns* in that they are rarely seen on a school campus yet they have many unique talents and characteristics to make an extraordinary impact. Whether engaging as a moral advocate on behalf of students or as a political advocate for adhering to state and federal policies, school psychologists, unique and powerful, are indeed real. The power of the unicorn lies in its uniqueness (Botting, 2015). Each school psychologist has unique interests, strengths, and focuses in their individual practices, as well as the skills and knowledge to conduct special education assessments and help guide educational programming. They engage in counseling services for children and families, crisis response, suicide prevention, parenting classes and family wellness, classroom management, positive behavior intervention supports, social-emotional-behavioral learning, program evaluation to improve MTSS practices, advocacy, and policy change, among other areas of expertise (National Association of School Psychologists, 2014; Dockweiler, 2016). Many find ways to incorporate their areas of skill and interests into daily and weekly practice while toeing the line for special education. Others get sucked into the monotony of assessment and are used to solely test and place students for special education due to high demand and low supply of school psychologists. School counselors, school social workers, school nurses, and teachers may share splinter characteristics, skills, and interests as school psychologists, and their professional duties may overlap in some limited ways. Yet no other educational professional can replace the background or perspective of the school psychologist when looking at schoolwide issues and individual differences.

School psychologists are among the first to realize when educational practices on a campus are not working. They can be a litmus test for school culture, can assist with getting to the bottom of complex issues quickly, and almost always have an evidence-based contribution on matters large and small. If school psychologists do not have a chair at the decision-making table, then they need to bring their own. However, even before they can bring their own chair, they need to be aware that a meeting is taking place. The *Three As* are required for having a seat at the decision-making table and participating in making decisions that impact the future and is true for all educators. *Awareness, access, and action are all necessary components of inserting the school psychologist's perspective into a school and community's ecosystem.* Input from the school psychologist is invaluable.

It takes psychology science to persuade people to engage in new endeavors and research-based change (Simonton, 2009). School psychologists need to get comfortable with resistance to change and use psychological strategies to help school teams bridge problems with solutions. Children do not typically change their behavior without the adults in their environment changing their behavior toward them, manipulating environmental variables, and altering reinforcement schedules. Adult-to-adult behavioral change is not dissimilar.

School psychologists have little to no leverage over colleagues at work because most are not employed in administrative positions within the school district hierarchy. However, they can use all their psychological tools and skills of persuasion to convince others to empower change within their environments, such as promoting a new research-based remedial program, teaching how to increase the positive reinforcement schedule for a student, and advocating for a comprehensive approach to systematic implementation and monitoring of remedial opportunities. School psychologists have more power than they realize and not as gatekeepers for special education eligibility determination. They have unique skills and training to persuade school teams to work collaboratively to systematically use best practices in smart groups to solve problems for all students at a school. A well-led school will appreciate and utilize these leadership qualities.

School psychologists must *advocate for their duty* to engage in psychological services in school systems. The role of a school psychologist at a school is frequently dictated by the school principal. Some school leaders support and promote the leadership of school psychologists, while others try to micromanage school psychologists to limit their professional activities. The only clearly consistent role school psychologists have across schools is the responsibility to guide special education eligibility assessments and determinations. In schools where no MTSS is in place and academic and behavioral supports are few and far between, teachers may grudgingly provide "documentation" of interventions and outcomes. This so-called documentation often comes with questionable validity, which may consist of random work samples, incomplete tests, dean's referrals, and failing grades. School psychologists may find themselves continuously reinventing the wheel with each individual student referral and with each individual teacher in an effort to ensure that students receive some sort of remedial opportunity and that teachers are collecting response-to-instruction data. The repetitious one-on-one consultation is not a productive use of time for the school psychologist or the school and does not systematically benefit students. When psychologists advocate for universal, systematic processes to address student deficiencies, with outcome measures and continuous improvement practices in place, they are helping *all* students on campus, not just the ones that they ultimately assess.

The more efficiently and flexibly school processes and personnel are able to respond to student needs, the more effective the school psychologist can be at identifying students with severe underachievement and atypical behavior patterns in an effort to obtain appropriate and timely treatment. The nationwide shortage of school psychologists (National Association of School Psychologists, 2016) has resulted in most school psychologists providing services at multiple school sites and increasingly growing numbers of students. It is not uncommon for one-school psychologists to have an assigned caseload of 2,000 to 3,500 students (Nevada Association of School Psychologists, 2018; Nevada Association of School Psychologists, 2016). There is no way one person alone can manage all the happenings on a large campus, let alone more than one campus. It is especially difficult for school psychologists to simultaneously manage multiple school sites with multiple school teams, cultures, and systems. Busy school psychologists need superpowers because they are responsible for students and school team functions even when they are off campus. Fortunately, *effective MTSS is a collective superpower* that all team members benefit from, especially school psychologists, in prioritizing school and student needs and making data-based decisions.

A healthy system of information exchange between MTSS team members increases the probability of a timely response with relevant and helpful feedback from the school psychologist. Staff members can actively support the school psychologist in the following ways:

- Sharing the updated Academic MTSS Student Database and Social-Emotional-Behavioral MTSS Student Database and corresponding case notes with the school psychologists after each MTSS team meeting (or provide them access if using a shared Google Folder)
- Supporting classroom teachers, grade-level representatives, and MTSS chairs to maintain organization and ensure that student deficit areas are matched with appropriate interventions and appropriate outcome measures
- Keeping the school psychologist in the loop during and after a crisis response, the event could be related to other relevant school safety and student issues. The school psychologist will be able to help mitigate situations through team collaboration, sharing student history, assessing the problem, observing and interviewing the student, de-escalating tense situations, and assisting with intervention design
- Including the school psychologist in school team meetings and administrative meetings that proactively address academic initiatives, school climate, and student safety

- Arranging meeting times to work with the school psychologists' schedule as they are often moving between multiple schools
- Making room at the table for the school psychologist to engage in team problem solving through awareness, access, and action
- Reimagining school psychologists as more than psychometricians. School districts that have marginalized school psychologists to testing centers or replaced them with psychometricians are missing out on the leadership, inclusiveness, and quality control school psychologists bring to a school culture.
- Providing administrative assistance to help school psychologists with the mounds of paperwork they must complete for compliance purposes. This frees the school psychologist to engage in more specialized activities such as additional problem solving, running student counseling groups, or engaging in positive behavior support planning for students and coaching for staff.

It takes a village to support school psychologists to maximize their effectiveness. School psychologists must advocate for such supports, and in turn, they must make themselves available and accountable to support team functions and follow through with team recommendations.

MTSS, and the paradigm of three tiers, can be used as a triage model in a school system, which enables MTSS teams to respond to the intensity of student problems with correspondingly intensive interventions. With all MTSS team members doing their part, enormous amounts of information on numerous students can be regularly sifted through and dispersed to relevant stakeholders in a timely manner. Few things are as upsetting to caregivers and school staff than when harm comes to children that is preventable. A combination of well-developed MTSS processes, including conscientious and accountable MTSS team members with strong team communication skills, is the closest thing schools will get to a magic crystal ball that can be used to predict students' futures. If present functioning and behavior are the best predictors of future performance, then fortune-telling should be a whole lot easier with several active MTSS team members' eyes on the ball.

When multiple sources of information get disseminated properly and in a timely manner, better decisions can be made for students. Teams must identify students who are at-risk and prioritize their response to minimize negative student outcomes. Getting student information updates to the right ears at the right time is paramount to serve students well. As will be discussed in Chapters 10 and 11, MTSS teams who work together effectively and communicate regularly can get ahead of students' emotional and behavioral problems before events happen that cannot be undone including assault to others, nonsuicidal self-harm, and suicide. And yes, assault to others, nonsuicidal self-harm, and suicide are present on our elementary school campuses. According to a study investigating rates of nonsuicidal self-injury in third, sixth, and ninth grade by sex (Barrocas, Hankin, Young, & Abela, 2012), researchers found that nonsuicidal self-harm was present in 6.8% of third-grade female students and increased to 18.9% by ninth grade. For males, the rate of nonsuicidal self-harm in third grade was 8.5% and decreased to 5.1% by ninth grade (Barrocas et al., 2012). While females and males may have somewhat similar rates of nonsuicidal self-harm in third grade, females have nearly triple the rate of incidences as males by ninth grade. Early identification and intervention with these female students are crucial.

In a recent study of 87 young children ages 5 to 11 who had successfully completed a suicide, 97.7% did so at home (Sheftall et al., 2016). These young students were less likely than older students, ages 12 to 14, to leave a note or to exhibit signs of depression. The top three precipitating events the students had recently experienced, in isolation or a combination of, were reported: some sort of relationship issue (60.3%), recent crisis (38.5%), and school problems (32.1%) (Sheftall et al., 2016). Again, early identification and recognition of the signs of internalizing problems, depression, and suicide, even in young children, is critical to providing them with the services and interventions they need to avoid tragedy.

It is assumed that school psychologists are responsive to student and school crises as part of the crisis response team, perhaps even leading in the efforts. However, if the crisis is on a day that they are not at the school, it is up to the school team to contact and notify the school psychologist so they can lend their expertise and assistance. Like Grandma always said, "an ounce of prevention is worth more than a pound of cure." School psychologists must manage their time to respond to the reality of overwhelming caseloads while balancing the desire to be proactive.

Some words for practicing school psychologists whose time is consumed with assessment and eligibility determination:

- Find ways to demonstrate your value to administrators, teachers, school staff, parents and families, and students outside of evaluation duties.
- Be the linchpin for students and connect them to resources to assist in their development and improve opportunities for positive school outcomes.
- Ask the school principal for processes or resources that you would like to see implemented. If the school psychologist does not voice their preferences grounded in evidence-based practices, somebody else may offer something less effective.
- Question established rules if it is in a student's or system's best interest.
- Be mindful of intensity versus volume of student needs and prioritize students who are a danger to themselves or others first, no matter how many other children you have on your referral waiting list. *Student and staff safety always comes first.*
- Listen to caregivers, school counselors, and teachers because their accurate and timely reporting increases the school psychologist's ability to synthesize large amounts of data to accurately identify and prioritize student problems, which leads to more effective and timely solutions.
- Nurture the growth of MTSS; school psychologists can have a positive on impact all students and adults in a school community.
- Build relationships with school staff, students, and community members to integrate the school psychologist's unique skills into the fabric of culturally responsive and proactive instructional practices.
- School psychologists are unicorns after all, and school communities need the services and input only school psychologists can offer, so advocate for the profession as well as best practices.

Attention Specialists

A school campus may have many individuals that fall under the functional category of specialist. Teachers on special assignment, special education teachers, school counselors, school social workers, school nurses, speech and language therapists, school psychologists, and other itinerant professionals may all fall under this category, depending on district classification, and have vested interests in supporting MTSS. Each position and perspective provide an important lens through which to filter student problems because each specialty has its own criteria for developmental expectations and unique remedies specific to areas of expertise. The school nurse is sensitive to organizing patterns of health symptoms into hypotheses about difficulties students may experience that are health-related. The speech and language pathologist would be particularly sensitive to developmental issues that are impacted by speech and language development in comparison to developmental milestones of communication. School social workers are experts at tracking down information and community resources for families, in addition to directly helping them overcome barriers to access resources. Special education teachers are valuable resources to any school campus because they are the masters of differentiated instruction and working with students who do not learn in typical ways. Each specialist is a necessary and esteemed member of the MTSS team.

As stated earlier, the importance of active participation of specialists in supporting appropriate educational opportunities for struggling learners cannot be overstated. Specialists fill needs that general education classroom teachers cannot. They target specific developmental skills and areas of need that cannot be addressed in the classroom or by any other team member depending on their specialty. Some duties overlap, such as sharing counseling responsibilities between the school counselor, school psychologist and school social worker, but most MTSS teams carve up team member responsibilities to ensure that the right professional is given the right job responsibilities. Specialists must be especially alert to evidence of students demonstrating low incidence disabilities, which do not require prior intervention and should be assessed for special education eligibility without delay if there is a demonstrated need for specialized services. Such eligibilities include, but are not limited to, intellectual disability, autism spectrum disorder, and visual impairment.

Classroom teachers work hard to teach the curriculum and manage behavior; they are also responsible for differentiating instruction to diverse learners. When they need help from colleagues to support them and their students, they should have easy access without having to go to great lengths for the help. When systems for accessing help become too complicated, or overly dependent on large amounts of prereferral paperwork, teachers are less likely to request assistance from specialists. MTSS team specialists are encouraged to create formats and brief forms that support documentation of information needed for referrals and for making decisions about students (see Chapter 6). Classroom teachers who believe that MTSS team members follow through with referrals in a timely manner and are responsive to requests for supports are much more likely to fulfill their own MTSS responsibilities.

Specialists doing their part and following through on MTSS team recommendations and referrals in a timely manner should be a given; however, expectations must be made explicit and emphasized. A message to specialists: support school MTSS teams by developing both proactive and reactive systems for supporting students. Develop streamlined procedures of communication with staff and user-friendly documentation from teachers so that you can make timely data-based decisions and provide direct services to increase student success. The MTSS team requires the expertise of specialists, and students benefit most from specialists who are looking out for student problems proactively. Specialists must step up and speak out on behalf of students, as they are excellent candidates for leadership positions advocating for MTSS on school campuses.

It is remarkable how powerful a fully functional MTSS can be on a school campus, and how many problems it automatically solves for students and school staff alike.

Teachers have a community to support struggling students and a recipe to follow when students need access to more help than can be provided within the general education curriculum alone. Students, regardless of their background, can get help when they need it instead of having to fail repeatedly for years to perform "low enough" for special education eligibility and to qualify for special education programming. The MTSS framework supports all students universally and has provisions in place for all types of learners. In a social justice context, special student populations' needs are not only considered but understood through a strengths-based lens and provided for along a continuum of relevant educational services for all. Implicit biases are confronted forthrightly and cognitive-behavioral mind-sets are checked and readjusted to ensure fair treatment of all students and staff, thus reducing overidentification and underidentification traps. Special education eligibility decisions can be complicated, and all variables must be weighed to make the most informed decisions and to effectively address individualized needs. School psychologists and specialists are uniquely qualified to train and support MTSS team functions, as well as provide a rainbow of alternative service delivery models depending on levels of administrative support, individual interests and areas of expertise, and the demands of caseload assignments and competing responsibilities. Last, school psychologists are highly qualified and uniquely talented educators whose talents and abilities to lead and support school changes should not be underestimated.

References

Abou-Rjaily, K., & Stoddard, S. (2017). Response to intervention (RTI) for students presenting with behavioral difficulties: Culturally responsive guiding questions. *International Journal of Multicultural Education, 19*(3), 85–102.

The Aspen Institute: National Commission on Social, Emotional, and Academic Development. (2018). *How learning happens: Supporting students' social, emotional, and academic development.* Washington, DC: Author.

Bal, A., Betters-Bubon, J., & Fish, R. E. (2017). A multilevel analysis of statewide disproportionality in exclusionary discipline and the identification of emotional disturbance. *Education and Urban Society.* Retrieved from https://doi.org/10.1177/0013124517716260

Barrocas, A. L., Hankin, B. L., Young, J. F., & Abela, J. R. (2012). Rates of nonsuicidal self-injury in youth: Age, sex, and behavioral methods in a community sample. *Pediatrics, 130*(1), 39–45.

Botting, E. H. (2015). Women's rights may be unicorns, but they can fight wicked witches. *Journal of International Political Theory, 12*(1), 58–66.

Carson, D. K., Klee, T., Lee, S., Williams, K. C., & Perry, C. K. (1998). Children's language proficiency at ages 2 and 3 as predictors of behavior problems, social and cognitive development at age 3. *Communication Disorders Quarterly, 19*(2), 21–30.

Center for Disease Control. (2016). *Sexual identity, sex of sexual contacts, and health-risk behaviors among students in grades 9–12: Youth risk behavior surveillance.* Atlanta, GA: Department of Health and Human Services.

Cummins, J. (2008). BICS and CALP: Empirical and theoretical status of the distinction. In B. Street & N. H. Hornberger (Eds.), *Encyclopedia of language and education* (2nd ed., Vol. 2, pp. 71–83). New York, NY: Springer Science + Business Media LLC.

Dishon, T. (2011). Promoting academic competence and behavioral health in public schools: A strategy of systemic concatenation of empirically based intervention principals. *School Psychology Review, 40*(4), 590–597.

Dockweiler, K. A. (2016). State association advocacy: Conversations about conversations. *Communiqué, 44*(7), 1, 32–33.

Dueck, M. (2014). The problem with penalties. *Educational Leadership, 3*, 44–48.
Fernald, A., Marchman, V. A., & Weisleder, A. (2013). SES differences in language processing skill and vocabulary are evident at 18 months. *Developmental Science, 16*(2), 234–248.
Forman, S. G., & Crystal, C. D. (2015). Systems consultation for multitiered systems of supports (MTSS): Implementation issues. *Journal of Educational and Psychological Consultation, 25*, 276–285.
Foucault, M. (1995). *Discipline and punish: The birth of the prison* (2nd ed.). New York, NY: Random House.
Francis, B., Mills, M., & Lupton, R. (2017). Toward social justice in education: Contradictions and dilemmas. *Journal of Education Policy, 32*(4), 414–431.
Garbacz, S. A., McIntosh, K., Eagle, J. W., Dowd-Eagle, S. E., Hirano, K. A., & Ruppert, T. (2016). Family engagement within schoolwide positive behavioral interventions and supports. *Preventing School Failure, 60*(1), 60–69.
Gershoff, E. T. (2010). More harm than good: A summary of scientific research on the intended and unintended effects of corporal punishment on children. *Law & Contemporary Problems, 73*, 31–56.
GLSEN, ASCA, ACSSW, & SSWAA. (2019). *Supporting safe and healthy schools for lesbian, gay, bisexual, transgender, and queer students: A national survey of school counselors, social workers, and psychologists.* Retrieved from www.glsen.org/sites/default/files/Supporting%20Safe%20and%20Healthy%20Schools%20-%20A%20Report%20on%20Mental%20Health%20Professionals%20%26%20LGBTQ%20Youth_0.pdf
Hobbs, N. (1982). *The troubled and troubling child.* New York, NY: Jossey-Bass.
House Bill 246, New Jersey 2019.
James, S. E., Herman, J. L., Rankin, S., Keisling, M., Mottet, L., & Anafi, M. (2016). *The report of the 2015 U.S. Transgender survey.* Washington, DC: National Center for Transgender Equality.
Kaplan, L. S., & Geoffroy, K. E. (1993). Copout or burnout? Counseling strategies to reduce stress in gifted students. *The School Counselor, 40*(4), 247–252.
Kincaid, A. P., & Sullivan, A. L. (2017). Parsing the relations of race and socioeconomic status in special education disproportionality. *Remedial and Special Education, 38*(3), 159–170.
Kosciw, J. G., Greytak, E. A., Zongrone, A. D., Clark, C. M., & Truong, N. L. (2018). *The 2017 national school climate survey: The experiences of lesbian, gay, bisexual, transgender, and queer youth in our nation's schools.* New York, NY: GLSEN.
Krashen, S. D. (1987). *Principles and practice in second language acquisition.* Upper Saddle River, NJ: Prentice-Hall International.
Krashen, S. D. (1988). *Second language acquisition and second language learning.* Upper Saddle River, NJ: Prentice-Hall International.
Ladd, H. F., & Fiske, E. B. (Eds.). (2008). *Handbook of research in education finance and policy.* New York, NY: Routledge.
Le Peletier, M. (1791). *Report on the draft penal code.* Retrieved from https://criminocorpus.org/en/exhibitions/death-penalty/history-death-penalty-france-1789-1981/debate-national-constituent-assembly/
McIntyre, A. (1984). *After virtue: A study in moral theory* (2nd ed.). Notre Dame, IN: University of Notre Dame Press.
Michael-Chadwell, S. (2010). Examining the underrepresentation of underserved students in gifted program from a transformational leadership vantage point. *Journal for the Education of the Gifted, 34*(1), 99–130.
Moore-Partin, T. C., Robertson, R. E., Maggin, D. M., Oliver, R. M., & Wehby, J. H. (2010). Using teacher praise and opportunities to respond to promote appropriate student behavior. *Preventing School Failure, 54*(3), 172–178.
Moorhead, L. (2018). LGBTQ+ visibility in the K-12 curriculum. *Phi Delta Kappan, 100*(2), 22–26.
National Association of School Psychologists. (2014). *Who are school psychologists?* Bethesda, MD: Author.
National Association of School Psychologists. (2016a). *ESSA and multi-tiered systems of support for school psychologists.* Bethesda, MD: Author.

National Association of School Psychologists. (2016b). *Safe and supportive schools for LGBTQ+ students*. Bethesda, MD: Author.

Nellis, L. M., Sickman, L. S., Newman, D. S., & Harman, D. R. (2014). Schoolwide collaboration to prevent and address reading difficulties: Opportunities for school psychologists and speech-language pathologists. *Journal of Educational and Psychological Consultation, 24*, 110–127.

Nevada Association of School Psychologists. (2016). *Statewide survey for read by grade 3*. Unpublished raw data.

Nevada Association of School Psychologists. (2018). *Notes from a presentation to the clark county school district board of trustees meeting*. Las Vegas, NV: Nevada Association of School Psychologists.

O'Connor, R. E., Bocian, K. M., Sanchez, V., & Beach, K. D. (2012). Access to a responsiveness to intervention model: Does beginning intervention in kindergarten matter? *Journal of Learning Disabilities, 47*(4), 307–328.

Payne, B. K., & Vuletich, H. A. (2017). Policy insights from advances in implicit bias research. *Policy Insight from the Behavioral and Brain Sciences*. doi:10.1177/2372732217746190

Peterson, J. S. (2006). Addressing counseling needs of gifted students. *Professional School Counseling, 10*(1), 43–51.

Pieretti, R. A., & Roseberry-McKibbin, C. (2015). Assessment and intervention for English language learners with primary language impairment. *Communication Disorders Quarterly, 37*(2), 117–128.

Robison, S., Jaggers, J., Rhodes, J., Blackmon, B. J., & Church, W. (2016). Correlates of educational success: Predictors of school dropout and graduation for urban students in the Deep South. *Children and Youth Services Review, 73*, 37–46.

Sadowski, M. (2016, Winter). More than a safe place: How schools can enable LGBTQ students to thrive. *American Educator*, 4–42.

Savage, T. A., Springborg, H., & Lagerstrom, L. (2017). An environmental scan tool to assess district and school readiness to support transgender and gender diverse youth. *Communiqué, 46*(1), 14.

Schonert-Reichl, K. A. (2017). Social emotional learning and teachers. *The Future of Children, 27*(1), 137–155.

Senate Bill 48, California 2011.

Sheftall, A. H., Asti, L., Horowitz, L. M., Felts, A., Fontanella, C. A., Campo, J. V., & Bridge, J. A. (2016). Suicide in elementary school-aged children and early adolescents. *Pediatrics, 138*(4). doi:10.1542/peds.2016-0436

Shinn, M. R. (2007). Identifying students at risk, monitoring performance, and determining eligibility within RTI: Research on educational need and benefit from academic intervention. *School Psychology Review, 36*(4), 601–617.

Shinn, M. R., & Walker, H. M. (Eds.). (2010). *Interventions academic and behavior problems in a three-tier model, including response-to-intervention*. Bethesda, MD: National Association of School Psychologists.

Shriberg, D. (2016). Commentary: School psychologists as advocates for racial justice and social justice: Some proposed steps. *School Psychology Forum, 10*(3), 337–339.

Shriberg, D., & Clinton, A. (2016). The application of social justice principles to global school psychology practice. *School Psychology International, 37*(4), 323–339.

Shriberg, D., Song, S. Y., Miranda, A. H., & Radliff, K. M. (2013). *School psychology and social justice: Conceptual foundations and tools for practice*. New York, NY: Routledge.

Shriberg, D., Wynne, M. E., Briggs, A., Bartucci, G., & Lombardo, A. C. (2011). School psychologists' perspectives on social justice. *School Psychology Forum, 5*(2), 37–53.

Siegle, D., Gubbins, E. J., O'Rourke, P., Langley, S. D., Mun, R. U., Luria, S. R., . . . Knupp, T. (2016). Barriers to underserved students' participation in gifted programs and possible solutions. *Journal for the Education of the Gifted, 39*(2), 103–131.

Simonton, D. K. (2009). Applying the psychology of science to the science of psychology: Can psychologists use psychological science to enhance psychology as a science? *Perspectives on Psychological Science, 4*(1), 2–4.

Sink, C. A. (2016). Incorporating a multi-tiered system of supports into school counselor preparation. *The Professional Counselor, 6*(3), 203–219.

Sprick, R. A. (2009). *CHAMPS: A proactive and positive approach to classroom management* (2nd ed.). Eugene, OR: Pacific Northwest Publishing.

Sprick, R. A. (2013). *Discipline in the secondary classroom: A positive approach to behavior management* (3rd ed.). Hoboken, NJ: John Wiley & Sons, Inc.

Staats, C., Capatosto, K., Wright, R. A., & Contractor, D. (2015). *State of the science: Implicit bias review 2015*. Columbus, OH: The Kirwan Institute for the Study of Race and Ethnicity.

Sullivan, A. L. (2011). Disproportionality in special education identification and placement of English language learners. *Exceptional Children, 77*(3), 317–334.

Tashman, W., & Song, S. (2018, February). *Websites and waiting rooms: Heteronormative discourse in school psychology services*. Practitioner conversation session presented at the annual convention of the National Association of School Psychologists, Chicago, IL.

Taylor, R. D., Oberle, E., Durlak, J. A., & Weissberg, R. P. (2017). Promoting positive youth development through school-based social and emotional learning interventions: A meta-analysis of follow-up effects. *Child Development, 88*(4), 1–16.

Verdugo, R. R. (2002). Race-ethnicity, social class, and zero-tolerance policies: The cultural and structural wars. *Education and Urban Society, 35*(1), 50–75.

Chapter 8

Early Childhood Recommendations

Key Terms

Teacher–Student Relationships
Intermediate Organizations
Decentralized
Early Childhood Curriculum Standards
Early Childhood Program Standards
Early Childhood MTSS

Chapter Concepts

In this chapter, readers will learn:

1. Long-term benefits for students who participate in early childhood programming.
2. How family structures contribute to the success and outcomes of early childhood students.
3. Potential barriers to early childhood programming and possible opportunities to overcome them.
4. Suggested nationally recommended early childhood curriculum standards and program standards.
5. How to integrate early childhood programming within the MTSS framework.
6. How to structure Early Childhood MTSS supports on an elementary or community school campus.

Supporting Multi-Tiered Systems of Support (MTSS) in early childhood is just as important as in grade school but is rarely recognized by state policy and school district practices. Indeed, early childhood should be considered not only a crucial part of Tier I academic and social-emotional-behavioral instruction for children ages 3 to 5, but a universal right of all children, laying the foundation to the success of a child's education. Depending on the state, education for young children may not be as specific as ages 3 to 5 and will cover young children from birth to age 8 (National Association for the Education of Young Children, 2009). When considering developmentally appropriate practice, there are three core factors: knowing about child development and learning, knowing what is individually appropriate, and knowing what is culturally appropriate. Within these domains, educators are regularly "(1) creating a caring community of learners, (2) teaching to enhance development and learning, (3) planning curriculum to achieve important goals, (4) assessing children's development and learning, and (5) establishing reciprocal relationships with families" (National Association for the Education of Young Children, 2009, p. 16).

Research clearly indicates the benefits of early childhood to include higher rate of school readiness for children entering kindergarten, improved social skills and resilience in later grades, and higher high school graduation rates compared to students who did not receive early childhood instructional opportunities (Bakken, Brown, & Downing, 2017; Schanzenbach & Bauer, 2016). Providing appropriate early childhood learning experiences for our youngest citizens has long-term benefits, especially in children from economically disadvantaged homes, including outperforming a matched control group on fourth-grade reading and math assessments, higher attendance rates, fewer discipline referrals, and significantly better social aptitude including more appropriate behaviors, social interactions, and emotional maturity (Bakken et al., 2017). The costs associated with providing free public early childhood as a society far outweigh the costs of remediating academic and social skills deficits in later grades, which contributes to the school-to-prison pipeline, especially in areas of high poverty and communities of color. In a study of prison inmates, the average response rate for those who had experienced adverse childhood experiences (ACEs) before the age of 18 was significantly greater than the response rate for those who experienced ACEs within the nonincarcerated population (Stensrud, Gilbride, & Bruinekool, 2018).

International research has confirmed the benefits of early childhood education to counter risk factors and increase protective factors in students (Centre for Community Child Health, 2000). Significant risk factors that impact students' long-term success include

> perinatal stress; difficult temperament; poor attachment; harsh parenting, abuse or neglect; parental mental illness or substance abuse; family disharmony, conflict or violence; low socioeconomic status; and poor links with the community. Important protective factors include: easy temperament; at least average intelligence; secure attachment to family; family harmony; supportive relationships with other adults; and community involvement. (p. 1)

Studies consistently report the benefits and cost-effectiveness of early childhood programs designed to target cognitive skills and preschool readiness, health and nutrition, caregiver and family education programs, community-based programs and outreach, and early intervention targeting family outcomes for children with delays in comparison to more expensive interventions in later development (Cascio, 2019; Bakken et al., 2017). In addition to improved behavior, long-term educational outcomes, and decreased incarceration rates, early childhood intervention programs also demonstrate economic benefits as well. "Well-designed early childhood interventions have been found to generate a return to society ranging from $1.80 to $17.07 for each dollar spent on the program" (Karoly, Kilburn, & Cannon, 2005, p. 1). Positive *teacher–student relationships* can help fuel the efforts of even the youngest students who can persist despite challenges and are resilient in times of adversity when the right level of support.

Enveloping the family in community and providing support to caregivers and the entire family, not only the young child, is critical. This is especially true in low-income, ethnically diverse families where the parenting profile of the caregiver can predict the student's likelihood of success in early childhood (Iruka, Jones-Harden, Bingham, Esteraich, & Green, 2018). Several caregiver factors contribute to this predictivity including family status, home language, maternal age, level of education, school/training status, and depressive symptomatology. Depending on the combination of these factors, the caregiver would fall into one of four categories: (1) low-enrichment, conflict-oriented, and distressed parent; (2) average-enrichment, conflict-oriented, and distressed parent; (3) low- to average-enrichment, emotionally close, and low distressed parent; and (4) high-enrichment, emotionally close, and low-distress parent. Students from families in category 4 had the highest predictive success and greatest outcomes in preschool (Iruka et al., 2018).

Research also emphasizes the relationship between class size and low student-to-teacher ratios to best improve cognitive and academic outcomes in early childhood students, with greatest benefits realized in classes with 15 students or less or in classes with a 7.5:1 or lower student-to-teacher ratio (Bowne, Magnuson, Schindler, Duncan, & Yoshikawa, 2017). In addition to appropriate class sizes and student-to-teacher ratios, factors such as the quality of the program and the use of evidence-based instructional curriculum also had an impact on the success of early childhood students.

Using a community-based approach to early childhood is extremely effective and can have a positive impact on prenatal to postnatal development, including prenatal health care, nutrition, immunizations, proactive parenting skills, daily and bedtime routines, language modeling, and behavior reinforcement in the home. Effective early childhood programming was correlated with school-based outcomes, including a reduction in identification for special education, a reduction in retention in later grades, and positive effects on high school graduation rates (Bakken et al., 2017; Centre for Community Child Health, 2000). Components of a high-quality early childhood program should also include curriculum taught by a licensed teacher with an endorsement in early childhood, use of developmentally appropriate screeners and assessments, and curriculum should be culturally, linguistically, and developmentally appropriate. Some of the most popular early childhood curriculum models have included the Montessori Method, the Bank Street Developmental Interaction Approach, High/Scope Curriculum, and the Dodge Creative Curriculum. Some curricula are highly structured with little room for flexibility while other programs have fundamental guidelines that teachers can choose the methods to teach best. The Reggio Emilia approach is an example that aligns well with MTSS in that instruction is informed by practice, experimentation, and feedback looping. The Perry Preschool Program has been found to be highly successful in teaching socialization.

Kindergarten has become mandatory in many states and is often the first exposure of children to a school setting. Over the past 20 years, curricula have been pushed down onto preceding grades, putting more pressure of higher developmental expectations to be taught to younger children, and kindergarten has become the new first grade. Kindergarten teachers are focusing more on advanced academics, standardized testing, and teacher-led discussions and less time on student-led activities, music, art, and play (Bassok, Latham, & Rorem, 2016). These often-unrealistic academic expectations have all but demolished the social model of kindergarten from years' past. Learning how to interact cooperatively with others has been the traditional model and aligned with the developmental skills of young students while exposure to academics was secondary to emotional regulation, friendship skills, and language and vocabulary development to provide the foundation for school success. While some benefits may be realized by exposing prekindergarten and kindergarten students to advanced academics, early academic experiences should be introduced proportionately with other developmental activities so as to not crowd out critical lifelong skills, such as social and emotional regulation, physical health, and cognitive reasoning (Bassok et al., 2016).

The benefits of early childhood programming are overwhelming, yet the public demand for universal early childhood education is tepid, and the costs to implement remain a significant barrier. This becomes an equity issue when children from higher socioeconomic status are all but assured access to high-quality early childhood learning experiences, tutoring, school preparation supports, technology, and environmental enrichment, whereas children of lower socioeconomic status have significantly fewer resources, experience barriers with transportation, do not have access to early childhood programs, or only have access to crowded or lower-quality early childhood programs, resulting in a lack of adequate exposure to school-readiness activities. Research on early childhood programs in impoverished and ethnically diverse neighborhoods indicates overwhelming support that early childhood improves school readiness and long-term outcomes for children (Bowman, Comer, & Johns, 2018).

Funding for early childhood programming, and education, in general, is highly complex and diverse across the country, even within states. Mainly, public early childhood programs receive braided funds from local, state, and federal governments depending on how their state's public school system is structured. They will then follow the regulations set forth from their corresponding licensing board. In some states, the Department of Education regulates education programs beginning in early childhood; however, in other states, community-based early childhood programs will fall under the jurisdiction of the state's Department of Health and Human Services (or similar department). Great variability can exist between the Department of Education and the Department of Health and Human Services regarding licensing requirements for early childhood teachers, teacher-to-student ratios, class size limits, and other regulatory requirements. *Educational achievement in the United State could be boosted through 12th grade if early childhood programs were universally available, properly funded, and adequately staffed.* Early childhood as a universal educational practice is gaining traction. It has taken decades for states to begin requiring that kindergarten-age students attend school, and most states still have not mandated education until a later age, such as age 7. Seventeen states, plus the District of Columbia, have some version of compulsory kindergarten attendance laws, the remaining 33 do not (Education Commission of the States, 2018).

Some school districts are largely tied to local property taxes with the wealthier neighborhood schools better funded than the lower socioeconomic status schools. Many charter schools and private early childhood programs tend to be located in suburban or higher-socioeconomic neighborhoods where families can afford the tuition, accommodate for transportation, and provide meals. This leads to inequities of access, programming, and services offered. To compound the problem, a high proportion of minority children and those learning English as a second language are living in poverty with their chances for upward mobility diminishing as schools in impoverished neighborhoods decrease in number and quality. These inequities lead to pervasive segregation. Early education opportunities should not be restricted to a particular demographic or community; rather, high-quality public preschool should increase dramatically across the board to make a greater impact and produce greater long-term outcomes for all our students.

Nationally, licensed and nonlicensed early childhood teachers tend to earn less money than their elementary- and secondary-level peers (U.S. Department of Education, 2016). With 97% of early childhood teachers being female, this also creates economic inequity between men and women (U.S. Department of Health and Human Services & U.S. Department of Education, 2016). These entrenched issues create inequities not only within the profession but also within the communities in which the schools serve. Low pay has an impact on the early childhood program's ability to attract and retain highly qualified staff and those with higher levels of training and education (U.S. Department of Education, 2016). Difficulties of recruitment, retention, and compensation all stand to have an impact on the quality of services the early childhood programs are able to provide.

How early childhood programs use their available human capital and allocate physical resources can help stretch limited resources and improve efficiency. Allocating resources to address the needs of an early childhood community using the MTSS framework can address equity issues by tackling access to appropriate levels of services depending on the needs of the child. At-risk early childhood programming's Tier 1 must include services touching on all of Maslow's hierarchy. Families living in poverty will have a greater number of children requiring support to have their basic needs met, in addition to a higher number of children living with issues such as trauma, parent incarceration, homelessness, and the higher risk of more adverse childhood experiences. Child refugees are also a special population of early childhood children who have been found to greatly benefit from early childhood programming to address their psychosocial needs, boost resilience, and remediate effects of trauma (Murray, 2019). Providing universal early childhood to all families is a highly supported evidence-based practice. In addition, resource mapping to better provide easy access to wraparound services includes health services, nutrition and food assistance, clothing, housing, and family counseling services for families that can bridge partnerships between community services, schools, and families to strengthen the bonds in the community.

While many cultures allow their youngest children to develop at their own pace, culture in the United States tends to accelerate expectations to obtain unrealistic developmental learning standards, which is not developmentally appropriate for all children. As we put more pressure on young children to read and perform on tests earlier, we are robbing them of crucial experiences that will help them learn to identify and regulate their emotions to become better able to cope with life's challenges. What early childhood curriculum should look like, and how academically proficient children should strive for are subject to debate. Harmful effects of pushing academics too early in young children when they are not ready to handle it emotionally could include anxiety, frustration, defiance, and avoidance of academic tasks that could last into later years, impacting attitude and effort. Some children may learn to read at age four, but the majority of children do not. It is not good practice to measure the success of early childhood students by academic growth that is not aligned with age-appropriate developmental indicators and is setting them up for feelings of failure and frustration when there is no need to create such stress so early in their educational careers. With the influx of aggressive marketing in commercials, mainstream media stations, and social media targeting the public's perception of appropriate toddler development and early learning, caregivers are questioning whether their very young children have learning disabilities from toddlerhood, where reading, math, and writing are the exception, not the norm. High ideals that are not connected with developmental milestone expectations can be the first step on the slippery slope of creating stress and anxiety in very young children, who benefit most from organic learning opportunities in the environment, language and music enrichment, social play with peers, and exposure to early academic skills, not requirement of mastery.

Children in early childhood benefit from exploration, multisensory learning experiences, social interactions with peers, and play-based activities to help them engage in developing a sense of self and to negotiate cooperative play with others. The value of play in early childhood cannot be underestimated (Hassinger-Das, Hirsh-Pasek, & Golinkoff, 2017). Children given access to play opportunities in early childhood were much more likely to demonstrate better classroom behavior in later grades. Of course, many educational factors contribute to long-term success in school. If students received prekindergarten education, participated in a social-emotional learning curriculum, had strong school–family engagement, or received primary intervention supports, they are more likely to experience success at the secondary level (Project AWARE Ohio, 2017; Williams, Landry, Anthony, Swank, & Crawford, 2012). Even in schools that support early childhood programs, early childhood is the most vulnerable to cuts in funding and increases for class size because there are no hard-and-fast rules and regulations supporting high-quality standards for early childhood nationally.

Due to the variability in early childhood funding from one school district to another, and early childhood being a privilege for some and not others, it is not surprising that early childhood is not considered as part of most schools' MTSS. However, it may be the most obvious, yet overlooked, Tier 1 component that could have the strongest long-term outcome for students in a school community. Strong and cohesive leadership across all levels, school, district, and state, is required for comprehensive support for MTSS structures and functions to ensure optimal elementary school student outcomes. Research on implementation of Early Childhood MTSS is becoming more prevalent and, in addition to this textbook, resources to guide teams on effective implementation are available (Carta & Young, 2019). Data suggest that strong state leadership and district-level systems that actively require accountability for administrators in the context of achieving MTSS framework benchmarks have a higher probability that funding, resources, and manpower will go toward evidence-based practices within MTSS. MTSS frameworks must have strong leadership at the district level to increase accountability and implementation fidelity (Freeman, Miller, & Newcomer, 2015). States and school districts without mandated and defined student improvement frameworks will be less likely to devote human capital, professional development, and investments in systematic processes for problem identification, intervention implementation, and progress monitoring (Morningstar et al., 2016; Masters, 2010).

Six Opportunities

Key barriers are evident as teams hurdle over the obstacles of addressing early childhood through an Early Childhood MTSS framework, on their elementary school campuses, and in their communities. With each hurdle comes the opportunity to reflect and revise the implementation process, including perceptions and metrics for measuring success. Six barriers and corresponding opportunities are present and include inclusion, state and district policies, federal law, funding, standards, and unions.

1. Inclusion

Hosting an early childhood program open to all community members is an incredibly inclusive concept. Data indicate that varying degrees of parent education contributes to early childhood attendance rates across the country:

> In 2017, the percentage of 3- to 5-year olds enrolled in preschool programs was higher for children whose parents' highest level of education was a graduate or professional degree (46 percent) or a bachelor's degree (47 percent) than for children whose parents' highest level of education was an associate's degree (36 percent), some college but no degree (34 percent), a high school credential (33 percent), or less than a high school credential (26 percent).
> (National Center for Education Statistics, 2019, p. 1)

Within these subsets, the quality and duration of the programming can also greatly differ. As the number of children who live in high-poverty neighborhoods increases, preschool opportunities are diminished and waiting lists for Head Start programs become long, making preschool inaccessible for many of our most vulnerable children. In certain urban and rural school districts, free preschool is only funded federally through the Individuals with Disabilities Education Act (IDEA, 2004), and parents must obtain an evaluation for special education resulting in the identification of developmental delays or another IDEA disability to get federally funded early interventions. This can lead to the overidentification of students for special education, especially those from ethnically diverse backgrounds.

Students can currently qualify for special education supports from birth to age 3 under Part C of IDEA and from the ages of 3 through 21 under Part B of IDEA. However, typically developing children also benefit from structured learning opportunities at all ages. School districts with limited early intervention services offered through Parts B and C of IDEA will struggle with equity in providing timely services to children with developmental challenges. Some families report feeling that they have been put in a morally compromising position to share truthfully about their children reaching developmental milestones during an early childhood special education evaluation in order to qualify for federally and state-funded early childhood programs. While they feel strongly that their child would benefit from early childhood programming, there are limited feasible options outside of early childhood special education and their child would not otherwise have access to early learning opportunities unless they qualify. Funding universal early childhood programs could alleviate overcrowding of IDEA-funded early childhood programs, though the high-quality instruction offered should be indistinguishable between the two program types.

Box 8.1

Voices From the Field

Ms. Washington is an expert early childhood teacher at a Title I elementary school. She is the designated lead general education teacher in a fully integrated early childhood and early childhood special education program. She shares teaching responsibilities with a licensed special education teacher and four instructional assistants. There are two large classrooms connected by open doors and bathrooms in between. Each room is segmented into distinct stations that children rotate throughout the day independently and as part of lesson plans. The space is highly organized and sectioned off with cubby cabinets and artificial barriers. The learning stations across the two rooms include (1) a living room with a library; (2) a math center with shapes and blocks embedded into fine-motor activities of building and creating; (3) a science center with exploration materials; (4) an engineering center with blocks, house construction materials, and toy furnishings; (5) a home–school connection center for clothes, play food kitchen, dress-up costumes; (6) an academic center with desks and a chalkboard resembling an elementary classroom; (7) a play area with dolls, toys, and games; (8) an open space for circle time; and (9) a table for snacks and meals. The structure of the classrooms creates the sense of continuity from one room to the next, as the program is designed to do. The special education students and early childhood students are engaged in a fully inclusive teaching environment.

The most remarkable thing about this early childhood program is that the teachers and teaching assistants are indefinable. There is such dynamic support among staff that they are virtually synchronized in their efforts. The teachers frequently and fluidly switch rooms, as do the assistants. Ms. Washington attributes that to them all being trained as safe professionals. The team of teachers and assistants plan all their lesson plans together from the very beginning of the school year. They use "The Solution Toolbox" from the Technical Assistance Center on Social Emotional Intervention with all forms available from the Center on the Social and Emotional Foundations for Early Learning (CSEFEL) website. CSEFEL is funded by the Office of Head Start and the Child Care Bureau and serves as a national resource center to disseminate research and evidence-based practices to early childhood programs across the country. CSEFEL uses the Pyramid Model for Supporting Social Emotional Competence in Infants and Young Children and directly aligns with MTSS. Teachers and assistants report liking the statewide framework for supporting equitable, rich learning environments for children, and they report that the best of evidence-based curricula had been selected. The assistants and teachers conduct all their behavioral planning together, and they all wear necklaces with a ring of teach-and-train pictures and concepts to remind students of behavioral expectations with consistent language and visual cues. The teachers and the aides work so well together that it is impossible to identify teacher from the assistant.

As with any program, this highly effective early childhood program has its challenges. First of all, it is a full-day program. Ms. Washington is not sure that full-day early childhood is all it is cracked up to be. More early childhood programming, five hours of instruction versus two-and-a-half hours of instruction, does not mean better outcomes. Longer days for very young children may be too long of a day and may not be developmentally necessary to achieve the best outcomes. Another challenge is that being a part of the elementary school resources, assistants may be poached for other school duties, leaving fewer adults supervising the large early childhood classes. For example, three of the six adults in the early childhood program are used for covering supervision of the schools' three lunch periods for elementary-age students. It is impossible to staff all the stations with half the adults present in the program. The lunch duty also interferes with a common planning period for the teachers and assistants, creating barriers to plan together and solve problems for students as a team. They have no preparation period the way their days are currently scheduled. Last, because the program is scheduled five full days a week, there is less time for family outreach and holding meetings with families for parent–teacher conferences, resource seminars, and special education meeting times during school hours.

Teachers worry that staff and resources will be cut from the program in the near future, as school district resources are geared toward improving school ratings and funding early childhood is less of a priority because early childhood students are not immediately contributing to the high-stakes test scores for school ratings. Despite all the barriers, Ms. Washington and her team love their jobs and make the most out of their program. In doing so, they provide incredible learning opportunities for the children and their families and set successes in motion for the future. A seedling with the right amount of sunlight, nutrients, and community in the forest will make a strong tree.

Opportunities

Until there is a cohesive and coordinated push at the national level to improve funding for universal early childhood programming as an educational right, there must be a local push to provide local services to young children and their families (see next section on State and District Policies). Brainstorm ways to increase awareness and access. Build a coalition with stakeholders. Create community events and recruit volunteers to increase the visibility and viability of early childhood activities and instructional opportunities. Find opportunities to incorporate inclusive materials into new or existing programming. For example, when planning inclusive school programs, schools need to ensure inclusivity of *all* families and have materials available to the children that represent the diversity of the families that they serve and who identify as LGBTQ+ or as coming from various cultures, ethnicities, or adoptive statuses (Frost & Goldberg, 2019).

2. State and District Policies

School practices often start at the state level with a policy that gets translated into a procedure at the district level and then carried out within some sort of program at the school level. At each level of bureaucracy, there are many different interpretations and attempts to implement the policy into a meaningful practice that accurately reflects the policy as written. Rarely does a policy get written as initially intended, there are too many competing influences and agendas. Compounding the policy-making process, potential landmines to negotiate around are the *intermediate organizations* that "operate between policymakers and implementers to affect changes in roles and practices for both parties" (Honig, 2004, p. 65). These intermediate organizations are typically not practitioners and their involvement can either impede or facilitate implementation depending on resources and motivations. When their understanding of the structure or subject matter is comprehensive and they have genuine motives for the policy's development, the intermediate organization will most likely be a helpful organization. However, if the intermediate organization is looking out for the best interest of their clients, not children or educators, they will most likely be a hindrance, especially if they have a lot of financial backing and social clout. The autonomy of schools to problem solve rigid laws and policies, such as seat-time rules, teacher licensure, and early childhood opportunities, is essential, and these intermediaries may be allies to help a school's ability to operate outside the box. They may also be able to assist schools and policy makers in examining unlikely allies or unintended consequences that may be detrimental to students and communities.

Opportunities

State and district policies are in place to guide educators in best practices that keep them working in accordance with laws in terms of curriculum, high-stakes testing, grading, discipline practices, and special education practices to name a few. Most of the time policies make sense, guide educators in best practices, and protect student rights. Sometimes procedures may be perceived as laborious or overly oppressive because there is little wiggle room for deviation from specific situations. Other times, some policies make little sense to the educators tasked with enforcing them, and they seem like barriers to common sense. It is important for school administrators to respect the intent of laws on the books while looking for ways to grow supports and services that could be supported by other existing policies. Title I schools often have more flexibility in maneuvering through policy to find funding solutions for struggling students (offering early childhood programming and parenting classes, hosting school-based mental health clinics, and offering extended wraparound services). Where there is a will there is a way to help children get an appropriate education. Best practices must be lobbied into state, district, and school policies.

When state, district, and school policies (and budgets) are on target, administrators are able to maneuver deftly to cover student needs with resource allocation, scheduling, and educator training and support, which is the intent of many policies. When policies miss the target and create insurmountable obstacles to best practices and common sense, unforeseen consequences may arise that have a negative impact on educators and students alike. These situations can be hard to accept and can create activists out of constituents. Empowered educators and students speaking up for common good such as school safety and inclusiveness, is a by-product of policies infringing on student rights and the well-being of the school and school personnel. It is not only a right to speak out against misguided state, district, and school policies but also a growing responsibility for affected communities to challenge the status quo of lawmakers to make laws that do not align with evidence- and research-based practices. Oftentimes, these laws are made out of ignorance; however, there are times when laws are passed that primarily benefit special interest groups.

3. Federal Law

It behooves educators at all levels and professional domains to stay abreast of federal legislation. While this may seem like a daunting task, it must be done because dangerous landmines of special interests get hidden in policy that have devastating impacts on funding and direct services at schools nationwide. Given that students' lives are complex and mostly take place outside the sole context of the school setting, it is also imperative to monitor federal policies outside education to obtain a more comprehensive perspective on what challenges and opportunities influence our students. *Many of our students are not coming to school to thrive; they are coming to school just to survive.*

Despite threats to eliminate significant portions of funding for Education in the President's 2019 budget, along with proposed cuts to several Every Student Succeeds Act (2015) Title programs, Congress provided additional funding for Education, increasing the 2019 education budget by $2.6 billion to $70.9 billion (Ujifusa, 2018). For example, Title II—Preparing, Training, and Recruiting High Quality Teachers and Principals, Part A was threatened to be eliminated in its entirety at a price tag of $2.1 billion. This cut would have had a dramatic impact on the grants offered to states for collaboration and the professional learning time of teachers. Collaboration and professional learning are key contributors to educators honing and refining their craft (Loughran, 2014). Elimination of these funds had the potential to result in unintended consequences of decreased student performance across the board academically, socially, emotionally, and behaviorally.

Social-emotional-behavioral learning is a significant instructional component that schools should be implementing as part of their Tier 1 instruction; however, the majority of teachers feel ill prepared to do so. There is an obvious need for continuing staff development in social-emotional-behavioral learning in all schools. Joint collaborative time allows educators to share, reflect, and revise teaching practices to enhance the learning opportunities for students. Often, innovative practices emerge during these professional learning times, as less effective teaching practices are identified and new skills are developed and rehearsed to replace them. The world in which we live is constantly evolving, as are the needs of our students and the teachers who teach them. Educators' practices evolve when regularly structured opportunities are provided for the growth of relevant new professional skills in a supportive environment. Cutting collaboration and professional development time cuts off growth opportunities and learning experiences for teachers and students alike, resulting in lower-quality instruction for students and lower educational outcomes.

Looking outside of federal education legislation to legislation emerging from other federal departments is essential to understand the scope of how legislation and policies intimately impact students in schools on a daily basis. For example, student health care and access to health care providers are monumental issues for students, especially those who come from low-income homes. Funding for programs such as Medicaid and CHIP (Children's Health Insurance Program) through the Department of Health and Human Services, Centers for Medicare and Medicaid Services is critical for students obtaining basic health care, as they subsidize access to care so children can qualify for health services, regardless of their parents' financial or insurance status.

Attempts have been made to improve community-based mental and behavioral health supports and facilitate ease of access through policy. A promising bill recently died in Congress due to lack of support, sponsored by the Department of Health and Human Services, H.R. 3770: Community Health Investment, Modernization, and Excellence Act (2017). It would have legislated a community-based approached to address the whole child, which is essential to ensure children's basic needs are being met within all levels of the child, school, and community ecosystems. Common sense would dictate that all elementary schools are afforded a community-based health center that allows students access to health care and mental health care locally. The fewer barriers for access, including funding and transportation to service providers, the greater the probability students and their families will obtain the care they desperately need.

Opportunities

Being proactive is the best approach to any policy whether it be at the federal, state, or local levels. Contacting congressional representatives, building relationships with representatives and their staff, and staying abreast of proposed federal policy is ideal. There are even websites, such as congress.gov, that will track bills and provide subscribers with immediate updates if there are changes to a bill that is of interest. Each state government also has a similar tracking system that interested individuals can sign up for without cost.

For example, as of the writing this book, there are two bills in Congress that support increasing mental and behavioral supports in schools and, if resources were allocated for early childhood, would benefit early childhood populations as well as school-aged populations of students. If passed, the two bills would be referred to as the Increasing Access to Mental Health in Schools Act and the Mental Health in Schools Excellence Program Act and would put into federal law school-based mental health pipeline opportunities (see Chapter 10 for more information). These proposed federal programs are great opportunities for states and individual constituents to advocate and show their desire for additional access points of service delivery and for professionals to enter the school-based mental health pipeline that will eventually equate to greater supports for students.

However, instead of being proactive and staying on top of legislation, school-based teams most often find themselves responding in a reactive manner, especially to federal policy. In such cases, states, districts, and schools must accommodate the new federal policy and build it into their existing budgets, programs, and policies. This often includes a reduction in staff and the elimination of programs, including early childhood. As with the case for the proposed federal mental health initiatives, being proactive is always the best pathway and educators will know that they did their part in sharing their voice, for example, advocating for more school-based mental health professionals. Whether it be school-based mental health professionals, teachers, administrators, or community members, the field of education needs more experts and "early childhood professionals engaging in developmentally appropriate practices, and more policy makers establishing policies and committing public funds to support such practices" (NAEYC, 2009, p. 23).

4. Funding

With budget shortages in districts across the United States, the addition of remediation courses is not only a budgetary issue but a time-constraint issue (Odden & Picus, 2014; Odden, 2012). Given the various demands placed on administrators and their budgets, priority decisions must be made. Typically, early childhood staff and resources are the first to be eliminated from the master budget because early childhood is not nationally or locally recognized as mandatory for funding. For example, many districts have had to close early childhood programs, leaving those that remain overcrowded and lacking a broad spectrum of resources. It is common for elementary schools to use any opening in their master schedule or to use any additional funding to find ways to help credit deficient students retrieve credits in order to meet promotion requirements. Many school districts have also reduced or eliminated early childhood outside of special education requirements.

Opportunities

Budgets are getting tighter for education dollars, and the allocation of dollars does not always make sense to all schools. As schools' processes are more decentralized, individual schools have greater opportunity to make allocations based on need. *Decentralized* is the transfer of power and decision making from central government to local government. Underfunding remedial supports and developmentally appropriate early childhood programs threatens long-term student outcomes, which has real-life consequences for students and hampers their access and opportunity for success in life. Advocacy for policies and budgets to fund mental health, social-emotional-behavioral programs, universal early childhood, and academic services is paramount. Like an initial deposit in the bank, those investments earn interest and dividends by increasing student well-being and safety, civilized behavior and problem solving, and independent living skills (The Aspen Institute: National Commission on Social, Emotional, and Academic Development, 2018). Investing early in early learning programming on the front end pays dividends on the back end down the road as the student transitions into adulthood.

5. Standards

Each state or district may have its own unique set of guidance on what learning standards are essential for young students ages 3 to 5; however, common developmental standards should include the following broad categories: social and emotional development, language and literacy, cognition, and perceptual, motor, and physical development (U.S. Department of Health and Human Services, 2015). Early childhood programs that teach curriculum standards should also follow program standards to ensure that the highest quality programming is delivered to young students. *Early childhood curriculum standards* are the developmental and learning expectations that young children are typically expected to meet within a chronological age bracket. *Early childhood program standards* set the quality levels in a variety of domains to ensure specific criteria are maintained on behalf of young children. The 10 program standards needed to obtain Early Learning program accreditation by the world's largest organization of early childhood professionals, the National Association for the Education of Young Children (2018), include relationships; curriculum; teaching; assessment of child progress; health; staff competencies, preparation, and support; families; community relations; physical environment; and leadership and management.

Opportunities

Standards are largely dependent on the political pendulum from conservative to less conservative measures of success. The advantage of professionals advocating for early childhood programming is that there is abundant opportunity to build evidence- and research-based curriculum and program standards into state and district policies from the ground up. Get a hold of state early childhood curriculum standards and compare them with national recommended best practice. Do the same for early childhood program standards. Where do state and nationally recommended curriculum and program standards align? Where are they different? What opportunities exist to align and incorporate national best practice recommendations?

Sometimes, lobbyists and private interest groups may advocate for a corporate business model of early childhood programming and indoctrinate the public through media and politics, which influences educational policy (Cooper & Randall, 2008). They do so to maximize profit and benefits to their private interests and to avoid the same accountability standards they helped create, which ultimately skews the public's perception and destabilizes trust in public schools. This mistrust creates a "need" for more competition in the market from for-profit schools and results in labeling public schools as underperforming in comparison based on standards that are not evenly applied, nor outcomes measured by the same tools.

Standardized testing for federal and state accountability is a multibillion-dollar industry whose influence in educational policy should not be underestimated. As a result, knowing that minority, second-language students, and students living in poverty will not necessarily achieve on these measures, efforts have been made, with varying levels of success, to grade at-risk schools on the growth model instead of criterion-referenced tests using cutoff scores for failure. The growth model has traditionally been the metric for early childhood programming and should remain so. Now more than ever, stakeholders have the opportunity to publicly advocate for early childhood programming with MTSS as the foundational framework to elicit and capture growth, and with quality control measures in place such as program accountability standards. As it stands, demonstrating incremental growth only goes so far in public opinion and policy is slow to catch up with best practices when it goes against public sentiment. Realistically, high-stakes tests are not going away and students need both test-taking skills as well as content knowledge ability, in addition to critical thinking skills. Rather than teach to the test, which has resulted in narrow standards and policies, it is important to grow resilient lifelong learners wherever their starting points are. The growth model is embedded in the function of MTSS, which can capture outcomes that inform data-based decision making and implementation feedback looping where high-stakes testing cannot.

6. Unions

Teachers' unions are under attack across the country, and the most influential unions are coming from large urban districts with hard to staff schools and less inviting work conditions (Fowles & Cowen, 2014). As teachers' working conditions, health insurance, and other monetary and nonmonetary benefits are disintegrating, and private interests are aggressively pushing legislatively to take public monies from public school funding equations, teachers are starting to push back as their livelihoods and professional duties depend on it. Teachers are entitled to a modicum of working conditions including scheduling that allows for "duty-free" preparation time and time to complete duties that do not involve direct teaching. Successful MTSS implementation not only requires flexibility in teaching standards but also includes creative scheduling and off-ratio teaching blocks to fit more relevant opportunities in the school day for students to get the remedial instruction they need while not losing out on required credit-bearing classes. Educators must be compensated for additional work hours, and most will be amenable to schedules that benefit students without infringing on their rights to breaks in the day and duty-free professional time.

While teachers' unions may be perceived as an obstacle with regard to scheduling, they serve to represent the teachers in this area by ensuring that the teachers are receiving their certain number of minutes a week of duty-free preparation time. This representation has proved to benefit not only the teachers but student achievement outcomes as well (Vachon & Ma, 2015). Scheduling priorities and demands are a constant struggle on a secondary campus; even with a modified block and extended class periods, it does little to reduce the ever-increasing curricular demands.

Opportunities

Teachers' unions and administrative unions have a vested interest in meeting the needs of students. The profession of teaching is under siege and entities outside of the education establishment are trying to seize public funding of education and privatize it to maximize profit. The only outcome measure that should be counted is student success. While *success* is a relative and widely debated term, it is still the primary outcome. Unions should focus on the well-being and health of teachers and administrators to nurture and care for children. In the coming technological age, where computers can store information, our children need to learn how to process information to understand meaningful relationships, solve problems, and exchange solutions in the context of becoming contributing members of society. Unions need to protect teaching positions with competitive pay and compensation packages, safe working conditions, safe learning conditions, and advocating for funding curriculum supports that meet the needs of all learners and compensates educators fairly. Teaching may be coming full circle back to the Socratic Method, or cooperative debate, in addition to utilizing technology advancements of our time.

Early Childhood MTSS Structure

MTSS in early childhood can be structured, with resources allocated to tiers of support, just as any other grade level within the elementary school. *Early Childhood MTSS* is the framework in which to provide young students and families with layers of supports at the student's developmental level. Given the young ages and developmental levels of the children, a comprehensive Early Childhood MTSS framework can be applied that addresses a variety of domains. Foundational to all support tiers within the multi-tiered system is an Effective Workforce (CSEFEL, 2018). Without adequate human capital, no MTSS would be able to get off the ground. After ensuring the subterranean foundational support of an Effective Workforce, the first layer (Tier 1) of support combines Nurturing and Responsive Relationships and High Quality Supporting Environments (CSEFEL, 2018). The second layer (Tier 2) is Targeted Social Emotional Supports while the top layer (Tier 3) is Intensive Intervention (CSEFEL, 2018).

Once an early childhood program has been established within the elementary school, a variety of pressures on kindergarten and first grades are reduced, including academic and language readiness as well as social-emotional-behavioral performance, because the students will have had the benefit of an additional year of educational learning experiences.

Quarterly universal screenings in early childhood can occur at the class level using a framework or developmental rubric to identify strengths and weaknesses in the eight Head Start Early Learning Outcomes domains with indicators for young children ages 36 months to 60 months of age (U.S. Department of Health and Human Services, 2015). The timing and sequence of developmental milestones will help determine the best learning experiences and needs of the student at the time of the screening and within a particular domain (Yates et al., 2008). While not a diagnostic tool, the use of a framework or developmental rubric or appropriate screening tool may provide guidance as to students who may appear to have significant developmental issues or require community interventions to address basic needs. Again, the core eight areas to address and screen for in an early childhood curriculum include social skills, emotional development, language and literacy skills, cognition, perceptual development, motor skills, and physical development (U.S. Department of Health and Human Services, 2015). Once students have been screened and strengths and weaknesses have been identified, the prioritization of each individual student's needs, and each corresponding goal, can occur, and targeted interventions can be matched to skills' deficits across developmental domains.

Early childhood should be considered the universal Tier 1 for all students, not just those with privilege, disadvantage, or those identified with disabilities. At Tier 1, universal early childhood should include a high-quality supportive environment with a nurturing and responsive environment (CSEFEL, 2018). Screenings are required to help identify children who are not adequately responding to Tier 1 opportunities and fall below chronological developmental according to the Head Start Early Learning Outcomes framework (U.S. Department of Health and Human Services, 2015) or similar developmental rubric. Early Childhood MTSS can provide opportunities to intervene early with all students, and can eventually help support identification of those who would benefit from an individualized family service plan, an individualized education program (IEP), or 504 plan, if warranted. Tier 2 supports would systemically identify students in need of intensified opportunities for small-group practice of social and emotional skill development, language and literacy rehearsal, cognition and reasoning, and perceptual, physical, and fine and gross motor development. Tier 3 supports should be offered to students on an individual basis as a tertiary intervention (National Center for Pyramid Model Innovations, 2018) and should focus on addressing skill deficits using targeted assessment tools if the deficits are suspected to be environmental in nature versus a manifestation of an underlying disability. For students not suspected of having a disability, these individual and intensive interventions should be met with incremental progress when provided with regular opportunities to have the desired skills modeled, guided, and rehearsed. Tier 3 supports should also envelop the family and include them in the intervention planning.

For students who are suspected of having a disability, the students should be referred for a special education evaluation congruently while receiving Tier 3 supports and, if eligible, could receive these Tier 3 supports as part of their IEPs. Clear procedures for what is a suspected environmental difference and what is a disability difference should be outlined for staff to avoid the overreferral, and potential overidentification, of young children with disabilities. However, when disabilities are clearly suspected, referrals should not be delayed. Specialized staff such as speech and language therapists, occupational therapists, physical therapists, and school psychologists are just a few of the professions that may be needed to support these Tier 3 young children with disabilities and schools can recoup some of the costs under the IDEA or by billing Medicaid. These financial components are realities and can support students who require their services as outlined in their IEPs.

Therefore, providing universal early learning experiences for young children will reduce school failure and increase long-term outcomes for students. Also, identifying students with special needs in early childhood and providing them with special education support leads to better outcomes for young children with identified delays. Early childhood supports all students and provides opportunities to identify and remediate developmental and environmental delays early in students' educational careers, leading to less expensive and intensive interventions and to greater successes in later grades. Early childhood teachers follow similar procedures that the rest of elementary MTSS follows, including screening their students, identifying individual needs, setting unique goals, collecting data, monitoring progress, and reviewing their students' progress at iterative cycles.

Support for the classroom teacher is another significant component of Early Childhood MTSS. Depending on the school and district, many individuals may play a role and have responsibilities to coach classroom teachers within this framework, including principal, assistant principal, a behavior coach, an instructional coach, or a site supervisor (Lemmer & Roberts, 2015). Coaching includes a preconference, coaching method/collecting data, and postconference. The coaching focus may include areas such as classroom behavior management, curriculum content, instructional delivery, or assessment and data collection. Throughout all phases of program implementation, iterative feedback looping on program effectiveness, and the response of the teacher to coaching supports, school leadership remains an integral component to the success of Early Childhood MTSS (Lemmer & Roberts, 2015).

The best remedy to specific site-based challenges is the development and support of highly trained educators to actively solve problems in smart teams; educators with specialties and subspecialties operationalizing problems, targeting evidence-based supports depending on needs of students and availability of resources at the school and in the community, and monitoring outcomes. Supports can be streamlined or structured uniquely depending on the school, as reflected by team decisions by major stakeholders. As explained in previous chapters, the more students there are on a campus, the more organized and automated processes have to be for MTSS practices to be effective and sustainable. The more staff members who are actively engaged in the culture of team collaboration and data-based decision making, the more efficient all processes will be within MTSS. Early Childhood MTSS can be reviewed systematically and iteratively using a framework such as the Preschool Program Quality Assessment (2003) to inform the capacity and improvement of the program in a variety of domains.

Lower-risk schools may not have as many students requiring intensified early childhood supports; however, they will still have students that require supports to achieve at developmentally appropriate levels. Even though lower-risk schools do not often have the intensity or frequency of issues higher-risk schools have, lower-risk schools still have at-risk and high-risk students to take into consideration and would also benefit from sticking to the MTSS recipe on a smaller scale. It would be an oversight to view teacher coaching, team development, and regular meetings as unnecessary in lower-risk and smaller schools because systematic team processes catch the students who may not succeed otherwise. Once automated, reviewing student data as a team and making data-based decisions for students takes less planning and preparation because the process of doing so becomes second nature and becomes institutionalized in the Early Childhood MTSS functioning.

Exercise 8.1

Early Childhood MTSS Implementation Considerations

- List the primary barriers to the implementation of early childhood on your elementary or community school campus.
- List the secondary barriers to the implementation of early childhood on your elementary or community school campus.
- Identify which mileposts of the Early Childhood MTSS framework appear most feasible in the short-term.
- Identify which mileposts of the Early Childhood MTSS framework are more feasible to build out in the longer term.
- Identify curriculum standards.
- Identify program standards.
- Identify evidence-based Tier 1 curriculum.
- Identify ways to make the curriculum and programming inclusive for all families.
- Identify universal benchmarking tool(s).
- Identify Tier 2 supports.
- Identify Tier 3 supports.
- Identify family-centric supports at each tier.
- Triangulate data for deficit/problem-area identification.
- Grow a network of evidence-based interventions taught with fidelity by highly effective teachers.
- Put regularly scheduled meetings in the master schedule.
- Conduct regular, highly structured team meetings.
- Use data-based decision making.
- Ensure reliable, reciprocal communication within and without professional learning communities and with families.
- Engage in iterative program evaluation cycles.

References

The Aspen Institute: National Commission on Social, Emotional, and Academic Development. (2018). *How learning happens: Supporting students' social, emotional, and academic development.* Washington, DC: Author.

Bakken, L., Brown, N., & Downing, B. (2017). Early childhood education: The long-term benefits. *Journal of Research in Childhood Education, 31*(2), 255–269.

Bassok, D., Latham, S., & Rorem, A. (2016). Is kindergarten the new first grade? *AREA Open, 2*(1). Retrieved from https://journals.sagepub.com/doi/full/10.1177/2332858415616358

Bowman, B. T., Comer, J. P., & Johns, D. J. (2018). *Addressing the African American achievement gap: Three leading educators issue a call to action.* National Association for the Education of Young Children. Retrieved from www.naeyc.org/resources/pubs/yc/may2018/achievement-gap

Bowne, J. B., Magnuson, K. A., Schindler, H. S., Duncan, G. J., & Yoshikawa, H. (2017). A meta-analysis of class sizes and ratios in early childhood education programs: Are thresholds of quality associated with greater impacts on cognitive, achievement, and socioemotional outcomes? *Educational Evaluation and Policy Analysis, 39*(3), 407–428.

Carta, J. J., & Young, R. M. (Eds.). (2019). *Multi-tiered systems of support for young children: Driving change in early education*. Baltimore, MD: Brooks Publishing.

Cascio, E. U. (2019). *Does universal preschool hit the target? Program access and preschool impacts*. Dartmouth College. Retrieved from www.dartmouth.edu/~eucascio/cascio_prek_latest.pdf

Centre for Community Child Health. (2000). *A review of the early childhood literature*. Report prepared for the Australian Department of Family and Community Services. Retrieved from www.dss.gov.au/sites/default/files/documents/early_childhood.pdf

Center on the Social and Emotional Foundations for Early Learning. (2018). *The pyramid model for supporting social emotional competence in infants and young children*. Retrieved from http://csefel.vanderbilt.edu

Community Health Investment, Modernization, and Excellence Act of 2017, H.R. 3770, 115 Cong. (2017).

Cooper, B. S., & Randall, V. (2008). Fear and privatization. *Educational Policy, 22*(1), 204–227.

Education Commission of the States. (2018). *50-state comparison: State kindergarten-through-third grade policies*. Retrieved from www.ecs.org/kindergarten-policies/

Every Student Succeeds Act of 2015, 20 U.S.C. (2015).

Fowles, J., & Cowen, J. (2014). In the union now: Understanding public sector union membership. *Administration & Society, 47*(5), 574–595.

Freeman, R., Miller, D., & Newcomer, L. (2015). Integration of academic and behavioral MTSS at the district level using implementation science. *Learning Disabilities: A Contemporary Journal, 13*(1), 59–72.

Frost, R. L., & Goldberg, A. E. (2019). The ABCs of diversity and inclusion: Developing an inclusive environment for diverse families in early childhood education. *Zero to Three, 39*(3), 36–41.

Hassinger-Das, B., Hirsh-Pasek, K., & Golinkoff, R. M. (2017). *The case of brain science and guided play: A developing story*. National Association of Education for Young Children. Retrieved from www.naeyc.org/resources/topics/play

Honig, M. I. (2004). The new middle management: Intermediary organizations in education policy implementation. *Educational Evaluation and Policy Analysis, 26*(1), 65–87.

Individuals with Disabilities Education Act, 20 U.S.C. § 1400. (2004).

Iruka, I. U., Jones Harden, B. P., Bingham, G., Esteraich, J., & Green, S. (2018). Profiles of parenting for low-income families and links to children's preschool outcomes. *Early Education and Development, 29*(4), 515–539.

Karoly, L. A., Kilburn, R., & Cannon, J. S. (2005). *Proven benefits of early childhood interventions*. RAND Corporation. Retrieved from www.rand.org/pubs/research_briefs/RB9145.html

Lemmer, S., & Roberts, R. (2015). *The main ingredients for an early childhood MTSS model*. RTI Innovations. Retrieved from www.rti-innovations.com/uploads/1/0/8/2/10825600/innovations_presentation__final.pdf

Loughran, J. (2014). Professionally developing as a teacher educator. *Journal of Teacher Education, 65*(4), 271–283.

Masters, G. N. (2010). *Teaching and learning school improvement framework*. Australian Council for Educational Research. Retrieved from https://research.acer.edu.au/monitoring_learning/16

Morningstar, M. E., Allcock, H. C., White, J. M., Taub, D., Kurth, J. A., Gonsier-Gerdin, J., . . . Jorgensen, C. M. (2016). Inclusive education national research advocacy agenda: A call to action. *Research and Practice for Persons with Severe Disabilities, 41*(3), 209–215.

Murray, J. S. (2019). War and conflict: Addressing the psychosocial needs of child refugees. *Journal of Early Childhood Teacher Education, 4*(1), 3–18.

National Association for the Education of Young Children. (2009). *Developmentally appropriate practice in early childhood programs serving children from birth through age 8*. Washington, DC: Author.

National Association for the Education of Young Children. (2018). *NAEYC early learning program accreditation standards and assessment items*. Washington, DC: Author.

National Center for Education Statistics. (2019). *Preschool and kindergarten enrollment*. Retrieved from https://nces.ed.gov/programs/coe/indicator_cfa.asp

National Center for Pyramid Model Innovations. (2018). *The pyramid model for promoting social emotional competence in infants and young children*. Retrieved from https://challengingbehavior.cbcs.usf.edu/Pyramid/overview/index.html

Odden, A. R. (2012). *Improving student learning when budgets are tight*. Thousand Oaks, CA: Corwin.

Odden, A. R., & Picus, L. O. (2014). *School finance: A policy perspective* (5th ed.). New York, NY: McGraw Hill.

Preschool Program Quality Assessment. (2003). High Score Press. Retrieved from www.cceifame.com/pdf/PQA_Form_A_Observation_Instrument_Preschool.pdf

Project AWARE. (2017). *Family engagement: Building school-family partnerships for behavioral and mental health*. Columbus, OH: Project AWARE Ohio.

Schanzenbach, D. W., & Bauer, L. (2016, August 19). *The long-term impact of the Head Start program*. The Brookings Institution. Retrieved from www.brookings.edu research/the-long-term-impact-of-the-head-start-program/

Stensrud, R. H., Gilbride, D. D., & Bruinekool, R. M. (2018). The childhood to prison pipeline: Early childhood trauma as reported by a prison population. *Rehabilitation Counseling Bulletin, 62*(4), 195–208.

U.S. Department of Education. (2016). *Fact sheet: Troubling pay gap for early childhood teachers*. Retrieved from www.ed.gov/news/press-releases/fact-sheet-troubling-pay-gap-early-childhood-teachers

U.S. Department of Health and Human Services. (2015). *Head Start early learning outcomes framework: Ages birth to 5*. Washington, DC: Author.

U.S. Department of Health and Human Services, & U.S. Department of Education. (2016). *High-quality early learning settings depend on a high-quality workforce: Low compensation undermines quality*. Washington, DC: Authors.

Ujifusa, A. (2018, March 23). *President Trump signs spending bill that includes billions more for education*. Retrieved from http://blogs.edweek.org/edweek/campaign-k-12/2018/03/president_trump_signs_spending_bill_increases_education_money_billions.html

Vachon, T. E., & Ma, J. K. (2015). Bargaining for success: Examining the relationship between teacher unions and student achievement. *Sociological Forum, 30*(2), 391–414.

Williams, J. M., Landry, S. H., Anthony, J. L., Swank, P. R., & Crawford, A. D. (2012). An empirically-based statewide system for identifying quality pre-kindergarten programs. *Education Policy Analysis Archives, 20*(17), 1–36.

Yates, T., Ostrosky, M. M., Cheatham, G. A., Fettig, A., Shaffer, L., & Milagros Santos, R. (2008). *Research synthesis on screening and assessing social-emotional competence*. Center on the Social Emotional Foundations for Early Learning. Retrieved from http://csefel.vanderbilt.edu/documents/rs_screening_assessment.pdf

Chapter 9

Family Engagement

Key Terms

Gerrymandering
Implicit Partnership Naïveté
Cultural Brokering
Ethnic Match
School-centric
Community-centric
Student-centric
Student Centered Academic Sessions

Chapter Concepts

In this chapter, readers will learn:
1. The roles of schools as safe harbors and service centers.
2. To be purposeful and inclusive in their definition of family engagement.
3. To use culture as an asset to negotiate healthy school and family connections.
4. How to invite, integrate, and value family input and collaboration instead of simply expecting it.
5. How to empower students and families to be leaders in the learning process.
6. Effective tools to promote family wellness and engagement.

Schools are community centers for social and cultural activities, as well as learning institutions. Family and community members are drawn to schools because that is not only where their children are but also where the future possibilities of their children are housed. Broadly speaking, public education in the United States is a vehicle to equalize inequities in society, and those with the highest levels of educational attainment often experience the greatest benefits, such as longevity, earning power, and social status (Freiman, 2016; Walsemann, Gee, & Ro, 2013; Marina & Holmes, 2009). Public schools aim to provide daily shelter, sustenance, and mind-expanding experiences for all children regardless of race, religion, social class, gender, or background. Schools are supposed to be neutral ground where children leave their circumstances behind and enter a world of knowledge and cognition dedicated to improving their life skills and to prepare them to successfully function in, and contribute to, society. All students deserve and require a safe environment that teaches self-discipline and provides opportunities for growth regardless of income level, social status, or individual abilities and disabilities. Public schools should be the islands of stability in the stormy seas of public division, class wars, and poverty. All families want to know that their children are physically and emotionally safe, valued, and loved. Once they genuinely feel this level of care from teachers and school staff members, family engagement barriers will begin to break away.

School and Student Realities

Children bring their families with them to school, whether other family members are physically present or not, and whether educators choose to acknowledge this fact. Students come to school with invisible backpacks that include a variety of experiences, values, and traumas that shape who they are, how they think, how they act and, ultimately, how they are going to interact with others on any given day. Students bring their family values and experiences to school without understanding that others have also brought their family values and experiences to school, which can lead to conflict within the school environment and without. Educators also bring their own invisible backpacks full of implicit biases regarding family engagement.

Some communities have gone to great lengths to minimize cultural and socioeconomic diversity to avoid the compromises that conflict creates. In the United States, many school districts have become, or remain, segregated because of racial districting that pushes out minority-based majorities into substandard school districts and segregated charter schools. Elite stakeholders are profiting from substandard charter schools with limited accountability (Hurst, 2017), and high-stakes testing has become a racially biased practice that disserves minority students (Au, 2015).

Lines are drawn on maps so that preferred students and communities are kept in while nonpreferred students and communities are kept out. Gerrymandered political regions have created haves and have-nots in the lottery of producing and supporting good schools and "exacerbates segregation" (Richards, 2014, p. 1119). *Gerrymandering* is when the geographic boundaries are manipulated to benefit one political party over another. Regardless of politics and quality of school, the neighborhood school is often considered the safest place for children to be, where children overcome their challenges and prepare for advancement in life.

Historically in the United States, children have worked with the civic belief that their industriousness served to prevent idleness and ending up in the poorhouse (Abbott, 1908). Such jobs for children entailed spinning yarn, carrying water, feeding chickens, and running errands. Immediately following the Civil War, freed slaves' children and child immigrants were employed as apprentices for training purposes and were basically reenslaved by former slave masters or patrons until laws challenging this practice were introduced during the Reconstruction period (Schuman, 2017).

The Industrial Revolution brought machinery that increased the capacity and output working children could produce. From the time of the Industrial Revolution to the passing of the Fair Labor Standards Act in 1938, which regulated the employment of children, the belief that children in the United States were expected to work continued. The mentality was that child labor kept children from being lazy and out of trouble, with the added bonus of substantial contributions to the family's income. These exploited child labor practices occurred across professions and several industrial sites, including mills, mines, and factories (Schuman, 2017).

In addition to the Fair Labor Standards Act, another contributing factor to the decrease in child labor was the increase in mandatory schooling, or compulsory education (Tyack, 1974). Common schools in the United States were conceptualized with a variety of motives, chief among them was to instill honest civic beliefs and individual moral character within the newly formed republics (Tyack, James, & Benavot, 1987). Students were to be taught moral character; however, over time, these values were overshadowed by gross inequities with respect to non-Whites and immigrants with prejudices that persisted for centuries. A democratic education was just not possible given the realities of social injustice. As one educator (as cited in Tyack, 1974) wrote about the conditions of education at the turn of the twentieth century, "[a]s long as Negroes [sic] are the victims of lynching, police brutality, disfranchisement, residential covenant, higher rents, segregation, unsanitary living conditions, meager recreational opportunities, and other forms of discrimination, the social-civic aim of education is defeated" (p. 218). This painful history cannot be changed but must be acknowledged, just as implicit biases must be acknowledged because they persist to this day. In our quest to devise one singular "best" system for educating our youth, we have created a system that ineffectively serves our poorest students *systematically* (Tyack, 1974). This deliberate and systematic exclusion of the unique characteristics of students and communities is damaging to individual children and society as a whole.

In addition to the ongoing evolution of a democratic education system, new changes are also taking place. With the rise of technology and artificial intelligence, some educators prognosticate that school buildings will become a thing of the past. Physical learning spaces are expected to be obsolete because students will be able to access technology and learning opportunities online or in ways not yet conceived. A compelling argument against this future for public schools lies in the fact that schools are already irreplaceable as a location for child care, and are becoming more so in times of uncertainty for family cohesiveness and public assistance.

Many schools have already transformed into community health centers, community food and clothing banks, and community social hubs. Schools are slowly taking over more roles and responsibilities for children than ever before, including providing basic needs and surrogate parenting. When other social safety nets fail, schools are expected to support and nurture children and, by proxy, their families, regardless of what needs they have. Public schools are being overtaken by the charter school movement as the fast-food-chain model of education service delivery, which reduces the health and funding of public schools. Defenders of public education must advertise their advocacy efforts and highlight their value to the public so that elected officials will hear loud and clear from constituents not to take away funding from public schools, funding that is necessary to reduce inequitable opportunities for already-oppressed communities. Educational policy must preserve free appropriate public education and put the same accountability standards on charter schools as on public schools.

Perhaps becoming safe harbors of society is not such a bad role for the school system. In times of alternative facts and civil discord, schools can safeguard civilization with visible support and care for others' well-being, social responsibility, emphasizing social reciprocity, community tolerance, and a sense of belonging for all community members. Instead of focusing on ways that students and communities are unique, a more culturally responsive approach would be to recognize and emphasize similarities that exist across cultures and build from there. Schools are already the heart of many communities and are the glue of civilized society, bringing elements together for the good citizenship of children. Future generations will probably be competing for jobs with robots, so education must be humanistic. The best schools are run like families, with the efficiency of factories.

Exercise 9.1

Family Engagement School Readiness Appraisal

- List challenges that families at your school are struggling with most.
- List the assets that families bring to your school.
- List the main reasons caregivers and families come to your school.
- Generate potential family engagement opportunities from a needs-based and asset-based perspective. Consider and list multiple opportunities for community members to join in evaluating, selecting, and developing targeted family engagement practices.

Shifting Perspectives

Family engagement is often cited by schools, districts, and states as a core value of their respective education systems. However, the quality, context, and implementation success of family engagement in schools, varies significantly along a spectrum, starting at one end of the continuum with schools that are below basic skill levels in their engagement and operate as Fortress schools to the other end of the continuum where schools that are proficient in family engagement and operate as Partnership schools (Henderson, Mapp, Johnson, & Davies, 2007). Fortress schools, resembling impenetrable castles surrounded by barricades, tend to make excuses for lack of family engagement and place blame on the caregivers for their perceived lack of commitment to the education of their children. Come-If-We-Call schools operate in a basic manner and use one-way communication to inform parents what the school year entails for their children. Open-Door schools tend to be fairly standard with established events held throughout the year in which families can come to the school and participate as an observer in their child's education. Partnership schools are proficient in effectively and meaningfully engaging families and involve families in the decision making that transpires with their child's learning and goals, schoolwide engagement opportunities and planning, and community connections.

Education leaders must be vulnerable and reflective enough to acknowledge that their traditional family engagement efforts may not be impactful, meaningful, or even respectful and culturally sensitive. Family engagement should never feel like an add-on or an additional program to implement as staff, and it should never feel like something that is being done to them as families. Instead, it should embrace "being" with families, creating a sense of belonging and shared values. Engaging with families should be a matter of regular practice, not just something that is done two or three times a year. Acknowledging this *implicit partnership naïveté*, or the inherent belief educators hold with regard to engaging the families they serve based on their own cultural experiences, expectations, and institutionalized assumptions, can be a source of empowerment and should not be viewed as a weakness or a source of shame for educators. Effective family engagement practices are not traditionally taught explicitly in teacher preparation programs or administrative leadership training and are typically assumed to be something that all school personnel inherently understand and can practice without preparation or skill development. By recognizing that implementation of effective family engagement practices are not universally taught in educator preparation programs and that is there no consensus about what effective family engagement looks like across schools or communities, professional learning opportunities can arise not only for school staff but for caregivers and community members as well.

Exercise 9.2

Family Engagement Mindset Survey

- Identify if your school operates as a Fortress, Come-If-We-Call, Open-Door, or Partnership school.
- Does this align with your goal of how you'd like your school to operate?
- What evidence exists that supports, and counters, the goal of how you'd like to engage families?
- List actionable ways in which your school can transition from a mind-set of family engagement as a program to family engagement as a daily practice or way of being.

Box 9.1

Voices From the Field

A few years ago, I was working at a low-income school that historically had a difficult time getting families to volunteer. There were two moms that consistently volunteered and ran the Community Engagement Club in lieu of a Parent–Teacher Association (PTA) since we did not have enough volunteers to form an official PTA board. This past year we made a concerted effort to engage volunteers and sent home sheets of paper in kids' backpacks that families could return if they were willing to volunteer, and the sheets were also made available in the front office and on the school's website. Throughout the year, the number of volunteers did not go up; however, toward the end of the year, it was reported that family members were either turned away or not called in to volunteer even after they submitted their sheet indicating that they would like to volunteer. It turns out the volunteer sheets were going directly to the Community Engagement Club (the two ever-present moms) who were stacking the sheets up without the intent to reach out to families or find ways for them to be involved. Eventually, the school administration found out and changed the process for the flow of volunteer sheet submissions. The forms were no longer going directly to the Community Engagement Club and instead went to a designated staff member who called the volunteers, thanked them for their time, and invited them on campus to find an activity for them to contribute to or participate in. A lack of coordinated oversight and targeted communication with the lead volunteer moms clearly had an impact on success and did not benefit the students, staff, or families who wanted to be part of a collaborative education process.

What Is Family Engagement?

Family engagement encompasses much more than parent–teacher conferences. The use of "family" engagement versus "parental" engagement is intentional and aligns with the realities of families in communities. The majority of families are not composed of biological parents at the helm but of blended families with an infinite number of configurations. Children are being raised by relatives, neighbors, and extended family even when parents are in the picture. Families are under more pressure than ever before to meet their basic needs and are facing incredible challenges in doing so. These basic needs, compounded by economic factors, mental illnesses and addictions, and less understood family systems, all undermine students' success at school. The need for family engagement is not limited to at-risk neighborhoods and many of the same challenges in getting families to support their children's education permeate all socioeconomic backgrounds. Families with higher-socioeconomic status often excel over their lower-socioeconomic counterparts in relation to advocacy and engagement as they often have access to, and knowledge about, how to maneuver effectively. Comparatively, families from lower-socioeconomic backgrounds often lack those same advocacy skills and maneuvering (Van Veslor & Orozco, 2007).

Systemic transformation and *cultural brokering* are needed to bridge socioeconomic and cultural barriers to family–school engagement (Ishimaru et al., 2016). In doing so, culture can be used as an asset and can be used to positively influence and bridge family and school relationships. Differences in language, social class, and ethnicity all require consideration through the inclusive lens of the LIQUID (Leadership, Implementation, Quality control, Universality, Implementation, Data-based decision making) Model. Similarities across all diverse groups on a campus should be considered and built into the fabric of a school's culture, climate, and family engagement practices. School providers must be proactive in addressing implicit bias that they or the educators on campus may have about families' commitment to support their children in school, as well as to bridge the divide from dominant culture's expectations to inclusive practices. Effective family engagement must contain six conditions: It must be relational and built on mutual trust, linked to learning and development, asset-based, culturally responsive and respective, collaborative, and interactive (Mapp, 2019).

In addition to addressing implicit partnership naïveté among school administration and staff, other factors contribute to an increase in family engagement. *Ethnic match* is one of those factors and occurs when a student's teacher and family both identify with the same ethnic background. Latinos have a lower rate of family engagement than other minority groups; however, when there is an ethnic match between the family and the teacher, family engagement increases considerably (Mundt, Gregory, Melzi, & McWayne, 2015). Special considerations must be given to immigrant families with primary languages other than English as they may be intimidated by the bureaucracy of a school system due to communication barriers and fear of authority. Other families may fear the deportation of some, or all, of its family members depending on immigration status.

Centric views must also shift to increase family engagement. Teachers tend to hold *school-centric* views of family involvement (Lawson, 2003) and how adults engage within an education system. However, instead of framing the narrative around how families can help schools to promote student education, the conversation should be *community-centric*, in the sense that a broader community influences and promotes student success

(Van Veslor & Orozco, 2007; Lawson, 2003). This community-centric perspective shifts the predominant narrative around the role of adults and can be used to increase family and learning supporters' engagement with schools. Reframing teacher attitudes and improving school climate to reflect a more inclusive view of *family* engagement must be part of this shift. Six community-centric strategies to increase family involvement include learn about the families of the children in the school, learn about the community where the students live, provide on-site services for caregivers, help caregivers address community concerns, offer in-service training for school personnel, and utilize family cultural capital (Van Veslor & Orozco, 2007).

Once schools are more inclusive and hold a community-centric view of the adults' roles in a child's education, a student-centric learning environment can then be cultivated. A *student-centric* learning environment is one in which the student remains at the core of all decision making and the adults surround that student in a circle of collaborative partnership. Students who are supported as partners in their own learning are more likely to be engaged in lessons, behave more responsibly, advocate for themselves, and reach their learning goals.

Communication with families must transition from a "school knows best" perspective to valuing and inviting the contributions and knowledge of families. The traditional hierarchical model of educators telling families what to do is not effective and promotes distrust and distance between families and schools (Weist, Garbacz, Lane, & Kincaid, 2017). Emerging is a partnership model of family engagement, which is much more effective. This model invites families' feedback on topics such as when convenient times to meet are and what engagement opportunities families would like to see transpire, instead of schools telling them when the engagement will take place and what it will look like. Traditionally, activities happen during the school and workday when caregivers are working. These caregivers are then shamed for not attending during these restricted hours; this shaming occurs across all socioeconomic strata and is incredibly counterproductive. Caregivers must work to meet the basic needs of their children and while they want to engage with educators, many cannot do it during school hours. Compensating teachers for meeting after school or on flexible hours is one way around this barrier. Other ways in which schools can foster a partnership paradigm of family engagement is by valuing family voice, their cultural strengths, and shifting the language used when describing the engagement of families from "including" families to "partnering" with families (Weist et al., 2017).

Family input is necessary when planning family engagement opportunities. Ideally, these data would be collected at the beginning of the school year and used to drive family engagement decisions throughout the year. There are a variety of ways to collect input from families and several mediums should be available. For example, surveys can be created and emailed out using a free platform such as Google Forms. The same survey can be made available as a QR code and sent out electronically or in paper form as part of a school newsletter, sent home in students' backpacks, or be posted throughout the school. Also, computers can be made available on campus for families to take the survey should technology be prohibitive. Similarity, efforts should be made to offer the survey in multiple languages so that language is not a barrier. Finally, parents should be encouraged to write notes to the school about what family engagement means to them and what they would like to see the school offer.

When using this information to inform on and plan family engagement activities throughout the year, it is helpful for the planning team to list out all the intended events. To avoid each event feeling like an isolated one-and-done activity, a universal yearlong theme can link each event creating connective tissue and cohesiveness. This planning team should include school staff as well as parents and students, especially students from the higher elementary grades. Planning should transpire at the end of the previous school year or at the very beginning of the current school year, ideally prior to a Back to School Night or Open House. In doing so, the theme can be launched at the Open House and carried over into all subsequent events, thus creating the connective tissue. For example, if the planning team is able to coordinate early and plan a yearlong theme of Road Trip to Learning, each family engagement event can have a theme of "Road Trip." Family engagement planning could include a Road Trip to the Ocean to learn about science or Road Trip to Student Learning Goals to learn about how to set and support their child with a particular academic goal. Each student could have a Road Trip booklet or map with each "stop" along the way representing each activity. Completed Road Trip booklets or maps could then be turned in for school tickets or other rewards and privileges in the context of class or schoolwide reinforcements. In general, by establishing the theme early, cohesiveness can be built, and Tier 1 family engagement will be supported.

There will always be families who are unable to attend family engagement events on campus for a variety of reasons, and accommodations should be made for these students to ensure that they are not inadvertently penalized or shamed. For example, some parents have work schedules or health problems that interfere with their availability to attend events, which may leave some children embarrassed about a lack of family support. Events planned at a variety of times could be planned for working parents, and if particular students are to be celebrated or particular families need reinforcement to come, the school principal or the teacher could make a personal call to the caregiver with the child present to deliver the good news or to extend the personal invitation. This gives the child a sense of pride and accomplishment without creating situations that are not perceived as rewarding.

Schools need to provide a welcoming and inclusive environment for students' families because there is a high correlation between family involvement and positive educational outcomes for students. Stanton Elementary in the District of Columbia experienced amazing results when the school addressed their implicit partnership naïveté and reimagined how family engagement could look like on their campus. After only one year, the school doubled its reading scores and experienced approximately a 50% growth in mathematics (Mapp & Kuttner, 2013). These findings are hardly surprising considering that the family system is arguably the true Tier 1 of instruction for a child. Bronfenbrenner (1979) placed the child at the center of his bioecological model of development to explain how interactions between the child and the environment help shape and influence how a child will grow. While the child is the microsystem, the family and school are the next immediate ring of influence at the mesosystem. According to this theoretical construct, individual and basic needs of a child must be addressed first and then further enhanced and supported by the school and family. In accordance with this model and integral to iterative evaluation cycles, obtaining student feedback that can be used as input for future planning is essential. See Exercise 9.3 for a sample Student Data Feedback Request Form with modified questions for younger students in parentheses. Such a form can be composed of open-ended questions, Likert scales, drawings, or combined-type questions and is very useful all the way down to kindergarten. For younger students, the teacher can read the questions aloud one at a time to the class and allow them to draw pictures that represent their responses. Given younger students' attention span, and to allow for illustrated responses, the questions can be asked one or two at a time over a series of days to allow adequate time for the students to complete their thoughts or drawings. Regardless of the specific information gathered or in what manner, obtaining student voice provides incredible insight toward the overall function, effectiveness, and perception of Multi-Tiered Systems of Support (MTSS).

Exercise 9.3

Student Data Feedback Request Form

- What do you like about school?
- What do you not like about school?
- What is the most difficult subject area for you? (What is the hardest part about school, and why?)
- What is your favorite subject area, and why? (What is the easiest part about school, and why?)
- Do you have a teacher or teachers you really like?
- What are you good at?
- Is there anything or anyone at school that makes you sad?

Basic needs are part of that Tier 1 foundation critical to a student's success, and a sense of belonging could be Maslow's (1943) most underrated and underappreciated basic need. Providing avenues for supporting parents and families, helping them to construct and use their voices, and encouraging them to participate in learning experiences and celebrations create a culture of responsiveness. Positively engaging families in a friendly, culturally respectful, and nurturing manner increases goodwill and collaboration. Therefore, earning the trust of families and finding pathways for them to participate in their children's education are paramount to understanding students' needs and helping them to overcome difficulties (Dotterer & Wehrspann, 2016).

Opportunities to Increase Engagement

Frameworks exist to build, enhance, and sustain relationships with families to promote academic and behavioral health between home and educational settings. Motivating school and family leaders to support academic and behavioral learning at home, as well as participate in school-based activities, indisputably increases student success at school. The intent of engagement and sustainability extends to the national level, and the U.S. Department of Education has recently appointed its first Family Ambassador. This Family Ambassador serves to promote the voice of families to liaise between families and stakeholders, including the U.S. Department of Education. To support this engagement and capacity, the U.S. Department of Education (2018) offers a framework for schools, families, and communities to follow.

An additional framework is the Dual Capacity-Building Framework for Family-School Partnerships that is intended to serve as a compass, rather than a scripted list of steps, to guide effective engagement and outlines four domains for school leaders to consider: The Challenge, Opportunity Conditions, Policy and Program Goals, and Family and Staff Capacity Outcomes (Mapp & Kuttner, 2013, Mapp, 2019). Nested within Opportunity Conditions are six process conditions that should be considered and endeavored toward when planning any family engagement activity (Mapp, 2019). The first is relational, the activity must be built on a mutual trust between the school and the families. Without this trust, the remaining five conditions are less meaningful and will gradually disintegrate as the trust dissolves. The second and third process conditions that must be met are engagement that is linked to learning and development and that is asset-based. If the "engagement" event is one-sided and simply explains to the families what the rules of the school are, then it does not allow the families to be viewed as having value to bring to the table to share in the learning and development of their child. Such an informational "engagement" event would be better video recorded to link through the school website or to go out in a phone message to families. The last three process conditions are culturally responsive and respectful, collaborative, and interactive (Mapp, 2019). When planning engagement activities, schools must strive to meet these three conditions and if they find themselves falling short or questioning whether they have achieved these conditions, odds are that they probably have not.

The Centers for Disease Control and Prevention (2012) also provides a framework that can be used to increase family engagement in school health: Parent Engagement Strategies for Involving Parents in School Health. This framework serves to connect parents with schools to support student learning and health, it engages families in opportunities to be involved with school and student activities, and it sustains engagement by overcoming barriers to building and maintaining relationships with families. It also includes a troubleshooting section with helpful hints to overcoming challenges related to family engagement.

At the school level, these frameworks exist to support students, families, teachers, and administrators. Teachers are understandably natural liaisons between home and school, but as their responsibilities grow along with their class sizes, they are less able to shoulder the burden of all duties. Teachers and administrators may have implicit partnership naïveté or may not have the tools to effectively engage families (or both), let alone sustain relationships individually. Inclusive MTSS practices automate some systems and processes to promote positive collaboration between school staff and families while providing a blueprint of a welcoming school environment for all.

Barriers to effective family–school engagement practices include parent and family factors, child factors, family–teacher interaction factors, and societal factors (Hornby & Lafaele, 2011). Using an additive view of family engagement, caregivers become involved due to their perceptions and constructs surrounding their role as an asset in educating their child, their sense of efficacy for helping their child, and the general engagement opportunities that exist at their child's school (Hoover-Dempsey & Sandler, 1997; Mapp & Kuttner, 2013; Mapp, 2019). Caregivers who feel that their involvement is as much valued as required at school and that family–school partnering increases the well-being of their children are more likely to be involved at school. Otherwise, family leaders will not prioritize school involvement as an effective use of family time or perceive school involvement as a resource to healthy child and family development. Even with a multitude of opportunities to engage, without improved parental perceptions of their role and increased efficacy for their level of support, family engagement will continue to suffer (Hoover-Dempsey & Sandler, 1997).

Child factors that may influence family involvement at school include individual differences, abilities and disabilities, and behavioral problems (Hornby & Lafaele, 2011). For example, children who demonstrate behavioral difficulties at school often demonstrate the same at home, and families may feel defensive, embarrassed, and unprepared to share their feelings with school professionals or seek input. On the other hand, families may be very vocal about difficulties and circumstances surrounding variables that contribute to or maintain maladaptive child behaviors but are not willing, or able, to change their own behavior to reinforce new variables in the environment that support change. Individual student strengths and challenges also pose unique circumstances for educators and families. Every child's needs are different, as is every family's ability to cope, and depending on the resources available in each school and district, what a school or teacher is able to provide may vary greatly.

Family–teacher factors may be influenced by perceived accessibility to one another. If families do not feel like they can communicate effectively with teachers or solicit advice without harsh judgment, they are less likely to request feedback. Alternatively, if teachers cannot reach families or do not feel supported by them with homework or consequences for misbehavior, teachers are less likely to make efforts to invite parental or caregiver input. Whatever the barriers may be, schools and educators need to do a better job partnering with parents and families in the school community. Oftentimes, it is as simple as *valuing* the input and participation of families, instead of expecting it.

The importance of positive relationships between school staff and families is indisputable and should focus on several key objectives. School campuses should focus on the primary family engagement tools of increasing communication between home and school, building positive home–school relationships, building reciprocal structures for support, increasing trust between community and school, encouraging families to motivate children, and valuing family culture and participation (Dotterer & Wehrspann, 2016; Cattanach, 2013; Neuman, 2013). Superseding these goals is the overall notion of working collaboratively with caregivers and sharing tools to create symbiotic structures to help guide and encourage their children. Families not only need to have regular opportunities to collaborate and be involved in their children's school lives; they also need to feel that their contributions are of value. Just another example of shifting the narrative of family engagement as a program to a daily practice. Family sessions focusing on wellness activities and providing a forum for addressing community concerns are avenues to building working relationships with families. Multiple opportunities for families to obtain basic services (e.g., health services, clothing, and food giveaways), attend open houses, enjoy celebrations, and participate in family engagement organization meetings attract families to get involved.

Methods to involve families come in all flavors and styles and how families are invited to events go a long way toward getting them to engage. Offering multiple modalities in which to engage families and framing the engagement as an opportunity to build capacity will increase the effectiveness of the partnership. Once on campus, providing a comfortable experience for families is strongly recommended. Higher-risk schools often have trouble attracting families to academic nights and events due to caregiver work schedules, child care for younger siblings, and difficulty organizing family functions with multiple family members. Oftentimes, educators are also not as diligent in reaching out to families and building partnerships in low social-economic environments because there is little accountability for them to do so. It is not uncommon for teachers to insist that they have called home because they know that the family does not have the social capital to challenge this. On the flip side, it oftentimes can be difficult to reach families from these environments because phone numbers truly do change every 30 days. However, if a strong partnership already existed between the teacher and the family, the family would immediately share that new phone number because it would be a priority to them that they are able to maintain that collaborative communication with the teacher.

> **Box 9.2**
>
> **Voices From the Field**
>
> As a principal, I get many complaints in a day, including from teachers. One day, a minor situation arose with a student, and I encouraged the teacher to call home and share with the family what had transpired. The teacher insisted that "we needed to do more to get these families engaged" and that she already had tried calling home and was demanding "something else" be done. While the two of us were in my office, I picked up the phone and dialed the primary contact number listed for the student and got the mother on the line after the second ring. After speaking with the mother, I had a discussion with the teacher about the importance of viewing our families as partners, not outsiders who were out to undermine our efforts. It was also made clear that subterfuge was not part of the culture of our school and that honesty was a core value to be respected. It was clear to me that as a staff, we had some work to do regarding our definition and application of family engagement.

In all communities, food, giveaways, and entertainment are a winning combination for bringing families in to events at school. Breaking bread, sharing a meal, or having a snack creates goodwill and brings in families with limited means. In general, food should be available at all family events, and accessibility to other community resources can be offered. Home visits by administrators, positive phone calls from teachers, and follow-up from caring specialists in a helping capacity (e.g., school social workers, counselors, psychologists) go a long way to earn trust and cooperation from parents (Tunison, 2013).

Typically, schools will have systematic functions in place that automatically invite families into the school to participate in activities and celebrations of students. The challenge is to make sure that the events follow the Dual Capacity Framework and are based on trust, linked to learning, relational, asset-based, collaborative, and interactive (Mapp & Kuttner, 2013; Mapp, 2019). Providing student-led entertainment also nearly guarantees that the families of those performing will be in attendance and is another technique for bringing in families. Open houses, parent–teacher conferences, band performances, and special events are some of the opportunities in place at most schools for family engagement. As previously mentioned in the Open House example about Road Trip to Learning, the theme of the event could be a springboard to cohesively unite future family engagement learning "stops" throughout the year. Building from this theme, if the Road Trip to Learning activities at Open House were student-centric and structured as a journey on their personal road map, it could be a fun way for families to engage and begin to build relationships with the teachers and staff who are central to their child's success. Additional stops along the way might include listening to the message from the school principal and reading or hearing the classroom and schoolwide expectations.

Welcoming messages from the school principal as well as introductions to the upcoming curriculum, classroom and schoolwide expectations, and school spirit are all typical components of an Open House event. However, what if these messages could be memorialized in a PDF document or a video message that could be posted to the school's website, sent home in an email, or accessed by QR code? By archiving these basic sources of information, families can easily reference them later if they have questions. Also, many families cannot attend Open House events, arrive late, or move to the school midway through the school year. Having this information available digitally is just another way for families to have access to the information while respecting the many factors that compete for their time. Making the information available outside a one-and-done presentation also levels the playing field and decreases the top-down communication hierarchy present in many schools.

Musical and theater performances, school club events, and sports practices or games compel families to campus like no other draw because the students are vested in performing and families are motivated to watch their children perform. Learning new skills, practicing new skills, achieving mastery of skills, and successfully applying learned skills is never better celebrated than at school performances and sporting events. If all learning activities could be similarly supported and celebrated by families and the school community, students might be much more excited and motivated to succeed academically. Educators can aim to capture the excitement and inclusionary spirit of school performances in other opportunities for families to support students.

Exercise 9.4

Family Engagement Opportunity Survey

- How does your school currently collect information from families about how they want to be engaged and at what times during the day and week?
- What opportunities do families currently have on your campus to be involved and excited about their students' learning and performance?
- How do you go about inviting families to campus, and how can you be more inclusive in your approach?
- What about these events do families and students most enjoy? How do you collect this information from them?
- Which of the preceding elements can your school leadership incorporate into academic functions and other family participation opportunities?
- What are ideas your school leadership can initiate to increase family outreach (e.g., phone calls, postcards, home visits) or quality of that outreach, among educators and other staff members?

Ideas to expand inclusive opportunities for family engagement on campus should be explored at least annually within the context of MTSS. Effective and high-impact family engagement should be a foundational Tier 1 support that all students receive, and it is the school's responsibility to engage as a Partnership school with families. School leaders can set the tone for what this engagement looks like and how to partner with families. Opportunities such as Student-Centered Academic Sessions, a family engagement center, and school events must all be visibly supported by the school administrator and have the buy-in of school staff. Mandates do not work, and the collective culture and climate of a school must shift to make foundational family engagement change.

Student-Centered Academic Sessions

Student-led information conferences, or *Student-Centered Academic Sessions* (SCASs), are a powerful evidence-based method to empower students and families to collaborate in the learning process (Conderman, Ikan, & Hatcher, 2000; Hackman, 1996). Conferences require self-reflection, identification of strengths and needs, and goal setting and monitoring, as well as organizational practice and communication skills. Such meetings are also powerful opportunities for families to have structured academic-based conversations with their children a few times a year, in addition to report cards and other traditional methods of communication between caregivers and the school. SCASs help students and families be collaborators in the learning process, be viewed as an active partner and asset, and can start conversations at home about empowering students to achieve academic goals. This type of approach aligns with the tenets of the Dual Process Framework in which family engagement is built on mutual trust, linked to learning and development, asset-based, culturally responsive and respectful, collaborative, and interactive (Mapp & Kuttner, 2013; Mapp, 2019).

SCASs are an opportunity to bring parents onto campus and to engage them in the goal setting and progress monitoring process for their child. Such sessions can either occur with the children present, especially for higher elementary grades, or without. For all grades, it is helpful to have a fun student activity, such as a movie and popcorn in the lunchroom, to allow teachers and families to have targeted discussions and to work on goal-setting and progress-monitoring techniques with fewer disruptions.

The school principal must be committed to SCACs by the beginning of a school year, as the session dates are memorialized in the master calendar so that teachers have the time and training to prepare for their families. Student-centered meetings are not part of the traditional parent–teacher conference cycle, which has a separate date and place. SCAC meetings occur approximately three times a year, immediately following each benchmark period and are paired with fun activities for students to increase attendance. Teachers prepare for their families by reviewing targeted curricular elements (not all subjects at once) and printing formative assessment results that can serve as a benchmark for the goal-setting exercise. Students are each given a number to eliminate identifying student information, and each family has a folder or packet prepared for them when they arrive. Within the classroom, students can use this identifying number in alignment with a transparent visual tracking system in which students can move their marker up a "mountain," through a "racecourse," or some other type of progressive system. This type of model is also referred to as Academic Parent–Teacher Teams, which was employed by Stanton Elementary to help bolster their reading and math performance in just one year (Mapp & Kuttner, 2013; WestEd, 2017; Mapp, 2019). On secondary campuses, a model in which students take a more active role in their goal setting and engagement with their families is referred to as Student-Led Informational Conferences (Clark & Dockweiler, 2019).

The first SCAC, held after the first academic benchmark period, includes the following artifacts: baseline information (selected work samples from across subject levels, tests and test scores, benchmarking scores or instructional-level fluency levels, or any other relevant assessment data), an identified academic goal domain (e.g., reading fluency, math computation, etc.), brief interventions that the family can implement at home to assist their child in reaching the established goal, quick assessment techniques that can be used periodically to informally assess growth, and sample worksheets families can use to record information. Families are guided by teachers to understand the curricular scope and sequence of the targeted academic skill, and they practice the brief interventions and assessment techniques until they feel comfortable. Students are brought in at the end of the session so that the families can review with the students what they will be helping to work on and reinforce at home. Students benefit from seeing their families and teacher working in partnership and reduces the opportunity for them to try to get away with anything because they know that their teacher and family are on the same page, in regular communication with each other. Subsequent SCASs can build off the curricular goal of the first SCAS or can dive into a separate curricular learning goal. During these subsequent sessions, teachers will have again prepared the folders or packets with individual student information, coded with numbers, with the same type of artifacts that were included in the first session. Additional information will include progress monitoring graphs or data collected by the school and the family may contribute a list or graph of scores that the student obtained at home. SCACs and other similar types of student-led conferences have a high validity for increasing student motivation and achievement (Conderman et al., 2000; Hackman, 1996).

SCACs take administrative commitment and planning, direct instruction in preparations, and reminders for each milestone. Teachers must have sufficient time to prepare materials, to calendar the SCASs, and to remind families of the sessions. Families must also have enough advanced notice to build the dates into their calendars or reschedule a time to meet with the teacher at a different date or time. Having clearly delineated procedures and timelines will help make SCAC events most effective.

Building positive relationships with the local business community is essential, and including them in school functions and celebrations will increase their generosity toward school families as they provide economic and social supports. Cultural celebrations can help cultivate relationships with local businesses investing in community health through local schools. In turn, businesses appreciate being publicly honored for community service, and students and families can patronize businesses that provide services and supports for them. A win–win for all.

Exercise 9.5

Student-Centered Family Engagement Inquiry

- How does your school currently engage families in the academic goal setting process?
- List short-term and long-term goals for improving this engagement.
- What cultural celebrations does your school currently practice?

- How can you grow culturally inclusive school celebrations at your school?
- Which businesses in the community might support school celebrations and relationships could be cultivated?

Family Center and Wellness Opportunities

Family wellness and parenting classes are popular opportunities for families to positively engage with school staff and share positive interactions with other families. An actual location on the school campus where families can be present in a structured manner gives them a sense of value and belonging to the school community. Resources to support basic needs, incorporating Community in Schools (where available), monthly family wellness classes, opportunities for enrichment and communication, and collaboration with community partners can be offered. For safety reasons, at most schools it is typically not feasible or allowed to have families walking around campus unsupervised by a staff member. The Family Center can be staffed by any number or combination of individuals including community liaisons, community family services workers, school social workers or other safe schools professional, school psychologist, school counselor, health teacher or coach, support staff or any educator fluent speaking in the dominant language of the families, such as Spanish. Community and school partnerships provide students and their families with basic needs' support including food, clothing, and health care.

A family center provides a comfortable location for family training and outreach functions, including welcoming community partnerships with organizations, such as Boys Town, and providing regular community education and enrichment. Some schools offer a business center for families who do not have access to computers, fax and copy machines, and supplies at home. A welcoming environment could include a children's corner with books, toys, and activities for young children to enjoy while their caregiver is involved in family center activities. Comforts may also include couches, tables, chairs, a water dispenser, coffee, snacks, and a refrigerator. Community resource information can be clearly posted and available for families to take copies.

Caregivers and families should also have universal access to the research-based curriculum in learning and practicing healthy parenting and family relationship practices. Monthly family connection meetings can be utilized to educate family leaders in more effective proactive positive parenting and less punitive and punishing practices. One particularly effective model can be taught in English and Spanish and presented in English and Spanish concurrently. Survival Skills for Healthy Families (Creighton, Doub, & Scott, 1999), now in its fifth edition "teaches, encourages and supports families, and those who work with them, to promote healthy communities. Practical skills are taught based on proven principles that strengthen, support and empower families" (p. 1). While Survival Skills for Healthy Families has proved effective, it is just one of many programs that are available for school teams to consider.

Goals of family connection meetings include increasing partnerships between families and schools, to support caregivers with engagement in student academic life, to provide families access to enrichment opportunities to improve family health, and to bridge the gap between families and community resources. Other goals may include providing English classes for families or caregivers who are not native English speakers and would like to learn the language, inviting community guest speakers, offering business or budgeting classes, offering small-group parenting classes, or hosting social opportunities, such as family dances. It is imperative that when offering these services or activities that the host always remain respectful and mindful of the culture in which it is seeking to engage.

Box 9.3

Voices From the Field

In my school, parent connection meetings are held monthly and presented by the school psychologist and bilingual health teacher. Survival Skills for Healthy Families (Creighton et al., 1999) is relevant for families of students of all ages (from preschool through high school), though our program discussions are geared toward middle school–age issues. Materials are provided in both English and Spanish, and all activities and discussions are also presented in both English and Spanish. Parents and caregivers are given multiple opportunities to reflect and discuss their personal parenting struggles with other parents, ultimately getting answers to their questions in the context of age-appropriate and developmentally relevant feedback from instructors. Family wellness is a well-established family education and family enrichment model for teaching skills, enhancing healthy family interactions, and connecting family members to each other and their community.

In addition, parents are offered opportunities to socialize with our school principal, other parents, and selected staff members each semester at our Principal's Potluck. Our principal sponsors a luncheon for parents, and we encourage parents to bring a dish to share, but it is not required to attend. The principal fosters discussions in a relaxed setting with parents providing a comfortable format to hear about challenges in the community from parents' perspectives. The Principal's Potluck allows parents a low-pressure opportunity to interact by breaking bread with the school principal at a family meal.

Quality family wellness or parenting programs, such as Survival Skills for Healthy Families (Creighton et al., 1999) or Strengthening Multi-Ethnic Families and Communities (Steele, Maringa, Tello, & Johnson, 1999) are designed to prevent child abuse, the mistreatment of children, and longer-term maladaptive generational family issues that stem from behavioral patterns passed along from parents to their children and to their children's children. Teaching family wellness and engaging in parent-level counseling interventions must be taught under a framework that includes both values and concepts (Prilleltensky & Nelson, 2000) and can be structured and allocated in the same way as all resources in MTSS.

Universal instruction is designed to provide opportunities for the entire school and family community to learn communication and discipline practices consistent with effective parenting highlighting family values and rehearsal of more functional parent–child interactions. Selective, targeted instruction and guided practice opportunities in smaller groups could be available for families with greater dysfunction and child behavioral problems. The highest tier of support would likely align with court-ordered interventions and out-of-home placement for child safety while children get individualized counseling and parents get rehabilitation services. A review of data on effective parenting (McKinney, Morse, & Pastuszak, 2014) has found that the benefits included improved parental empowerment and competency, increased positive parenting practices, increased social connection, improved child behavior, improved parent–child interactions, improved parental mental health and well-being, and decreased use of corporal punishment and risk of child abuse. Using parents and guardians as mentors, making cultural adaptations and actively engaging families was also recommended.

Box 9.4

Connection to Practice

Who is involved in the planning, implementation, and evaluation of the family wellness curriculum?

Many different individuals can serve in this role. It is optimal if the teacher, school counselor, social worker, school psychologist, or administrator planning to implement a family wellness curriculum attends training in the parenting practices they are teaching, or even better, holding an advanced certification. Like effective teaching, training parents and families in best practices requires a highly qualified instructor. As mentioned earlier, at one school, the school psychologist was also a certified family wellness instructor and led family engagement sessions. The planning and implementation of Survival Skills for Healthy Families were led by the school psychologist and supported by a co-presenter, the bilingual health teacher. The co-presenter translates English to Spanish and Spanish back to English, as well as engages in role-plays, facilitates discussions, and brings her own wealth of knowledge and experience to the training. Supporting school staff members are involved in trainings, and events included involvement of the safe schools professional, Community in Schools staff member, a learning strategist, Title I specialist, school counselors, the school nurse and first-aid safety assistant, and office managers. The school principal also attended meetings and supervised all functions. Parents were given surveys at the end of each session to evaluate topics and presenters.

How is this practice funded?

The family center and family connection meetings, community and school partnerships, and Survival Skills for Healthy Families training were all funded by Title I, through state-dedicated funding streams, and from the strategic or flexible spending school budget.

How does the practice link to student outcomes?

- To improve student behavior at home and at school
- To increase communication between home and school
- To build trust between community and school
- To build on home–school relationships

- To give families tools to guide, support, and encourage their children
- To teach families how to make small changes in their parenting that will have big payoffs
- To increase student and staff pride

How is this practice evaluated? What has been learned from this evaluation?

The family center connection meetings that present Survival Skills for Healthy Families is evaluated by parents after every session. These meetings have occurred monthly for the past four school years and parent feedback has been 100% positive. Parent responses on Title I evaluation forms are reviewed after every session. In addition, the school principal, her supervisor, and other school district administrators have also attended meetings and given positive feedback. The school has learned that its family wellness trainings have been very worthwhile. Parents love the practical advice and family problem-solving model. Administrators and teachers love the high energy of meetings and relevant discussions with parents in a culturally sensitive and safe environment.

What advice would you offer to someone wanting to implement the practice?

All schools would benefit from hosting a parent–family center and parent connection meetings using the Survival Skills for Healthy Families curriculum or another evidence-based curriculum. Investing in a comfortable and welcoming place for families on a school campus says a lot about a school's culture. Engaging with parents in a friendly, nurturing manner increases goodwill, a sense of pride, and collaboration with families. It also demonstrates the value schools and teachers believe that caregivers bring to the table. This shift toward a community-centric, versus school-centric, dynamic is essential to achieve positive family engagement. Families want to do better, and presenting family leadership skills in a fun way increases the chance that caregivers will try strategies at home.

Listening to families talk about their needs allows school personnel to address small problems before they become big problems and vice versa. Organization and preplanning are key to any new program in terms of who does what, when, and how. The outstanding professionalism of staff members working together collaboratively to proactively engage with parents increases opportunities for parents to feel connected to our school and staff members. Families are educators' best allies in fostering academic and emotional growth in students. Teaming up with families gives educators the best odds of meeting the needs of all their students.

A common logistical challenge for any family wellness program is getting caregivers to attend meetings. Some solutions to work around this issue include polling families at the beginning of the school year about what they would be interested in learning about, scheduling meetings in the evening to accommodate working families, scheduling later in the morning to allow caregivers to take younger siblings to school first, and videoing sessions that can be live-streamed by caregivers or available for online viewing. Other outreach efforts include advanced notifications of upcoming meetings, personalized calls to families in their native language to encourage attendance the week of the meeting, parking lot campaigns to give families meeting information while they drop off and pick up their children, providing delicious breakfasts and snacks at all family connection meetings, offering gift card drawings at the end of meetings, combining food giveaway opportunities on same day as meetings, and allowing opportunities for parents or caregivers to discuss personal problems individually with instructors after meetings.

Depending on the demographics, industry, and social factors of a community, some caregivers may be more apt to attend during the day or the evening. At one school, it was more difficult to get families to attend in the evening than during the school day, but at other schools, communities may find that evening and weekend meetings work best. Ideally, older students are able to attend skills sessions with their families as well because they benefit from learning strategies to develop individually and how to get along better with others, including better communication with parents and how to ask for and respect boundaries. Taking students out of class to attend meetings with their families is always a challenge because students might miss important class content. Evening meetings allow children to attend meetings with their families without interruption to class. Student schedules, teacher lesson plans, family work schedules, and student behavior all impact whether students are able to attend sessions held during the school day.

Last, a major challenge is freeing up personnel from other duties to engage with families during contract hours. Meetings that occur during school hours require planning to cover the teacher's classes during sessions, scheduling other important meetings around Family Connection meetings, and effectively communicating with staff and students about the importance of family engagement. Aligning with the culture of compensating staff for the extra work that they do, the school principal can also provide extra-duty pay to cover educators' prep buy-out and planning times. This is a great incentive for staff to be involved above and beyond school duties. Prioritizing the teaching of positive parenting practices by highly qualified, and personally invested, site-based educators sends a clear message to the community the importance of school–family engagement and relationship building, which increases the probability of sustainability of reciprocal support. Schools can also outsource their family wellness training to have parenting skills taught on campus by persons from outside agencies. However, parenting services presented by providers outside of school staff may turn into missed opportunities, and could potentially miss the point of building and sustaining school–family relationships, which cannot be outsourced. If the outside organization is framed as an opportunity to build school–community–family partnerships, this can be a positive experience for all parties involved.

References

Abbott, E. (1908). A study of the early history of child labor in America. *American Journal of Sociology, 14*(1), 15–37.

Au, W. (2015). Meritocracy 2.0: High-stakes, standardized testing as a racial project of neoliberal multiculturalism. *Educational Policy, 30*(1), 39–62.

Bronfenbrenner, U. (1979). *Ecology of human development: Experiments by nature and design.* Cambridge, MA: Harvard University Press.

Cattanach, J. (2013, March). Support parents to improve student learning. *Phi Delta Kappan,* pp. 19–25.

Centers for Disease Control and Prevention. (2012). *Parent engagement: Strategies for involving parents in school health*. Retrieved from www.cdc.gov/healthyyouth/protective/pdf/parent_engagement_strategies.pdf

Clark, A. G., & Dockweiler, K. A. (2019). *Multi-tiered systems of support in secondary schools: The definitive guide to effective implementation and quality control*. New York, NY: Routledge.

Conderman, G., Ikan, P. A., & Hatcher, R. E. (2000). Student-led conferences in inclusive settings. *Intervention in School and Clinic*, *36*(1), 22–26.

Creighton, F. P., Doub, G. T., & Scott, V. M. (1999). *Survival skills for healthy families* (2nd ed.). Holly Springs, NC: Family Wellness Associates.

Dotterer, A. M., & Wehrspann, E. (2016). Parent involvement and academic outcomes among urban adolescents: Examining the role of school engagement. *Educational Psychology*, *36*(4), 812–830.

Freiman, C. (2016). Poverty, partiality, and the purchase of expensive education. *Politics, Philosophy & Economics*, *16*(1), 25–46.

Hackman, D. G. (1996). Student-led conferences at the middle level: Promoting student responsibility. *NASSP Bulletin*, *80*(578), 31–36.

Henderson, A. T., Mapp, K. L., Johnson, V. R., & Davies, D. (2007). *Beyond the bake sale: The essential guide to family-school partnerships*. New York, NY: The New Press.

Hoover-Dempsey, K. V., & Sandler, H. M. (1997). Why do parents become involved in their children's education? *Review of Educational Research*, *67*(1), 3–42.

Hornby, G., & Lafaele, R. (2011). Barriers to parent involvement in education: An explanatory model. *Educational Review*, *63*(1), 37–52.

Hurst, D. (2017). The end of public schools? The corporate reform agenda to privatize education. *Policy Futures in Education*, *15*(3), 389–399.

Ishimaru, A. M., Torres, K. E., Salvador, J. E., Lott, J., Cameron-Williams, D. M., & Tran, C. (2016). Reinforcing deficit, journeying toward equity: Cultural brokering in family engagement initiatives. *American Education Research Journal*, *53*(4), 850–882.

Lawson, M. A. (2003). School-family relations in context: Parent and teacher perceptions of parent involvement. *Urban Education*, *38*(1), 77–133.

Mapp, K. L. (2019, June). *Building the capacity for effective family engagement*. Presented at the Executive Leadership Academy at the Public Education Foundation, Las Vegas, NV.

Mapp, K. L., & Kuttner, P. J. (2013). *Partners in education: A dual capacity-building framework for family-school partnerships*. U.S. Department of Education. Retrieved from https://www2.ed.gov/documents/family-community/partners-education.pdf

Marina, B. L., & Holmes, N. D. (2009). Education is the great equalizer: Or is it? *About Campus*, *14*(3), 29–32.

Maslow, A. (1943). A theory of human motivation. *Psychological Review*, *50*, 370–396.

McKinney, C., Morse, M., & Pastuszak, J. (2014). Effective and ineffective parenting: Associations with psychological adjustment in emerging adults. *Journal of Family Issues*, *37*(9), 1203–1225.

Mundt, K., Gregory, A., Melzi, G., & McWayne, C. M. (2015). The influence of ethnic match on Latino school-based family engagement. *Hispanic Journal of Behavioral Sciences*, *37*(2), 170–185.

Neuman, S. B. (2013, May). The American dream: Slipping away. *Educational Leadership*, 18–22.

Prilleltensky, I., & Nelson, G. (2000). Promoting child and family wellness: Priorities for psychological and social interactions. *Journal of Community & Applied Social Psychology*, *10*, 85–105.

Richards, M. P. (2014). The gerrymandering of school attendance zones and the segregation of public schools: A geospatial analysis. *American Educational Research Journal*, *51*(6), 1119–1157.

Schuman, M. (2017). History of child labor in the United States – part 1: Little children working. *Monthly Labor Review*. Retrieved from www.bls.gov/opub/mlr/2017/article/history-of-child-labor-in-the-united-states-part-1.htm

Steele, M. L., Maringa, M. K., Tello, J., & Johnson, R. F. (1999). *Strengthening multi-ethnic families and communities: A violence prevention parent training program* [Facilitator manual, parent manual and materials, workshop manual]. Los Angeles, CA: Consulting and Clinical Services.

Tunison, S. (2013). The Wicehtowak partnership: Improving student learning by formalizing the family-community-school partnership. *American Journal of Education*, *119*(4), 565–590.

Tyack, D. B. (1974). *The one best system: A history of American urban education.* Cambridge, MA: Harvard University Press.

Tyack, D. B., James, T., & Benavot, A. (1987). *Law and the shaping of public education, 1785-1954.* Madison, WI: University of Wisconsin Press.

U.S. Department of Education. (2018). *Family and community engagement.* Retrieved from www.ed.gov/parent-and-family-engagement

Van Veslor, P., & Orozco, G. L. (2007). Involving low-income parents in the schools: Communitycentric strategies for school counselors. *Professional School Counseling, 11*(1), 17–24.

Walsemann, K. M., Gee, G. C., & Ro, A. (2013). Educational attainment in the context of social inequity: New directions for research on education and health. *American Behavioral Scientist, 57*(8), 1082–1104.

Weist, M. D., Garbacz, S. A., Lane, K. L., & Kincaid, D. (2017). *Aligning and integrating family engagement in positive behavioral interventions and supports (PBIS): Concepts and strategies for families and schools in key contexts.* Center for Positive Behavioral Interventions and Supports (funded by the Office of Special Education Programs, U.S. Department of Education. Eugene, OR: University of Oregon Press.

WestEd. (2017). *Academic parent-teacher teams: What is APTT?* Retrieved from www.wested.org/wp-content/uploads/2017/03/services-appt-brochure.pdf

Chapter 10

School Safety and Student Well-Being

Key Terms

Trauma-Informed Care
Contagion Effect
Threat Assessment Team
Mental Health Transition Team
Reentry Plan
Incremental Correction System
Restorative Justice
Change Agents

Chapter Concepts

In this chapter, readers will learn:

1. The necessity for rehearsal and the repeated opportunities for cognitive-behavioral corrections.
2. The underlying role adverse childhood experiences have on all aspects of a child's life and the importance of trauma-informed care.
3. Examples of federal and state-level school safety and student well-being initiatives.
4. The need for smart team training to build capacity and efficacy for helping vulnerable students transition back to campus.
5. Red flags for students on the path to an attack.
6. A range of prevention and intervention models available to address the multiple facets of school safety and student well-being.

Behavioral and mental health services are increasingly becoming a necessary function of school systems. Schools are the de facto mental health hospitals for children just as prisons are the de facto mental health hospitals for adults. School shootings, school violence, student killings, extreme bullying, student suicide, and harsh discipline procedures against minority students have been blasted across the social consciousness in an alarmingly increasing number of incidences (Mazer et al., 2015). Educators help keep students safe every day despite the challenges of managing hundreds of students with individual personalities and problems on one school campus. Some students are more challenging to manage than others, and as is often the case, the small percentage of students with the most severe emotional and behavioral problems can cause the most mayhem in an educational setting.

Critical thinking skills and cognitive-behavioral strategies must be nurtured in students, as well as cultural sensitivities and tolerance. Likewise, educators must be cognizant of their own implicit bias and mind-set when handling diverse students' issues competently to reinforce resiliency and to ensure equity in discipline and corrective behavioral practices (Brooks, Brooks, & Goldstein, 2012). Changing implicit bias is easier achieved through changing social contexts rather than trying to change peoples' beliefs (Payne & Vuletich, 2017). In this framework, improving the school climate and culture goes a long way toward reducing educators' own implicit biases with consistent implementation of proactive practices toward all students. Systematically teaching social-emotional-behavioral (SEB) strategies increases the probability that students will feel more connected to others, become more resilient, and lead more meaningful social lives (Aspen Institute: National Commission on Social, Emotional, and Academic Development, 2018). Research suggests that childhood resilience is linked to long-term outcomes, and "clinicians should begin to focus on the development of resilience or protective factors for the most vulnerable youth" (Naglieri, Goldstein, & LeBuffe, 2010, p. 354).

The danger of not having frequent guided socialization opportunities from early childhood on, with explicit and appropriate modeling, is that children who do not know how to play well with others grow into big kids and adults who do not play well with others. In some elementary schools, recess in kindergarten and beyond is all but a thing of the past due to mandatory academic seat time and test preparation with skills drills, which robs students of social skills development and social problem-solving opportunities that unstructured play allows. In 14 states, explicit teaching of social-emotional learning (SEL) skills, such as socialization and self-awareness, are required as part of the K–12 curriculum; this is up from only 1 state in 2011 (Collaborative for Academic, Social, and Emotional Learning, 2018). Illinois was the first state to mandate SEL standards in 2004 and in 2013 added early childhood SEL standards as well (Illinois State Board of Education, 2019). If students have not learned appropriate classroom behavior after first grade, the intensity of punitive measures increases as grade levels rise without guarantee of targeted learning experiences to address underlying skills deficits. Students who should be "old enough" to know how to act right but clearly do not behave within expected norms must have repeated exposure to appropriate modeling and rehearsal with reinforcement of new behaviors to improve coping skills, anger management skills, or social skills deficits. Instead of punishing students with skills deficits, students need to be retaught and given enough time and reinforcement to acquire, rehearse, and sustain new behaviors. Many students will respond to direct behavioral instruction for all, some will require targeted skills practice in smaller groups, and a small percentage will require intensive instruction and individualized support.

Consequences for social-emotional and behavioral issues can be very punitive and applied inequitably in schools, especially for, but not limited to, at-risk minority youth. Such students are often viewed through a school's discipline lens to control crime; these at-risk students face greater consequences of exclusion and harsher punishment than their less at-risk peers (Hirschfield, 2008). Three factors appear to contribute to the bureaucratic default of the discipline lens to crime control in higher-risk schools: "a troubled domestic economy, the mass unemployment and incarceration of disadvantaged minorities, and resulting fiscal crises in urban education" (Hirschfield, 2008, p. 79). Severe punishment of children from communities experiencing economic disadvantages, negative cultural bias, and a high risk of incarceration further exacerbates the poverty cycle and school-to-prison pipeline. The need for inclusive, proactive practices in all schools and communities has never been more evident.

Trauma and Emotional Response

Students are faced with numerous adverse childhood experiences (ACEs) and traumas that permeate all aspects of their lives throughout development. Examples of ACEs include physical abuse and neglect, sexual abuse, emotional abuse and neglect, parental violence, substance abuse in the home, mental illness in the home, caregiver divorce, and caregiver incarceration (Substance Abuse and Mental Health Services Administration [SAMHSA], 2017). Students tend to experience ACEs in clusters, with more than 50% of children experiencing at least one ACE, nearly 40% experiencing two or more ACEs, and 12.5% experiencing four or more ACEs (Felitti et al., 1998). Research suggests that it is not the severity of any one ACE that a child experiences, it is the *number* of ACEs a child experiences that has the greatest impact on his or her functioning (SAMHSA, 2017). Knowledge of students and relationship building between school staff and students and their families are essential for understanding and addressing the underlying basic needs of students.

Supporting students with ACEs and trauma is an expanding responsibility for educators. There are core strengths which children need to be healthy socially-emotionally and behaviorally, including attachment, self-regulation, affiliation, awareness, tolerance, and respect, which lead to student resourcefulness and resilience in the face of adversity (Perry, 2002). The Neurosequential Model of Therapeutics (Perry & Hambrick, 2008) is an example of an evidence-based practice to train educators and build school capacity to provide safe learning experiences in a compassionate way by working sequentially to systematically nurture and heal regions of the brain impacted by trauma, in precise order, from the lowest level at the brain stem to the diencephalon to the limbic system to the highest level at the frontal cortex. The Neurosequential Model of Therapeutics emphasizes that the best biological interventions for students with behavior problems are a safe environment, human interactions that do not retraumatize the brain, and positive relationships with others, which reorganize and heal trauma-related brain impairment over time. Focusing treatment on brain health, and targeting treatment on the correct part of the brain, in the correct sequence, will have a direct and positive impact on behavior. Creating an atmosphere of physical and emotional student safety and relationship building are the primary roles for all educators in the social-emotional-behavioral health of students and in providing trauma-informed care (Cavanaugh, 2016). *Trauma-informed care*, broadly, is an organizational framework that can be used to guide responsiveness to various types of trauma.

When intervening on behalf of students who have experienced some form of trauma, care must be given to understanding the role of the limbic system that guides the internal organization and neuronal connections of the brain (Braak, Braak, Yilmazer, & Bohl, 1996). It is important to note that prefrontal cortex interventions that involve thinking and reasoning, such as listening and talking coherently with a teacher or administrator, do not work well when hypervigilant students interpret events as threatening because their brains easily downshift into their limbic systems, engaging their flight-or-flight responses. This tug-of-war between the limbic system and the prefrontal cortex interferes with human choice making in the present at the potential expense of future consequences (Schüll & Zaloom, 2011). Cortex functioning is impaired when the limbic system takes over. When students are upset or angry, no matter the cause, one of two *involuntary* limbic system responses are activated including flight (i.e., withdrawal, putting head down, hoodie over eyes, hiding under desk, leaving class) or fight (i.e., verbal altercations with other students and teacher, throwing objects, shoving or assaulting people, destroying school property, and other explosive combative behaviors). Whether a threat is physical or psychological, the limbic system limits decision making to fight or flight. Emotionally and behaviorally dysregulated children tend to get the adults around them to act *just like them* because adults get upset in response to student behavior and downshift into *their* limbic systems. The only chance educators have to keep a step ahead is to remain in their own cortexes by planning ahead and remaining calm, which neurologically allows them to have the capacity to be strategic in choosing which variables to reinforce in anticipation of students' behavior.

Box 10.1

Voices from the Field

Stefan was supposed to be sitting at his desk but was wandering around his first-grade classroom while 22 other students drew pictures of their winter-break activities and were writing sentences describing the pictures. Stefan refused to go back to his seat when the teacher told him to. When the teacher impatiently asked Stefan to participate and pointed out the open containers with pencils, markers, and crayons that students were sharing to make colorful artwork, Stefan grabbed a container and threw it on the ground. The teacher engaged in a power struggle with Stefan over picking up the items scattered across the floor. Instead of cleaning up the mess, Stefan ran around the room and grabbed more containers of supplies and threw them across the room. Stefan's behavior ramped up as he destroyed the room, knocking books off shelves and items off surfaces. The teacher evacuated all the other students from the classroom for safety purposes and called the front office for assistance. With all the other students safely out of harm's way and an adult to supervise them in another location, the teacher was able to focus her full attention on Stefan, who was hiding under a desk. Stefan sat under the desk for about five minutes before he was ready to come out and talk. Stefan could not really explain why he got so upset but started picking up the pencils and markers scattered across the room and helped the teacher clean up. He made an excuse that the teacher never called on him when his hand was raised, but the teacher could not recall that happening.

A meeting with Stefan's guardians, his maternal grandparents, revealed that he never knew his father and that his mother lived across the country. His mother had rare contact with Stefan, but he found out over break that she had recently had another baby and was not coming back for him as she had promised. In addition, he was exposed to heavy alcohol and drug abuse in utero, and he had always been a fussy baby and toddler. This background information shed some light on his developmental predispositions and what may have triggered Stefan's emotional and behavioral reaction to the assignment, assumed to be abandonment issues and feelings of rejection from his mother. Stefan engaged in fight (yelling, throwing items, destroying the environment) and then flight (hiding under the desk). The first-grade teacher had never worked with a child who threw such destructive tantrums and required coaching from administrators on which behaviors to attend to and reinforce and when administrative intervention was truly warranted. With coaching and guidance, the teacher was better able to look for early signs, or triggers, of distress in Stefan so she could intervene early before his behavior got out of control. The next time, the teacher would look for these triggers and try to manipulate variables for better outcomes. If Stefan's behavior escalated, she would not engage in a power struggle and would give praise and attention to other students, ignoring the meltdown so as not to throw grease on the fire. She would provide unemotional brief, preplanned statements to redirect him to a designated location to allow him to calm himself. Instead of immediately calling the administration for support, the teacher was taught to utilize an incremental correction system. Stefan was taught to use a designated "chill out" zone where he could go when he was feeling angry and upset, where no additional demands would be placed on him, and he could earn preselected rewards from a menu if he could calm down and recoup without trashing the classroom. Stefan's emotional regulation issues ultimately required a formal behavior plan, daily communication between home and school, and coordination with the grandparents to obtain community services, including psychiatric consultations and family counseling.

In order to overcome limbic system havoc, repeated rehearsal of expected behavior is critical for the student as well as the teacher. Both must be retaught behavior and learned responses in order for the intervention to be effective and for the student and teacher to attain successful outcomes. A limbic system intervention gives a student time and space to recoup without additional prefrontal cortex demands that may be further interpreted as threatening, which, as an unintended consequence, may keep the child in limbic system mode. Taking a break, going to a designated quiet area in the classroom, deep breathing, using relaxation techniques or visual imagery for self-calming gives the brain time to feel safe again, which must happen before any thinking, reasoning, or learning can take place. If the student is able to rehearse these coping skills in advance, including a secret signal between student and teacher when the teacher suspects that an upcoming event may trigger the behavior, the student can exhibit the desired practiced behavior on cue, based on trust and safety, which decreases the probability of limbic system responses and seemingly impulsive aggressive behavior. When students have overactive limbic systems, they are not making bad choices; they are making the only choices their brains will allow them to make, fight or flight. Giving students a sense of safety and trust is the best offense and defense for educators working with hyper-aggression in students.

Young students may not be able to accurately recognize their emotions or be able to generalize coping skills rehearsed in advance to current situations and frustrations. This is especially true for young students who have been exposed to drugs and/or alcohol in utero and/or with executive functioning issues. However, once students turn 8 years old, training them in cognitive behavioral skills using developmentally appropriate language becomes more effective and a feasible reality (Minde, Roy, Bezonsky, & Hashemi, 2010). Intervention training can include responding to misbehavior unemotionally, giving them limited choices to help them feel like they have some control, and using shaping techniques to reinforce what they are partially doing right (starting where they are successful), and building on it will increase the probability of fewer limbic system responses over time. Adults reinforcing students' small steps forward is more effective for emotionally labile students than commenting on misbehavior. For example, "You are facing in the direction of your chair; when you are sitting in your seat, you will be on target!" versus "Why are you out of your seat? How many times do I need to ask you to sit down? Move your clip from yellow to red." It also increases the probability that those students will respond positively instead of downshifting into their limbic system.

Behavioral and Mental Health Policies in Schools

School security and student well-being are at the height of social consciousness. School shootings, such as those that transpired at Sandy Hook Elementary in Newtown, Connecticut and Marjory Stoneman Douglas High School in Parkland, Florida, along with other school tragedies, have risen the level on the barometer of awareness of, and response to, the confluence of variables that keep our children safe while on school campuses. Since the Parkland shooting, 27 states have proposed school safety initiatives ranging from arming school personnel, developing emergency response plans and drills, increasing the number of and access to school resource officers, strengthening building security, increasing access to mental health services, or a combination of the aforementioned initiatives into comprehensive school safety bills (National Conference of State Legislators, 2019).

While there seems to be two primary trains of thought being sensationalized on the approach to school safety, namely, arming teachers or not, the most impactful approach has nothing to do with guns or hardening schools, which are not research-based or evidence-based (Fiddiman, Jeffrey, & Sargrad, 2018; National Association of School Psychologists, 2018; Tanner-Smith, Fisher, Addington, & Gardella, 2017). Conversely, these studies favor behavioral and mental health prevention policies and practices as demonstrating the greatest long-lasting and positive impact on the safety of students, schools, and communities.

Box 10.2

Connection to Practice

Senate Bill 89 (2019) was a comprehensive school safety and student well-being omnibus bill that recently passed in Nevada and was drafted by the Nevada Department of Education and members of a Statewide School Safety Task Force. The 25 members were experts in their respective professions and were appointed to serve in 2018 by Governor Sandoval. The group worked for nearly a year with unwavering leadership from the Governor's Office and the Department of Education to collect and determine the best evidence- and research-based practices for both physical infrastructure and student well-being. The end result was a bipartisan school safety law that was built by experts to increase student well-being and the safety of schools. It was an absolute honor to have been appointed to serve on this task force as a mental health care professional.

Everyone appointed was extremely knowledgeable, experienced in their respective fields, and wanted to be there to problem solve the complex issues; no one was apathetic about the work we were doing. When the larger group split up into two working groups, physical infrastructure and student well-being, I volunteered for the student well-being group. As a school psychologist, my lens was whole child–centered and focused on the organizational structures needed within the state education system to keep students safe and to help them thrive. Having worked in the schools for 14 years, understanding the unique needs of our state, surveying national trends, and scouring through research on the most efficacious approaches to school safety and school-based mental health services five key recommendation domains emerged from my findings: (1) human capital, (2) implementation and action planning, (3) perspectives surrounding behavior, (4) preventative support structures, and (5) accountability standards.

The student well-being working group colleagues heard my recommendations, found their merit, and brought them back to the task force, including them in our working group's comprehensive list of recommendations. The cumulative members of the task force approved the recommendations, and they were passed along to be included in the overall School Safety Task Force Omnibus bill, Senate Bill 89, that was drafted and put forth to the legislature. Following are details of the five unique domains identified and the recommendations made, and passed into law, to address each of the needs.

Human Capital. There just are not enough school-based mental health professionals in our state to begin adequately addressing the needs of our students, let alone to be proactive and to assist with preventative supports. School psychologists, school counselors, and school social workers are staffed at over four times nationally recommended ratios. The long-term solutions will require collaborative buy-in and commitment from a variety of stakeholder groups, but the first step to set the expectation that our human capital needs must be remedied (Cowan, Vaillancourt, Rossen, & Pollitt, 2013). As a result, Senate Bill 89 (2019) was passed requiring the State Board of Education to make recommendations regarding the ratio of students to specialized instructional support personnel (namely, school psychologists, school counselors, and school social workers) that align with their respective national recommendations.

Implementation and Action Planning. In order to begin adequately staffing our school-based mental health profession, there must be a systematic manner in which to permanently achieve better ratios, not providing a Band-Aid fix. It will not happen overnight, and thinking that it can will set districts up for failure. Systemic change will require new higher education training infrastructure, career pathways, defined scopes of practice, and a school-based mental health pipeline. As such, a long-term plan must be established that folds in a variety of stakeholder groups. It was recommended and passed into law that each school district's board of trustees will develop a 15-year strategic plan in which to achieve the recommended ratios.

Perspectives Surrounding Behavior. As a nation we are beginning to shift our perspectives on behavior. Behavior is a learned skill, and school systems have traditionally penalized students for poor behavior when, in fact, the student may have never been taught appropriate behavior or seen it modeled. This lack of explicit training and modeling is unfortunately becoming more the norm as families are experiencing increasing numbers of traumas and unstable living and work conditions. Schools must begin to integrate behavior into the preventative and proactive supports offered to students, not reactively lump it in exclusively with discipline. This resonated with the Task Force and the addition was made, and passed into law, to include behavior not only with discipline practices but also with preventative integrated student supports (ISS), the state's terminology for Multi-Tiered Systems of Support (MTSS).

Preventative Student Structures. Integrated student support frameworks, or MTSS, are ideal for addressing students' internalizing and externalizing behaviors in a proactive manner. While initially just capturing social and emotional learning, it was passed into law that the state's ISS framework must now also include behavior, along with screenings, interventions, and progress monitoring to help better identify and remediate student difficulties. While this process may look different at each school, these mandated screening, intervening, and progress monitoring requirements are essential to ensure that social-emotional and behavioral supports are adequately addressed within the integrated framework.

Accountability Standards. When working toward a desired goal with an understood minimum acceptable threshold, it is important to set accountability standards so that the implementors of a program or initiative know exactly what it is that they are to be implementing and to what degree. While acknowledging that flexibility must be allowed due to the great variability of student need and school resources across districts, there still needs to be a basic understanding of how the ISS framework should be implemented. Through experience with previous legislation, when these basic benchmarks are not made clear or are not required, the fidelity of implementation goes out the window. As such, it was recommended and passed into law that administrator accountability standards be established to ensure the coordination and implementation of ISS.

Aside from these key student well-being recommendations, additional recommendations were made regarding crisis response and physical infrastructure supports. These recommendations include, but are not limited to, composition and requirements of school crisis teams, reporting and accountability of school crisis teams, methods for evaluating and improving school climate, provisions related to anonymous reporting using SafeVoice, requirements for each school to have a school safety specialist, changes in the classification of school police officers, a requirement for each school to develop a restorative discipline plan, changes in reporting with state agencies, and the appointment of a statewide standing School Safety Committee. Based on national research and best practice, the physical infrastructure supports were in the form of improved crisis procedures, human capital of school police officers, and reporting and coordination with the Division of Emergency Management and the Department of Public Safety.

Every member of the task force had insightful and significant contributions to improve the safety of our schools and the well-being of our students; my voice was just one of the many voices. The persistent leadership and commitment from the Governor's Office and the Department of Education was exemplary and spanned two bipartisan administrations as an election had transpired from the task force's creation to the legislature's passage of the bill; much appreciation is offered to all. Recently elected Governor Sisolak signed Senate Bill 89 into law on June 12, 2019, confirming his commitment to school safety and student well-being.

> I constantly encourage parents and educators to speak up and share their perspective and expertise, and this process reinforced to me the importance and value of doing so to have a positive impact on the educational system and outcomes for students. In addition to the work of the task force members, many others contributed to the eventual legislation as well. Parents, teachers, school counselors, school social workers, school psychologists, administrators, community members, and students attended meetings, spoke up during public comment, wrote letters, and shared what they felt would improve school safety and student well-being. Their collective voice was heard and is reflected in the law.

States that adopt educational policies and practices that have not been validated by research violate our children's and educators' emotional and physical safety. Such is the case with Indiana and the policy that resulted from their recent school safety initiative, now Public Law 197 (2019), and includes live shooter drills. The practice of "live-shooter" drills and other simulated, real but not real, traumatic events are being forced unnecessarily on students and educators with no educational value and result in lasting damaging effects. Caution must be used during implementation as many staff and students may have already experienced significant trauma, and there should always be an opt-out when simulations will be used (National Association of School Psychologists, 2017). The increase of posttraumatic stress, anxiety, and other emotional issues has skyrocketed in students and educators suffering from these ill-conceived, highly unregulated operations. The recently publicized instance of Indiana teachers being held in a mock "hostage situation" went too far, with physical and emotional harm of educators occurring during an out-of-control experiment hampered by a lack of ethical standards, educational research, and adequate training (Zraick, 2019).

Knee-jerk policy reactions can result from the spike of awareness on the school safety barometer of public consciousness; however, like any other public health crisis remedies should be thoroughly vetted before unleashing cures that do not solve the crisis and instead compound the problems. No ethical doctor or scientist would ever rush into treating a disease and forcing a treatment on groups of people, which has no evidence of working as intended, let alone a treatment that results in more problems. "Live-shooter" drills should be eliminated immediately from public practice until they are recalibrated and vetted through research as having a positive impact on school safety. The previously mentioned live-shooter simulation that happened in Indiana is an example of policy gone wrong, causing more harm than good. Instances such as this are reminiscent of the Stanford Prison Experiment (Zimbardo, Haney, Banks, & Jaffe, 1971) in which a social experiment went out of control quickly when the volunteer "prison inmates" were subjected to a variety of abusive treatments from volunteer "prison guards" during researchers' attempt to explore how social roles influence behavior, except these active-shooter drills are not an isolated experiment in a college basement restricted to relatively few students, and there is no telling how many children and educators have been traumatized *or will be* traumatized by this harmful practice.

Nine states in the United States allow for the arming of school personnel including the arming of teachers (Erwin, 2019). Florida is one of the most recent and publicly controversial states who have passed legislation, Senate Bill 7026 (2018), allowing teachers to carry guns to school. Hardening schools with metal detectors, added police presence, random searches, and making schools look and feel more like prisons have not led to students feeling safer at school and lead to negative emotional outcomes; however, increasing mental health supports in schools have resulted in positive emotional outcomes for students (Fiddiman et al., 2018; National Association of School Psychologists, 2018; Tanner-Smith et al., 2017). It is estimated that "75%–80% of children and youth in schools in need of mental health services do not receive them. Of those who do receive assistance, 70%–80% receive mental health services in schools" (National Association of School Psychologists, 2016, p. 1). The data are clear: Mental and behavioral supports are essential in the school setting.

In order to implement proactive and preventative behavioral and mental health policies and practices, schools must have the school-based mental health staff coordinate and lead the work. U.S. Senator Tester (D-MT) has proposed federal legislation with Senate Bill 1642, the Increasing Access to Mental Health in Schools Act, to increase retention and recruitment of school-based mental health professionals. Similarly, U.S. Representative Fitzpatrick (R-PA) is drafting proposed federal legislation, the Mental Health in Schools Excellence Program Act, to help with tuition support to incentivize students to enter higher education school-based mental health programs such as school psychology, school counseling, and social work.

Despite the current political appetite to fix or destroy the Patient Protection Affordable Care Act of 2010 (PPACA, 2010), the PPACA promotes school-based health center programs and cites that addressing students' mental health outcomes in a school setting has become a priority. It is also noted in PPACA language that evidence-based programs and evidence-based interventions are frequently underimplemented in school settings. More than 1 in 6 students experience mental health issues, with those in the foster care system experiencing even greater rates, yet only approximately 1 in 10 of these students receive treatment (Maag & Katsiyannis, 2010). Given easier access to highly lethal weapons, more mentally and emotionally unstable students and adults are targeting schools and children specifically to cause massive harm on a large scale (Bonanno & Levenson, 2014). Alarmingly, threats to schools are increasing. Only a coordinated and systematic approach to social-emotional and behavioral supports in schools, in conjunction with family outreach, community health services, and law enforcement efforts, can effectively address the challenges of preventing school violence and mitigating effects of the aftermath.

Schools are traditionally safe places for children; however, in recent years, high-profile acts of school violence have been sharply on the rise. Preventative and administrative measures are needed to decrease this violence and the resultant discipline issues in our schools (Whitford, Katsiyannis, & Counts, 2016). At the school level, a behavioral threat assessment and management (BTAM) model can be used to reduce or block imminent threats to others and "to connect a student of concern (and potential victims) to continually available resources" (Reeves & Brock, 2017, p. 1). At the student level, communication is key in prevention and crisis response. Teachers and families can use certain techniques when speaking to children to help them understand and work through the aftermath of threats or acts of violence. This includes reassuring children of their safety, making time to talk to them about what happened, keeping explanations developmentally appropriate, limiting exposure and time on social media, observing their emotional state immediately following and after a traumatic event, reviewing safety procedures, and keeping up with normal routines (National Association of School Psychologists, 2017). During times of crisis trying to locate loved ones can add to the trauma. National and local organizations, such as the I Love You Guys Foundation, can help with school and community safety and with family reunification in times of crisis.

Addressing student behavior and mental health needs in smart teams on elementary campuses will improve informed decision making, which will result in more equitable decisions for students. There has to be a clear process in place to address concerns about students' SEB stability so that mental health supports can be provided in a timely manner. An obstacle for preventing some student suicides, or other preplanned violence, is when adults and students who have valid concerns about erratic behavior and emotionality of other students do not know who to tell or how to tell others about what they know ahead of time, let alone know how to ask for help for themselves. An inhibition to report is especially true when a child who suspects a pending act of violence has been a victim of violence themselves or has previously witnessed violence (Zaykowski, 2012). Schools that have clearly defined procedures on how to report, and respond to, social-emotional and behavioral concerns will be more sensitive to those reports and more accountable for acting on potential threats. They will also be better prepared to deal with the contagion effect that often follows suicide completions. Mandated educational policies have emerged after tragedies to provide clear procedures previously lacking, which school staff must follow to keep students safe.

For example, in Nevada, a middle school student named Hailee Lamberth died by suicide in 2013 after a series of severe bullying incidences went unaddressed over a prolonged period. Hailee's parents had no idea that bullying was taking place, even though evidence indicated that complaints of Hailee's bullying had been reported to a teacher and on the school district's website allowing for anonymous reporting. Her parents were never notified about the bullying until reading Hailee's suicide note. After the student's death, her family sued the school district and won. In 2015, Nevada became the 20th state in the union to pass antibullying legislation with Senate Bill 504. Antibullying policies were determined, providing a host of supports and procedures for school districts. Mandates were put in place for bullying complaints to quickly travel up the chain of command. School staff must immediately report any complaints of bullying to a school administrator, in which case the school principal is required to immediately stop the bullying and ensure the safety of victims. Principals must formally respond to the complaint by the end of that day or the next school day, with required phone calls to all parents of students involved in the bullying. In addition, principals must maintain written documentation of incidences. Failing to follow procedure could result in immediate termination for school staff members. In Nevada, Senate Bill 504 (2015) is referred to as Hailee's Law.

Policies such as Hailee's Law could be generalized to include reported acts of violence and mandating administrative accountability for following up on threats of pending acts of violence. Keeping students emotionally and physically safe is a reality for educators in all schools. Barriers should be low for students to be referred for behavioral and emotional supports, and barriers should be even lower for reporting safety concerns to school staff with the expectation that the threat will be assessed and addressed in a reasonable amount of time. School safety measures are replicable and should be required to have uniform components applied at all schools. Procedures and processes can be standardized so students have a basic understanding of how to get help no matter which school they attend. When school procedures for identifying and acting on potential threats are established and followed, the next challenge is accountability for coordinated community resources with caregiver and family follow-through.

There are many other state-level policies that can support student behavior and mental health. State representatives can pass legislation that includes the Safe2Tell program that originated out of Colorado. Individual states may call it something different; for example, Nevada has legislated and renamed the model SafeVoice under Senate Bill 80 (2019). Safe2Tell is an anonymous reporting system and protects reporters of bullying and other acts of violence from retaliation by the perpetrators. This type of system can prevent tragedies, connect individuals with interventions and resources, and help save lives.

School Safety

School safety is a multifaceted problem that requires many moving parts to work well together. The number of variables that must be accounted for in school safety is as staggering as the potential number of threats our students face. Our buildings can be quite secure while our students are in danger in the community due to ecological factors beyond the control of the school. For example, the growing phenomena of sex trafficking and the practice of luring children away from school campuses and prostituting them for financial gain are increasing (U.S. Department of Education, 2015). Students who are victims of sex-trafficking are not necessarily abducted and never seen again. School officials need to monitor evidence of odd patterns of attendance, students returning to school with inappropriate or expensive clothing, signs of abuse, and sexualized behavior to identify warning signs of sex-trafficking. More metal detectors and arming teachers do not protect students against the nature of these types of threats. The physical security of a school site must be addressed in terms of school site layout, limited entry points, limited access to students, and school safety drills; however, what keeps children most safe inside schools is relationships with educators resulting in student connections to staff and other students. The effects of increasing security measures in schools are not clear, and some efforts, such as metal detectors, may decrease students' feelings of safety (NASP, 2018). Schools with positive cultures of supports for all students, such as those with positive behavioral intervention supports and MTSS in place, systematically evaluate school incident data and make data-based decisions to make schools safer in smart teams.

School safety is comprised of both physical infrastructure and student well-being. Falling within both groups is human capital. Within the physical infrastructure domain, there are components such as security devices, management and crisis plans, technology supports, and school resource officers to guide and implement the procedures. Within the student well-being domain, there are universal benchmark screenings, a social-emotional learning curriculum, positive behavior supports, proactive classroom management, school cultural incentives, counseling groups, behavior intervention plans, reentry and transition plans, progress monitoring data, and school-based mental health professionals to coordinate, collect, and analyze efforts as part of a comprehensive proactive and preventative effort.

Red Flags

There are red flags in student behaviors that require immediate attention. Aside from average hyper-aggressive students making impulsive threats that can often be quickly assessed and ameliorated, there are patterns of behavior that can arguably be predictive of which students will initiate school violence and possibly school shootings. As researched by the U.S. Secret Service and the U.S. Department of Education (Fein et al., 2004), there were consistencies between perpetrators of mass school violence and warning signs that should be monitored, communicated, and acted upon. The SEB MTSS team is tasked with evaluating the threat level of students, intervening accordingly, and closely monitoring outcomes. The SEB MTSS team, as well as all staff members on campus, should monitor reports from students regarding patterns of troubling behavior and emotionality of older siblings and family members. Such reports could require contact with caregivers and other school campus safety teams for further investigation. It is possible that elementary-aged students may see and hear things that can tip off school staff that an older sibling or someone closely related to their family is headed down a path of attack. There is no valid profile of a school shooter; however, such individuals share commonalities, including a history of mental health difficulties, engaging in social isolation, perceptions of having experienced a catastrophic loss, and having access to weapons (Bonanno & Levenson, 2014). Using the threat assessment approach, as would be used by SEB MTSS teams, teams must consider previous interactions with a potential attacker and history of stressful events, the current situation, and any identified target or targets (Fein et al., 2004). Key findings reported in two U.S. Secret Service and U.S. Department of Education (Vossekuil, Fein, Reddy, Borum, & Modzeleski, 2004; Fein et al., 2004) reports indicate the following about those who have engaged in school attacks:

- Incidents of targeted violence at school are rarely sudden, impulsive acts.
- Prior to most incidents, other people knew about the attacker's idea and/or plan to attack.
- Most attackers did not threaten their targets directly prior to advancing the attack.
- There is no accurate or useful "profile" of students who engage in targeted school violence.
- Most attackers engaged in noticeable behavior that caused concern, or indicated a need for help, prior to the attack.
- Most attackers were known to have difficulty coping with significant losses or personal failures. Many had considered or attempted suicide.
- Many attackers felt bullied, persecuted, or injured by others prior to the attack.
- Most attackers had access to and had used weapons prior to the attack.
- In many cases, other students were involved in some capacity.
- Despite prompt law enforcement responses, most shooting incidents were stopped by means other than law enforcement intervention. (Fein et al., 2004, p. 17)

Warning signs that a student is on a "path toward an attack," which requires immediate investigation, threat assessment, and interventions initiated and monitored by the SEB MTSS team include

- ideas or plans about injuring him- or herself or attacking a school or persons at school;
- communications or writings that suggest that the student has an unusual or worrisome interest in school attacks;
- comments that express or imply the student is considering mounting an attack at school;

- recent weapon-seeking behavior, especially if weapon-seeking is linked to ideas about an attack or expressions about interest in an attack;
- communications or writings suggesting the student condones or is considering violence to redress a grievance or solve a problem; and
- rehearsals of attacks or ambushes. (Fein et al., 2004, p. 50)

Students who display violent behavior verbally, imaginatively, and overtly must be evaluated by threat assessments to determine if they have plans and access to weapons, or means, to carry out acts of destruction. According to studies, individuals with a history of a previous suicide attempt are four times more likely than first-time attempters to successfully complete a later attempt (Christiansen & Jensen, 2007). Recent major losses and/or pending major losses often tip the scales in favor of students acting rashly, especially when it is perceived there is no other way to solve the problem or end their suffering. Such emotions are not restricted to any one gender, race, or ethnicity. However, these feelings of hopelessness and the corresponding suicide attempts and lethality rate are higher for Black Americans than for White Americans (Durant et al., 2006). Teams must be especially alert to students who have actively been seeking weapons and rehearsing attacks or who report such behavior of older siblings or extended family members. It is important to ensure that barriers are low to report behavioral concerns to school staff by students, parents, and the community. Threat assessment, crisis response, and monitoring follow-up are important functions of the SEB MTSS team to prevent school violence, respond to crises, and increase school safety. The PREPaRE training curriculum (NASP, 2017a) is one such crisis response model. A more preventative approach is the comprehensive Framework for Safe and Successful Schools that outlines the various tiers of intervention as part of an MTSS system and has been developed in partnership with, and vetted by, several national organizations: the National Association of School Psychologists, the American School Counselors Association, the School Social Work Association of American, the National Association of School Resource Officers, the National Association of Elementary School Principals, and the National Association of Secondary Schools Principals (Cowan et al., 2013).

In July 2018, the U.S. Secret Service National Threat Assessment Center released an operational guide for preventing school violence, *Enhancing School Safety Using a Threat Assessment Model: An Operational Guide for Preventing Targeted School Violence*. The call for a "comprehensive targeted violence prevention plan" (p. 2) is composed of eight steps that directly align with building and sustaining systematic SEB MTSS teams and functions in every school:

Step 1: Require each school to form a multidisciplinary threat assessment team, which meets on a regular basis, includes team members from a variety of disciplines, has a specifically designated leader, and has clearly established protocol, roles, and procedures.
Step 2: Define prohibited and concerning behaviors, which includes understanding the continuum of concerning behaviors, a low threshold for access to interventions, and assessing concerning statements and actions.
Step 3: Create a central reporting mechanism.
Step 4: Determine the threshold for law enforcement intervention.
Step 5: Establish assessment procedures.

Step 6: Develop risk management options.
Step 7: Create and promote safe school climates, with teachers actively building trusting relationships with students and helping students feel connected to one another and the school.
Step 8: Conduct training for all stakeholders.

These steps are accounted for in a school with a functional implementation of SEB MTSS.

All evidence supports SEB MTSS teams' structure, functions, and processes in a school setting. It is clear that MTSS is the ideal framework in which comprehensive, targeted violence prevention plans may come to fruition. The SEB MTSS team outlined in this book more than meets the minimum standard for a multidisciplinary threat assessment team as described in the U.S. Department of Homeland Security and the United States Secret Service report and should become the gold standard in both secondary and elementary schools.

Behavioral and Mental Health Prevention

Regardless of age, all students, especially those with social, emotional, and behavioral deficits, should be given SEB learning opportunities in a school setting. Lack of adequate screening procedures and classrooms full of students with SEB problems are some of the leading causes of teacher burnout and job dissatisfaction (McCarthy, Lambert, Lineback, Fitchett, & Baddouh, 2016; Benner, Kutash, Nelson, & Fisher, 2013). Teachers who feel unprepared to adequately manage students in the classroom are at the highest risk of leaving the profession (Charner-Laird, Kirkpatrick, Szczesiul, Watson, & Gordon, 2016; Brezicha, Bergmark, & Mitra, 2015). While some teachers remain apathetic to students' social, emotional, and behavioral needs, teachers are not always to blame for their lack of interest or preparedness. Not all higher education teacher preparation programs adequately prepare preservice teachers about social-emotional-behavioral issues and how to identify, intervene, and monitor performance. Most higher education training programs do not offer or require such a class as part of their course syllabi, nor is it required for state licensure. The need for investing in teacher skill development and competencies to support students behaviorally in the classroom cannot be overemphasized. Educators must have interdisciplinary skills, be experts in content areas, and be masters of their own cognitive behavior in choosing which variables to reinforce in the environment for students, regardless of personal experiences, feelings, or opinions. Ideally, educators are perfect role models for students, remaining calm and collected through all situations; realistically, they are people with personal experiences, feelings, and opinions.

Teachers should be mindful not to accidentally reinforce inappropriate behaviors, thus increasing the likelihood of those undesirable behaviors occurring in the future. For example, giving too much attention and power to disruptive students or sending them to the office for misbehavior which the students know will allow them to avoid unpreferred tasks can be a negative behavior–consequence cycle. When student behavior crosses the threshold from off-task to atypically disruptive, behavior problems can have an impact on the academic growth of self and others. When students misbehave, their attention is diverted from instruction and often diverts other students' attention from instruction resulting in a contagion effect when other students become off-task and disruptive. *Contagion effect* refers to a replication of a particular behavior by others, due to proximity or social media exposure. Relationship skills, positive interactions with students, and improving teacher classroom management skills to reinforce and increase on-task behavior are some of the most important and effective strategies for having a positive impact on student learning in the long term.

The administration of most screenings takes very little effort for students and teachers; however, following up with higher-risk students will require the attention and expertise of school-based mental health service providers to the exclusion of performing other duties during that time period. The perception at the school level is that schools do not have the capacity to support the potentially high number of students identified with moderate to high-risk factors. Identifying students who are at-risk for suicide and self-harm without having anywhere or anyone to send them to in the community for treatment could leave school districts and states open to liability issues for not properly responding to students with identified risk factors. This is why it is important for teams to have intervention supports in place at all tiers and to have established wraparound services readily available in which to refer at-risk students. Without these supports, sole responsibilities then fall on parents and families to closely monitor emotionally unstable children, requiring constant adult supervision and locking up medications, guns, chemicals, knives, tools, and anything that can be used as a weapon to ensure they do not have access to potentially harmful elements.

A lack of capacity of mental health supports in schools and in the community is a public hazard and a perceived barrier in the administration of universal SEB screeners in some school communities. Nonetheless, SEB universal screenings are one of the most powerful tools schools can use to quickly and accurately identify vulnerable students who require mental health supports most acutely. In addition, how teachers feel about their comfort, commitment, and culture of supports in administering and using these measures has a significant impact on their success (Brackett, Reyes, Rivers, Elbertson, & Salovey, 2011).

Effective proactive and reactive practices can be ingrained in school culture, ultimately protecting student rights, improving school safety, and saving lives. Highly charged emotional and behavioral situations can be minimized, or negative outcomes mitigated, if handled effectively; likewise, unfortunate and permanent damage can result if such situations escalate despite, or as a result of, actions taken to intervene. Advanced training in de-escalation techniques is critical for school staff members for knowing how to decode student behavior, identify the function of behavior, determine the skill deficit, and apply the right intervention, such as described in the research-based curriculum of Life Space Crisis Intervention (Long, Wood, & Fecser, 2001). Sometimes, the escalation of student behavioral issues can be more gradual over time and likely outcomes predicted. Long-term damage to students on the wrong path may be reduced, if not prevented, when one caring adult is paying attention and has the power to actively make changes to the student's probable trajectory by building a trusting relationship. When adults are trained to actively promote treatment within the school setting and out in the community, students' support networks increase. Students with behavioral and mental health issues can be especially exhausting for teachers to manage long term, which is why a network of support in the school setting is so critical. Even a tenacious, well-intentioned staff member may not get too far in garnering support for advocating for a student's mental health care alone, as there can be a maze of steps to get services. This is why the supportive embrace and support of the school-based SEB MTSS team is so critical.

In a school setting, a smart team approach capitalizes on individual strengths and collective responsibility in reaching common goals as an organization and in functional discrete units, consisting of experts in adaptive team configurations. The size of each team depends on the size of the task, yet are interconnected with other teams. The SEB MTSS team is composed of mental health, medical, administrative, and teaching experts on campus. The tasks of this large team are comprehensive in proactively and reactively supporting SEB health on campus. Smaller units of this team, in multiple configurations, can work together as separate but overlapping smart teams to work on discrete components of SEB health. For example, the threat assessment team and mental health transition team are micro-teams of the overall SEB MTSS team. Each team has overlapping members that are all part of the macro SEB MTSS team. A *threat assessment team* most often includes the school psychologist, school counselor, school social worker, and school nurse conducting an assessment of whether a student is an immediate threat to self and/or others, although not all team members are necessarily a part of a specific threat assessment at the same time. A *mental health transition team* often includes the same school-based mental health professionals as the threat assessment team, as well as any other professionals required by the school district or state, and assists to put supports in place for students who transfer back to campus from a residential treatment facility. The combination of professionals present to participate in discrete smart team functions depends on many factors, including what other crises are going on at the same time, who is available to respond, and a lack of access to professionals because of funding and shortages issues. Mental health transition teams are activated when students who have been hospitalized for mental health issues (most often suicidal attempts) come back to the school setting and require a reentry plan to support the student proactively in coping successfully in coming back to school. The *reentry plan* is the specific plan devised by the mental health transition team to support the student who transitions back to campus from a hospital or residential treatment facility. The mental health transition team includes the student and parent or legal caregiver, in addition to the designated team members from the SEB MTSS team. Reentry mental health transition plans are developed by the team and disseminated to the classroom teacher and specialists, just like any other behavior plan, intervention plan, or individualized education program (IEP). The reentry plan may include, but are not limited to, specifics regarding personnel involved, how to handle transitions in the hallways, designated "safe zones," and updated de-escalation procedures.

Box 10.3

Connection to Practice

As a volunteer for a national burn charity that focuses on burn prevention and burn survivor support, I had the opportunity to visit our local burn care unit, where the charity was holding an informational gathering for families to learn more about camp, a therapeutic camp that addresses the specific psychological and emotional needs of children with burn injuries. At the gathering, I met the burn unit's child-life specialist and the licensed family therapist, both of whom worked closely with children and their families on the unit. When they found out I was a school psychologist for the local school district, they shared with me their frustrations in communicating with schools after a child has been admitted to the burn unit. Some caregivers got truancy notices and other upsetting calls regarding student absences, even after parents notified the school of the students being hospitalized. They had difficulty getting timely release of information forms signed by caregivers between the hospital and schools, impacting the burn unit staff's ability to be proactive with continuing educational services while at the hospital, as well as transitioning back to school after discharge. In further discussion, the burn care specialists reported running up against barriers to obtaining home-bound services for patients and did not understand the steps involved to bridge community and school services.

After assessing the situation, scheduling follow-up meetings to listen to hospital staff, talking with school-based officials, and considering both sides of the problem, I realized that existing school district practices and policies could be aligned to address the need for effective communication among hospital staff, caregivers, and local schools. I helped the burn specialists set up a protocol for every child who entered the burn unit. First, they had parents sign a school district release of information form as soon as possible, not a hospital form (even though it should not matter) so it would be immediately recognizable and familiar to school staff when they got it. Parents were encouraged to sign two releases (1) so that the hospital could communicate with the school and (2) so that the school could communicate with the hospital. This would enable the burn unit staff to send a written letter addressed to the school's nurse regarding the student's situation. A barrier for communication was that many parents were emotionally unable to engage in effective dialogue with school officials due to grief, so the letter from the hospital to the school formally notified school officials about the student's specific needs and would set supports in motion at the school level. Next, it became apparent that the hospital did not know who to contact within the school district to liaise. The hospital reported that it had reached dead-ends multiple times. It only took me two phone calls to find the correct person in home-bound services the hospital could contact directly for guidance to overcome barriers of home-bound support of its patients. Connection made. Last, the burn unit staff was trained in how to request and participate in reentry planning with the school-based mental health transition team upon hospital discharge. I provided them an example of a reentry plan and familiarized them with how to participate in the planning team, including how to overcome barriers when the schools seem unresponsive. I advised them to call the school nurse to request a reentry plan. If they did not hear back, call the school counselor. If they did not hear back, call the school psychologist, and then start over with the school nurse if, for some reason, no one followed up with them. I assured them that one, if not all, of those professionals would respond, as leaving a message with the school's office secretary may not get them anywhere.

Our local schools are required to provide reentry plans for suicidal students coming back from hospitalization with district forms and procedures administratively in place to address the needs of these specific students returning to school. However, there is no procedure for reentry planning for students who have been hospitalized for reasons other than suicidal ideations and attempts. This remains a barrier, but there is no need for a separate procedure. Parents can request a reentry plan at the school, which may not guarantee one for their child because the school district does not require staff to create a reentry plan for burn victims, as is the case for suicidal students. However, SEB school-based mental health professionals in our school district understand the value of these support plans, are already trained in the process, and are highly unlikely to decline a parent request for a valid reason. In the end, the burn unit staff members understood who to ask, what to ask for, and how to ask for supports for their clients in relation to school supports after burn injury, hospitalization, and transition back to school in our school district. This is a perfect example of a school-based and community collaboration.

In addition to environmental and emotional supports, reentry planning for children with burn injuries includes educating staff members, informing classmates and other peers in what to expect (that children may look different on the outside and disfigured by scars but are the same inside), and address how to support and include children with burn injuries socially and emotionally. The burn foundation has a specific reentry protocol for burn survivors they share with schools, which can be considered and incorporated into the school reentry plan as deemed appropriate. The mental health transition team's functions at a school can support all students returning from hospitalization, not solely suicide attempts, but can include any trauma such as burn injuries, rape and assault, and any other tragedies that turn children into survivors. Expanding the scope of reentry planning for all students who need it is another example of how existing school procedures can be aligned with SEB MTSS goals and functions, with overlapping smart teams supporting students inclusively.

Connecting with students and helping them with access to resources they need can be extremely time-consuming. Finding quality community mental health service providers who have openings in their schedule and take caregivers' insurance takes time. Insurance issues, a lack of ability to provide a copay to providers, a lack of transportation, parent denial of severity of issues, and a host of other factors can be barriers to students getting timely treatment, which requires educators' patience, encouragement, and finesse to gently push families into community sector supports when student mental health needs exceed the scope of school interventions. Teachers, administrators, and support staff are probably not going to have the time or ability to help students this way.

There truly is power in teamwork, sharing strengths and shouldering burdens together. Mental health providers in schools, including school psychologists, school counselors, school nurses, and school social workers, are needed in every school so they can prioritize risks for students and assist families by making connections with appropriate resources in the community. Unfortunately, most school districts do not have near enough school psychologists, school counselors, school nurses, or school social workers, who are critical to bridging supports and services among school, home, and community. Whether or not local education agencies or states prioritize mental health supports for students in schools, the need is there, and overworked, underpaid educators are left carrying the burden of supporting all students with mental and behavioral health problems, and their families by proxy.

Behavioral and Mental Health Prevention Now

Schools can prioritize mental health and student safety by empowering an SEB MTSS team to lead school practices to identify, prioritize, intervene and monitor students with Tier 2 and Tier 3 SEB needs on an elementary school campus. SEB MTSS enables a team of highly specialized educators to systematically evaluate student behavioral data and monitor the social-emotional and behavioral functioning of the highest-risk students on campus. Sources of information include discipline records, teacher report, parent report, student report, school counselor report, school nurse report, school social worker report, school psychologist report, and administrator report. Regular meetings guarantee all parties regularly share pertinent student information allowing the team to work together cohesively to address student SEB issues head-on by sharing responsibilities and actively promoting appropriate supports and services for students within and out of the school setting.

Referrals for Tier 2 and Tier 3 behavioral supports can come through staff recommendation or through the regular SEB MTSS team's triangulation of data sources, including student SEB screener scores. Schools with universal SEB screenings can get ahead of the ball by identifying and tracking students with the most severe externalizing and internalizing behavioral and emotional issues quickly. Schools that do not use universal SEB screeners are at a disadvantage because responses to behavioral and mental health issues are going to be more reactive and less proactive. Students who act out or have extreme externalizing problems usually come to the attention of school administration on their own. Others are brought to the attention of school counselors through a teacher request for assistance, a parent report, a peer report, and a self-report. The goal of a school-based SEB MTSS team is to engage in active problem solving to minimize the impact of mental illness, behavioral disorders, and maladaptive behavioral functioning, which is often compounded by family, environmental, and socioeconomic stressors, and to use a coordinated approach to connect the most socially-emotionally and behaviorally unhealthy students to the supports and services they require. Anyone can refer a student to the SEB MTSS team, but typically, school counselors and school psychologists on an elementary campus are in the best position to lead triangulation efforts to help determine whether students require Tier 2 or Tier 3 supports, or something beyond what the school can provide exclusively. Students requiring case management by this team are selected because they are deemed a high risk of threat to themselves and/or others. Whether students are managed by the SEB MTSS team or not is a team decision based on data triangulation, experience with the student, and professional judgment.

The SEB MTSS team monitors all the most severe SEB problems and high-risk students on campus, regardless if a student is already receiving special education support. The majority of students monitored by the SEB MTSS team may never be referred for special education evaluations because of a variety of situational and environmental factors, severe attendance issues, or high transience. Bottom line is that emotionally fragile students can break with pressure if not adequately supported. The question is not whether potentially dangerous students are on elementary school campuses, the question is whether these students are going to cause significant damage to self or others before they get help or if they can be identified and provided services prior to unfortunate, yet potentially predictable, events, including assaults on students and others, self-harm, and threats to do the same. Children are vulnerable to inconceivable horrors, such as abuse, neglect, sexual assault, sex trafficking, drug additions, bullying, gang violence, and horrifying family situations. Many parents struggle to survive with their own issues and have no idea how to protect their children, let alone successfully navigate the challenges of raising children with severe mental and behavioral health problems.

Systematically watching out for traumatized, behaviorally and emotionally unstable students; actively solving problems for them at school; and connecting students and families to community services could be a matter of life and death and is a necessary component of safe schools.

Who Now

Elementary classroom teachers and school counselors are the most likely school professionals to directly monitor students' performance and behavior on an elementary campus. They often communicate and collaborate on how best to address student concerns. In large schools and school systems, the sheer number of students can be difficult to keep track of when teachers and counselors have large caseloads to monitor. Usually, the students with the most inappropriate, aggressive, or disruptive behavior have already come to the attention of the school-based mental health professionals and school administrators. Discipline alone does not correct chronic behavior problems that are better addressed in the long term with comprehensive positive behavioral instructional supports. It is especially negligent for elementary schools to default to a punishment model instead of an incremental correction model to improve behavior because student behavior is much more malleable in the younger years and least resistant to change. Educators must provide an unlimited number of trials for cognitive behavioral corrections; as a master educator emphasized, the correct number of trials it takes to learn something is the exact number of trials it takes and no less. School discipline reform is much needed, which is a nuanced function of technical tasks such as resource utilization, normative processes such as conflict resolution, and political maneuvering to shift power (Wiley et al., 2018). Incremental correction systems are flow charts of specific cognitive-behavioral correction opportunities and include when to offer them and under what conditions. It is used prior to discipline procedures and offers the student various opportunities to engage in pretaught coping, self-awareness, and self-management techniques that can be modeled, rehearsed, and positively reinforced.

Teachers are required to do their progressive discipline procedures and implement incremental correction systems, school administrators are required to do their progressive discipline procedures, and school counselors are stuck in the middle with no control over outcomes. School counselors, trying to support students by providing social-emotional learning experiences and helping support families with referrals to community agencies, may also feel pressured into being a part of the progressive discipline plan. Most school counselors on elementary campuses prefer to be associated more positively and proactively with students than as a necessary part of the negative reinforcement cycle of discipline procedures.

Rather than relying on progressive discipline and ultimately removing elementary students from campus, a more effective approach is to use restorative justice. *Restorative justice* is a strengths-based approach to student behavior in which students are active participants in changing their own behavior through a series of cognitive-behavioral techniques. In this manner, the behavioral change is not something that happens *to* them; it is something that they actively help to facilitate and lead the action on. Incremental correction systems support this strengths-based approach and provide necessary opportunities for students to correct their own thinking and actions.

The administrator in charge of discipline usually knows every child with a behavioral challenge on campus by name and knows their caregivers' phone numbers by heart. They have as much, if not more, pertinent information on students with social-emotional and behavioral challenges than any other school staff member. Communication between the administration and school counselors seems like a natural relationship, as counselors help students with getting through emotional and social crises, as well as communicating with caregivers, monitoring credit attainment, and attending parent–teacher conferences. However, relationships between discipline and counseling are sometimes strained, with two opposing desired outcomes if the administration is not completely on board with the SEB MTSS program or they do not buy in to restorative justice practices.

Discipline depends on consequences, and harsh consequences are sometimes warranted. However, mediation, understanding, social skill development, character building, and second chances may also be warranted and can be achieved through restorative circles or other opportunities to review and revise behavioral choices (van Woerkom, 2018). Facilitating restorative circles helps students identify their emotions, to become more self-aware, and to process how to handle them in a safe and supportive environment. Whose decision is it to give students more chances, more counseling, harsher discipline, or even consideration of eligibility for special education services when facing students with severe and chronic emotional and behavioral problems? Are second chances applied fairly? Are harsh punishments applied equitably? Oftentimes, such decisions are made unilaterally, often by the teacher or the administrator in charge of discipline. Who ensures that discipline practices are applied equitably? How much more equitable could student outcomes be if a team of mental health–based school professionals worked together regularly to actively manage students with wraparound services within the school and extended out to home and community? Schools can operate more inclusively with established restorative practices that have been agreed upon and practiced within a school environment, which decreases the tension that arises in emotionally charged situations.

Having a SEB MTSS team in place is necessary to systematically monitor students who are severely struggling emotionally and behaviorally; which, in turn, has positive impacts on student outcomes and increases school safety. The SEB MTSS team's structures and functions will provide the backbone to systematic procedures to increase interventions and monitoring in the lives of students with the most severe emotional-behavioral issues. Each role on the SEB MTSS team has unique and overlapping responsibilities. Members of the SEB MTSS team often include many of the individuals who can help facilitate change on campus. Required team members include all school administrators, all school counselors, the school psychologist, the school nurse, the school social worker, community and school advocates, and any other behavior mentor who has a close relationship with the target students.

Making the Change

According to the National Implementation Research Network (2017), there are three main categories that affect implementation: organizational issues (resources and procedures), leadership practices (budgeting and staff motivation), and competency issues (staff training and development). Successful implementation of MTSS is affected by each of these categories. Academic interventions may be perceived as easier to implement with fidelity than behavioral interventions because teachers feel more prepared to address the former over the latter. However, the very systems of universal screening, systematic monitoring of students' data, growing intervention opportunities, data-based decision making, and streamlining documentation into manageable procedures for teachers and other educators can be amended for students' behavioral and mental health needs from the Academic MTSS model.

Systematically monitoring and proactively intervening with the highest-risk students increases school and student safety (Benner et al., 2013). Elementary school teams that effectively implement a data-based decision-making model for academics will have a much easier time adapting to SEB MTSS roles and functions because the processes overlap in many ways. The organizational issues are exactly the same in terms of procedures: scheduling time and space in the master calendar for regular meetings and locations, ensuring meetings take place and are conducted professionally, having a chair-lead team discussions and document case notes, ensuring member preparedness to present data to the team at meetings, and making data-based decisions and communicating to those who need to know. The SEB MTSS team meetings mirror the format of Academic MTSS team meetings except for different required team members and sources of data discussed.

Data sources, referral procedures, and team members' functions differ somewhat from Academic MTSS processes, but the format is almost identical. Students selected to be managed by this team demonstrate social-emotional and behavioral needs that exceed what can be provided through universal Tier 1 and targeted Tier 2 supports. Only students with the most severe SEB difficulties, usually a small percentage of students requiring Tier 3–level supports, will be actively managed by this team and includes students who have been identified in the highest-risk category of potential harm to themselves and/or others. Regular meetings are necessary (every other week) to provide an opportunity for the team to draft, review, and revise treatment plans, present new information, document behavioral status, and add or terminate services and resources. The regular meeting schedule for SEB MTSS is preferably every other week because it allows a cushion for meetings to get moved back a week in cases of having to cancel or reschedule without sacrificing bimonthly team attention to emotionally and behaviorally fragile students. In larger schools, teams may find that they need to meet weekly to address all students requiring the most intensive interventions, support, and monitoring. Larger schools have more students and may need to meet more often to address the volume of students' needs. Meetings should not typically go over 45 minutes or so in duration because longer meetings compete with other essential professional responsibilities of team members. School teams must ultimately choose the best SEB MTSS team meeting schedule, taking into account school realities and student populations while supporting regular meetings to ensure the success and sustainability of team functions and communication.

Change Agents

As implementation science can verify, getting people to change their practices in a professional setting is easier said than done (Bryk, Gomez, Grunow, & LeMahieu, 2016). This MTSS framework for implementation describes the content, procedures, and empirical nature of interventions in relation to the individuals implementing program practices, known as change agents. *Change agents* influence innovation and make decisions that align with the central mission of an organization. They are external experts who engage in the system to help diffuse innovative practices and processes

(Hall & Hord, 2006). Ideally, change agents in schools are school administrators, but that is not always the case. Often, school psychologists, school counselors, and teachers take leadership roles in MTSS to move current practices to new practices with better outcomes. It cannot be stated enough that if the school principal does not actively support school leaders in leadership roles, school staff will be much less likely to respond or comply with new practices. The principal depends on networks of many individuals to support the school's overall MTSS framework including Academic MTSS and a unique team to support SEB MTSS. By administratively supporting the change agents on campus, desired initiatives have a better chance of succeeding. Change agents must be empowered to act on school improvement measures and deliver the message of expected professional duties within the structures and functions of MTSS.

Exercise 10.1

SEB MTSS Team Development

- Who are your current natural leaders and change agents on your school staff?
- How are change agents empowered to actively grow school community participation in best practices and new practices?
- What supports can be implemented to improve the reinforcement, power, and effectiveness of change agents?

There are several barriers to overcome in developing behavioral and mental health supports and an SEB MTSS model in schools. Potential barriers to changing mental health support structures in schools include the following:

- Too many students and not enough time to get to know each individually
- Not enough training for teachers to adequately inquire and understand the backgrounds and issues of their students
- Too few people trained in mental health supports in schools: shortages of school psychologists, school counselors, school social workers, school nurses, special education teachers, and culturally competent role models
- A lack of communication between staff members
- Stigma associated with mental and behavioral health. Oftentimes, adults want to ignore red flags in children not because it is best for the child but because it is more palatable than confronting the realities about behavioral and mental health disorders that require active professional management and possibly lifelong treatment.
- Different agendas of staff members (i.e., discipline vs. restorative justice)
- A lack of staff commitment and follow-through in response to safety issues
- Resistance to cultural change. A team approach to mental and behavioral health issues feels like one more responsibility to team members who may not appreciate more meetings or responsibilities.
- A lack of adequate training. Teachers and staff must be trained to recognize warning signs of student instability and know how to report concerns and observations of poor student hygiene, bizarre student perceptions, and risky behavior.

- Inconsistent expectations and implementation of procedures. Oftentimes, students and staff are aware of which students are struggling emotionally and behaviorally, but they do not know how to get help. Who to tell? Where to go? How to do it? School staff can be accountable for following clear procedures.
- A lack of adequate screening and data-triangulation procedures. Depressed students are underidentified without universal screenings, externalizing behaviors, or peer reporting.
- Overuse of zero-tolerance policies. Most hyper-aggressive students get expelled or suspended before help happens and restorative practices can occur.

Barriers to behavioral and mental health programming and supports in school can and must be addressed. There will always be barriers at both the micro- and macro-levels; however, with adequate time, planning, and partnering, these barriers can be overcome.

Exercise 10.2

SEB MTSS Barrier Survey

- What are barriers to behavioral and mental health supports at your school?
- What are some solutions to barriers at your school?
- What additional supports or resources are needed?
- How is stigma being addressed and neutralized?

Box 10.4

Connection to Practice

The LIQUID Model to Social-Emotional-Behavioral Health in Schools

Leadership

Effective school leaders provide ongoing opportunities for students, staff, and families to build competence and relationships to achieve personal and community social-emotional and behavioral health. Key components of Leadership to SEB health in schools include the following:

- Prioritizes emotional health and well-being, proactive, listens to staff and community members' concerns, effectively addresses issues, and dedicates the right level of support
- Fully committed to funding Tier 1 social-emotional and behavioral learning opportunities and building Tier 2 and Tier 3 supports
- Sets performance goals, for example, lowering expulsions and lowering student to student violence
- Treats staff, students, and parents with dignity giving voice, giving comfort
- Supports community resource networking
- Values competencies, visibly supports, and empowers SEB MTSS team members and functions

- Has an administrative presence and support at SEB MTSS team meetings
- Requires and reinforces SEB benchmark screenings throughout the year to help identify and track student behaviors
- Supervises SEB instruction to ensure fidelity of implementation

Inclusiveness

Making school relevant using culturally competent practices is a priority. Prevention, family outreach, community-based services, and lowering barriers to treatment improve access to supports and services. Key components of Inclusiveness to SEB health in schools include the following:

- Universal, high-quality SEB learning experiences from kindergarten through 12th grade
- Explicitly taught community and social skills
- Implementation of valid behavioral interventions improves equity
- Higher accountability for educators enforcing discipline fairly
- Implicit bias must be addressed openly and directly
- Nurture critical thinking using cognitive-behavioral strategies, incremental correction systems, increased cultural tolerance, and improved sensitivity and empathy
- Culturally competent teaching practices

Quality Control

Standardized processes and procedures are implemented to automate required components (scheduling, intervention class curriculum, documentation of data within tiered supports), and teams have confidence in the system and the quality of the interventions provided. Students get the help they need when they need it, with functional systems to provide timely services, and with reflective and corrective practices in place. Key components of Quality Control to SEB health in schools include the following:

- Universal, high-quality SEB learning experiences from kindergarten through 12th grade are implemented with fidelity.
- Evidence-based Tier 1, Tier 2, Tier 3 SEB learning opportunities are accessible and implemented with fidelity.
- Leaders conduct random fidelity checks of SEB curriculum and activities.
- The quality control experts are school leadership and the school-based mental health providers (in accordance with evidence-based practices). All school administrators, the school psychologist, the school counselor, the school nurse, the school social worker, additional specialists, and mentors.
- Meeting regularly to discuss mental and behavioral health schoolwide issues, identify and monitor the management of the highest-risk Tier 3 students, and liaise with offsite stakeholders.
- Regular communication between team and staff in the care of and planning for students *requiring intensive Tier 3 supports and services* is well coordinated.
- Responding to teachers and families who have students with difficult behaviors.
- Engaging in crises response planning, implementation, and debriefing
- Following a continuous improvement model with feedback looping
- Building and growing supports; solve problems oftentimes with limited resources
- Keeping barriers low for accessing SEB services

Universality

Schoolwide access to Tier I SEB instruction, with targeted and intensive supports available as needed. All students have access to the intensity of instruction they require. Regardless of the severity of the academic or behavioral issue, each student is receiving quality support at their individual level. Every student, every quarter has their SEB temperature checked to determine if follow-up services may be required. Continuous care and monitoring for those who need it, supports, and functions are in place to allow the opportunity for *all* students to access instruction. Key components of Universality to SEB health in schools include the following:

- All students participate in the universal SEB benchmark screenings, whether they have a history of problems or not
- All students have access to supports and services if they have a demonstrated need
- Social-emotional and behavioral skills will be taught to all students using evidence-based practices at corresponding developmental age levels at Tier I. For example, all students receive social-emotional learning opportunities, and they learn expectations across all areas on campus (classroom and schoolwide) and the implementation of positive behavioral instructional supports (PBIS).
- Tier I practices must meet standard criteria to align with evidence-based practices and teaching competencies.

Implementation and Feedback Looping

Schools must have structures, functions, and processes in place to support student SEB development and remediation. The MTSS and Behavioral and Mental Health MTSS teams work together to provide case management and actively solve problems for students demonstrating the need for additional SEB support through data sources. Staff and school community member input is valued and all are encouraged to freely contribute to the feedback loop of how responsive systems are to the needs of the school community. Program evaluation cycles allow for examining practices resulting in improved service delivery. It is imperative for teams to stay on top of resource mapping and create a referral database of the most current reliable and effective resources available to support student SEB health. Key components of Implementation and Feedback Looping to SEB health in schools include the following:

- Put structures and functions in place to support all students behaviorally and develop social-emotional learning opportunities at Tiers I, 2, and 3.
- Select evidence-based SEB learning curricula and schedule delivery times in the master calendar.
- Support MTSS school functions by providing continual learning opportunities for teachers in classroom management and relationship building with students.
- PBIS and SEL health are integrated and embedded in school culture to improve socially just practices.
- Build and support a mandatory site-based SEB MTSS team who share responsibilities for managing high-risk students. This team serves as the quality control panel

for site-based problem solving and resource networking as it pertains to student behavioral and mental health, specifically, and student and school safety, in general. The team is responsible for examining and improving practices.
- Use feedback looping cycles, both single loop and double loop, to inform on routine daily implementation and long-term program sustainability (see Chapter 12).

Data-Based Decision Making

Using a variety of data sources to make informed decisions about students, the efficacy of implementation of the MTSS framework, school culture, and staff procedures and processes helps teams prioritize and implement adequate supports to the needs of their unique schools. Data informs and leads the discussions of whether practices are effective or not based on data trends, and the fidelity of implementation must be ensured before accurate data-based decision making can occur. If trends indicate that systems or treatments are ineffective, then new solutions must be tried and closely monitored for quantitative and qualitative outcome data. Key components of Data-Based Decision Making to SEB health in schools include the following:

- Students are screened three times a year at regular benchmark intervals to strategically monitor their SEB performance levels.
- Students are systematically monitored for a number of indicators across data sources. When triangulated data suggest that interventions are required or new treatment is warranted, help happens, and changes are made to address student deficits.
- Specialized, highly confidential data used by the SEB MTSS team in solving problems for students with SEB issues may include, when applicable, behavioral, health, and developmental histories; scores on SEB benchmark screeners, counselor documentation and impressions; history or reports of trauma; psychological and psychoeducational evaluation reports; police history; medical/psychiatric report and records; parent/caregiver report; student reports to teachers and staff; nurse's report; school psychologist report; discipline report; response to behavior plans/supports and progress monitoring data; teacher report and anecdotes; and reports of current events or problems on and off campus.
- The team meets at least twice a month to discuss the entire caseload, new developments, and new directions for supports and services. They communicate regularly on *all* irregular student activities, major losses and disruptions, or events that may impact behavioral and mental health.
- SEB MTSS team members are responsible for communicating with families, guardians, and outside agencies (with proper releases signed); and for actively contributing to feedback looping by mapping and evaluating the usefulness of resources based on how well the services and service providers respond to needs of students referred to them.
- Barriers are addressed to improve access to care for students with SEB issues.
- Data-based decision making for SEB occurs according to the MTSS Evaluation Frequency and Intensity Framework (see Chapter 12).

References

Aspen Institute: National Commission on Social, Emotional, and Academic Development. (2018). *How learning happens: Supporting students' social, emotional, and academic development.* Washington, DC: Author.

Benner, G. J., Kutash, K., Nelson, J. R., & Fisher, M. B. (2013). Closing the achievement gap of youth with emotional and behavioral disorders through multi-tiered systems of support. *Education and Treatment of Children, 36*(3), 15–29.

Bonanno, C. M., & Levenson, R. L. (2014). School shooters: History, current theoretical and empirical findings, and strategies for prevention. *Sage Open, 4*(1). Retrieved from ttps://doi.org/10.1177/2158244014525425

Braak, H., Braak, E., Yilmazer, D., & Bohl, J. (1996). Topical review: Functional anatomy of human hippocampal formation and related structures. *Journal of Child Neurology, 11*(4), 265–275.

Brackett, M. A., Reyes, M. R., Rivers, S. E., Elbertson, N. A., & Salovey, P. (2011). Assessing teachers' beliefs about social and emotional learning. *Journal of Psychoeducational Assessment, 30*(3), 219–236.

Brezicha, K., Bergmark, U., & Mitra, D. L. (2015). One size does *not* fit all: Differentiating leadership support to support teachers in school reform. *Educational Administration Quarterly, 51*(1), 96–132.

Brooks, R., Brooks, S., & Goldstein, S. (2012). The power of mindsets: Nurturing student engagement, motivation, and resilience in students. In S. L. Christenson, A. L. Reschly, & C. Wylie. *Handbook of research on student engagement* (pp. 541–562). New York, NY: Springer.

Bryk, A. S., Gomez, L. M., Grunow, A., & LeMahieu, P. G. (2016). *Learning to improve: How America's schools can get better at getting better.* Cambridge, MA: Harvard Education Press.

Cavanaugh, B. (2016). Trauma-informed classrooms and schools. *Beyond Behavior, 25*(2), 41–46.

Charner-Laird, M., Kirkpatrick, C. L., Szczesiul, S., Watson, D., & Gordon, P. (2016). From collegial support to critical dialogue: Including new teachers; voices in collaborative work. *Professional Educator, 40*(20), 1–17.

Christiansen, E., & Jensen, B. F. (2007). Risk of repetition of suicide attempt, suicide or all deaths after an episode of suicide: A register-based survival analysis. *Australian & New Zealand Journal of Psychiatry, 41*(3), 257–265.

Collaborative for Academic, Social, and Emotional Learning. (2018). *State scan scorecard infographic.* Retrieved from https://casel.org/wp-content/uploads/2018/09/CSI-infographic-9-7-18-v4.jpg

Cowan, K. C., Vaillancourt, K., Rossen, E., & Pollitt, K. (2013). *A framework for safe and successful schools.* Bethesda, MD: National Association of School Psychologists.

Durant, T., Mercy, J., Kresnow, M., Simon, T., Potter, L., & Hammond, W. R. (2006). Racial differences in hopelessness as a risk factor for a nearly lethal suicide attempt. *Journal of Black Psychology, 32*(3), 285–302.

Erwin, B. (2019). *School safety: Guns in schools.* National Conference of State Legislatures. Retrieved from www.ncsl.org/research/education/school-safety-guns-in-schools.aspx

Fein, R. A., Vossekuil, B., Pollack, W. S., Borum, R., Modzeleski, W., & Reddy, M. (2004). *Threat assessment in schools: A guide to managing threatening situations and to creating safe school climates.* U.S. Department of Education. Retrieved from www2.ed.gov/admins/lead/safety/threatassessmentguide.pdf

Felitti, V. J., Anda, R. F., Nordenberg, D., Williamson, D. F., Spitz, A. M., Edward, V., . . . Marks, J. S. (1998). Relationship of childhood abuse and household dysfunction to many of the leading causes of death in adults: The adverse childhood experiences (ACE) study. *American Journal of Preventative Medicine, 14*(4), 245–258.

Fiddiman, B., Jeffrey, A., & Sargrad, S. (2018). Smart investments for safer schools. *Center for American Progress.* Retrieved from www.americanprogress.org/issues/education-k-12/reports/2018/12/19/464445/smart-investments-safer-schools/

Hall, G. E., & Hord, S. M. (2006). *Implementing change: Patterns, principles, and potholes* (2nd ed.). Boston, MA: Pearson Education.

Hirschfield, P. J. (2008). Preparing for prison? The criminalization of school discipline in the USA. *Theoretical Criminology, 12*(1), 79–101.

House Bill 1004, Indiana 2019.

Illinois State Board of Education. (2019). *Social-emotional learning standards.* Retrieved from www.isbe.net/Pages/Search-Results.aspx?k=SEL%20standards

Long, N. J., Wood, M. M., & Fecser, F. A. (2001). *Life space crisis intervention: Talking with students in conflict* (2nd ed.). Charlottesville, VA: Pro-Ed.

Maag, J. W., & Katsiyannis, A. (2010). School-based mental health services: Funding options and issues. *Journal of Disability Studies, 21*(3), 173–180.

Mazer, J. P., Thompson, B., Cherry, J., Russell, M., Payne, H. J., Kirby, E. G., & Pfohl, W. (2015). Communication in the face of a school crisis: Examining the volume and content of social media mentions during active shooter incidents. *Computers in Human Behavior, 53,* 238–248.

McCarthy, C. J., Lambert, R. G., Lineback, S., Fitchett, P., & Baddouh, P. G. (2016). Assessing teacher appraisals and stress in the classroom: Review of the classroom appraisal of resources and demands. *Education Psychology Review, 28,* 577–603.

Minde, K., Roy, J., Bezonsky, R., & Hashemi, A. (2010). The effectiveness of CBT in 3–7 year old anxious children: Preliminary data. *Journal of the Canadian Academy of Child and Adolescent Psychiatry, 19*(2), 109–115.

Naglieri, J. A., Goldstein, S., & LeBuffe, P. (2010). Resilience and impairment: An exploratory study of resilience factors and situational impairment. *Journal of Psychoeducational Assessment, 28*(4), 349–356.

National Association of School Psychologists. (2016). *Mental health infographic.* Retrieved from www.nasponline.org/resources-and-publications/resources-and-podcasts/mental-health/school-psychology-and-mental-health

National Association of School Psychologists. (2017a). *Best practice considerations for schools in active shooter and other armed assailant drills.* Retrieved from www.nasponline.org/resources-and-publications/resources-and-podcasts/school-climate-safety-and-crisis/systems-level-prevention/best-practice-considerations-for-schools-in-active-shooter-and-other-armed-assailant-drills

National Association of School Psychologists. (2017b). *Talking to children about violence: Tips for parents and educators.* Retrieved from www.nasponline.org/resources-and-publications/resources/school-safety-and-crisis/talking-to-children-about-violence-tips-for-parents-and-teachers

National Association of School Psychologists. (2018). *School security measures and their impact on students.* Retrieved from www.nasponline.org/Documents/Research%20and%20Policy/Research%20Center/School_Security_Measures_Impact.pdf

National Conference of State Legislators. (2019). *How states are addressing school safety.* Retrieved from www.ncsl.org/blog/2018/04/05/how-states-are-addressing-school-safety.aspx

National Implementation Research Network. (2017, August 8). Retrieved from http://nirn.fpg.unc.edu.

Patient Protection Affordable Care Act of 2010, 42 U.S.C. § 18001 et seq. (2010).

Payne, B. K., & Vuletich, H. A. (2017). Policy insights from advances in implicit bias research. *Policy Insight from the Behavioral and Brain Sciences, 5*(1), 49–56.

Perry, B. D. (2002). *Training series 2: Six core strengths for healthy child development.* Houston, TX: The ChildTrauma Academy.

Perry, B. D., & Hambrick, E. P. (2008). The neurosequential model of therapeutics. *Reclaiming Children and Youth, 17*(3), 38–43.

Reeves, M. A. L., & Brock, S. E. (2017). School behavioral threat assessment and management. *Contemporary School Psychology.* Retrieved from https://doi.org/10.1007/s406880017-0158-6

Schüll, N. D., & Zaloom, C. (2011). The shortsighted brain: Neuroeconomics and the governance of choice in time. *Social Studies of Science, 41*(4), 515–538.

Senate Bill 504, Nevada 2015.

Senate Bill 80, Nevada 2019.

Senate Bill 89, Nevada 2019.

Senate Bill 1642, Congress 2019.

Senate Bill 7026, Florida 2018.

Substance Abuse and Mental Health Services Administration. (2017). *Adverse childhood experiences*. Retrieved from www.samhsa.gov/capt/practicing-effective-prevention/prevention-behavioral-health/adverse-childhood-experiences

Tanner-Smith, E., Fisher, B. W., Addington, L. A., & Gardella, J. H. (2017). Adding security, but subtracting safety? Exploring schools' use of multiple visible security measures. *American Journal of Criminal Justice, 43*(1), 102–119.

U.S. Department of Education, Office of Safe and Healthy Students. (2015). *Human trafficking in America's schools*. Retrieved from https://safesupportivelearning.ed.gov/sites/default/files/HumanTraffickinginAmericasSchools.pdf

van Woerkom, M. (2018). Building community with restorative circles: A technique for proactively building the skills and relationships students will need when challenges arise. Retrieved from www.edutopia.org/article/building-community-restorative-circles

Vossekuil, B., Fein, R. A., Reddy, M., Borum, R., & Modzeleski, W. (2004). *The final report and findings of the safe schools initiative: Implications for the prevention of school attacks in the United States*. U.S. Department of Education. Retrieved from www2.ed.gov/admins/lead/safety/preventingattacksreport.pdf.

Whitford, D. K., Katsiyannis, A., & Counts, J. (2016). Discriminatory discipline: Trends and issues. *NASSP Bulletin, 100*(2), 117–135.

Wiley, K. E., Anyon, Y., Yang, J. L., Pauline, M. E., Rosch, A., Valladares, G.,. . Pisciotta, L. (2018). Looking back, moving forward: Technical, normative, and political dimensions of school discipline. *Education Administration Quarterly, 54*(2), 275–302.

Zaykowski, H. (2012). Reporting physical assault: How experiences with violence influence adolescents' response to victimization. *Youth Violence and Juvenile Justice, 11*(1), 44–59.

Zimbardo, P., Haney, C., Banks, W. C., & Jaffe, D. (1971). *The Stanford prison experiment: A simulation study of the psychology of imprisonment*. Stanford University Press. Retrieved from https://web.stanford.edu/dept/spec_coll/uarch/exhibits/Narration.pdf

Zraick, K. (2019, March 22). Indiana teachers were shot with pellets during active-shooter drill, union says. *The New York Times*. Retrieved from www.nytimes.com/2019/03/22/us/indiana-teachers-shot.html

Chapter 11

Social-Emotional-Behavioral MTSS

Key Terms

SEB MTSS
SEB MTSS Team
SEB MTSS Student Database
6–13–13–6 Benchmark Windows
About Me Everywhere
About Me Care-to-Share
Phase I Prioritization
Phase II Prioritization
Data-Triangulation Chats

Chapter Concepts

In this chapter, readers will learn:

1. The importance of providing comprehensive SEB programming.
2. How a SEB MTSS team functions and what roles the key members have.
3. How to conduct universal SEB screenings, identify indicators of SEB risk, provide tiered interventions, and monitor student response under SEB MTSS.
4. How the LIQUID Model is embedded within SEB MTSS.
5. The implementation components of *Healthy Minds, Safe Schools*: an integrated SEB MTSS Model.

Evolving from the ever-present need to increase school safety and student well-being comes Social-Emotional-Behavioral (SEB) multi-tier systems of support (MTSS). *SEB MTSS* is built on the familiar framework of Academic MTSS with the focus shifting from Academic identification, prioritization, intervention, and monitoring, or IPIM, to SEB IPIM. The SEB MTSS framework helps identify students with internalized and externalized social, emotional, and behavioral issues. At the secondary level, this model is commonly referred to as Behavioral and Mental Health MTSS; however, due to sensitivities at the elementary level, the more commonly used term is SEB MTSS. Both terms can be used interchangeably and preference is determined by school administration and response from families and staff.

SEB MTSS

A *SEB MTSS team* is needed to support students with social-emotional and behavioral issues and is composed of highly trained individuals tasked with school safety and addressing the behavioral health and emotional well-being of students in a school and community setting. As previously mentioned, depending on the comfort level of the school and community, some may find the term *social-emotional-behavioral* more palatable than *behavioral and mental health*. In reality, the teams function the same. However, many families of young children do not support the idea of their child participating in a schoolwide mental health program, no matter how preventative and proactive it may be.

The SEB MTSS framework must follow the same tiered support system as the academic intervention framework, and SEB MTSS team members are typically selected by the administrator under the hybrid committee selection model outlined in Chapter 5. It is critical to emphasize that evidence-based behavioral practices in a school setting need to start at Tier 1 before Tier 2 and Tier 3 can be effectively implemented and evaluated, as is the case in academic tiers of support. Building capacity for training and supports at Tier 3 only is a thinking error many school teams make, focusing interventions solely at the highest-risk offenders in a reactive versus proactive manner. However, implementing quality social-emotional and behavioral Tier 1 and Tier 2 instructional opportunities as soon as feasible would alleviate the need for expensive and effort-intensive Tier 3 interventions much of the time. Tier 3, individualized behavior plans for high numbers of misbehaving students in classes can be difficult to implement, at best, and highly disregarded, at worst, because of the complexity of implementation and documentation requirements. Regular education teachers are not typically prepared to manage multiple students with individualized behavior intervention plans (BIPs) in one class and benefit from the support of the SEB MTSS team when faced with that situation.

In general, the behavioral health of students in a classroom is largely dependent on the skill of the teacher. Educators who teach behavioral expectations and strategically pay more attention to students when they act civilly, rather than uncivilly, are most likely to have students who behave within classroom expectations (Sprick, 2009, 2013). These strategic reinforcements are brief, preplanned corrections that follow the expectations established by the teacher at the beginning of the year and align with schoolwide expectations. While each classroom teacher will have his or her own behavior management system, there should be some alignment to the schoolwide incremental correction system regarding when teachers are to call home, which offenses require family engagement, when to have the student reflect on their actions within the classroom and then out of the classroom, and when the situation is so severe that administration should be called. For nearly 100% of offenses the administration should not be the first number to call, the parents or guardians should be. Proactive classroom management is considered Tier I behavioral instruction, as are explicit teaching methods of schoolwide expectations through positive behavioral instructional supports (Sprick, 2009, 2013). Environments in which expectations have been clearly taught by caring educators who strive for positive relationships with students and who reinforce, or manipulate, the right variables in the classroom and throughout the school trump individualized behavior plans for most students most of the time. When these expectations are reinforced in the home through partnerships with the families, they are even more successful.

Universal Tier 1 instruction in social-emotional and behavioral (SEB) functioning, from prekindergarten through high school, should be as valued in school as academic rigor. Intervention programs that specifically target behavioral interventions (the B in SEB) have been correlated to a decrease in antisocial behavior and an increase in prosocial behaviors, while programs that focused on social-emotional learning (SEL; without the B in SEB) demonstrated less impact and less rigorous investigations into behavioral variables (Sabey, Charlton, Pyle, Lignugaris-Kraft, & Ross, 2017). Even with the significant impact SEB intervention has, SEB screening only occurs in approximately 2% of schools (Harrison, Vannest, & Reynolds, 2017). Children need to be taught behaviors that are conducive toward living socially and emotionally healthy lives. Learning prosocial behavior is dependent on learning in the home environment through family values and social structures into the community but should not be depended on as the sole source of instruction in civil behavior.

As evidenced by the increasing numbers of students who do not have good role models of proper civil behavior at home and who do not demonstrate appropriate social behavior at school, school-based solutions are needed. While many at-risk students exhibit poor coping skills and problem solving in the face of frustration in increasing numbers, they are not the only ones, and *all* students would benefit from research-based SEB learning experiences in the school curriculum. Ideally, states not only would adopt SEB standards, but SEB MTSS would also be mandated from kindergarten through 12th grade, like academic content for subject levels. SEB programming that is implemented with fidelity will benefit all students through clear expectations, fair discipline practices, and socially just behavioral interventions. Fidelity of instructional delivery will be intrinsically reinforced with the teaching staff as they see the benefits reaped within their classrooms. Students who perceive that discipline is fairly distributed by teachers who care about them are more likely to accept natural consequences, which may increase their cooperation with efforts to replace behaviors that are maladaptive with more functional behaviors to meet their needs.

Explicit SEB Instruction and Intervention

Students must be given more opportunities to learn social-emotional regulation skills if they do not learn them naturally or from positive and negative consequences in the general environment. These core SEL competencies include self-awareness, self-management, social awareness, relationship skills, and responsible decision making (Collaborative for Academic, Social, and Emotional Learning, 2018) and should be integrated into the proactive and preventative practices of SEB MTSS. At Tier 2, interventions for behavioral and emotional regulation must provide a more targeted approach, including exposure to appropriate behavioral modeling and rehearsal of new behaviors with guided feedback. This level of intervention is typically delivered in the form of small-group counseling with like-risk students, such as those with issues of poor anger management, social skills, sadness, or relationship building. Depending on the specific intervention, Tier 2 students are monitored weekly and their level of risk, or response to the intervention provided, is reevaluated after completion of the six- to eight-week counseling group session. A weekly self-monitoring log can help students receiving these Tier 2 interventions with self-awareness as well as self-management. This type of intervention, along with check-in–check-out programs and evidence-based social skills curriculum taught by school social workers, school counselors, or other trained educators to small groups of students can be very effective for targeted instruction (Ross & Sabey, 2014). One example of a proven research-based tool is Sanford Harmony, which is composed of stories, activities, and lesson plans that can be taught in isolation or embedded within the existing instructional curriculum and focus on prosocial and problem-solving skills surrounding relationships, empathy, confidence, and choice making. Whichever curriculum is used, there must be repeated opportunities for students to practice new skills with guided feedback. Accommodations including limbic system interventions, pressure passes (allowing students to leave stressful situations for a predetermined safe place), extended processing time, and alternative work locations, if warranted, can all be part of Tier 2 behavioral supports leading up in intensity to Tier 3–level supports, if required regularly and specifically.

As found in earlier chapters of this text, scheduled Tier 2– and Tier 3–level SEB interventions, such as scheduled academic intervention blocks, provide the added bonus of simplified documentation of interventions with lesson plans and attendance logs. Block scheduling allows for creative "blocking" of intervention times and allocates specific time within the master schedule to provide evidence-based interventions that can be monitored by administrators for fidelity. It is important to note that learning a new habit or behavior requires daily rehearsal for long enough to become part of one's behavioral repertoire. The formation of new behaviors takes an average of 66 days, or 9 to 10 weeks (Lally, van Jaarsveld, Potts, & Wardle, 2010) or more, for students who do not rehearse the desired behavior on the weekends.

In a perfect world, funding for SEB MTSS programs would be budgeted for the target students' entire school year, but school budgets are tight. At the very least, intensive supports through SEB MTSS programs should be funded for at least one full semester at the beginning of the school year for students who are functioning at a Tier 2 and Tier 3 level with less costly maintenance programs built in for the rest of the year. The positive outcomes of building community partnerships and building relationships with organizations such as Big Brothers Big Sisters, the United Way, and the 100 Black Men should not be underestimated either. School districts should pay now for culturally competent teaching practices and adequate SEB MTSS in schools, or society will pay later for building more prisons for all the children the system will fail generationally. All students must be given ample opportunity to learn successful SEB skills.

A small percentage of students will demonstrate behavior that is atypical, maladaptive, and resistant to proactive management strategies over prolonged periods of time across settings so as to provide evidence for suspicion of a lower-incidence disability (i.e., emotional disturbance) under Individuals with Disabilities Education Act (IDEA, 2004). These students may require an individualized education program (IEP) with a BIP, or a 504 plan if deficits can be addressed with accommodations alone. SEB interventions must provide the requisite documentation of prior interventions and responses needed for IDEA services. This documentation includes any interventions implemented on behalf of the student, behavioral notations and progress monitoring reports, attendance logs, discipline history, counselor's notes, and individualized behavior improvement plans or any anecdotal documentation by teachers or other educators in regards to frequency, intensity, and duration of behavioral episodes.

BIPs are considered Tier 3 territory as are recurring direct school counseling services, individualized incentive planning, behavioral charting, and supports that are intensive in the community, including psychological and counseling supports, psychiatric supports, medical supports, and mandatory court interventions for students with a history of problems with law enforcement. Students receiving Tier 3 SEB supports require that behavioral performance be monitored daily. Many schools already have MTSS teams, behavior teams, and individualized education planning teams to support these functions.

General referrals to SEB MTSS for behavior, and social or emotional problems, outside of the universal SEB screening process, should be collected and managed through an automated referral system. The person designated as the collector of these referrals, whether it be the school counselor or some other specialist on campus, must then loop back with the referring teacher to determine the level of severity and the true nature of the referral. Referrals are then brought to the appropriate grade-level team or the SEB MTSS team for documentation and support in Tier 2 or Tier 3 intervention planning, as well as coordination with caregivers, classroom teachers, and school counselors. Some students requiring Tier 3 may qualify for special education services or are already receiving special education supports.

Students who already qualify for special education support may be identified as requiring Tier 2 and Tier 3 supports. For those who already qualify for special education, contact must be made between the classroom teacher and the special education teacher of record to ensure the student displaying problem behaviors is having their needs met, which is information that would be captured in present levels as well as goals, benchmarks, and accommodations in the IEP. If the student does not currently have a BIP, this would be a great opportunity to identify targeted and preferred behavior and put a plan in place. If the student already has a BIP, the classroom teacher and special education teacher of record can come together to brainstorm ways to make the plan more effective and to ensure that the current plan adequately addresses the student's presenting needs.

A very small percentage of the most acute students requiring Tier 3 intensity supports, whether they have an IEP or not, will require active case management by a school team that specializes in overseeing the treatment plans of the most severe Tier 3 caseload. This particular smart team includes individuals with highly concentrated talent working in coordination with other related or overlapping highly skilled teams, communicating systematically to work together efficiently in identifying, assessing, and managing potential threats and intervening early. In this light, a school's SEB MTSS team is positioned to be incredibly smart.

The SEB MTSS team is considered the most intensive SEB support team, comprised of all school personnel licensed to conduct suicide protocols and threat assessments and all administrators on campus, to actively manage the most dangerous students, as in a triage model. This team engages in Tier 3 problem solving, proactive treatment efforts, and reactive problem solving. Administratively, it is wise to remember that if a student is *suspected* of having an educational disability that student has the same legal protections and rights as the students who have already been identified with the disability, including disciplinary protections against expulsion as a consequence of behaviors that appear to be a manifestation of the suspected disability.

Exercise 11.1

Grow Your SEB Supports

- List Tier 1 SEL, behavioral supports or any initiatives currently in place at your school to teach behavioral expectations to all students.
- Team exercise: Research curriculum options, family engagement activities, and brainstorm possible SEB learning opportunities that could be incorporated into the current curriculum.
- List Tier 2 SEL, behavioral supports or any initiatives currently in place at your school to teach behavioral expectations to a selected number of students requiring more intensive reteaching.
- Team exercise: Research curriculum options, family engagement activities, and brainstorm possible SEB learning opportunities that could be incorporated into the current curriculum.
- List Tier 3 SEL, behavioral supports or any initiatives currently in place at your school, or in the community, to teach behavioral expectations to high-risk and special-needs students.
- Team exercise: Research curriculum options, family engagement activities, and brainstorm possible SEB learning opportunities that could be incorporated into the current curriculum.

Where to Start

Ready or not, educators will have students whose behavior and affect range from the norm to highly atypical and dysfunctional. Teachers who do not have positive proactive classroom management skills are going to struggle with even the most benign behaving students in otherwise structured settings. Ideally, the school administration will provide training to the entire staff on positive school culture, positive classroom management, the incremental correction system, and discipline plan. Teachers with higher student referrals to the office or administration, especially in at-risk populations, should be provided mandatory classroom behavior management coaching and skill development opportunities, both formal and informal, to improve classroom management skills and, ideally, get individually coached by a colleague trained in accomplished teaching with at-risk populations (Cannata, McCrory, Sykes, Anagnostopoulos, & Frank, 2010). When a student is not succeeding in a classroom environment sometimes the problem lies in a lack of understanding, compassion, or skill on the part of the student, teacher, or both.

Teachers with highly effective management skills, who do not respond to student behavior emotionally, are always the best choice for students with special behavioral needs. Administrators should be mindful that the most effective teachers often get tapped out quickly with extra duties on campus, in addition to managing the most difficult students on campus, which leads to burnout. Some students are unstable, unpredictable, disruptive, and highly explosive no matter who is teaching. *Of course, not all students who make threats or act threatening are actual threats to student safety, just as not all students who are actual threats to student safety make threats or behave volatilely.* It is important to have systems in place for observation, communication, and problem solving to quickly identify and support students who are at risk of engaging in behaviors that lead to dangerous situations for themselves, other students, school staff, and those in the community.

Staff members must be trained to perform quick screenings to skillfully identify students with internalizing and externalizing problems, leading to quicker identification of those with moderate to imminent risk of suicide, self-harm, and risk of harming others, as well as those who would benefit from follow-up with less urgent, but very serious, needs requiring mental health and community supports. These schoolwide SEB MTSS benchmark screenings are led by trained school-based mental health professionals and are recommended to occur at least twice a year; ideally, they would correspond to academic benchmark or assessment periods three times a year. There are several free tools available to schools, in addition to programs for purchase, with some assessments administered via teacher report and others administered via student report. In the elementary setting, the general recommendation is for teachers to complete the screenings; however, each school is going to have to select the measure and rater system that works best for their individual needs and the intent that they are trying to achieve. For purposes of a schoolwide universal SEB screener, a lengthier assessment does not always equal better as schools and districts will also need to consider whether active parental consent, passive parent consent, or opt-out will be required. The fewer barriers to universal screening of students, the better.

Some schools and school districts use universal SEB screenings to help identify high-risk, emotionally fragile students and those in need of more immediate and intensive interventions for signs of depression and signs of suicide. The screenings can also help identify students who may be at risk for anxiety or poor social skills. For example, schools within Boston Public Schools use universal screening methods to ask straightforward questions about students' thoughts and feelings about their behavioral and mental health (Boston Public Schools, 2017). Universal screenings cast a wide net and allow educators to systematically sift through responses of student risk indicators to focus attention on students who fall within the at-risk range or significant risk range for internalized and externalized behaviors. Using teachers as raters on the universal screeners allows for coordinated administration of the screeners, which can be administered during staff meetings and allows for short administration times (depending on the tool) and immediate results (depending on the tool).

Schools conducting universal SEB screenings can use results to examine Tier 1, identify students for Tier 2 and Tier 3 programming opportunities and as mid- and postscreenings to measure SEB functioning, intervention response, and perceptions over time. Larger schools may be reticent about implementing SEB screenings due to fears that the screenings may automatically lead to a tremendous spike in the number of suicide protocols and other types of threat assessment, which could overwhelm school-based mental health supports and referrals to community medical and mental health care facilities. Rather, the screenings should be viewed as a temperature check on students' SEB status, which helps inform and guide grade-level teams and the SEB MTSS team in their formation of Tier 2 and Tier 3 interventions. Campuses may not feel they have the resources to conduct full-scale SEB screenings; however, many screenings can be administered and scored electronically, and schools often find that the proactive value of identifying at-risk students and increasing opportunities to intervene early outweighs the up-front inconveniences of scheduling and manpower it takes to conduct the screenings.

SEB MTSS Team Members

Pinpointing types of services provided by team members, and wraparound resources provided by the school, will improve the automaticity, sustainability, and effectiveness of SEB MTSS (National Resource Center for Mental Health Promotion & Youth Violence Prevention, 2017). Building effective relationships within the school environment and among community agencies will increase the probability that students in need will receive appropriate and timely services, thus increasing student and campus safety. The SEB MTSS team operates at the highest level of student confidentiality, and according to Family Educational Rights and Privacy Act (FERPA), confidential information can be shared with team members who have a *legitimate educational interest* (Family Educational Rights and Privacy Act, 1974) in the student; however, it is important to safeguard student confidentiality, as would be expected in any mental health or educational setting, unless students intend to hurt themselves or someone else. Confidential personally identifiable information is most often shared among the SEB MTSS team members throughout the school day, during meetings, and in the form of the SEB MTSS Student Database shared at meetings. Teams need to follow information sharing policies and be mindful to ensure that student privacy is protected because information collected by this team may not be found anywhere else in educational records and is only used for real-time problem solving to protect students from themselves and others. Teams may elect to put an information-sharing policy in writing specifically for this team. Some things they might consider include (1) establish procedures for storing and sending sensitive SEB information digitally that can be accessed by other parties; legally, this is a gray area because many districts use Google Drive and related products in which the intellectual property rights remain with the individual, but Google technically has a worldwide license to use the content (Google, 2018); (2) store private records and notes about students' identifiable information in a secure and locked location; (3) reduce or destroy personal notes and identifiable data of students when it is no longer necessary to provide services for the students; and (4) protect confidential information of individual students monitored by the team that does not directly pertain to their educational services. Highly confidential information is shared among the SEB MTSS team members, and most of that information cannot be discussed outside of the team unless the person, such as classroom teacher, has a legitimate educational interest and it is relevant for that teacher to know. For example, in discussing a student who has aggressive behaviors at school, the school psychologist or school counselor may conduct an interview with the caregiver that revealed details of a history of sexual abuse. Not all the child's teachers would need to know this information unless it had a specific impact in the classroom. Even then, the classroom teacher would most likely be given an abbreviated briefing on the history or told generally that there had been abuse, not the specific details that were revealed during the caregiver interview. The specialist teachers, such as those for art or physical education, may also witness the child having anger problems but would not necessarily need to know about the history of abuse. In the case that the same student was dressing or acting provocatively and lying frequently, then specialist teachers would need to know that they should take great care to never be alone with the child and be given the background information to avoid compromising situations for the teachers or other students. It all depends on who needs to know and why they need to know. The reason this point is so pertinent is because information shared in a timely manner is the currency of SEB intervention effectiveness, but placing extra emphasis on the need for privacy of students' personal information, including details of their tragic lives, must not only be respected but highly guarded.

Administrators

School administrators must actively lead and support SEB MTSS, to create a culture and climate of tiered supports. All the school administrators on campus are automatically part of the SEB MTSS team, whether or not they attend meetings. As in the beginning of any new initiative on a school campus, the school principal is strongly urged to take an active interest in the performance of SEB MTSS. *When the principal visibly supports this team, the message to other administrators and staff members is that SEB MTSS is a school priority and that working to support students with behavioral and mental health issues is a school priority.* The principal's regular attendance at SEB MTSS meetings, at least initially, commands professional behavioral standards at the meetings. Assistant principals are required to communicate with school counselors and other SEB MTSS members on matters relating to discipline issues, administrative actions, and teacher regulations pertaining to interactions with students and caregivers, which may be relevant in team decision making.

At some point, the school principal can nominate another administrator or school leader to attend SEB MTSS meetings to speak on behalf of the school administration so that not all administrators have to attend all meetings. Ideally, the individual representing all the school's administrators at meetings will be able to contribute information and provide support to the team with the understanding of teachers' needs and the knowledge and experience of schoolwide expectations for discipline issues and can liaise with the principal for decision making or has the authority to made decisions on the spot. At least one school administrator or representative is required to attend every SEB MTSS meeting, but all have an open invitation to discuss students of concern at any meeting.

Administrators contribute in many ways including communicating with counselors about students who are chronically coming to their office for discipline and with the special education department if a student has an IEP to ensure that disciplinary suspensions do not exceed limits before compensatory time is owed. Administrators also contribute by observing and reporting unusual student behavioral patterns, reporting SEB incidences regarding target students to the team, handling anonymous reporting of safety through Safe2Tell or any other similar system, providing insights into the function of student behavior, making executive decisions for student and staff safety, and ensuring restorative practices are applied equitably. School administrators will be called on to support school-based mental health professionals' decision making in times of crisis. Each state and each district has different laws and procedures; however, policies do exist for school administrators to legally have students hospitalized for observation and treatment without parent presence or consent in the most extreme cases.

School Counselors

School counselors are an integral part of a school's behavioral and mental health supports. Counselors help students through issues large and small; giving students second chances and avenues to make their way back when they have gotten off track. School counselors are often aware of students' personal histories, adverse childhood experiences, successes and failures in social circles, family issues, and many other facts about students that few others may collectively know. *All school counselors on campus are required to be on the SEB MTSS team and attend all meetings.* In most schools, school counselors interact with all age levels of students throughout the day, including supervision duties, in-class lessons, and other responsibilities that bring them in direct contact with students. Counselors have their "frequent fliers" and usually know the frequent fliers to the administrator's office and nurse's office, as well. They communicate with numerous students on a personal level throughout the day and hear all kinds of reports from students about what is happening on campus. School counselors have skilled eyes and ears to process and prioritize SEB information from various sources. School counselors often handle significant student issues independently, sometimes administratively, and occasionally with other mental health professionals. Some students have problems that are more chronic and more severe than a typical student going through hard times. While school counselors can assist with any manner of SEB issues, one of their greatest values is working in conjunction with the school psychologist to provide comprehensive and well-rounded supports. School counselors may begin to address the social-emotional, or internalized, issues of students while the school psychologist addresses the behavioral, or externalized, issues of students. Responsibilities to students can be negotiated among team members, and with the addition of school social workers and improved ratios among the school-based mental health professionals, students have better access to direct interventions.

Students whose mental and behavioral health issues exceed the universal supports offered at Tier 1 may get referred to their grade-level team, the SEB MTSS team, or may be identified for further data triangulation on the SEB screener. School counselors are responsible for: student counseling duties at Tier 2 and Tier 3, contributing to incentive planning with students, coordinating behavioral planning with the school psychologist and the special education teachers, helping keep track of students who are frequently out of class for SEB issues, reporting SEB incidences regarding high-risk students to the team, monitoring student data, and partnering with families to provide consistency of supports outside of school. *Depending on the school district, shared responsibilities among school counselor, school psychologist, school social worker and school nurse include* providing counseling services, assisting with behavioral planning; consulting with teachers on SEB strategies, providing insights into the function of student behavior, communicating with families about concerns and team discussions, conducting threat assessments and crisis management strategies, helping provide mental health follow-up within the school and in the community, and obtaining release of information and communicating directly with mental health services providers. School-based mental health providers also communicate with school police officers and school resource officers when necessary, and assist when there is an acute need to have a student admitted to a community mental health treatment center when warranted.

School Psychologists

School psychologists are natural leaders and participants on this committee. Their advanced-level training in normal and atypical development, school psychology, counseling, assessment, and educational research puts them at the top of the human capital food chain at a school in terms of skills requisites for participating in the SEB MTSS team. They are very qualified to chair the team, provide training for other team members, lead team discussions, make recommendations, and record significant case notes on individual students for the team. *School psychologists are sensitive to psychological issues that have an impact on students and staff and have the relevant background knowledge to weigh in on prioritizing student needs and assisting in obtaining relevant services for students at school and in the community.* They are often experts at narrowing issues quickly and generating probable hypotheses by reviewing criteria of known mental illness and educational disability criteria. As stated previously, special education eligibility is never the goal of Academic MTSS, nor is it the goal of SEB MTSS. However, SEB MTSS will lay the groundwork for adequately documenting problem behaviors and response to interventions, which will more than cover legal requirements for evidence-based interventions and documentation of outcomes needed for special education eligibility determination, if warranted. In addition to the previously mentioned overlapping responsibilities with other school-based mental health professionals, other responsibilities for school psychologists on this team involve consulting with parents about target concerns, exploring strategies and treatment options, monitoring intervention implementation and frequency/intensity of data, bringing referrals to the multidisciplinary team for special education evaluation, conducting comprehensive or short-term psychoeducational assessments, communicating with special educators, and providing support and counseling for school staff when debriefing after traumatic incidences. Other supports psychologists might provide include trauma-informed counseling, family engagement or parenting sessions, and sharing assessment information and recommendations with community service providers. The school psychologist is required to attend all meetings, and it is highly recommended that the SEB MTSS team make every effort to schedule meetings on days the school psychologist is on campus to facilitate their participation with access to meetings.

School Nurse

The school nurse is the local medical expert on campus. He or she has access to the medical information of all students including health histories, medical diagnoses, and physician contact information. *They are natural liaisons between home and school regarding students' health.* School nurses have an understanding of the side effects of medication that could have an impact on behavior or school performance. In addition to overlapping responsibilities with other team members, they are responsible for sharing pertinent student medical information with the SEB MTSS team; contacting parents to discuss medication issues and recommendations for physician follow-up; monitoring students for acute signs of mental illness and abuse, hygiene problems, and/or substance abuse requiring immediate medical attention; helping keep track of frequency of students in the nurse's office for somatic issues; and reporting SEB incidences regarding target students to the team. Nurses are often able to help parents get reduced cost or insurance covered medical referrals, free or reduced-cost medicines, state Medicaid applications, free glasses and dental services, and other health-related community services. The school nurse is strongly encouraged to attend all meetings, and it is recommended the SEB MTSS team schedule their meetings when the school nurse is on campus.

Social Workers and Other Licensed Service Providers

Other helpful participants on the SEB MTSS team include the school social worker, community partner advocate (available in many urban areas), or any other mentor on school campus, including teachers on special assignment with knowledge of a student. Mentors and teachers, including school police, can attend parts of meetings pertaining to discussions about students they have working knowledge of but should be excused after they have participated so as not to violate FERPA/Health Insurance and Portability and Accountability Act (HIPPA, 1996) for students' records they do not need to know about because they do not have a legitimate education interest. *As mental health providers, social workers can engage in counseling services directly with students and can support the student's family as an extension.* The school social workers often have the most flexibility in scheduling and can allocate a bigger percentage of time to engage in community outreach compared to school counselors, the school psychologist, and the school nurse. Creating relationships with caregivers and families, providing referrals for community resources, making home visits, problem solving with families, finding ways for students to get medical and mental health care regardless of a lack of insurance and transportation barriers, resource mapping the most relevant and responsive service providers, and developing working relationships with those service providers are critical to the team's functions and can be facilitated by the school social worker. In addition, school social workers share many overlapping skills and responsibilities with school counselors, school psychologists, and school nurses, as much as their licenses allow. If the school is located in an at-risk neighborhood, school social workers might work closely with community partner representatives who bring fresh fruits and vegetables, free food giveaways, a community closet, basic toiletries, and other information and services to connect families to resources. Social workers are strongly encouraged to attend all meetings and, again, SEB MTSS meetings should be scheduled to accommodate their schedules to the best extent possible.

Community partners are critical and complement school-based mental health supports, providing qualified and caring coordinators who serve as stabilizing factors by offering nurturing relationships with students and assistance with basic needs (Villarreal & Castro-Villarreal, 2016). The more adults at a school who strive for positive relationships with students and families, increase the positive ratio of interactions with troubled students specifically, and are good role models within and out in the school community, the better the outcomes for students.

Exercise 11.2

SEB MTSS Team Member Survey

- Who are your SEB MTSS team members?
- What are their individual strengths and weaknesses?
- What are their collective strengths and weaknesses?
- What expertise is your team missing? How can you fill that gap?
- Identify areas of training that could benefit team member decision making.

Essential SEB MTSS Team Functions

Engaging in resource mapping of school and community resources and assessing the needs of a school are proactive ways to support all students' behavioral needs (National Resource Center for Mental Health Promotion & Youth Violence Prevention, 2017;

Sprick, Booher, & Garrison, 2009). It is important to define basic services, establish consent and release policies, agree on basic roles and expectations, participate in community partner meetings, and identify agencies who support students in terms of mental health crises, health issues, social work support, counseling, and wraparound services. It is also helpful for site-based SEB MTSS teams to have an emergency list of reliable professionals and support staff who can help de-escalate students within the school using evidence-based practices, such as Life Space Crisis Intervention (Long, Wood, & Fecser, 2001). Enlisting collaboration with community agencies and growing relationships with outside service providers will ensure a more fluid response to student mental health crises, during and after extreme behavioral episodes. Resource mapping will require constant updating to reflect the needs of the school, the skills of staff members, and the qualitative experiences with community service providers to establish a preferred list of responsive and effective services for students and their families in the community. School teams must aim to increase student access to quality treatment options in the community for the most mentally, emotionally, and behaviorally unhealthy students.

SEB MTSS Meetings

Once structures, functions, and processes are in place to identify and prioritize the highest-risk students, the real work begins with interventions and progress monitoring. Several things will now be taking place, such as the school administration will have made the mental and behavioral health of students a school priority with vision and action. Like Academic MTSS, the master calendar has been considered, team meeting dates and locations are memorialized, Tier 1 curriculum has been selected, and intervention opportunities with research-based SEB programming have been identified. Grade-level teams have been trained in data triangulation and risk prioritization. SEB MTSS team members have been trained in roles and functions, the team chair has been selected, and procedures for SEB universal screening and student referrals have been reviewed. School staff have also been trained to spot and report potential red flags as they arise and have been instructed on the importance of student-centered relationship building skills, communication, and team problem solving. Given the comprehensive nature of this framework, the planning and training of SEB MTSS usually begins prior to the school year in which it is to be implemented.

SEB MTSS team members will lay the groundwork for resource mapping within the school and out in the community: empowering change agents, creating safe spaces on campus, teaching students how to access supports, and growing relationships with community service providers and neighborhood community leaders. Family buy-in to SEB MTSS is critical, as are engagement efforts to encourage communication and collaboration between home and school. It is essential that everything and everyone is in place to identify high-risk students and to support them.

A universal schoolwide SEB screener will help detect indicators of internalizing and externalizing factors proactively, which leads to data-triangulation meetings and scheduling of SEB interventions and supports for Tier 2 and Tier 3 students who are monitored by the SEB MTSS team. If students with severe SEB issues are not already getting the maximum Tier 3 supports on campus, they should be implemented immediately. This is especially true for high-risk students who transfer in midway through the school year outside a universal benchmark period. As previously mentioned, the SEB MTSS team's caseload is determined by data-triangulation chats during grade-level professional learning communities, with input from the school counselor, school psychologist, teachers, administration, and other mental health service providers on campus. Triangulation of data sources ensures that students do not slip through the cracks or receive unnecessary interventions for having a bad week or two. Some students who do not have a history of severe behavioral or mental health issues but are in the midst of situational stressors that would adjust perceptions of SEB outbursts as falling within the range of normal response, such as homelessness or death of a family member, which would require patience and care to get through the difficult time period. Some socially-emotionally and behaviorally unstable students do not demonstrate academic delay or have overarching issues such as attendance problems, which might preclude them from rapid identification to be monitored by the Academic MTSS team. High-risk SEB-involved students sometimes come up before the Academic MTSS team and sometimes not. When students with Tier 2 and Tier 3 academic issues actually have underlying mental health and/or behavioral needs those students typically go on to be monitored by, or in conjunction with, the SEB MTSS team. In doing so, students would still have access to resources allocated through Academic MTSS, including academic supports, progress monitoring, and convenience of documentation of interventions through lesson plans and attendance logs. Many processes are virtually identical to Academic MTSS, and some students may require the supports of both the Academic and the SEB MTSS teams.

The *SEB MTSS Student Database* is the warehouse of all relevant factors that may have an impact on students' SEB functioning. Such factors may include information and columns for student name, identification number, grade, classroom teacher, brief documentation of pertinent history, SEB benchmark screener scores, any known adverse childhood experiences, academic benchmark scores, any medical diagnoses and medications, current behavioral performance and events, any interventions and progress monitoring data, recommended next steps, and who will be responsible for following up. A Microsoft Excel spreadsheet or Google Sheet can be used. The SEB MTSS team chair, or designee, records and updates relevant case notes in real time for the team and distributes at meetings, which team members would be expected to store securely if they are keeping for their personal professional notes and records. It is not advised to send such confidential information by email or electronically for privacy purposes. Some teams may project the information on a whiteboard to discuss individual students, while other teams may distribute copies of the SEB MTSS database for discussion but collect at the end of meetings. In all cases, the SEB MTSS database information and case notes should be destroyed when they are no longer needed. All the same historical factors as Academic MTSS are reviewed for significance, including enrollments, attendance, grades, health, and discipline history. Data sources indicating functional levels across multiple settings, in addition to students' family ecology and home environment, are also considered.

Once the SEB MTSS Student Database is up to date, team members can refer to it at subsequent meetings. The team chair need not comprehensively verbalize student case notes but may briefly review presenting problems, review action steps recommended from previous meetings, report student progress toward intervention(s) implemented, check in with team members who were tasked with follow-up, and share updates of how well things are going. These decisions are evidenced by data sources, including progress monitoring data and reports, current discipline referrals or restorative practice opportunities, documented response to Tier 2 and Tier 3 interventions, and, if relevant, any medical updates, parent–teacher conferences, teacher reports, counselor reports, special education updates, law enforcement actions, and other information relevant to decision making.

SEB MTSS team members are focal points of student information, similarly to Academic MTSS case managers, gathering subjective and objective reports from school personnel, caregivers, and community service providers who have pertinent student information that may have an impact on team decisions. For example, the school psychologist is a natural liaison with Academic MTSS and special education teams regarding students identified with educational disabilities or suspected of such. Sharing team recommendations with interventionists and special educators in the implementation of Tier 2 and Tier 3 supports needed will allow school staff to effectively coordinate efforts. School counselors are natural liaisons to teachers who are likely to report experiences of abnormal student interactions to them. Likewise, school counselors can communicate with teachers regarding recommendations from the team that will impact students in the classroom. They may also take the lead in parent-teacher conferences or directly share plans with caregivers. Each SEB MTSS team member may be assigned follow-up responsibilities that are specific and overlap. Typically, the SEB MTSS team chair will ask for volunteers or assign responsibilities based on presenting variables that match strengths, schedules, as well as roles, of team members.

School-based mental health providers will share burdens and take on tasks as team players rather than only supporting the team with one specific duty or function. These dynamics will vary campus to campus depending on the relationships of school service providers and their ability or availability on any given day. Collegial support and leaving personal egos out of problem-solving processes are required, which builds trust and improves effective communication among team members. Using a growth mindset and accepting that no one person can know it all or do it all, the adults on a school campus can be leaders and learners together. Reflective practices and feedback looping will inform whether practices are working as intended or revisions are required for implementation. Effective collaboration between SEB MTSS team members and school staff help teachers feel supported by administration in an effort to help students with the most severe SEB difficulties and, as a by-product, creates a culture of team problem solving, professional collaboration, and trust. Students and schools are safer when all professionals on a campus are systematically looking out for at-risk students, are actively problem solving together, engaging in outreach and growth of support networks, providing case management and care, and are closely monitoring outcomes.

Healthy Minds, Safe Schools

Healthy Minds, Safe Schools is an example of putting initiative into action using the SEB MTSS framework and LIQUID (Leadership, Implementation, Quality control, Universality, Implementation, Data-based decision making) Model, which is adaptable to the unique characteristics of individual school environments and aligns with the recommendations of the Framework for Safe and Successful Schools (Cowan, Vaillancourt, Rossen, & Pollitt, 2013). *Healthy Minds, Safe Schools* (see Figure 11.1) began in select urban schools as a comprehensive model to systematically implement SEL *and* positive behavioral interventions (PBIS) in high-need schools (Dockweiler & Clark, 2018). At the elementary level, the flagship *Healthy Minds, Safe Schools* elementary school has seen

Healthy Minds, Safe Schools is a trademark of Dockweiler & Clark, 2018.

Figure 11.1 Healthy Minds, Safe Schools Model
Note
Healthy Minds, Safe Schools is a trademark of Dockweiler and Clark (2018).

tremendous results with a 64% decrease in school violence since implementing the program (Dockweiler & Clark, 2019). At the middle school level, student-to-student violence has been demonstrated to decrease by 28% (Dockweiler & Clark, 2018).

The marrying of SEL and PBIS tenets into a combined SEB framework is a novel approach supported by research as one of the most impactful ways to improve student mental and behavioral well-being (Cook et al., 2015). While SEL and PBIS alone result in impactful outcomes, combining the two has an impressive effect size that exceeds 1.0 and far outperforms the implementation of either program individually (Cook et al., 2015). The SEB approach of *Healthy Minds, Safe Schools* methodically addresses internalized and externalized behaviors on both elementary and secondary campuses and is conducive to a phased rollout. It is a flexible model for schools to customize based on the unique needs of their campuses from a selection of various programming and curricular options.

Healthy Minds, Safe Schools seeks to increase students' protective factors, resilience, problem-solving skills, emotional regulation, and behavioral performance; to reduce office referrals; and to reduce student-to-student violence (Dockweiler & Clark, 2018). It aligns with esteemed and well-known evidence-based practices of the Aspen Institute (2018), the Collaborative for Academic, Social, and Emotional Learning (2018), and PBIS (Sprick, 2009) and provides SEB instructional support to teachers with coaching through the Principles of Accomplished Teaching (National Board for Professional Teaching Standards, 2016). Community support and family engagement are critical pieces of the framework that provide an additional layer of protective supports for students and staff.

Middle School B began implementing *Healthy Minds, Safe Schools* due to an overwhelming increase in the number of students thinking about, threatening, and attempting suicide. The school team could no longer afford to use short-term reactionary fixes to solve their students' SEB problems. A comprehensive, long-term solution was called for; school teams knew *what* the problem was and *why* addressing it was important. What they did not have was the *how*. *Healthy Minds, Safe Schools* was birthed from evidence-based practices as the *how* and has since expanded to encompass elementary campuses as well.

Box 11.1

Connection to Practice

Elementary School A began implementing *Healthy Minds, Safe Schools* with a two-year phased rollout. Elementary School A is a Title I school with approximately 950 students, with 55% being eligible for free or reduced-price lunch; 11% being limited English proficient; and a population that was 24% Hispanic, 24% Caucasian, 22% Asian, and 17% Black (Nevada Report Card, 2018). Four months into the two-year rollout, the school had already decreased its office behavioral referrals by 33.7% (Dockweiler & Clark, 2018). By the end of the first full year of implementation, the school had realized a 64% collective decrease in student violence since the initial implementation. Data collection efforts are underway targeting internalized as well as externalized behaviors, teacher efficacy, school culture and leadership, and how behaviors are linked to student academic achievement.

At the student level, analysis reveals a 50% decrease in externalized behaviors in students identified as having significant risk and who were continuously enrolled for the entire school year ($N = 856$). Similarly, there was a 75.2% decrease in internalized behaviors in students identified as having significant risk and who were continuously enrolled for the entire school year ($N = 856$). At the teacher level, initial results suggest a significant increase in teachers' reported self-efficacy for implementing social-emotional curriculum and making data-based decisions. At the administrative level, similar increases have been found in the perceived ability for data-based decision making. School culture has improved since initial implementation as has academic achievement (Dockweiler & Diamond, 2019).

Box 11.2

Connection to Practice

Middle School B is an urban Title I school with a population of approximately 1,350 students. The student population is 96% eligible for free or reduced-price lunch, and 95% are limited English proficient; the student population is 84% Hispanic and 11% Black (Nevada Report Card, 2018). The transiency rate has been near 50% for the past 10 years. Middle School B already had a healthy culture for Academic MTSS, so when the waves of students in crisis peaked, the Behavioral and Mental Health MTSS grew to respond to the intensity and volume of student need. Tier 1 and Tier 2 included evidence-based curriculum delivered during homeroom universally and during scheduled Tier 2 SEB classes. Tier 3 supports were layered incrementally to individually address student needs, in addition to increasing outreach to community resources.

The Behavioral and Mental Health MTSS team met regularly to discuss and actively manage the highest risk students. Over the next two years, student-to-student violence decreased 28% with the implementation of *Healthy Minds, Safe Schools* (Dockweiler & Clark, 2018). To put this 28% decrease in perspective, nearly half of all discipline incidences statewide fell under the category of Violence to Other Students. This number of incidences has remained virtually unchanged (decreased 0.81%) in the last decade (Nevada Report Card, 2018). For Middle School A to decrease its student-to-student violence rate by 28% in two years is quite significant and has become a sought-after model to scale.

Universal Screening Cycles

The *Healthy Minds, Safe Schools* model requires universal benchmark screenings three times a year. Screenings conducted only twice a year are just not frequent enough to capture new students to the school, students' continually changing needs, or to provide data on student performance in a timely manner. These screening windows correspond to the academic universal benchmark windows and semester dates, with the first screener occurring approximately 6 weeks into the school year, the second one happening 13 weeks later near the end of first semester, and the last one occurring 13 weeks after that or approximately 6 weeks before the end of the school year. This *6–13–13–6 benchmark model* is a guideline for schools that follow a traditional 38-week academic calendar. Screening dates, of course, can be shifted as they transpire during a "window" versus a perfectly prescribed calendar.

On a typical campus, it is recommended that universal screeners take place no sooner than six weeks into the school year. This allows staff to get to know their students and to reduce the number of false positives and false negatives of students identified. Caution, just because the weeks have passed and teachers and students have spent time together, it does not mean that the teachers actually *know* their students. It is recommended that prior to the beginning of the school year the SEB MTSS school leadership team create a common *About Me Everywhere* tool for teachers to use as a guide to get to know their students. One version is tailored for the lower grades, kindergarten through second, and one version for the higher grades, third through fifth. This tool helps capture relevant student data without being intrusive and is especially helpful on larger campuses or with schools from larger communities; it then becomes the springboard in which to have unique student conversations. On one side of the About Me Everywhere paper is a place for students to draw a picture of their family and on the backside are questions relating to any pets in the house, things they like to do that make them happy, what they find motivating or reinforcing, and anything that may make them sad or upset. These types of questions will work for all elementary-age students and allow younger students to draw their responses if necessary.

After completing the About Me Everywhere forms the teachers are ready to review the information individually and confidentially with the students. The teachers can sit down with each student and ask them to "tell me about your drawing," making mental notes of anything that may seem odd or exceptional. Notes should not be taken during the conversation but later so that all attention can be devoted to students and they do not feel like they are being quizzed. In asking the students to tell about the drawing, it is not leading the student to talk about any one particular aspect but allowing a student-led dialogue. From there, the teacher and the student can talk about the questions and corresponding answers on the back of the form. It may take a week or so to get through all the students but the time invested will certainly be worth it. These one-on-one teacher–student conversations, or *About Me Care-to-Share*, help build rapport and facilitate a deeper understanding of what the students' experiences are on a daily basis outside of school. This process aligns with the National Board for Professional Teaching Standards (2016) and will help curtail issues down the road. For example, at one school before incorporating About Me Care-to-Share conversations into the *Healthy Minds, Safe Schools* model, when grade-level teams met to review their students' benchmark data and have data-triangulation chats to identify, prioritize, and divvy up students into intervention groups, the teachers were ill prepared to engage in such dialogue. As the school psychologist and school counselor led the teachers through the discussion, the teachers had a difficult time answering basic questions, such as Who does the child live with? What do they like to do outside of school? and What do they find rewarding? At no fault of the teachers, they truly came to the meetings feeling like they "knew" their students; however, when asked questions through a different lens, they were not able to answer them. In creating the About Me Everywhere and using it as a common guide for About Me Care-to-Share, teachers were better equipped to engage during data-triangulation chats and make more informed decisions regarding their students.

After the six weeks have passed, the About Me Everywhere forms have been completed and the About Me Care-to-Share conversations have taken place, the universal screeners are conducted. On an elementary campus, every teacher completes a screener for each of the students in his or her class. This means that each teacher would complete screenings for approximately 30 students, depending on actual class sizes. Teachers-as-raters are preferred and are more reliable because students may not have the reading skills or self-awareness to accurately self-report, and parents-as-raters create a host of challenges including participation rates and misinterpretation of intent. To be clear, the universal screeners are not lengthy and tedious questionnaires; they are brief surveys used to reorganize information already known about the student. The preferred tool used by *Healthy Minds, Safe Schools* is the Student Risk Screening Scale for Internalizing and Externalizing Behaviors (Lane et al., 2015). It not only contains an elementary and secondary version to provide consistency over time; it is composed of only 12 questions, it self-scores, and it has zero cost associated with using it. The brevity of the tool is part of its beauty and allows entire school campuses of 1,000 students to be screened simultaneously in approximately 15 minutes.

After screening, the scored data can be exported to a screener database (if the screening tool does not have a built-in database component) that serves as a warehouse for students' SEB universal screener scores. Each grade level has a tab on the database with self-contained special education programs having a tab as well. When stated that the whole school is screened, that means the *whole school*. One person is designated as the keeper of SEB universal benchmarking data or "the warehouse"; however, that person does not need to be the SEB MTSS chair. The chair will need to have access to the database, as will the core members of the SEB MTSS team (administration, school counselor, school psychologist, and school social worker), but the chair does not need to be the one to maintain it exclusively. Anyone on the leadership team with a strength for delving into data and who enjoys the tedious nature of maintaining large sets of information with fidelity can fill this role.

Data-Triangulation Meetings

Once all the data has been exported to the SEB universal screener database, or the warehouse, *Phase I Prioritization* occurs. This is simply a basic sorting and ranking of students who scored high for (1) externalized and (2) internalized behaviors, by grade. The keeper of the SEB warehouse data would typically conduct this first step of prioritization. The prioritization list from Phase I is then taken back to each grade-level SEB data-triangulation meetings for *Phase II Prioritization*, which further refines who, from the initial sorting and ranking, does indeed need additional supports, and discussion transpires as to what kind. Each grade level reviews its own grade's list of prioritized students, not the entire school. *Data-triangulation chats* occur during the meeting and remove false positives and add false negatives to the initial prioritization list. Information not captured by the screener is incorporated, such as the information discussed during the About Me Care-to-Share. By the end of the grade-level data-triangulation meeting, grades will have identified which of their students will require Tier 2 and Tier 3 interventions.

These data-triangulation chats are used to not only eliminate false positives and negatives and to prioritize students and their needs; it is also used to empower teachers to assist in the decision-making process for their students. For example, students may come up high on the externalized portion of the SEB screener if they are constantly out of their seat, are disrupting instructional time, and are argumentative. This is different from students who are socially isolated, are withdrawn, and appear chronically depressed. For the disruptive student, task avoidance and academic deficiency may be the root of the behavior, not an underlying behavioral disorder. For the student identified as having significant internalizing problems, after the data-triangulation chat with the teacher, the student may be asked if he or she has had thoughts of suicide and self-harm and if he or she is engaging in high-risk behavior or behaviors that put others at risk of harm. This probing causes the teacher to reflect and think about his or her student's behavior differently, which aligns with the Accomplished Teaching Body of Knowledge, including the resource What Teachers Should Know and Be Able to Do (National Board for Professional Teaching Standards, 2016). It also builds capacity for teachers' self-efficacy and data-based decision making when it comes to SEB issues.

Interventions and Progress Monitoring

The time between screening and Phase I is approximately one week, the time between Phase I Prioritization and Phase II Prioritization is approximately one week, and the time between Phase II Prioritization and the start of intervention implementation is approximately two weeks. Therefore, 4 weeks into the 13-week window have passed between the screener and official intervention implementation, leaving approximately 9 weeks to implement the intervention(s), progress monitor, and modify as necessary before the next benchmark period. This is just a guideline and is certainly not to say that students do not receive interventions during that four-week window, they *do*, and they *can*, especially the most at-risk students. However, when mobilizing large-scale SEB interventions, it takes time to systematically identify, document, prioritize, and intervene with students. Once this happens, it requires human capital to create interventions, obtain parental consent for some interventions such as counseling groups, and coach teachers on implementation techniques. Many school-based mental health professionals are assigned to multiple campuses and are not afforded the opportunity to spend 100% of their time at one school. To adequately meet the needs of students and educators, school-based mental health professionals should be staffed at their nationally recommended ratios. That would be 1:250 for school counselors and school social workers and 1:500 to 1:700 for school psychologists (American School Counselor Association, 2016; School Social Work Association of America, 2013; National Association of School Psychologists, 2010).

Broadly speaking, students who are ranked high for externalized behaviors will already be known to the teachers and some may already have some sort of behavior management system in place within their classroom. Students who score high for externalizing problems will most likely require an individualized BIP and, depending on any underlying issues, a small counseling group as well. Externalizing interventions tend to be supported by the school psychologist, interventionists, and special education staff. Special education teachers are masters at writing behavior plans, implementing interventions, collecting data, and reviewing that data on an ongoing basis. They can provide invaluable leadership support and coaching to general education teachers who have high-needs behavioral students. The classroom teacher is the primary point of contact with families and communicates the need for behavioral intervention. They partner with families to discuss meaningful reinforcement rewards and offer the plan to families so that families may also implement the plan at home to offer consistency of behavioral expectations and response.

Students who are ranked high for internalizing behaviors will most likely have their intervention needs met through the school counselor in the form of six-week small-group counseling. School counselors will need to reach out to families to obtain written permission to provide this service and act as the main point of contact with the family. Teachers will certainly also be involved; however, due to confidentiality, school counselors and school psychologists can only share so much with teachers. Some teachers may find this challenging and open dialogue between the teacher and school counselor is strongly recommended so that both parties can be comfortable with the level of sharing that they are engaged in.

Students with IEPs who come up high on the screener will require follow-up between the general education teacher and the special education teacher of record. If a student is ranked high for externalized behaviors, the team needs to consider adding or modifying an existing behavior plan or updating the IEP. While the specific decisions made by the IEP team do not need to be documented within the SEB MTSS Student Database, the date that the SEB MTSS team made the recommendation to the IEP team to review and update the student's services is recorded. The goal is to meet the student's needs and to document attempts to do so.

The SEB MTSS team meets every other week to discuss the highest need students. These are students who are not responding well to their BIPs even with repeated modifications to the plan and the increased reinforcement schedule. New interventions or alternatives are brainstormed and explored for these high-needs, high-resistant students. Students receiving only Tier 2 small-group counseling may not be discussed until after the six-week session as the school counselor will be making modifications weekly depending on the topics discussed. If the school counselor continuously makes modifications, yet the student still is having difficulties, the school counselor will bring the student to the SEB MTSS team to request additional support, problem solving, and to investigate external community-based resources. All decisions are documented in the SEB MTSS Student Database.

Iterative Phases

During the second universal benchmark screening period, the process is repeated. Screen, record, Phase I Prioritization, data-triangulation meetings and Phase II Prioritization, and then implement and monitor progress. It is at this time that the manager of the SEB MTSS Student Database analyzes the change in student scores, for those students who were continuously enrolled, from the fall benchmark to the winter benchmark. Data are disaggregated at various levels: whole school, grade level, males, females, special education, or any other category that was built into the database. Data are then used to inform the SEB MTSS leadership team and then, ideally, the whole school. Knowledge is power, and if the teachers are able to see statistical results, as well as an improved culture and climate on campus, they will continue to be motivated to implement the program with fidelity.

During the third and final universal benchmark period, the process is largely the same. Screen, record, Phase I Prioritization, data-triangulation meetings, and Phase II Prioritization, and then implement and progress monitor. The biggest difference lies with the implementation and progress monitoring piece. Given that there are only a few weeks of school left at this point the implementation and progress monitoring is more of a triage with new at-risk students or the highest-need students being managed and intervened upon. Hopefully, over the course of the school year, the SEB MTSS team has been able to positively intervene and reduce the risk of the majority of students on campus.

A final piece of the third universal benchmark period cycle includes using the data to support students over the summer and to immediately support them once they return to school in the fall. For students who are identified as being at risk but have been successfully managed all school year, the classroom teacher makes sure that the families have a copy of the BIP and clearly understands how to implement it. For students receiving small group counseling, the school counselor provides families with a tip sheet for how to best support good decision making, self-regulation, and anger management (or any other relevant issue). The school counselor will also make sure that the students he or she has been working with have a tip sheet reminding them how to self-regulate and manage their own behavior and thoughts with regard to the topic(s) that they had been working on. More globally, the SEB MTSS team or a team leader puts together an end-of-the-year newsletter for families or add a column to an existing school newsletter, with local community-based resources available over the summer. This newsletter is sent home in paper copy and/or in an email link and is added to the school's website. It includes links to basic socialization opportunities, such as summer camps; to child psychologists or marriage and family therapists for individualized *or* group supports; and to residential treatment facilities for intensive individual situations. Finally, the list of students identified as being at risk for externalizing and internalizing behaviors during the third and final universal benchmark period will help guide teachers and the SEB MTSS team in their prioritization of student interventions from the first day of school in the fall. Since the first universal benchmark period is not for six weeks into the school year, this list of students will carry over, and they will receive supports (if still warranted) once school starts.

Healthy Minds, Safe Schools is currently being scaled out at both the elementary and secondary levels and is receiving praise for its comprehensive and customizable approach to addressing students' SEB needs on campus. This proactive approach, based on the SEB MTSS framework, is showing great success in the reduction of internalized and externalized behaviors in elementary school.

References

American School Counselor Association. (2016). *Student-to-school counselor ratio 2015–2016*. Retrieved from www.schoolcounselor.org/asca/media/asca/home/Ratios15-16.pdf

Aspen Institute: National Commission on Social, Emotional, and Academic Development. (2018). *How learning happens: Supporting students' social, emotional, and academic development*. Washington, DC: Author.

Boston Public Schools. (2017). *What is CBHM?* Retrieved from http://cbhmboston.com/what-is-cbhm
Cannata, M., McCrory, R., Sykes, G., Anagnostopoulos, D., & Frank, K. A. (2010). Exploring the influence of national board certified teaching in their schools and beyond. *Education Administration Quarterly, 46*(4), 463–490.
Collaborative for Academic, Social, and Emotional Learning. (2018). *Core SEL competencies.* Retrieved from https://casel.org/core-competencies/
Cook, C. R., Frye, M., Slemrod, T., Lyon, A. R., Renshaw, T. L., & Zhang, Y. (2015). An integrated approach to universal prevention: Independent and combined effects of PBIS and SEL on youths' mental health. *School Psychology Quarterly, 30*(2), 166–183.
Cowan, K. C., Vaillancourt, K., Rossen, E., & Pollitt, K. (2013). *A framework for safe and successful schools.* Bethesda, MD: National Association of School Psychologists.
Dockweiler, K. A., & Clark, A. G. (2018, April). *Multi-tiered systems of support: Behavioral and mental health in schools.* Paper session presented at the Nevada Department of Education Mega Conference, Las Vegas, NV.
Dockweiler, K. A., & Clark, A. G. (2019, May). *Healthy minds, safe schools: A multi-tiered system of support for mental and behavioral health.* Paper session presented at the Nevada Department of Education Mega Conference, Las Vegas, NV.
Dockweiler, K. A., & Diamond, L. L. (2019). *Healthy mind, safe schools program evaluation data analysis reports.* Unpublished raw data.
Family Educational Rights and Privacy Act of 1974, 20 U.S.C. § 1232g. (1974).
Google. (2018). *Google drive terms of service.* Retrieved from Google www.google.com/drive/terms-of-service/
Harrison, J. R., Vannest, K. J., & Reynolds, C. R. (2017). Social acceptability of five screening instruments for social, emotional, and behavioral challenges. *Behavioral Disorders, 38*(3), 171–189.
Individuals with Disabilities Education Act, 20 U.S.C. § 1400 (2004).
Lally, P., van Jaarsveld, C. H. M., Potts, H. W. W., & Wardle, J. (2010). How are habits formed: Modelling habit formation in the real world. *European Journal of Social Psychology, 40*(6), 998–1009.
Lane, K. L., Oakes, W. P., Swogger, E. D., Schatschneider, C., Menzies, H. M., & Sanchez, J. (2015). Student risk screening scale for internalizing and externalizing behaviors: Preliminary cut scores to support data-informed decision making. *Behavioral Disorders, 40*(3), 159–170.
Long, N. J., Wood, M. M., & Fecser, F. A. (2001). *Life space crisis intervention: Talking with students in conflict* (2nd ed.). Charlottesville, VA: Pro-Ed.
National Association of School Psychologists. (2010). *Model for comprehensive and integrated school psychological services.* Bethesda, MD: Author.
National Board for Professional Teaching Standards. (2016). *What teachers should know and be able to do.* Arlington, VA: Author.
National Resource Center for Mental Health Promotion and Youth Violence Prevention. (2017, August 8). Retrieved from www.healthysafechildren.org/sites
Nevada Report Card. (2018). Retrieved from http://nevadareportcard.com/di
Ross, S. W., & Sabey, C. V. (2014). Check-in check-out + social skills: Enhancing the effects of check-in check-out for students with social skill deficits. *Remedial and Special Education, 36*(4), 246–257.
Sabey, C. V., Charlton, C. T., Pyle, D., Lignugaris-Kraft, B., & Ross, S. W. (2017). A review of classwide or universal social, emotional, behavioral program for students in kindergarten. *Review of Educational Research, 87*(3), 512–543.
School Social Work Association of America. (2013). *National school social work practice model.* Retrieved from www.sswaa.org/copy-of-school-social-worker-evalua-1
Sprick, R., Booher, M., & Garrison, M. (2009). *Behavioral response to intervention.* Eugene, OR: Pacific Northwest Publishing.
Sprick, R. A. (2009). *CHAMPS: A proactive and positive approach to classroom management* (2nd ed.). Eugene, OR: Pacific Northwest Publishing.

Sprick, R. A. (2013). *Discipline in the secondary classroom: A positive approach to behavior management* (3rd ed.). Hoboken, NJ: John Wiley & Sons.

United States. (2004). *The Health Insurance Portability and Accountability Act (HIPAA)*. Washington, DC: U.S. Dept. of Labor, Employee Benefits Security Administration.

Villarreal, V., & Castro-Villarreal, F. (2016). Collaboration with community mental health service providers: A necessity in contemporary schools. *Intervention in School and Clinic, 52*(2), 108–114.

Chapter 12

Program Evaluation and Feedback Looping

Key Terms

Brokers
Iterative
MTSS Evaluation Frequency and Intensity Framework
Outside Evaluator
Feedback Looping
Peer Coaching
Logic Model

Chapter Concepts

In this chapter, readers will learn:

1. How to integrate a program evaluation schedule into their implementation efforts.
2. How to analyze data from the evaluation cycles to inform continuous improvement to the model.
3. How to use an MTSS Evaluation Frequency and Intensity Framework to guide evaluation cycles.
4. The importance of feedback looping and iterative evaluation mechanisms.
5. How the conditions of LIQUID are met through program evaluation and feedback looping.

A program is only as successful as its evaluation, reflection, and revision. No program can remain nimble and continue to meet the needs of those it serves without the capacity for refinement. New programs require courage and innovation to work things differently, and refinement processes occur simultaneously with implementation through lessons learned on the way. It is always recommended to reevaluate practices comprehensively at the end of each school year, but the school year need not be over to reflect and revise. Established programs require tenacity to sustain successful systems and processes while replacing ineffective practices with targeted solutions. Knowing the solution to a systemic problem in an organization does not mean that the solution will be implemented and the problem solved. *Brokers* are people within an organization who keep people working together, alleviating tension, and moving forward by cultivating relationships, negotiating respectful conflict, and ultimately getting consensus to solve problems. They are the human capital who intervene, care for, and contribute to the overall shift of culture and climate in a school and are a school's strongest assets. In this chapter, readers will learn the importance of integrating a program evaluation schedule into the implementation of their Multi-Tiered Systems of Support (MTSS) and how brokers can negotiate practices for improved team decision making. These regular evaluation cycles will serve to inform on the effectiveness of the program and ensure that no time or energy is spent needlessly (Yuen, Terao, & Schmidt, 2009).

Program Evaluation

Unintended consequences, poor treatment effect, and negative trends are all possible outcomes in program implementation, but these are risks teams must be willing to take and are not permanent conditions in a system of continuous improvement. Productive reflective processes strengthen organizations and professional relationships with collective experiences designed to strengthen the organization and professional relationships. When analyzing data trends for decision making, relationship skills with team members may become complicated. Some team members may have differing agendas or may be attached to certain outcomes, or they may come to different conclusions about causes and effects. Counterproductive behaviors and attitudes, such as finger-pointing and blaming, may also occur.

When data demonstrate students' growth and improvement, joy and celebration occur. When the data demonstrate students' lack of growth or academic or behavioral decline, educators may feel discouraged or entrenched in faulty assumptions and thinking patterns. They may try to "fix" problems without adequately evaluating all the components of program and service delivery before making targeted changes. Quick fixes or short-term appeasements are never long-term solutions and rarely serve the best interests of the child. If anything, they might often serve the best interests of the school or district but eventually are detrimental to the long-term outcomes of the student. Effective instruction relies on a multitude of variables and methods for measuring those variables, which have an impact on outcomes. School problem-solving teams must have confidence that they understand those variables, have the ability to influence and voice to select those variables, and are using the right outcome measures to inform practices. Determining which changes to make, and how to make them, requires interpersonal skills to negotiate team discussions resulting in decisions that can be supported by all within the organization. A respectful, collaborative professional environment allows for delivery and support of corrective actions with regard to implementation fidelity of high-quality curriculum. Instruments selected for feedback looping, including both qualitative and quantitative measures, may be used for different purposes. Some will be used as a broad measure to evaluate total outcomes, while some will be selected due to their sensitivity in identifying and detecting changes in the trajectory of discrete skill development, cultural attitudes, and systems that support those discrete skills.

A program implemented without constant reflection and evaluation will not last, nor will it be successful while it is in operation. Implementing a program, or a framework, without an established evaluation cycle results in entropy, much like letting small children run loose on a playground: Some will branch off and play alone, some will run in circles, one might climb the fence and run away, and others may play in groups, collaboratively or combatively, with no clear organization or goal. Without regular check-ins and structured evaluative and problem-solving systems with timeframes in which to regroup, a program can run amok quickly.

Program evaluation begins before the program even starts. Key members of the program evaluation team include the school administration, representation from the MTSS teams who have an interest or expertise in program implementation or data collection, and the school psychologist. The program evaluation team may select a planning measure, such as the Hexagon Tool (Blase, Kiser, & Van Dyke, 2013), to evaluate the implementation readiness of their program before rolling it out. The Hexagon Tool investigates six components: needs, fit, resource availability, evidence, readiness for replication, and capacity to implement. If a team is lacking any of these critical components, then they have an opportunity to bolster their weak areas before the school year starts to see that their MTSS program is a success once it is introduced to staff in the fall. It is recommended that members of the program evaluation team be assigned one or more of the six components, collect relevant data, and report back to the team (Blase et al., 2013). The team then completes the corresponding Hexagon Tool rubric to determine their score, or level of readiness, in each of the six categories. Whether or not a team selects a specific planning measure, it is important to consider the fundamental questions of which needs will be targeted, how the targeted needs will be supported systematically, what resources are needed, which outcome measure(s) will be monitored, and whether evidence supports continuing or revising practices over time.

MTSS Evaluation Frequency and Intensity

There are several components of an MTSS program that must be evaluated on an iterative cycle. *Iterative* refers to a repeated process that occurs at regular intervals with the purpose of achieving an established goal. Comparing the actual rate of improvement to the expected rate of improvement at consistent intervals over time will guide teams in their decision making with regards to maintaining or replacing current practices. *Programs must regularly be refined to maximize efficacy and effectiveness.* In an effort to find solutions with substantial and immediate outcomes, educators often throw the baby out with the bathwater when instead they should give the baby some time to grow with proper nutrition and care. Oftentimes, a program is deemed ineffective when, in reality, if it had undergone another round or two of iterative feedback, it would have been successful (Epstein & Klerman, 2013). Program evaluation can be accomplished in MTSS through the use of an MTSS Evaluation Frequency and Intensity Framework (see Figure 12.1). Under the *MTSS Evaluation Frequency and Intensity Framework*, some practices must be evaluated universally, or on a regular basis, largely through formative assessment measures. Others must be evaluated on a targeted basis, for example during benchmark windows, while some will require intensive, in-depth, and thorough investigation, such as an annual report of the program.

Data must be collected and evaluated on an iterative basis to effectively inform on the MTSS program and to enhance service delivery at all levels of intensity: student, staff, and school. At the core, efforts must be made to collect information from the micro- to the macro-levels, and at various frequencies, throughout the school year. Data collected at each of the three intensities can be analyzed in isolation, as well as how they contribute to the larger MTSS program, depending on what outcomes the

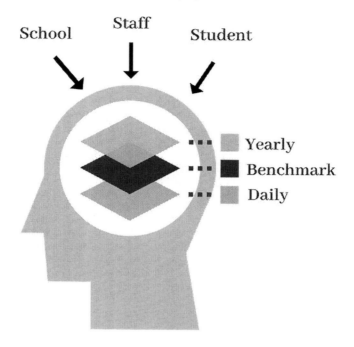

Figure 12.1 MTSS Evaluation Frequency and Intensity Framework

team is looking to reflect on. Some practices must be evaluated universally, on a regular or daily basis, largely through formative assessment measures. Some practices must be evaluated on a more intensive, targeted basis, such as at benchmark periods, while others will require intensive, in-depth, and comprehensive investigation, such as an annual report of the program.

Working backward from the macro-level, the intensive investigation may include an end-of-the-year program summary that can summarize the program's goals and the school's progress toward meeting those goals. This document is a compilation of multiple data collection cycles and sources and can be used for planning purposes and to share with stakeholders, including state departments of education, individual school districts, or community interest groups. If the MTSS work is being conducted under a grant, or receives funds as part of a larger grant project, this type of intensive reporting is typically conducted and reported by an outside evaluator. This *outside evaluator* is an impartial person hired to collect data and report on the program's progress toward its stated goals; the report may include information about resource utilization, efficiency, effectiveness, and fiscal allocations. If the work is not being conducted under a grant, as outside funding is not necessary to restructure and repurpose the existing resources on a campus, it is still best practice to have an annual meeting to review the MTSS goals, progress, barriers, and opportunities.

Targeted program evaluation would occur at regular intervals such as quarterly or at benchmark cycles, depending on how the school or district is calendared. This information would be collected to inform on student progress, teacher efficacy, or program targets. For example, at the student level, regular benchmark data can be collected to determine student progress in the key content areas, any specific academic domain of concern, or students' social-emotional-behavioral functioning. At the staff level, if the school is implementing a new math intervention curriculum, pre-, mid-, and postsurveys can be given to determine the teacher's efficacy in implementing the new intervention program to give school leaders an idea of where training opportunities may lie or where they may need to direct their efforts. At the school level, regular benchmarking can be used to monitor the rollout of MTSS components. For example, if a school decides to implement a Social-Emotional-Behavioral MTSS program but does not have the resources to implement all three tiers with fidelity, or if they do not have sufficient planning time to build the entire program before the school year starts, establishing a rollout calendar with preset benchmarks and targets will help keep the school team on track as stages of implementation develop. There may be unanticipated barriers that can threaten the implementation schedule, which requires stakeholders to review and revise the rollout schedule. Comparing actual progress to desired progress at regular intervals will help keep a program's overall implementation schedule on track. Active problem solving by the leadership team, with a sense of urgency to stay on schedule, can often be the tipping point for successful incremental growth and sustainability.

Universal program evaluation must occur at the micro-level on a regular basis to ensure that universal instruction is being provided, that interventions are being implemented, and that progress monitoring probes are being executed with fidelity. *The universal level of an MTSS program is its foundation and without proper implementation, the structure falls apart.* Each member on campus must hold him- or herself accountable to implement universal learning opportunities with fidelity on a daily basis, and if members are not sure how to implement a piece of the curriculum or program, they must have the confidence to ask through an established pathway in which to seek advice.

Checks and balances can be used to reinforce this daily fidelity. In the classroom, this includes randomized observations and drop-ins from school leaders. Administrative and mentor observations can inform on the general instructional techniques and content delivery of the staff. It can also serve to inform on the classroom management, or lack of management, style in the classroom. This can be an opportunity for peer coaching if there is a specific piece of the universal foundation that is missing from a teacher's repertoire. *Peer coaching* is a valuable tool to reinforce sound instructional practices from one teacher leader to another. On elementary campuses, this may be in the form of a Pineapple Board in which teachers can invite their peers into their classrooms to observe them teach specific lessons. It can also be something more explicit, such as a special education teacher providing leadership and guidance as to how to write and implement individualized behavioral plans.

Frequent checks should also be made during intervention and progress monitoring sessions. If the intervention probes are not being conducted according to the standardized procedures, then the data collected becomes questionable and cannot be deemed valid for making decisions about students. For example, in both the elementary and secondary settings, when delivering reading, writing, and math fluency probes, the teacher must follow the standardized administration procedures for the particular probe. There have been cases where the teacher sat a student down next to him or her and had the student read the passage directly from the teacher's computer screen instead of having the student sit across from the teacher so that the student could not see the screen or what the teacher was marking. As the student misread a word, the teacher clicked on it and marked it wrong. This violates the standardized procedures of this particular assessment and has a negative impact on the student's psyche. Such an instance must be reported to the school administrator who needs to address this issue with the teacher and offer opportunities for training. If practices are not upheld with fidelity, the entire integrity of the program suffers, and quality control diminishes.

Evaluation Tools

There are several tools available to evaluate programs depending on the unit under investigation. For example, if a school is implementing a program to reduce students' problematic behaviors, the School Wide Positive Behavior Intervention Support (Algozzine et al., 2014) evaluation tool can be used to determine the effect of the program schoolwide. For social-emotional status, regular screeners can be used to determine the trajectory of reported internalized and externalized maladaptive behaviors over time. For academic evaluation, schools often determine the success of their intervention program by an increase in student performance on high-stakes tests. However, these measures may not be sensitive enough to pick up on positive student growth, and other tools are recommended to celebrate incremental gains and progress. If the school has a particularly high transiency rate, the team will want to take this information into account and may want to consider comparing the progress of only the students who have been in attendance at that school since the very beginning of the school year and have had the full benefits of MTSS supports.

Feedback looping is integral to any type of evaluation and is a prevalent tool used by institutional organizations, which includes the bureaucratic field of education (DiMaggio & Powell, 1991). *Feedback looping* is when the outputs of a reflection or outcome are used as inputs to inform and improve on the next phase of the cycle. Feedback looping can be either a single loop or a double loop; each serves a specific purpose (Hanson, 2001, 2003). Single looping is feedback on the updating of routine and repetitive aspects of a program (Argyris, 1999; Hanson, 2001). In the school setting, this may be likened to the universal, micro-level components such as instruction, program delivery, and daily check-ins. Double looping involves acquiring new knowledge to promulgate the long-term success of an organization or program in an ever-changing environment (Argyris, 1999; Hanson, 2001). This may include an annual review of cumulative evaluative measures, benchmark trends, and staff efficacy reports. In this vein,

> [s]mart organizations are also cognizant that all acquired knowledge is not equal when it comes to organizational learning for problem solving. With single-loop learning, the acquired knowledge is for the short term and intended to facilitate routine day-to-day problem solving. Double-loop learning, on the other hand, is intended to ensure the long-term future of the organization by analyzing core issues and making policy judgments.
>
> (Hanson, 2001, p. 658)

Before the school year starts, the school's leadership team should determine what evaluation tools to use, how often to use them, who will be responsible for their execution, what feedback loops exist and what new ones may need to be created, who will be responsible for the data, and how the data will be used. It is helpful to calendar these evaluative meetings before the school year starts so that other priorities do not get in the way. If a school establishes quarterly or thrice-a-year benchmark assessments to monitor student progress (academic, social-emotional-behavioral), it is recommended that the leadership team meet at a similar interval. That way, after the students are benchmarked, the team can sit down, review all the data, and make decisions about the program and students.

At the macro-level, the team can determine if the procedures and programmatic tools are aligning with the preestablished program benchmarks. Any major issues can be discussed and, through feedback looping, be used as inputs for improvement moving into the next quarter of MTSS implementation. At a less aggregate level, grade-level or classroom data can be reviewed to determine if there are any significant irregularities. For example, if third and fifth graders are showing progress with their basic reading skills but fourth graders are not, perhaps there is an underlying issue with the quality of curriculum or delivery of instruction in fourth-grade teaching practices that the MTSS team will need to evaluate and address. At the micro-level, the team can determine which students are making progress, who can be exited from programming, and who may need an intervention change.

All data collected can be used to inform program decisions and assist in making causal inferences by way of a logic model (Epstein & Klerman, 2013). A *logic model* can be used as an effectiveness framework to ensure inputs are leading to desired outputs in the short and long term. There are a variety of models available for teams to adopt, and they can be customized depending on the needs, inputs, and outputs a team deems necessary. The MTSS team will want to assign one or two people to the duties of collecting data that can be used to inform the logic model. This information can be collected during each of the evaluation meetings that follow the regular benchmarking periods. They may also engage researchers from research institutes of higher education to assist with the data collection and analysis. The better the school is able to understand data and translate that data into meaningful interventions for students, the greater the opportunities and outcomes are for students.

School leadership may identify improving the capacity of the school leadership team to make data-driven decisions with efficacy as an area to monitor while increasing intervention opportunities and outcomes for students. In this case, a pre- and posttest Data-Driven Decision-Making Efficacy and Anxiety Inventory (3D-MEA; Dunn, Airola, Lo, & Garrison, 2013) may be used. Depending on the resources of the team, including any researchers or research institution partners, success can be measured using the 3D-MEA, as well as any subsequent analysis of variance investigations or content analysis of open-ended teacher reports.

At the teacher level, an evaluation tool can be selected to determine the teachers' efficacy in implementing a program. For example, if a school is implementing a school-wide social-emotional learning program as part of a social-emotional-behavioral program, the Social and Emotional Learning Beliefs Scale (Brackett, Reyes, Rivers, Elbertson, & Salovey, 2012), can be used. In conducting a pre- and posttest, the Social and Emotional Learning Beliefs Scale can be used to determine teacher comfort (sense of confidence), commitment (desire to participate), and culture (schoolwide support) for implementing social-emotional learning in their classrooms. Based on feedback from the scale, teams can make decisions about what professional learning opportunities may need to be offered, how committed their teachers are to the social-emotional learning program, and what additional supports may be needed that will ultimately increase outcomes for students.

Regardless of the tool used to measure program progress and performance, several constants must be present:

- A planning assessment must be conducted to determine if the program can feasibly be rolled out.
- Iterative feedback looping must transpire at regular intervals to hone and improve the program once it has been rolled out.
- The MTSS Frequency and Intensity Framework must be followed.
- The team must decide what programmatic goals it would like to measure and select corresponding data collection tools.
- Regular meetings must occur to analyze, record data and progress, and make improvements.
- Team relationship-building opportunities must be supported annually or more often as warranted. This may be in the form of maintenance workshops, effective teamwork activities, or team problem-solving retreats.

As part of the program evaluation and iterative feedback cycle, all components of the LIQUID (Leadership, Implementation, Quality control, Universality, Implementation, Data-based decision making) Model are constantly in a state of analysis. Leadership, inclusiveness, quality control, universality, implementation and feedback looping, and data-based decision making do not function independently; rather, they are all part of each other at various points of implementation. With regard to the second "I", implementation and feedback looping, this must be integral within each of the other components. Reflection on the overall implementation of MTSS and using feedback as inputs to drive future decision making are critical to leadership. Using these data, the school principal can make decisions not based on emotion but based on evidence and can steer the MTSS team in the necessary direction. Inclusiveness based on feedback looping is a key goal of MTSS practices and can be used to build a more socially just system. Without cultural competence embedded in teaching practices and school culture, the effectiveness of instruction will be significantly attenuated. Implementation and feedback looping are also critical to quality control; without it, the MTSS recipe would fall short and the cake would be flat. Universality addresses all students' needs with quality learning experiences and screens them for possible deficits allowing for early intervention. These educational practices are monitored by feedback looping for implementation fidelity. Data-based decision making permeates all ingredients of the MTSS recipe and goes hand in hand with implementation and feedback looping. MTSS requires constant evaluation, reflection, and revision to ensure that elements are the right proportion to make school equitable and relevant for each and every student.

References

Algozzine, B., Barrett, S., Eber, L., George, H., Horner, R., Lewis, T.,. . Sugai, G (2014). *School-wide PBIS tiered fidelity inventory*. OSEP Technical Assistance Center on Positive Behavioral Interventions and Supports. Retrieved from www.pbis.org

Argyris, C. (1999). *On organizational learning* (2nd ed.). Malden, MA: Blackwell.

Blase, K., Kiser, L., & Van Dyke, M. (2013). *The hexagon tool: Exploring context*. Chapel Hill, NC: National Implementation Research Network, FPG Child Development Institute, University of North Carolina at Chapel Hill.

Brackett, M. A., Reyes, M. R., Rivers, S. E., Elbertson, N. A., & Salovey, P. (2012). Assessing teachers' beliefs about social and emotional learning. *Journal of Psychoeducational Assessment*, *30*(3), 219–236.

DiMaggio, P. J., & Powell, W. W. (1991). The iron cage revisited: Institutional isomorphism and collective rationality in organizational fields. In P. J. DiMaggio & W. W. Powell (Eds.), *The new institutionalism in organizational analysis* (pp. 63–82). Chicago, IL: University of Chicago Press.

Dunn, K. E., Airola, D. T., Lo, W., & Garrison, M. (2013). What teachers think about what they can do with data: Development and validation of the data driven decision-making efficacy and anxiety inventory. *Contemporary Educational Psychology*, *38*, 87–98.

Epstein, D., & Klerman, J. A. (2013). When is a program ready for rigorous impact evaluation? The role of a falsifiable logic model. *Evaluation Review*, *36*(5), 375–401.

Hanson, M. (2001). Institutional theory and educational change. *Educational Administration Quarterly*, *37*(5), 637–661.

Hanson, M. (2003). *Educational administration and organizational behavior*. Boston, MA: Allyn & Bacon.

Yuen, F. K. O., Terao, K. L., & Schmidt, A. M. (2009). *Effective grant writing and program evaluation: For human service professionals*. Hoboken, NJ: John Wiley & Sons.

Chapter 13

Advocacy and Policy Making

Key Terms

Stakeholder Networks
Lever
Tactical Advocacy Steps
Connector
The Why
The Ask
Unfunded Mandates
Braided Funding
Formula Funding
Discretionary Grant Funding
Base Funding
Categorical Funding
Dedicated Funding

Chapter Concepts

In this chapter, readers will learn:

1. Where to begin their advocacy efforts and with whom.
2. How advocacy efforts differ at various levels of government.
3. The importance of identifying and integrating the why of others.
4. How to allow the initiative to evolve and grow by starting advocacy efforts early.
5. The importance of relationship building and maintenance.
6. What funding sources are available and why some options are better than others depending on the initiative.

Quality programming for students, along with structures and supports for staff, is not divorced from advocacy and policy making. As experts in their fields, education leaders have a duty to share evidence-based practices and research with others. If data and evidence are not driving the conversation, something else will. Pet projects, emotionally driven practices, and "that's just the way we do things" are all too common and can be replaced by better policies and practices when educators advocate for, and demand, change.

This chapter delves into promoting best practices at the state and district levels and advocating for policies that reflect these practices. Once a team's Multi-Tiered Systems of Support (MTSS) is up and running smoothly, how can it ensure that funding will remain available to support the program (Odden & Picus, 2014)? How can teams partner with stakeholder groups to advocate and promote MTSS programs; what examples currently exist (Dockweiler, 2016)? Who in a team's stakeholder network can elevate MTSS awareness, and who in the network may be detrimental to its success and should be avoided like the plague? Understanding the perspectives, needs, and "whys" of stakeholder groups will help teams better navigate the complicated political arena and leverage existing relationships (Rigby, Woulfin, & Marz, 2016; Robinson, 2015). Advocating for, and legislating, evidence-based programs may not sound like a key piece of the recipe for MTSS success; however, it is critical for long-term student success.

Where to Begin

Different advocacy is required depending on the level of government. MTSS advocacy is not only a federal or state policy issue; it is also relevant at the district and school levels (Morningstar et al., 2016). At the district or school level, it might be as simple as presenting the MTSS concept to the school principal and gauging their level of buy-in. Similarly, at the district level, it might be as simple as presenting the notion to the local school board or superintendent. Stakeholder networks are vital to the success of initiatives. *Stakeholder networks* "are based on a common understanding and extend beyond a single stakeholder group, which can lead to greater impact in times of need" (Dockweiler, 2018, p. 26). They are a web of stakeholders who share similar interests and who can reach out within, and across, their own networks to spread news and help build support for an initiative.

In general, the further up the advocacy chain, the more stakeholders and community support will be needed. If the advocacy is at the school level, the stakeholders may include other respected educators, the school leadership team, or parent group(s). At the district level, stakeholders may include the local teachers' union, local administrators' union, nonprofit organizations, and county associations. At the state level, stakeholder groups are going to include those with members statewide, for example, the state administrators', teachers', and support staff's unions; state professional organizations (school boards, superintendents, school psychologists, speech and language pathologists, school nurses, school social workers, school counselors, etc.), state nonprofit organizations, and state-level for-profit businesses. When advocating at the federal level, having a local voice with a coalition of other state organizations, is going to be beneficial. The local voice will be beneficial to the specific congressional representative that covers that constituent base, whereas the coalition is going to lend strength to the breadth and depth of an issue. *A general rule of thumb: The higher the level of government or bureaucracy, the greater quantity and diversity of representation are going to be beneficial to push an agenda item through.*

Wherever the level of advocacy, whether it be school, district, state, or federal, the first thing an education leader must do is identify what the desired initiative is and what structures need to be put in place. From there, a map can be developed consisting of what's missing, or preventing (either inadvertently or blatantly), in the initiative and devise a plan. *Barrier identification is key because each barrier is going to need a unique and specific plan of attack to bring that barrier down.* Each specific barrier identified within an initiative may also have a separate *lever*, a bureaucratic layer, person, or organization, in which support for change must be sought. Some strategies may be similar or linked, but until each barrier is identified, the problem cannot be comprehensively addressed or solved. As part of the strategy building, stakeholders and other individuals or professionals who are experiencing similar barriers can be brought in to strengthen the efforts and build a coalition. The five *Tactical Advocacy Steps* that need to take place on the front end of planning before any actual advocacy work can even begin:

- Identify the desired initiative.
- Identify the necessary level of advocacy.
- Identify the barriers.
- Identify the levers and strategies to eliminate barriers.
- Begin coalition building.

These steps may take place organically, or they may take a more structured format. Often, one or two key individuals will recognize a problem and will walk through these five steps without even knowing they are doing it. Other times, a group of leaders or an association may get together and require more structured guidance as to how to best begin their efforts. The organic or structured format does not always correlate to the level of advocacy. Great state-level advocacy efforts have been born from one person saying, "This isn't right."

Central to advocacy, coalition building, and demonstrating value is credibility. As professional educators, practitioners have the actual boots-on-ground experience of being "in the field" with the ability to accurately report on what they see happening daily from their credible perspectives in schools. While experience can build credibility, poor behavior and presentation can strip it away. Be mindful of not only what you say but also of who you say it to and in what manner. Written (email, Twitter, Facebook, other social media), verbal (formal and informal conversations), and nonverbal (body language and personal presentation) communication must always be respectful, professional, and tactful. Any transgressions can immediately erase an educator's credibility and result in the death of an educator's advocacy efforts or being blacklisted. Messaging is critical and finding ways to get a point across without being confrontational or accusatory can take time but is essential to advocacy and coalition building.

How to Offer Value

Once the barriers and strategies have been identified and the coalition has been built, the individual(s) or group(s) must immediately begin formulating and offering solutions. It is not enough to simply say, "We want an MTSS program in our district"; the group must show value and be a resource to stakeholders. Whoever is spearheading the efforts must offer viable solutions to remediating specific problems; while pathway A may be the preferred course to get to MTSS, also offer pathways B, C, and D as options because you never know what may resonate with those in decision-making positions and may align with other initiatives that may currently be underway.

A word of advice for those educators for whom advocacy and diplomacy do not come naturally: Do not do what *you* would do; do what you believe someone *should* do. This may feel a bit like acting at first and will be very uncomfortable, as it is out of most people's typical scope of work; however, it is absolutely necessary. Whether you are a parent who disagrees with a particular law or practice at your child's school or an educator who sees the unintended consequences of a policy day in and day out, it is your duty to stand up for your children. If you will not, who will? The old cliché is true: If it were easy, everyone would do it. *However, if it is uncomfortable, you are learning and growing, which will only serve to benefit your cause and children.*

Educators cannot be experts in all things. Bring in those with experience and expertise that differs from the norm who can offer unique perspectives. If funding is a major issue for an initiative, seek out an accountant, banker, lobbyist, or anyone else who is familiar with funding and funding streams. If you have a legal question, seek out a lawyer. Chances are, within your coalition, someone has a friend, or has a friend of a friend, or is related to someone who knows someone. *Leverage existing relationships to maximize the reach and strength of the collective group.* In education, the initiatives being proposed are (hopefully) in the best interest of children. Most people do not mind donating a few hours of their time to lend their professional expertise to an initiative that will benefit students. Sometimes what groups need is a *connector* in their organization or coalition, someone with high social capital who can put the group in touch with other likeminded individuals or with individuals who have a specific skill set that can benefit the initiative.

Consider solutions from many angles and from many perspectives. The group of education leaders who want to implement academic MTSS may have a different "why" than their principal, the superintendent, or the school board. *The why* is the individual's purpose or motivations behind his or her actions. The teachers' *why* may be "We have students who are failing and we need to help them." The principal's *why* may be "Students are struggling and bringing down the overall ratings of my school." The school psychologist's *why* may be "Few of the referrals for special education testing are appropriate because no interventions have been put in place or have been documented." The parents' *why* may be "My child is frustrated with school and doesn't want to go." While this is an oversimplified example of considering the whys, motivations, or purposes, of various stakeholders, if a solution, or ask, can be presented that positively addresses each stakeholders' concerns, it is a win–win for everyone. *The ask* is a specific request made from one individual or group to another. In this particular case, the ask would be a systematic manner in which to identify gaps in learning, provide interventions, and monitor student progress, in other words, an MTSS infrastructure with multiple levels of high-quality universal and targeted learning experiences. This particular ask may be made by educator leaders to the school principal, district representatives, or state representatives, depending on what level they are advocating for.

Typically, the whys of groups are often complicated and may be kept close to the vest, at least the *true* why behind what they are trying to achieve. Stakeholders are not necessarily duplicitous on purpose, but the messaging of their why may change depending on their audience. This is true for education leaders as well. For example, knowing that the why of the principal is overall school performance, when teacher leaders approach the principal with their ask, they can frame the conversation around their why of noticing student failure, and they can also incorporate the why of the principal into the dialogue. In doing so, the teacher leaders have demonstrated their value and have essentially solved a problem for the principal. If they can take it one step further and discuss solutions to funding, staff training, and scheduling, their value and resourcefulness will be even further amplified.

Advocate Early

Just as district- and school-level planning for the next school year begins before the current year ends, so does state legislation. If a group of leaders thinks it can begin building relationships with legislators during the legislative session and request that bills be filed, they are sadly mistaken. Leaders are cautioned to be mindful of bill draft timelines and to plan accordingly. For example, if state legislators can begin putting in bill drafts December 1, they will be looking for ideas and having conversations with organizations and individuals during the spring and summer prior, if not sooner. This allows them time to research the initiatives and bring together stakeholders that share similar concerns so there are not multiple bills being proposed that say nearly the same thing. It also gives them time to keep an eye out for competing initiatives. If a group has the ear of a legislator, continue to maintain a relationship with them and demonstrate value in and out of legislative sessions.

Ideally, relationships will be maintained so that new relationships will not need to be forged each session. *Relationship building is essential and time-consuming, and it is easier to maintain a relationship than build a new one.* However, depending on the state or district, term limits may have an impact on the length of time someone stays in office, such as on the local school board or state legislature. There are pros and cons to term limits and election cycles with revolving-door relationship building certainly being one of the biggest downsides. Once a group has built a relationship with a legislator, school board member, or key decision maker, it is more likely to have their ear when issues arise. The key is to build relationships early, and outside times of crisis or necessity, so organizations or individuals can access that relationship in times of need. This access goes both ways and allows elected officials and other stakeholder groups to reach out to educator leaders when questions or concerns arise. Relationships must be maintained and sending informational emails updating the elected official as to what a group is doing is one quick and easy way to keep a presence.

Never take "no" for an answer. Sometimes "no" is simply "not yet," "not in this form," or "not with these people." Never accept "no". This point cannot be stressed enough; perseverance and flexible problem solving are essential to advocacy. Yeses can be found down the road even when the nos are presently inevitable. Advocating early allows groups time and space to strengthen their efforts, gather more information, or take their initiative to someone else who sees the vision in the work. Oftentimes, initiatives arise out of a need to counter an existing proposal or practice. It can be a full-bodied response that screams, "We cannot do this to our children!" and as a result, a counter practice, program, or policy is initiated. Be mindful that most policy is not devised from people with foresight sitting around a conference table thinking about all the good that can be done. More often, policy arises to fill a need or a gap in existing practice that was not even evident until something less than desirable happened. For example, many states and districts do not have mandated social-emotional-behavioral programming in place. These programs have been used infrequently by some schools in the form of social-emotional learning or positive behavior intervention supports but were not brought to the front of America's consciousness until the recent years' school shootings, such as Parkland, Florida, and Santa Fe, Texas. Now parents, educators, and communities are screaming for increased mental-behavioral health supports and school safety policies. Social-Emotional-Behavioral MTSS (Chapter 11) is a great way to systematically address the social-emotional-behavioral needs of students and is a critical infrastructure for school leaders to advocate for at all levels of bureaucracy.

Having a window of opportunity to advocate for a particular initiative due to a recent crisis or a sudden public awareness benefits the advocacy process. Kingdon (1984) refers to this phenomenon as policy building through multiple streams, with the three streams being the problem, the solution, and the political will. Political change cannot happen without an initiative reaching the political agenda. Kingdon argues that these three streams must converge at a given point in time in order for this change to happen. If a problem has been identified and the perfect solution has been found, it will not make it into the public's consciousness without the political will. Until a legislator can be found to champion the cause, a bill draft will never be submitted let alone heard before a committee. And one legislator is not enough. Many legislators from both political parties must be on board and must be prepared to push the initiative through multiple committees, including finance if needed, in order for a bill to pass out of the legislature successfully and to be signed by the governor. Ultimately, if the governor is not on board, a bill will not become law, even with legislative support.

Funding

Depending on the level and type of programming, various funding streams may be available and may vary significantly state by state. At the school level, certain programming options can be written into the school's budget. As long as the costs are not too exorbitant, school-level programming options can typically be funded, especially if the planning is done during the prior school year so priority can be given to the new program or initiative.

District level initiatives are costlier and are better received by individual schools, administrators, and staff if they are adequately funded. *Unfunded mandates* are statutory requirements or regulations imposed without funds provided to carry out the directive. These unfunded mandates, or underfunded mandates, are seen at the federal level with requirements put on state education agencies, and they are also seen at the state level with requirements put on the local education agencies. Unfunded mandates are some of the most difficult for schools to implement as they are often expected to do more with less. Again, planning is key, as districts and school board representatives can prepare, budget, and plan for new initiatives if they see them coming. Reactionary measures are taken when they are caught off guard, lose lawsuits, or are forced to make drastic cuts. Arbitration decisions with local unions also make a difference in what districts are required to pay, which, in turn, have an impact on the amount of money they have in their budgets for initiatives. Staff are a school's greatest asset and compensating them for their time, education, and expertise is essential. Local teachers' unions have been holding walkouts in states such as Arizona, California, Colorado, Illinois, Kentucky, Oklahoma, and West Virginia in protest of low educator pay, and this has resulted in many educators receiving higher compensation. This compensation must come from somewhere, and if money is pulled from a district's budget to (rightfully) increase educator pay, something else in the budget must be decreased.

At the state level, a variety of funding sources are available from the federal budget, to supplement the state budget, for programs and human capital. *Braided funding* is the weaving of funds from multiple sources and is useful in maximizing impact without relying too heavily on any one funding source. The multiple sources can include the various funding levels of federal, state, or local and may include private and public funds. State education agencies can use federal funds and grant monies to offset and supplement local education agencies' costs. The majority of states, 90 percent, use formula funding to cover education costs (Tilsley, 2017). In a very broad sense, *formula funding* is the dollar amount assigned from the state to each district based on various computed factors. To ensure equity and transparency of dollars spent, the majority of states

> use data-driven, cost-based education funding formulas to meet these goals. Most of these formulas use accurate student data, account for differences among school districts, direct funding to address those differences, and do so with a goal of ensuring all students have adequate funding to meet state standards.
>
> (Klehr, Presson, Schaeffer, & Zelno, 2013, p. 1)

Discretionary grant funding is money that is awarded through a competitive application process. Such grants are typically available at the federal level and have specific stipulations about who can apply, the amount of funds available, and what the funds can be allocated toward. In addition to federal public grant monies, state grant monies and private grant monies may also be available for qualifying organizations. Oftentimes, when applying for grant monies, in addition to the actual application, a budget must also be submitted that outlines where each dollar requested will be spent. Formula funding may be better for long-term planning of initiatives due to the temporary nature of grant funds. If a state receives federal grant funds for a particular program or initiative, after the grant expires, the funds are no longer available. If possible, it is ideal to get funding for a new statewide initiative into the governor's budget as this ensures that monies will already be allocated to support it. As a result, when the bill is heard before the legislature, the likelihood of it passing increases as decisions about whether to fund a bill or not are less of an issue.

Looking at the Social-Emotional-Behavioral MTSS discussed in Chapter 11, several different funding scenarios may be present at the state level. First, a bill may be introduced into the legislature that requires each school in the state to implement a Social-Emotional-Behavioral MTSS model. Even if the model presented is data-driven and evidence-based, who is going to pay for its creation and implementation in the schools? Staff training would be required and materials would need to be purchased; there are many different ways in which schools would benefit from financial support to implement the initiative. If a bill does not pass out of committee, it will die. If a bill passes out of the introducing committee, it could still die in the finance committee without the motivation of the committee chair and committee members to allocate monies to support it. If the bill does manage to pass through all the necessary committees without funds attached to it to support its implementation, and the governor signs the bill into law, then districts could be faced with an unfunded mandate.

Looking at another scenario with the same Social-Emotional-Behavioral MTSS bill, the bill could also pass into law but could come with funding provided by the state. If the governor of a state knows when he or she is designing their budget that X is going to be a priority, specific funding amounts can be earmarked. Similarly, state legislatures can pass funding and budgeting requests, and the process for doing so will vary state by state. Various funding streams may be available to support education initiatives, such as base, categorical, and dedicated. *Base funding* is the amount of money a state sets aside to cover the basic costs of education. *Categorical funding* is reserved for a very specific program or purpose: "[W]ith categorical funds, priorities are set by the state to enact what state officials view as the most desirable programs. By its nature, categorical funding is narrowly directed, and as such, district flexibility is limited" (Smith, Gasparian, Perry, & Capinpin, 2013, p. 1). In the example of the implementation of a Social-Emotional-Behavioral MTSS program, categorical funds set aside for this could not be used by districts on other types of programs. Common uses for categorical funding may also include special education, gifted and talented education, and class-size reduction. *Dedicated funding* in a broad sense is somewhat similar except the monies are dedicated for a specific purpose, such as teacher salaries, through a dedicated funding source, such as specific tax revenues. Both have a practical use, and it just depends on the initiative as to which is more appropriate.

A third, and optimal, scenario for the Social-Emotional-Behavioral MTSS legislation example is that the governor of a state recognizes the initiative as an upcoming priority and puts money aside in their budget, *and* the state uses federal funds to back the initiative. In the case of mental-behavioral health and school safety, there are three suggested federal funding sources to investigate. First is Title I of the Every Student Succeeds Act (ESSA; 2015). This is a formula fund that passes monies from the state education agencies to the local education agencies. Monies from this funding source can go toward implementing schoolwide programs, such as Social-Emotional-Behavioral MTSS, and to fund counseling and school-based mental health supports (National Association of School Psychologists [NASP], 2018). Title II of ESSA is also a formula fund for states to pass down to local education agencies, and funds can be used for professional development on a variety of topics surrounding student well-being and safety. Title IV-A of ESSA is another formula fund for state education agencies to pass down to local education agencies surrounding the implementation of trauma-informed practices, comprehensive mental and behavioral health systems, and violence prevention programs; the training of intervention and prevention programs for students at risk; and the development of restorative justice and positive discipline strategies versus exclusionary and punitive discipline (NASP, 2018). These various federal formula funds are also relevant to investigate for other related initiatives, not just those related to Social-Emotional-Behavioral MTSS.

Federal grants that support behavioral and mental health are also a good source of additional funds and worth exploring. Additionally, if a state currently does not have existing pathways for their school psychologists and other school-based mental health professionals to bill for Medicaid services, it would behoove the state to look into establishing this avenue as a funding source (Ekland, von der Embse, & Minke, 2015).

Moving Forward

If given the opportunity to assist in the writing of legislation, opt to use policy language that is written in the form of a commissive, not a directive. In doing so, the effectiveness and impact of policies can better be determined (Dockweiler, Putney, & Jordan, 2015) and can lend information for iterative, data-based decision making. Also, in writing state policies with commissive statements, state-level accountability will be easier to determine. Many state education policies are written in the form of a *directive*, which tells the local education agencies what to do, rather than of a *commissive*, which commits itself to action (Dockweiler et al., 2015; Dockweiler, 2012). Policies that are written in the form of a directive make implementation fidelity difficult to determine; however, when policies are written in the form of a commissive, it is easier to determine if the intended actions have indeed been carried out (Dockweiler et al., 2015; Dockweiler, 2012). Typically, state legislative council bureaus, lawmakers, or noneducators write state education policies. Being involved in the policy writing process is a great opportunity for educational leaders to advocate for policies that are written using commissive statements and have state-level accountability measures built in.

Box 13.1

Voices From the Field

It was the day after the 2016 presidential election. Ten weeks earlier, our Title I middle school staff, students, and families had been informed that our school could be forced into a newly formed Achievement School District (ASD) by the end of the year due to persistently low high-stakes test scores and a newly passed law under Senate Bill 448 (2015). Most of our students were English language learners, living well below the poverty line, and our school had a transiency rate that hovered around 50%. Unbeknownst to us, there was a hidden time bomb tucked into the law established during the previous legislative session, which would force all public school district employees out of selected schools, while the school building, computers, and all equipment inside the school would be turned over to a selected for-profit charter organization to turnaround school achievement for select schools in the state. The criteria for qualifying for the ASD included the schools with the highest percentage of students who scored at the bottom 5% statewide on the annual high-stakes test, Smarter Balanced Assessment Consortium (SBAC), and our school fell within this range.

All neighborhood children would be forced to attend the charter school unless they could get their own transportation to attend the next closest public school. The school principal, teachers, support staff, students, and neighborhood families were stunned that our community school could be forcibly taken over, and an out-of-state charter school with no vested interest in the neighborhood or community would be given all the power to do with our children whatever it wanted or needed to do. Research on charter schools in places such as New Orleans, North Carolina, Arizona, Rhode Island, and Chicago does not indicate empirically better outcomes and indicate a confluence of intermediaries and financial variables that contribute to charter school operations (DeBray, Scott, Lubienski, & Jabbar, 2014; Chingos & West, 2015; Paino, Renzulli, Boylan, & Bradley, 2013; Teresa & Good, 2017; Wronowski, 2017). The extracurricular activities and clubs that students depended on for enrichment and engagement would no longer be offered. None of the supports and services helping our families and children, including assistance with basic needs, disabilities, and behavioral-mental health problems would be guaranteed for students the following year. Our whole community was horrified and turned otherwise benign constituents into activists.

A minimum of six schools from across the state were to be selected to forcibly participate in the ASD. A long list of schools put forth by the state Department of Education turned into a short list of schools to be considered. All the schools identified for takeover in the state happened to be located within a 20-mile radius of the poorest section of the largest county in the state, with the highest number of minority and second-language students. Local schools were pitted against neighboring local schools in the fight to get off the list. Led by our tenacious school principal, staff, students, and parents testified at the State Board of Education meetings to have our school removed from the list of potential ASD schools. Our students and staff went on a letter-writing campaign. We were in the newspapers and on television, speaking out at every opportunity against the flawed concept of bringing in an unknown out-of-state charter school vendor to turn our neighborhood school into nothing more than what we imagined would be prison-style experiences.

The "Save Our School" rally was one of the most extraordinary experiences in my career. Our families and parent center team worked with students and teachers to make signs, which were plastered all over the front of the school and carried by every single person. Our orchestra set up on the sidewalk and played. Our cheerleaders cheered up and down the sidewalks. Our teachers, students, and parents walked arm and arm, chanting to save our school. We had at least 75 people at our school rally, and then the media showed up. More people came. Local politicians spoke out on our behalf. We were televised live on all three major television news stations and Telemundo broadcast across the country. News helicopters filmed us from overhead, as it was the largest local school rally to date. The news world heard our voices. The Nevada Department of Education heard our voices. The Nevada legislature heard our voices. Shortly after the world witnessed our continuing dedication to our community and our school with a successful rally, we were taken off the list for consideration of the ASD. I am still in awe of that day. Everything went perfectly in terms of safety, organization, and teamwork. We could never have planned the media's response and the compassionate light they shined on us. I will never forget the power harnessed by our community that day, like harnessing lightning.

In the end, the selection of the six schools was put on hold due to contentious community backlash when the disreputable behavior of the chosen ASD charter organization was revealed, as evidenced by a Federal Bureau of Investigation raid charging fraud, fiscal mismanagement, and misuse of public monies meant for schoolchildren. Efforts to repeal the ASD were not successful during the 2017 legislative session, but, with tenacity, they succeeded in 2019 with Assembly Bill 78. An amendment was added toward the end of the session that if an existing ASD school wanted to continue as a charter, it could, but public school takeovers by outside organizations would not be forced on communities against their will. Our staff and school community learned the hard way that education policy will impact a school community directly, intimately, and invasively. If it can happen to us, it can happen to any school, when community and staff members in the field are not working together to lead discussions to develop better solutions. If educators are not leading the charge, then other people with agendas of their own will drive decisions in their best interests that do not necessarily align with evidence-based practices or student and community well-being. That school year we all learned the importance of advocacy and policy making as a required part of educator responsibilities in school practices.

References

Assembly Bill 78, Nevada 2019.
Chingos, M. M., & West, M. R. (2015). The uneven performance of Arizona's charter schools. *Educational Evaluation and Policy Analysis*, *37*(1), 120–134.
DeBray, E., Scott, J., Lubienski, C., & Jabbar, H. (2014). Intermediary organizations in charter school policy coalitions: Evidence from New Orleans. *Educational Policy*, *28*(2), 175–206.
Dockweiler, K. A. (2012). *Language of instruction policies: Discourse and power*. University of Nevada, Las Vegas University Libraries. (ISBN 9781267755230).
Dockweiler, K. A., Putney, L. G., & Jordan, T. S. (2015). Enhancing the policy analysis process: Case studies using the layers of analysis framework. *Journal of Ethnographic and Qualitative Research*, *10*(4), 87–103.
Dockweiler, K. A. (2016). State association advocacy: Conversations about conversations. *Communiqué*, *44*(7), 1, 32–33.
Dockweiler, K. A. (2018). Responding to tragedy through stakeholder communication networks. *Communiqué*, *46*(7), 26.
Ekland, K., von der Embse, N., & Minke, K. (2015). School psychologists and school-based Medicaid reimbursement. *National register of health service psychologists*. Retrieved from www.nationalregister.org/pub/the-national-register-report-pub/the-register-report-fall-2015/school-psychologists-and-school-based-medicaid-reimbursement.
Every Student Succeeds Act of 2015, 20 U.S.C. (2015).
Kingdon, J. W. (1984). *Agendas, alternatives, and public policies*. Colchester, UK: The Book Service.
Klehr, D., Presson, E., Schaeffer, B., & Zelno, S. (2013). *Funding, formulas, and fairness: What Pennsylvania can learn from other states' education funding formulas*. Education Law Center. Retrieved from www.elc-pa.org/wp-content/uploads/2013/02/ELC_schoolfundingreport.2013.pdf
Morningstar, M. E., Allcock, H. C., White, J. M., Taub, D., Kurth, J. A., Gonsier-Gerdin, J., . . . Jorgensen, C. M. (2016). Inclusive education national research advocacy agenda: A call to action. *Research and Practice for Persons with Severe Disabilities*, *41*(3), 209–215.
National Association of School Psychologists. (2018). *Framework for safe and successful schools: Considerations for action steps* [Brief]. Bethesda, MD: Author.
Odden, A. R., & Picus, L. O. (2014). *School finance: A policy perspective* (5th ed.). New York, NY: McGraw Hill.
Paino, M., Renzulli, L. A., Boylan, R. L., & Bradley, C. L. (2013). For grades or money? Charter school failure in North Carolina. *Educational Administration Quarterly*, *50*(3), 500–536.
Rigby, J. G., Woulfin, S. L., & Marz, V. (2016). Understanding how structure and agency influence education policy implementation and organizational change. *American Journal of Education*, *122*, 295–302.
Robinson, S. (2015). Decentralisation, managerialism and accountability: Professional loss in an Australian education bureaucracy. *Journal of Education Policy*, *30*(4), 468–482, doi:10.1080/02680939.2015.1025241
Senate Bill 448, Nevada 2015.
Smith, J., Gasparian, H., Perry, N., & Capinpin, F. (2013). *Categorical funds: The intersection of school finance and governance*. Center for American Progress. Retrieved from www.americanprogress.org/wp-content/uploads/2013/11/CategoricalSpending1-brief-4.pdf
Teresa, B. F., & Good, R. M. (2017). Speculative charter school growth in the case of UNO chart school network in Chicago. *Urban Affairs Review*. Retrieved from https://doi.org/10.1177/1078087417703487
Tilsley, A. (2017). *How do school funding formulas work?* Urban Institute. Retrieved from https://apps.urban.org/features/funding-formulas
Wronowski, M. L. (2017). Beacon charter school needs a school: A case of capital outlay of charters in a public district. *Journal of Cases in Educational Leadership*, *20*(3), 56–64.

Chapter 14

Troubleshooting Guide

> **Chapter Concepts**
>
> In this chapter, readers will learn:
> 1. How to problem solve a variety of issues that they may encounter as they seek to implement MTSS or experience once they've already begun implementation.
> 2. How to navigate obstacles related to leadership, staff, and gatekeepers.
> 3. Ways to creatively work around resource needs and funding constraints.
> 4. How to problem solve issues of fidelity, tier prioritization, and program transferability.

There are many obstacles to effectively implement Multi-tiered Systems of Support (MTSS) on a school campus. Some remedies are easily identified, while other solutions seem elusive and out of reach. It is important to identify barriers to implementation and barriers to change on your school campus (Forman & Crystal, 2015). As mentioned in Chapter 5, if the school principal is not actively solving problems in this process, your success in a systematic implementation of supports is in serious jeopardy. If the principal is passively allowing MTSS at your school, other issues will arise (Averill & Rinaldi, 2011). Obstacles to organizational change in bureaucratic institutions are all but assured, and the key to success in building and sustaining best practices is responsive adaptability. Nurturing team functions and supporting team decisions are the responsibility of all stakeholders and each educator must fill a role. This chapter introduces the most common barriers to implementing and sustaining MTSS, as well as solutions for teams to help identify, and troubleshoot past, the obstacles.

18 Common Barriers to Implementation of MTSS

1. The School Does Not Have a Principal Who Is on Board With Supporting MTSS

This situation is the worst-case scenario for an effective implementation of MTSS. Ideally, state- and district-level leadership is not only backing MTSS efforts but also leading efforts with advancing the framework that includes accountability standards built into performance goals for school leaders. School principals are the key to laying foundational supports for scaling MTSS at their schools and maintaining the system once it is started. There are several critical incidences that are associated with positive change in practice and the principal is associated with each: "multidisciplinary leadership, access to professional development, consistent language and/or practices, consultation with external partners, and a focus on student outcomes in evaluation and planning" (Charlton et al., 2018, abstract). Additionally, teachers report wishing that they had greater access to individuals who had more expert knowledge and training surrounding MTSS and had more effective interventions available to them (Charlton et al., 2018).

Outside active high-level leadership, including state- or district-level mandates directing the school principal to build tiers of support, the responsibility to convince the school principal to allow MTSS usually falls to the school psychologist, school counselor, literacy specialist, or other motivated educator leader. Most school principals understand that major eligibility criteria for special education are dependent on prior interventions, and many can agree that intervention implementation and making data-based decisions to determine students' response to instruction makes sense, at some level. What many are not willing to commit to is investment in evidence-based practices, supports to structure intensified instruction, assistance in organizing or training teachers in implementing interventions or team development, and providing assessment tools to measure outcomes consistently across teachers and grade levels (Anyon, Nicotera, & Veeh, 2016; Cavendish, Harry, Menda, Espinosa, & Mahotiere, 2016; Averill & Rinaldi, 2011).

Getting agreement in principle with the principal about the MTSS framework is always the first goal of building MTSS, as it is instrumental in determining the success of new practices (Printy & Williams, 2014). If that fails, the next step is to attempt to obtain support for one part of MTSS, such as Academic MTSS. Success may be had with the principal's support for small-scale or part of Academic MTSS, such as one grade level, using curriculum-based measures to measure the progress of Tier 2 and Tier 3 readers in third grade. Staff buy-in and implementation goals may need to be incremental, and small successes can help to get a foothold in the school for teachers to build on.

If efforts to obtain principal buy-in are not effective, then the task becomes enticing teachers and support positions to work intervention magic on a small scale, with an individual teacher or teachers implementing and documenting interventions and outcomes within their class(es). In large schools, small-scale individualized efforts are rarely sustainable. Small-scale efforts that grow because of popularity, effectiveness, and relationship building with stakeholders, other than the school principal, may lead to a leadership crisis for the school principal, who must either publicly back the initiative or, more likely, crush outward practices that threaten leadership priorities or self-image. When this happens, intervention implementation and documentation go underground, and experienced teachers who have concern for lower-performing or suspected special-needs students will continue to collect Response to Intervention data quietly to support students and to build evidence for eligibility. This can create a hostile school climate and good teachers will eventually leave the school in search of a more supportive administrator (Boyd, Grossman, Lankford, Loeb, & Wyckoff, 2011). School psychologists, special education teachers, school counselors, speech therapists, learning strategists, and other supporters can advocate, educate, and demonstrate the benefits of MTSS as often as possible at all leadership levels.

2. The School Does Not Have a Principal Who Actively Leads MTSS on Campus

The disorganized and disengaged principal is worse than it sounds and is almost as difficult a scenario as the principal not backing MTSS at all. Like a teacher with students, the school principal sets priorities for the staff and reinforces desired teaching practices, or not. When it comes to classroom management, teachers who are comfortable with chaos are the most difficult to help motivate to change their own behavior in how and when they reinforce variables in the classroom environment. Students in such teachers' classes basically do whatever they want, whenever they want, and sometimes the teacher gets upset for no clear reason because expectations are never clear. Teachers who are comfortable with chaos are extremely unlikely to be successfully coached by peers or administrators in positive behavioral supports. For the school psychologist who seeks to assist in helping teachers change their selective attention and behavior strategically to have a positive impact on students, successful coaching of comfortable-with-chaos teachers is nearly impossible. Such teachers are not bothered enough, or motivated enough, to become self-disciplined and make the effort to change themselves.

When teachers are *uncomfortable* with classroom chaos, they are often willing to make substantial effort to reinforce the correct variables to increase the probability of positively impacting student behavior, which, in turn, improves classroom climate and productivity. These classroom behavior management efforts are most successful when they align with the schoolwide positive behavior intervention framework. If a schoolwide positive behavior framework does not exist, it is recommended that one be put in place with the principal leading the charge. Increasing the rate of positive reinforcement of students and using preplanned unemotional responses to address misbehavior are cognitive-behavioral tasks for the adults managing them. Improving teaching practices, like learning and rehearsing anything new, takes sustained mental effort, and if the goals are not perceived to be worth the effort, then the quality of effort will suffer. Like teachers, comfortable-with-chaos administrators will struggle with the efforts required to build and actively manage MTSS. Changing staff beliefs and behaviors toward the structures and practices of MTSS are among the greatest barriers to implementation (Anyon et al., 2016).

Principals who are comfortable with chaos also lack leadership, and others will not follow them, resulting in teachers basically doing whatever they want, whenever they want, because performance expectations are never clear. The outcome of leadership chaos is a leadership vacuum that attracts someone else to the top of the heap to create "order," much as in the book *Lord of the Flies* (Golding, 1954). When your school campus is run by Lord of the Flies, school culture suffers, and educators find themselves trying to please all or none. Welcome to Bolman and Deal's (2017) jungle. Building and sustaining relationships with the "quasi"-administrators to influence cultural attitudes toward better practices is required for stakeholders wishing to improve student outcomes through generating useful, evidence-based solutions to school problems. Fortunately, school psychologists and other leaders on staff are adaptable, and convincing self-appointed tyrants to try different things is all part of the job.

Some very laid-back principals can still clearly be in charge. Under a distributed leadership model, administrative responsibilities may get shifted to assistant principals, specialists, and teacher leaders in quasi-administrative positions. With proper implementation, distributed leadership is correlated to teacher's positive feelings about their school and their desire to remain and be a part of the organization (Ross, Lutfi, & Hope, 2016). Under this type of model, collaboration and decision making usually transpire within the leadership team on executive resolutions that have an impact on MTSS.

The administrator in charge may be part of this decision-making team, or he or she might make decisions unilaterally. It is important to get agreement in principle of the MTSS framework with both the principal and the administrator overseeing MTSS (if they are not the same person). If accomplished, then the school psychologist and MTSS teams would work with the appointed administrator in the same capacity as the principal. If the principal and administrative appointee do not agree in principle to the MTSS framework, the need to educate, demonstrate, and advocate would apply to build consensus. As long as the principal agrees in theory and supports funding efforts, all possibilities for MTSS implementation are on the table. Administrators must see MTSS as an embodiment of the school, not something separate from the school or an add-on (Averill & Rinaldi, 2011). This becomes a matter of relationship building with stakeholders within the school and not compromising who, what, where, when, and how supports are implemented. Starting MTSS processes is not the most difficult part; growing and sustaining effective practices through teamwork from stakeholders and adapting responsively to address challenges are the ultimate accomplishments of successful MTSS.

3. The School Lacks Research-Based Curriculum or Interventions

School principals get much of the heat for not implementing best practices, when as often, if not more often, state-level decision-making bodies, school boards, and school districts sabotage efforts of MTSS intentionally and inadvertently. Policy makers jump on bandwagons without looking at implications of research-based outcomes from the national level to the state level. When disregard for evidence-based practices in school settings is evident throughout the country, it is no wonder that school principals have a difficult time weighing the cost-to-value ratio of instructional practices. Principals and school teachers do not like wasting time with practices that do not work. Sometimes, ineffective practices are mandated by school districts and school boards for political reasons, and there is little principals can do except supplement teachers with additional tools to fill in gaps that the curriculum does not touch.

MTSS advocates can build support for teachers in the classroom with teaching supplements, online resources, and documentation or charting tools that produce and capture measurable outcomes, many of which are free. A lack of effective intervention material is cited by teachers as a challenge that, ideally, could be remedied in their schools (Charlton et al., 2018). There are also grant opportunities that can fund supplements, supports, and human capital that do not impact the school's budget. Success is a motivating factor for students and teachers alike, and successes create a stronger appetite for investment in interventions that work. Working on a small scale with individual teachers willing to try something new is progress no matter how small, and those efforts often lead to other teachers becoming interested or taking initiative in implementing helpful and easy to use processes.

Growing best practices one teacher at a time is a virtue, especially when the school principal(s) does not make MTSS processes a priority and turns their back on supervision and visible support. Schools with similar populations often look to each other to find promising solutions to similar issues. Educators leading and learning with other educators, despite a lack of coordinated leadership efforts, is challenging but can lead to successes on a smaller scale. Feedback looping, unfortunately, will not be maximized for evaluating intervention implementation until the issues of systematic service delivery are ironed out. Otherwise, each teacher is re-creating intervention magic on an individual basis, which mostly relies on professional judgment in program evaluation to cover for reliability and validity issues.

Picking a target skill, choosing a research-based method to address the skill deficit, recording the amount of time the student is getting the intervention, and progress monitoring outcomes can be accomplished by a classroom teacher. Without systematic supports, these individual efforts are most often the case. However, when systems are in place for teachers, at-risk students are more quickly identified, and teachers are more likely to implement intensive instructional supports systematically and with integrity. They can do this because they are not scrambling to find time to squeeze interventions in the instructional day, find lower-level materials, maintain intervention logs for each student, or measure outcomes with alternative assessments. Teachers who have to create remedial opportunities for their students on an individualized basis have to go to many extra efforts to put it all together, which is a barrier to implementation and results in fewer students getting help when they need it. The more teachers and other educators who advocate for systems in their schools to address student needs, the more open school leaders may be to provide supports in a systemic fashion. Educating, demonstrating, and advocating the benefits of evidence-based practices schoolwide, districtwide, and statewide are required.

4. The School Has Teachers Who Are Resistant to MTSS Despite Training Efforts

The teachers who are resistant to MTSS may not be convinced that the promised outcomes justify the efforts or may not have received sufficient training to carry out the initiative. When educational fads come and go, teaching practices change with the direction of the wind and the only constant thing is change, teachers lose heart in the "next best thing." Teacher buy-in is a crucial milestone for successfully implementing MTSS, and teachers belong in leadership positions to make decisions that have an impact on their daily teaching practices (Brezicha, Bergmark, & Mitra, 2015). It is difficult to argue with the need for evidence-based practices, but there is hardly consensus on how to best choose or implement evidence-based teaching practices. Guidelines for supporting the implementation of best practices include following a research-based framework, selecting practices with sufficient data to support effectiveness, and using data to guide decision making (Mazzotti, Rowe, & Test, 2012).

As discussed at length, teachers have amazing skills and must be masters of curriculum and behavior management to survive teaching successfully. Effective teaching requires purposeful intent and sustained effort. Requiring educators to do more with less is one thing, but asking them to do differently with more supports is another. When given a choice to do more work without administrative support, additional compensation, or celebration, why would teachers choose more work? Because the majority of teachers honestly want to help their students, which is why they got into education. Most teachers would be happy simply to have current textbooks for students and enough classroom supplies without spending their own money. But, of course, the celebration and compensation of educators to engage in best practices, which lead to the best outcomes, should be the gold standard.

If school leaders provide the tools and structures to implement MTSS practices to grow extraordinary learning opportunities for all students, and teachers let those opportunities go to waste because of a lack of skill or motivation, then the solution is to provide greater training or supervision. One possibility could be to include the resistant teachers on the problem-solving team to help them understand the needs of others and allow *them* to find solutions that work for everyone. Complainers can turn those frowns upside down by being a part of the solution, and actively working with the school team to address the issues. Things change constantly in education and change is hard for people sometimes. When changes are unpalatable, allowing others to simply have a seat at the table can be part of the solution. Another way to ensure the buy-in and support of the teachers is to have them contribute to the building phases of the school's MTSS. When they feel that their input was heard they will feel validated and will be more likely to support MTSS when it is up and running.

Administrative guidance is the best remedy for resistant teachers. Compliance with effective teaching practices is often reflected in teachers' annual evaluations, which should determine corrective actions and, in extreme cases, possible professional discipline and behavior restoration. Barring administrative oversight, teachers are influenced by other teachers' success with students, participating in a distributed leadership model, and making extra-duty pay. Administrators who reward change agents publicly and provide plenty of opportunity for staff collaboration and development will see the greatest movement of resistant teachers toward best practices. In schools that have a well-run MTSS, life gets easier for everyone because the staff have what they need to get the job done and the students get what they need when they need it.

5. Interventions Are Not Being Implemented With Fidelity

Supervision of teaching methods falls squarely on the school principal and school administration. When teachers are not implementing interventions with fidelity, it is up to the school administration to provide leadership as to how the interventions should be implemented through reteaching, modeling, or guided practice. A lack of intervention fidelity may include not using a research-based curriculum, providing interventions consistently for the recommended amount of instructional time, or not using the curriculum as prescribed.

Tier 1 must always be implemented with fidelity and must be addressed first before evaluating Tier 2 and Tier 3 practices. The selection of intervention tools and methods at Tier 2 and Tier 3 is a function of the MTSS administrative team with professional learning community feedback or goodness of fit (Cheney & Yong, 2014). If teachers are not adequately trained in the prescribed teaching methods, then they need more opportunity for skills development in instructional strategies, and doing so will also increase the likelihood of teacher retention and decrease of attrition from the teaching field (McCarthy, Lambert, Lineback, Fitchett, & Baddouh, 2016). If teachers do not have enough time to use the methods as validated, then more time must be carved out of the students' day to be exposed to the interventions.

Supplementing research-based tools without using the method with fidelity cannot be counted on for positive results, nor can the results be blamed due to the efficacy of the method because it was not implemented as directed. Physicians have the same problems with patients who do not take their prescriptions as directed. When the antibiotics did not cure the infection, doctors cannot blame the treatment because the patient did not take all the doses for the amount of time that is statistically needed to remedy the problem. Educators cannot blame the curriculum if they did not follow the prescribed method with the length of exposure to materials statistically needed to remedy the problem. Not using intervention tools as directed is simply a waste of time and money, and no reliable inferences can be made whether the method works or if a student is responding adequately to it. School administrators must ensure integrity with teaching practices through supervision, monitoring, and professional feedback and guidance.

6. Interventions Are Not Being Documented Adequately

Documentation for large numbers of students is laborious at best and impossible at worst. If large numbers of students are not responding to instruction and require interventions, the effectiveness of Tier 1 instruction must be addressed. Teachers who find that school structures do not support systems of interventions, such as a scheduled intervention block, and have to find "free time" to remediate student skills' deficits, have a bigger problem than just documentation. Students who receive interventions through an intervention-based scheduling design outperform their peers who receive interventions ad hoc or not at all (Dallass, 2017). Getting hold of research-based interventions and scheduling ample time for implementation are the true challenges. If the intervention method is preselected as meeting criteria for being evidence-based and intervention blocks are scheduled and adhered to, attendance logs, along with lesson plans, suffice as documentation of having participated in the session. When teachers have to cobble together their own intervention plans, find their own tools for interventions and progress monitoring, and write notes about what they're working on sporadically, with 10 minutes here, 10 minutes there, intervention logs are much less reliable. In such cases, documenting the interventions is as much of a challenge as implementing the interventions regularly with fidelity. The solution to one problem solves the other.

7. The School Staff Perceives MTSS as a Function of Special Education Eligibility Outcome, Not as a Path to Solutions for Student Difficulties in and of Itself

You have to start somewhere. If the principal's and teachers' initial buy-in to MTSS is for special education eligibility purposes, start there. Squeezing in evidence-based practices for one student improves accessibility to evidence-based practices for all others as a by-product. A common mistake that occurs on campuses where teachers collect response to intervention data solely for special education eligibility purposes is that curriculum-based measurement (CBM) data are collected repeatedly over time, yet the instructional opportunities are rarely intensified during that period, interventions to target skills' deficits are not documented, and/or interventions are not valid or implemented with fidelity. For example, a student's math computation fluency graph is flat for a whole year, yet no interventions were documented, and there is no way to confirm whether they occurred at all. Academic MTSS teams and school psychologists can build on that. Teachers are already dedicating time and effort to progress monitoring, yet that effort is wasted because documented interventions to intensify instruction did not occur along the way to determine if anything more intensive worked. Adding intervention opportunities in classrooms already utilizing CBM is a small leap compared to the initial step of implementing regular CBM assessment in data-based decision making. This staff is halfway there. Educate, advocate, and demonstrate the benefits of evidence-based practices and MTSS processes to more productive outcomes.

8. The School Does Not Have Sufficient Funding to Address MTSS Adequately in Terms of Personnel and Resources

Like having a baby, you are never really 100% sure if you are ready. The underlying insecurity is whether there will be enough resources (money, time, energy) to support the baby. Babies are expensive and a lot of work. MTSS is also a lot of work and requires significant investment. Unlike the unpredictability of raising children, MTSS can be grown in incremental manageable steps. Low-cost practices that depend more on staff buy-in and effort can be implemented to begin the mind-set needed for change that will ultimately lead to better practices. Team building can begin in the context of solving site-based issues with existing resources. Not all evidence-based interventions are expensive, many free or low-cost supports can be found online. Some such examples include intervention.org, rtiforsuccess.org, interventioncentral.org, xtramath.org, Interventions for Math Difficulties, easycbm.org, Florida Center for Reading Research, Reading A-Z, What Works Clearinghouse, PBIS.org, the National Center on Intensive Interventions, and PBIS World. Some fee-based online interventions also allow free trials or limited-use trials.

Schools starting MTSS from scratch have many things to consider. They should begin with the following six items: (1) picking universal screeners (Academic and Social-Emotional-Behavioral) and determining how to identify at-risk students, (2) scheduling at least one intervention block per grade with an intensified curriculum, (3) ensuring implementation fidelity of evidence-based practices, (4) selecting which diagnostic and progress monitoring tools to use, (5) identifying who is going to monitor outcomes, and (6) identifying who is going to make data-based decisions on behalf of students with support of classroom teachers. Leaner teams can operate efficiently until they need more hands on deck based on the number of referrals. During the intervention block, students performing below grade level attend intervention. Students at or above grade level attend enrichment. Each student is receiving the content he or she needs at his or her instructional level. Depending on the size and needs of the school, a teacher from a high-risk school may have up to 10 students in their intervention group. Ideally, small-group Tier 2 instruction would not have that many students, but reality often dictates practice, not the other way around. Similarly, with Social-Emotional-Behavioral MTSS, there may only be the capacity to offer one counseling group per grade, but start there. Start lean and grow.

9. The School Does Not Engage in Universal Benchmarking, nor Are Progress Monitoring Tools Being Used Consistently for Data-Based Decision Making

This is a fairly common situation and a thinking error on part of many school leadership teams. School administrators may be unaware of its necessity, or they may want to save money and time. Or they wrongly believe that mandated high-stakes tests can serve as student benchmark data. However, investing in the cost of human capital resources and tools to appropriately implement universal screenings to root out underperforming students actually saves time and money because benchmarking quickly identifies students who may not come to the attention of teachers as requiring remediation until much later in the school year, if at all. Old-fashioned methods rely on parent or teacher referral requests, which often occur after prolonged academic failure, and may be compounded by the amount of time it takes to track down and sort through student data by cross-referencing sources. Only the most persistent educators track down student records from previous schools. Schools without universal benchmarking are going to be on the reactive end, supporting underachievers, rather than at the proactive end, where they are able to quickly identify at-risk learners and target and remediate skill deficits. The reactive approach does not align with research and best practice and often violates states' laws requiring the use of screening measures to identify and remediate student deficits early in their academic careers (Salinger, 2016). The toll of wasting instructional and behavioral remediation opportunities resulting in prolonged school failure is much higher than the initial deposit of money and human capital it takes to be proactive using universal benchmarking to identify at-risk kids and invest in evidence-based interventions, progress monitoring tools, and human capital to professionally monitor and manage outcomes.

10. The Teachers Are Overwhelmed, Cannot Take on New Responsibilities, and Do Not Have Time to Engage in Professional Learning Activities Pertaining to MTSS

MTSS is a framework that allocates school resources in a proactive manner and as a triage model. State laws and district-level protocol for adhering to evidence-based practices should guide implementation at the school level, but sometimes required practices at the school level prove to be labor-intensive with no clear benefits. Continuing to pile on responsibilities to teachers' workloads, including mandating new duties, more paperwork and time-intensive activities, only serves to be counterproductive. Giving teachers more work without taking anything away from their job responsibilities leads to less compliance with all job duties. There are only so many hours in a day and job requirements can tap teachers' reserves only so much, as generations of teachers can attest. Obviously, compensating teachers with financial and nonfinancial benefits for their extra time and efforts is a certain motivating factor and well earned. The rest lies in common sense. Educators must prioritize which tasks require immediate attention and those that can wait, tasks that have the most impact on students and those that have less impact, and tasks that make the most sense and those that make less sense.

MTSS is a framework designed to address the needs of all students. The framework requires evidence-based Tier 1 instructional practices first and foremost, which has an impact on everyone. The MTSS framework also provides the path for actionable steps to follow in times of academic and behavioral difficulty for students requiring Tier 2 and Tier 3 supports. By shifting perceptions from MTSS as "more" work to "more effective and efficient" work, school teams will realize that practices actually become *less* labor-intensive with automaticity as it becomes embedded in the schools' culture of functions and processes to support all students.

The first-time practices are changed universally on a school campus may be shocking to the community as some people can be resistant to change. Time passes, and new practices become established practices. Like money in the bank, investing in teacher and educator development, supports, and services earns interest like no other down payment. Leaders must evaluate school priorities, eliminate unnecessary or duplicative processes and paperwork for teachers, and foster a culture of shared responsibility for problem solving by automating as much of the process as possible embedded within the school culture. Barriers should be low for teachers to advocate for help for students, and intervention efforts should be celebrated and compensated. *A little love and support for educators go a long way toward helping them help their students.*

11. The School Psychologist Does Not Honor Teachers' Intervention Implementation or Documentation, Which Makes Referral for Special Education Evaluation and Ultimate Eligibility Determination, Almost Impossible

School psychologists are in the unenviable position of being perceived as *gatekeepers* to special education. If the school psychologist does not conduct an evaluation, the target student is definitely not going to be eligible for any additional services; thus, "letting students in" or "keeping them out" of special education, like a gate. Closer to reality, the challenge school psychologists face includes the often-unavoidable position of unilaterally evaluating MTSS practices in schools with no control over intensifying supports for students without pursuing special education eligibility. Nationally, there is a shortage of school psychologists practicing in the field, as well as professors and higher education training programs (National Association of School Psychologists (NASP), 2016). If shortages of school psychologists could be addressed, there could be enough school psychologists to work proactively, guiding teamwork in the development of layers of supports and networks within the tiers of academics, social-emotional and behavioral functioning, family engagement, special education, mental health, and resource networking. A reasonable school psychologist caseload, that aligns with the nationally recommended 1:500 to 1:700 ratio (NASP, 2016) would allow school psychologists to engage in these essential prevention and intervention services (Bocanegra, Grapin, Nellis, & Rossen, 2017).

School psychologists may not be able to get to all referrals immediately and must prioritize their referral list based on intensity or need, which is why supports and services should not be dependent on one person as a gatekeeper. The time and expertise of the school psychologist are a valuable human capital resource, and more should be invested in school psychological services. The school psychologist can sort through large amounts of student data to generate hypotheses about student functioning and variables that maintain dysfunction, which leads to highly educated recommendations for solutions. Proactively prioritizing student need and providing supports within MTSS not only benefits individual students; it also aligns with the Every Student Succeeds Act, as it can improve school climate and safety and it benefits *all* students on a school campus (NASP, 2017). When MTSS systems are automated, everyone does their part because structures are in place to allow each professional to do their part; and active problem-solving processes are in place so that everyone can figure out how to do their part despite obstacles and unexpected situations.

When school psychologists have to literally run down teachers to plead for MTSS documentation and data, it is never an efficient use of limited time. When interventions are on the master schedule, when data can be accessed remotely by all stakeholders, and when meetings occur regularly to engage in problem solving for students over time, then teams can run efficiently. These systematic processes can be relied on and prevent school psychologists from the untenable task of tracking down or squabbling over unreliable documentation and making judgment calls. Systematic processes help protect teachers, school psychologists, and students and ensures that everyone's time is used wisely and efficiently.

The question ultimately is whether the student demonstrates a lack of adequate progress and performance over time in response to highly intensive instruction with severe enough underachievement to warrant eligibility. The difference between MTSS being in place or not for the student referred for eligibility is that in the end, students who do not meet criteria for special education eligibility will *still* get assistance at the level they need because the school offers other levels of support within the functions of MTSS. Whereas in schools without MTSS, special education eligibility is the only way for underperforming students to get differentiated instruction to meet their needs. The worst thing for the school psychologist–teacher relationship is when the school year is over and the student is even more behind, the teacher blames the school psychologist for the child not getting more help and the school psychologist blames the teacher for not having the acceptable documentation to meet legal criteria for eligibility to adequately address suspicion of disability in terms of prior interventions.

Practices need to change, and one shift that can occur is for school psychologists to be more flexible in working with teachers to negotiate and problem solve intervention practices that provide evidence to meet criteria for eligibility determination. You got to give a little to get a little. When the school psychologist is an active and participating member of the MTSS team, issues of documentation tend to be eliminated as the school psychologist has been guiding and supporting intervention processes every step of the way.

12. The Parents or Guardians Do Not Want Interventions; They Want Special Education Eligibility Determination

Rarely is this the case. The most common thread in parental requests for assistance is that they want help for their child(ren) in the school setting and beyond. Oftentimes, when parents or family leaders make a request "for an IEP (individualized education program)" for their child, they do not know what they are asking for, what the process is to be found eligible, or what eligibility even means in the long run. Families who need help for their children can and should be persistent in requesting supports, services, and documentation of outcomes. Parents who write a letter requesting a psychoeducational evaluation or an IEP, including third-party requests from counselors, lawyers, parent-advocate groups, and physicians (often in the form of prescriptions) are simply proxy parent requests asking for help from the school psychologist and teachers for the child's benefit.

Occasionally, caregivers seeking financial public assistance consider special education eligibility as an income-generating proposition, but only a tiny fraction are out for Social Security Income. In reality, what they are unknowingly seeking is an advocate in the system to promote best practices to ensure the welfare of their child in a school setting. If students can get the help they need with an added intervention or a layer of support without eligibility and without waiting periods, most caregivers are on board. Help the students when and where they need it. Educating parents and families about

MTSS may be time-consuming on the front end but pays off in the long run. Strong family–school partnerships will also lower barriers for families when they are seeking help as they will feel more comfortable going directly to the school rather than through a third party. In rare cases when special education evaluation *is* warranted and the team is delaying the evaluation, then caregivers have the right to ask for a timely assessment in writing with a response provided by the school within a reasonable amount of time.

13. The Behavioral Supports Are Too Complicated to Implement Systematically or They Do Not Exist at All

One of the biggest mistakes school systems make is providing behavioral supports only at Tier 3, often in the form of reactive discipline procedures. Systemic behavior supports at Tier 1 and Tier 2 have been shown to have a significant positive impact not only on students' behavior but also on students' academic performance; especially for those students with emotional-behavioral disorders (Lewis, McIntosh, Simonsen, Mitchell, & Hatton, 2017). Beginning at Tier 1 means everyone has exposure to learning experiences and everyone has equal opportunity to earn rewards and positive reinforcement. Classroom management gets the biggest bang for its buck on a school campus, closely followed by schoolwide positive behavior intervention support (PBIS) practices. Integrating and aligning the two are optimal for student and staff success. There are many variables to consider in PBIS, and it is recommended to keep things as streamlined as possible.

Ideally, a systematic process can be built during the year prior to full-scale implementation; however, they can also be built in incrementally year by year. Start with a solid foundation, like Tier 1 social-emotional-behavioral opportunities, and build in Tier 2 and Tier 3 intervention blocks or supports. Without comprehensive planning and troubleshooting for all three tiers a year in advance, it is recommended to get good at the first layer before building on the next layers too heavily. Growing practices incrementally is far more sustainable than revamping and rebuilding constantly, which is ineffective and leads to fatigue and burnout. Layers of support are very likely occurring at Tier 2 and Tier 3 on your campus but are not being captured systematically with data and monitoring. Schools often operate as a system of teams; through better identification and understanding of the underlying motivations, school leadership can better predict successful system performance and processes (Rico, Hinsz, Burke, & Salas, 2016). Look around campus and find out what is happening in terms of school counselors, mentors, and teachers putting in the time to build relationships, building skills to offset academic frustrations, and teaching critical thinking and problem solving to students. Every little bit counts. Tweaking current practices to add evidence-based methods is a smaller leap than starting from scratch. New initiatives must be weighed by the MTSS team to make the best decisions for a particular campus.

14. The High-Needs Students Are Frequently Absent or Tardy for Classes

Students who experience school failure and are frequently absent or tardy are usually not the culprits on an elementary school campus. Oftentimes, it is the caregiver who fails to put the child to bed, wake him or her up, and ensure that he or she arrives at school on time. These adult problems soon become student problems and compound year after year without remediation. Getting the caregivers to change their behavior can be a huge barrier to overcome as the caregivers themselves often experienced failure at school and do not place much value in education. In these cases, one intervention rests in dealing with the caregiver and coming up with creative ways to help. There is always the threat of educational neglect; however, these threats are often empty, and most districts do not pursue a legal course of action unless in the very most extreme cases. Another option is to send truancy officers to the house to see what is going on and transport the student if necessary. However, this is only a short-term solution and only buys a little time while looking for a more permanent solution to the student's absence and tardy issue.

In the early elementary grades, kindergarten through second grade, students are more at the mercy of their parents. When they reach the upper elementary grades, third through fifth grades, school staff can teach them valuable life skills such as how to set an alarm clock, how to go to bed at a set time each night, how to shower and pack a backpack the night before, and how to get ready and out the door in the morning. If there are multiple children in the family, the older siblings can assist the younger siblings in getting ready and sticking to this routine. For students who are in walking distance of the school, and they are in a safe place to walk, they can transport themselves. If the school is not within walking distance, helping the students to learn the bus routes can help ensure they arrive on time each day.

Students ultimately need employable skills and remaining in school increases their chances for success. Individually, "dropouts are significantly disadvantaged compared to high school graduates with respect to employment, earnings, avoiding crime and incarceration, avoiding teenage childbearing, parenting children within wedlock, having good health, civic engagement, well-being, and intergenerational upward mobility" (Hoffer, 2015, p. 81). In addition to the individual consequences, there are also economic and social consequences of dropping out, including "reduced economic activity from unemployment and reduced tax revenues from foregone higher earnings associated with high school completion; and higher costs to society of increased crime, increased welfare use, and increased use of public health insurance" (Hoffer, 2015, p. 81). Teaching good home-to-school routines early and placing a practical emphasis on education can assist some students in persisting year after year when they might have otherwise dropped out.

Family outreach and supporting families to help their children get to school with free bus passes, attendance contracts and incentives, and enabling relationships with families so that they allow their children to participate in extracurricular and community learning opportunities to increase engagement. Considerations should also be made by the team to identify, and support, students who may be homeless as their educational access and self-advocacy may be compromised (Ausikaitis et al., 2014).

15. Tier 1 Instructional Practices Are Not as Effective as They Should Be and Getting Tier 3 Supports for Students Takes Too Long

This is the most common framework error, party foul, and saboteur of success at other tiers. How can a building withstand weight and gravity without a proper foundation? Tier 1 systems of a school should be the theoretical blueprint with sufficient tons of iron rebar and cement underground to hold up a skyscraper. If the base of the building is unstable then nothing built on top is going to be stable either. Tier 3 solutions do not fix problems at Tier 1, but Tier 1 solutions can resolve and prevent issues at Tier 2 and Tier 3. Scheduling, building layers of support, providing access to supports based on need, decision-making models, growing data sources and tools, universal benchmarking, teaching behavioral expectations proactively, providing a school culture of achievement and shared responsibility all have an impact on the success of Tier 2 and Tier 3. Hopefully, through these strategies, processes, and practices schools can keep students out of Tier 3 because they are engaged in Tier 1 and are receiving remediation in Tier 2.

Family engagement and parents' or guardians' voices are often louder than educators' voices within a system and can advocate for Tier 1, 2, and 3 supports more effectively than all other advocates. Family advocacy groups are important contributors to schools and are most successful when there is a collaborative and proactive rapport with staff and school leadership (Matthews, Georgiades, & Smith, 2011). Nationwide parent-advisory councils are gaining decision-making powers at school organizational levels, and parents and guardians must be educated about best practices so they can advocate for those practices locally and nationally.

16. The Administrator Has Decided that Intervention Blocks Cannot Be Scheduled and That Interventions Should Be Taught Within the Classrooms at the Teacher's Discretion

All school administrators should have high expectations of teachers, although some may underestimate the power of supporting teachers with smart teams to grow better teaching practices. Especially with the reality of teacher shortages and having undertrained and under-prepared teaching staff, it is really difficult for teachers to take ownership of identifying underachievers and implementing solutions in the classroom without the help of an MTSS team and systems. Teachers *should* take ownership of student outcomes in the classroom. By all means, classroom teachers should know their students' instructional and performance levels and should be making data-based decisions, which is why systems are needed to continually support teachers in their practice. In situations where the administrator is not going to support schoolwide MTSS teams, the grade-level teams will become autonomous micro-level MTSS problem-solving teams. Work-arounds and Tier 3 intervention planning will now fall on the shoulders of each grade-level team, and they will need to advocate on behalf of the highest at-risk students in their grades. At-risk students require a focal point of advocacy on large and small campuses, and classroom teachers often benefit from having a second advocate, or grade-level team, who can speak to a student's needs.

Target students can be monitored by classroom teachers, and those teachers could be responsible for problem solving at grade-level collaborative team meetings. Block scheduling can work well if the interventions are scheduled into the differentiated learning segments documented in lesson plans to ensure enough class time for using the evidence-based curriculum with fidelity. Breaking up intervention blocks this way works just like scheduling additional intervention periods and supervision can occur to monitor implementation, which always increases compliance. A drawback is that, if not paced adequately, instructional time can be wasted during block-scheduled classes.

17. Even Though All 50 States Have State Policies That Allow for Academic MTSS, Our Local Education Agency (LEA) Prefers Identification for Specific Learning Disabilities Based on Cognitive–Achievement Discrepancy Model Reliant on Strengths–Weaknesses Processing Deficits Versus Academic MTSS

LEAs that persist in choosing a practice that goes against evidence-based practices will require advocacy and action from stakeholders at the micro- and macro-levels. LEAs that were able to overcome the draconian cognitive-achievement discrepancy with processing deficits model for specific learning disability (SLD) eligibility for special education created a new normal when they moved to the more humane practices of determining eligibility based on resistance to documented high-quality instruction. First and foremost, switching from the discrepancy model to the Academic MTSS model creates the duty to evaluate the quality of instruction at all levels of intensity beginning with Tier 1, which is a school improvement issue. It also creates the need for responsive systems to support teachers and students, which requires significantly more effort; a greater deal of planning, organizing, and documenting of teacher and student performance over time is required, and less emphasis is placed on student performance during an evaluation period for eligibility. The requirement of determining processing deficits as the sole determination of SLD was changed years ago (IDEA, 2004) and most states now have more flexible eligibility options including MTSS. A nonsensical formula to determine whether a discrepancy between a child's predicted and actual achievement is statistically severe and assigning a processing deficit as the presumable cause to warrant special education eligibility may make the decision making much more clear-cut at an eligibility meeting, but is it ethical to make educational decisions based on faulty logic because it seems easier to justify? Is it not our professional responsibility to challenge unethical practices? *Faulty policies did not get in place by themselves, and they will never change without stakeholder intervention to amend the policy.* The first misconception is at the practitioner level, when school psychologists feel like policies are imposed on them, and they follow the state policies instead of challenging them. As practitioners, we may not think it is our place to slow things down at the school level when it comes to being testing machines that churn through evaluations. No one can force a school psychologist in a school to test 100 students for initial SLD evaluations every year. If school psychologists are able to increase their time spent working on coaching, increasing coalition networks, and building systems and structures of alternative supports in a school, then teachers will have tools and supports they need to reach all students and fewer students will need testing for special education. In the meantime, students will be receiving the level of intensity of instruction they need with or without special education eligibility, and they get what they need as a result of the school psychologist effectively being proactive, which was time well worth spent. The second misconception is with regard to advocacy and the faulty thinking that we do not have the experience or power to speak up. Constituents become activists and school psychologists can become advocates for best practice in state policy. It is a *must*. Get comfortable with showing up, writing your legislative representatives, building relationships with policy makers, and speaking up about unjust practices in schools at the legislative level. You can do it!

18. The Principal Has Left the School, Will Any of the MTSS Infrastructure That Was Created Last?

The truth is that it depends. With personal vision and priorities, new building principals choose to do things differently. Hopefully they will evaluate existing programs and improve on what works. Sometimes when school administrators move on from a school, large numbers of staff also leave with them or move on themselves. When the educators with the MTSS leadership skillset leave a campus, new training opportunities must be established for new staff if the system has any chance of sustainability within a school culture. A principal who has experience and success with MTSS is much more likely to be open-minded to keeping systems in place and to improve on those systems than an incoming principal who does not. It is almost guaranteed that a new building principal will change some systems and processes. MTSS is transferable principal to principal if the incoming administrator already buys into it and has the skills to be responsively adaptive and actively support staff leadership positions and team problem-solving activities. MTSS is replicable, yet it rarely is replicated exactly. Finding functional and sustainable MTSS is rare indeed but does not have to be.

References

Anyon, Y., Nicotera, N., & Veeh, C. A. (2016). Contextual influences on the implementation of a schoolwide intervention to promote students' social, emotional, and academic learning. *Children & Schools, 38*(2), 81–88.

Ausikaitis, A. E., Wynne, M. E., Persaud, S., Pitt, R., Hosek, A., Reker, K., . . . Flores, S. (2014). Staying in school: The efficacy of the McKinney-Vento Act for homeless youth. *Youth and Society, 47*(5), 707–726.

Averill, O. H., & Rinaldi, C. (2011). Multi-tier systems of support. *District Administration, 9*, 91–94.

Bocanegra, J. O., Grapin, S. L., Nellis, L. M., & Rossen, E. (2017). A resource guide to remediating the school psychology shortages crisis. *Communiqué, 45*(6). Retrieved from www.nasponline.org/publications/periodicals/communique/issues/volume-45-issue-6/a-resource-guide-to-rem ediating-the-school-psychology-shortages-crisis

Bolman, L. G., & Deal, T. E. (2017). *Reframing organizations: Artistry, choice, and leadership* (6th ed.). San Francisco, CA: Jossey Bass.

Boyd, D., Grossman, P., Lankford, M. I. H., Loeb, S., & Wyckoff, J. (2011). The influence of school administrators on teacher retention decisions. *American Educational Research Journal, 48*(2), 303–333.

Brezicha, K., Bergmark, U., & Mitra, D. L. (2015). One size does *not* fit all: Differentiating leadership to support teachers in school reform. *Educational Administration Quarterly, 51*(1), 96–132.

Cavendish, W., Harry, B., Menda, A. M., Espinosa, A., & Mahotiere, M. (2016). Implementing response to intervention: Challenges of diversity and system change in a high-stakes environment. *Teachers College Record, 118*, 1–36.

Charlton, C. T., Sabey, C. V., Dawson, M. R., Pyle, D., Lund, E. M., & Ross, S. W. (2018). Critical incidences in the scale-up of state multitiered systems of supports. *Journal of Positive Behavior Interventions*. Abstract retrieved from https://doi.org/10.1177/1098300718770804

Cheney, D. A., & Yong, M. (2014). RE-AIM checklist for integrating and sustaining Tier 2 social-behavioral interventions. *Intervention in School and Clinic, 50*(1), 39–44.

Dallass, W. P. (2017). Systemic sustainability in RtI using intervention-based scheduling methodologies. *Learning Disability Quarterly, 40*(2), 105–113.

Forman, S. G., & Crystal, C. D. (2015). Systems consultation for multitiered systems of supports (MTSS): Implementation issues. *Journal of Educational and Psychological Consultation, 25*, 276–285.

Golding, W. (1954). *Lord of the flies*. London: Faber and Faber.

Hoffer, T. B. (2015). Dropping out: Why students drop out of high school and what can be done about it. *Contemporary Sociology: A Journal of Reviews, 45*(1), 80–82.

Individuals with Disabilities Education Act, 20 U.S.C. § 1400. (2004).

Lewis, T. J., McIntosh, K., Simonsen, B., Mitchell, B. S., & Hatton, H. L. (2017). Schoolwide systems of positive behavior support: Implications for students at risk and with emotional/behavioral disorders. *AERA Open, 3*(2). Retrieved from https://doi.org/10.1177/2332858417711428

Matthews, M. S., Georgiades, S. D., & Smith, L. F. (2011). How we formed a parent advocacy group and what we've learned in the process. *Gifted Child Today, 34*(4), 28–34.

Mazzotti, V. L., Rowe, D. R., & Test, D. W. (2012). Navigating the evidence-based practice maze: Resources for teachers of secondary students with disabilities. *Intervention in School and Clinic, 48*(3), 159–166.

McCarthy, C. J., Lambert, R. G., Lineback, S., Fitchett, P., & Baddouh, P. G. (2016). Assessing teacher appraisals and stress in the classroom: Review of the classroom appraisal of resources and demands. *Education Psychology Review, 28*, 577–603.

National Association of School Psychologists. (2016). *Addressing shortages in school psychology: Resource guide*. Bethesda, MD: Author. Retrieved from www.nasponline.org/resources-and-publications/resources/school-psychology/shortages-in-school-psychology-resource-guide

National Association of School Psychologists. (2017). *ESSA and multitiered systems of support for school psychologists*. Bethesda, MD: Author. Retrieved from www.nasponline.org/research-and-policy/current-law-and-policy-priorities/policy-priorities/the-every-student-succeeds-act/essa-implementation-resources/essa-and-mtss-for-school-psychologists

Printy, S. M., & Williams, S. M. (2014). Principals' decisions: Implementing response to intervention. *Educational Policy, 29*(1), 179–205.

Rico, R., Hinsz, V. B., Burke, S., & Salas, E. (2016). A multilevel model of multiteam motivation and performance. *Organizational Psychology Review, 7*(3), 197–226.

Ross, L., Lutfi, G. A., & Hope, W. C. (2016). Distributed leadership and teachers' affective commitment. *NASSP Bulletin, 10*(3), 159–169.

Salinger, R. L. (2016). Selecting universal screening measures to identify students at risk academically. *Intervention in School and Clinic, 52*(2), 77–84.

Chapter 15

Moving Forward Together

> **Chapter Concepts**
>
> In this chapter, readers will learn:
>
> 1. How to nurture and grow the six components of the LIQUID Theory into their school's MTSS practices.
> 2. Pathways in which to be forward thinking and for reimagining schools systems as they could and should be.
> 3. How to be a practice leader in the implementation of MTSS.
> 4. The urgent need to advocate for socially just programs and practices to promote the fundamental rights of all children.

Multi-Tiered Systems of Support (MTSS) is a living garden that requires constant attention and care and, in return, provides the manna to build and sustain the nutrition of all students, staff, and school community. MTSS gardens can be ignored and starved, which leads to mangled educational practices with no solid root system. MTSS practices that only provide sunlight to the top of the tiers may also get root rot and die. Schools that neglect Tier 1, the root system, will never have rich enough soil or strong enough seeds to grow sustainable best practices to support all students. Only school systems that commit to growth will survive changes in weather and be healthy enough to meet community needs into the future. The ingredients of LIQUID support MTSS growth and sustenance just as plants need water to grow and survive. Good educational outcomes are the result of good educational practices. Good educational practices are the result of strong **L**eadership; **I**nclusive practices; **Q**uality control through supervision, educator development, and team empowerment; **U**niversal practices; **I**mplementation of evidence-based curriculum valid for academic and social-emotional-behavioral instruction at Tiers 1, 2, and 3 with engagement in feedback looping; and **D**ata-based decision making.

Leadership

Viewed through the Leadership lens, every decision made on a school campus reflects the vision and quality of the school principal and administrative team to carry out school-level initiatives in compliance with federal, state, and district guidelines. MTSS requires high competence in leadership qualities of organization and supervision in order to put structures, functions, and procedures in place, as well as maximize human capital and most effectively budget to allocate scarce resources. Restructuring existing roles, responsibilities, and resources to enable highly specialized collaborative communities to flourish improves school culture, increases the effectiveness of communication and personal responsibility, and helps with budgeting. Principals with strong organizational management skills who can inspire, motivate, and reward educators are more likely to reach schoolwide goals (Grissom & Loeb, 2011; Stetler, Ritchie, Rycroft-Malone, & Charns, 2014). Investing in human capital, evidence-based curriculum, and having a clear blueprint for building and sustaining best practices are all required for effective leadership. School leaders are required to actively solve problems to ensure barriers to implementation of MTSS are successfully overcome. Leaders must continually review and revise all practices to keep on course with evolving student and staff needs and realities of circumstances. When leadership makes MTSS a school priority, then it shall be a guiding framework on a school campus.

Inclusiveness

When decisions on a school campus are viewed through the Inclusiveness lens, leaders and staff members must take into account how existing and proposed educational practices have an impact on all individuals with differing ethnicities, languages, cultures, religions, backgrounds, and beliefs. If a current practice is not universally implemented nor equitably applied, groups of students, families, staff, and community members could be alienated by not having equal access to supports or having legal protections equitably applied to all. When the rights of one are institutionally violated, the rights of all are violated with a risk of disintegration of all said rights. Procedures must align with best practices to expect them to work as intended. Cultural competence is required to provide a respectful and adaptively responsive learning environment to the needs of diverse populations. School leaders support inclusive practices by continually challenging educators to challenge their own implicit biases, effectively building relationships with people from different backgrounds, and creating learning opportunities to grow more inclusive practices through staff development and community outreach. Restorative justice is a perfect example of an inclusive practice that provides an effective alternative to ineffective discipline procedures with zero tolerance. School psychologists are poised to positively consult and contribute to these efforts on school campuses (Song & Swearer, 2016). Increasing cultural competence and using restorative justice practices benefits all stakeholders.

Quality Control

Quality control is the overarching construct for maintaining the fidelity of implementation of any program or practice on a school campus. Ensuring that practices are evidence-based and that teachers are implementing instruction with fidelity is paramount. Every day, educators are faced with more responsibilities, more requirements, and more seemingly pointless roles. Educators want to work smarter, not harder. With every new practice in a school, a competing less effective practice should dissipate for educators in order for them to have the time and energy to comply with new expectations. Yet, rarely is that the case. It makes no sense to add more criteria to what teachers are required to do without addressing the obstacles to policies with unintended consequences that make teachers' work less meaningful. Evaluating current practices, through measurable outcomes, is required to shed ineffective practices; however, selling educators on new roles and responsibilities is not a simple task. *Quality control of resources is much simpler than quality control of human capital.* Nonetheless, data-based decision making is at the crux of quality control of effective systems in schools. The way to initiate and sustain quality control measures relies on the continuous improvement model of implement–review–revise (Bryk, Gomez, Grunow, & LeMahieu, 2016). Leadership must constantly be supervising practices for fidelity to ensure quality control because directives that are not enforced through active supervision are never sustained. Most teachers simply do not have enough time, resources, or administrative support to build or sustain new complex systems without states, school districts, and school administrators actively solving problems at the point of service delivery. Research-based practices are grown when there is room to grow, and the way to make room for new practices should include reducing unnecessary paperwork, reducing unnecessary meeting times, reducing the unreasonably high levels of pressure of teaching to the test, and reducing busywork required of administrators and educators for high-stakes testing.

Universality

Universal is best described as "all means all." Every student counts, and every student should have a place in a high-quality school. Giving equal opportunity and equal access is the foundation of social justice in education. Beyond that, individualizing educational supports for students is required for many to be successful presently and is the wave of the future in education. Providing evidence-based instruction with fidelity for all students should be the goal of every school. Educational practices that have the biggest impact on a school are those that all students benefit from. For example, students benefit from practices that are aligned with MTSS, and there is a level of support for all students who have a range of needs. Students are screened universally to help identify those at risk proactively, which saves instructional time for them when they are given opportunities and remedial interventions as quickly as possible in their educational careers. All students require low barriers to access the level of support they need to be successful in school.

Implementation and Feedback Looping

The Implementation and Feedback Looping lens of educational practices magnifies the nuts and bolts of the what, when, why, where, and how educational practices are rolled out. Oftentimes, the idea behind an educational practice is noble, but the implementation of it is a disaster. When this is the case, the product or outcome does not meet the hype of promised results and administrators may become discouraged. When results are not as desired, school leaders may have the inclination to throw the baby, or the educational practice, out with the bathwater without having evaluated implementation integrity. It goes back to best teaching principles and using evidence-based instructional practices to maintain quality control in terms of supervision fidelity. Staff motivation and positive reinforcement of positive practices and outcomes are at the heart of the Implementation lens. Feedback looping must occur constantly to determine the efficacy of practices, which is tied to quality control. The only way to grow best practices is to give a voice to those implementing those practices to review and revise the practices as necessary to adjust and adapt or stay on course. Once again, success breeds more success, as does empowering and rewarding educators who deliver the what, when, why, where, and how.

Data-Based Decision Making

Data-based decision making is the engine of MTSS. Data should drive instruction and most other decisions on campus. The Data lens is the tool for a hyper-focus on outcomes, indicators, trends, trajectories, and systematic feedback. Multiple sources of information and observational opportunities must be triangulated to get the whole picture of instructional quality. Instructional decisions based on one source or one type of assessment may drive assumptions that are faulty or misleading. If the curriculum is of high quality, if teachers are implementing with integrity, if the data collection methods are sound, then the outcome data should be reliable. To gain a clearer picture of practices at a school, or in the classroom, a variety of instruments should be used, both formative and summative. Relying on one measure, such as high-stakes testing, may not give an accurate reflection of whether instructional practices and educators are effective or not. Systems must be designed to manage the rich sources of data available to continually renew and update in real time so that timely decisions for students may occur. Practices not supported by a positive impact on achievement data should be reevaluated for fidelity of implementation before being abandoned completely. The quality controls of MTSS depend as much on quality data as stringent supervision of implementation fidelity.

The Basics

Administrative accountability is inevitable. School principals, school district administration, and school boards must be accountable to the public for providing adequate supports to their schools' multi-tiered support systems. The days of optional evidence-based services in the field of education should be as frowned on as instances of physicians not washing their hands before conducting surgical procedures. Best practices should be supervised for accountability because they will never otherwise be adequately built or sustained. As evaluation standards for teachers and other licensed educators are beginning to align with national teaching and other professional standards, administrative job performance evaluations for principals, as well as for high-level school district administration, and school boards should also be aligned and measured by more transparent standards, especially in failing schools and districts.

High-stakes tests often fail to measure true gains of high-risk, high-poverty populations. Including benchmarks and goals in the growth model on administrators' annual evaluations will allow district superintendents and state superintendents to hold administrators, as well as teachers, accountable for student growth. These accountability assessments also serve as a self-reflection tool for administrators to gain a better understanding of where their implementation strengths lie and where there may be cracks in the foundation or building. The politics should be taken out of schools, and fair evaluation standards should apply. Any school taking any amount of public school dollars for students should be held to the same standards. School principals should have MTSS criteria on their evaluation rubrics to ensure that such practices are taking place. When the school principal refuses to provide, or inadequately provides, supports for all, they are not serving their students or the community justly. Nearly everything can be broken down to a leadership issue in education. School principals who value professional learning and training in evidence-based practices can take steps to implement MTSS and create a better school culture that produces greater opportunity for all students. Change takes time, and children are usually the least resistant to change in comparison to the adults supporting them.

Teacher motivation and compensation are huge factors in the success of MTSS. Expecting more of educators without taking away other burdens is not a long-term solution. Taking advantage of salaried workers only goes so far before the quality of service suffers. Educators need a comfortable salary and health benefits so they do not have to work two and three jobs, as has been indicated by teacher walkouts from West Virginia, Kentucky, and Oklahoma to Arizona, Colorado, Illinois, and California, with varying levels of success, in the past couple of years. Professional compensation and valuing educators' specialized skills that lead to positive educational outcomes for all students is the best way to get high-quality efforts from the educational workforce. Extra work should come along with extra pay. Extra-duty compensation, additional pay from longer school days or school years, and comp time are only fair.

Administrators are forced to make hard decisions, such as cutting budgets and staffing positions, because many states do not fully fund education as fully as they should. However, until the day that highly trained educators working directly with students are treated like the venerable developmental experts they are and compensated accordingly, schools will continue to face issues of staff attrition and quality. It is time to restructure the way schools are funded and the way educator pay is allocated. In the meantime, MTSS can grow incrementally if it is a priority. Once the new practices take root in a school, automaticity dramatically increases the likelihood of sustainability. MTSS practices built from scratch can be sustained, as long as best practices are supervised for implementation fidelity and positively reinforced.

A motivated and well-trained school staff can accomplish the impossible with students. Whether children have disabilities or high giftedness, building and sustaining relationships with teachers as positive role models increase students' critical thinking and prosocial skills. Healthy children need adults as leaders and as models (Creighton, Doub, & Scott, 1999), and today's children especially need guidance in a safe space so they can make judgment errors in a confusing world without lasting repercussions. With social media and instant publishing of personal images and private moments, children are growing up in a very unforgiving world. Information on the internet lasts forever. Schools have become less forgiving as well, if they ever were at all. Kicking children out of school, through expulsion, takes away their rightful opportunity to receive guided practice in a forgiving environment. Mistakes are guaranteed in life, especially in childhood, which is why zero-tolerance discipline policies are so unfair to so many students.

Situations get out of hand quickly in emotionally charged moments, and training educators, support staff, and school police to deescalate, rather than escalate, with students is key. Using these conflict situations as teachable moments for empathy and social skills problem solving should be a national priority. Research suggests that authenticity and empathy are expected of both students and teachers, yet these skills are not explicitly taught or actualized by both parties at the same time (Bialystok & Kukar, 2017). Furthermore, this can create competing demands and tensions that undermine a socially just education system. The less students understand themselves and each other in childhood, the less understanding they will have in adulthood. Children with a history of trauma and emotional and environmental instability, mixed with gaps in school attendance, severe underachievement, and poor impulse control or understanding of social expectations, have little hope for positive outcomes in a system that prepares disadvantaged children for prison instead of remediating the problems through humanistic treatment and culturally competent teaching.

Some solutions are very expensive, unfortunately. Mental and behavioral health services in the community cost a fortune, Medicaid and insurance will cover less and less, and service providers are limited in how many low-cost patients they can support. Many of the most talented psychiatrists, psychologists, and mental health providers in the private sector accept cash only for treatment due to laws of supply and demand, in addition to the constantly changing challenges of medical billing that service providers would rather avoid. Another barrier to treatment, in addition to the cost for services, is transportation. It is becoming more apparent that schools with community health centers are a necessity. Behavioral health, psychiatric services, and therapeutic counseling for children and families at school sites could solidify schools' role as the safe harbors in society and should be funded as the pillars of the community that they are. Helping caregivers and family leaders with advocacy for behavioral and mental health treatment is key for schools to succeed in interventions for mentally and behaviorally unhealthy students who grow to be mentally and behaviorally unhealthy adults otherwise.

Where to Start

The place to start, of course, is wherever you are. Evaluate your resources. Determine what you have and what you should keep in place when the data supports that it is working. All school administrators should strive to improve Tier 1 instructional practices. Many realize that the needs of Tier 3 easily overwhelm resources on a campus and may need to start with a major investment there and grow out Tiers 1 and 2 as byproducts of necessity. Bottom line is that better practices can lead to better practices in both directions, although growing from the foundations of strong leadership and effective Tier 1 is healthier and more sustainable. Realistically, all three tiers grow together.

With established MTSS, solid Tier 1 can ensure that fewer students require Tier 2 and Tier 3 instruction. However, Tier 3 cannot fix problems with Tier 1. Poor instruction or intervention, in combination with apathy and other risk factors, can create lifelong learning problems in students, which are perpetuated systemically through chronic issues in schools. Realistically, not all educators at any one school are exceptional, and they are not all bad either. Most schools have a mix of many accomplished and less accomplished teachers. Administrators are tasked with increasing the skills of less accomplished educators, nurturing the talents of teacher leaders, and improving the delivery of evidence-based practices across all educators. No matter the etiology of student delays, evidence-based skills curriculum, spiraled throughout kindergarten through 12th grade with multiple opportunities to learn the same skills, will give each child the correct number of guided instructional opportunities to master developmental benchmarks.

Starting with Tier 3 is a common place to build supports because students who are low academically are less likely engaged in class and are more likely disruptive, destroying the learning environment for everyone else. Students who externalize behaviors and present as a danger to themselves and others will require intensive interventions and support immediately. Supporting a healthy Tier 3 is also an equity factor for students with educational disabilities and those with potential or unidentified disabilities. Students with the highest needs require individualized supports with progress closely monitored, which requires the most coordination of resources and regular communication between staff members.

Putting together a Social-Emotional-Behavioral MTSS team may seem like a good place to start, especially in light of recent mass shootings and violence in schools nationwide. The recent urgency has cast the spotlight on the need for increased school safety measures; however, what is at the heart of prevention of school violence is a comprehensive and coordinated mental health model which includes proactive and crisis procedures to maximize school safety. While some schools may not feel prepared to implement Social-Emotional-Behavioral MTSS, they probably already have more supports in existence than they realize. *MTSS systems that are clearly understood, have automated processes and procedures, and have coordinated administrative vision and supervision to build and sustain evidence-based practices, will be most likely to be implemented.* Schools that implement Academic MTSS will already have a school culture that supports Social-Emotional-Behavioral MTSS and should find less resistance to new roles and responsibilities from educators.

School administrators and leadership teams must ultimately decide for themselves which issues to tackle first, from attendance to social-emotional-behavioral screenings. There is no correct answer for where a school should get started on building MTSS, just that it should be "built to last" as part of a growing and sustainable comprehensive system. The superstar administrator might take action to add multiple new initiatives at once, while another administrator may find it difficult to take action to add more than one new initiative at a time knowing that every new piece added to MTSS requires active problem solving and supervision to begin and sustain. *Starting with low-hanging fruit is often a good place to build success.* Increase educators' earning potential for motivation. Empower collaborative teams with leadership opportunities to grow under a distributed leadership model and reward problem solvers on your campus. Institute quarterly or thrice-a-year benchmarking to quickly identify underachievers and students with social-emotional-behavioral indicators, schedule reading and math intervention blocks in the master calendar with researched-based curriculum, provide social skills curriculum and counseling groups, and monitor student growth over time. Make things easier for teachers by automating data collection with easy-to-use tools for decision making. Schedule regular team meetings in the master schedule to get school experts working on problems. The sooner stakeholders feel the positive benefits of new practices, the more likely new practices will be embraced and sustained.

Exercise 15.1

Get Started Now!

- What are your schools' low-hanging fruit, easy-to-fix problems, or obvious solutions?
- Survey your staff, prioritize, and fix those small problems while increasing motivation and positive support of all staff members

- List and rank your schools' problem priorities 1 to 5 (i.e., attendance, teacher retention, high rate of suspensions/expulsions, low academic rigor or achievement, a lack of qualified educators/too many long-term subs, low morale, etc.).
- Pick one initiative at a time and let the problem solving with your smart teams begin.

Just Do It

When to start MTSS structures and functions is never as important as what or where to start. The beginning of the year is always a great time for new initiatives, but any time is a good time for best practices to occur. Schools need not wait for the beginning of the year to address a problem systematically. Schools are more likely to put things in place incrementally so as not to bite off more than can be chewed in terms of incorporating and managing new professional expectations. Some principals can systematically restructure a school all at once, in a dramatic turnaround fashion. For the high-achieving, blue-ribbon principals who will use this guide to affirm current educational practices already in place or to reconsider different options and build or improve on ideas, kudos to these superstars in education. Unfortunately, these superstar leaders may have inherent leadership skills, and the transformative results they obtain may not necessarily be intuitive to others, which is why a framework or road map is needed to reach the same destination. See Table 15.1 for examples of the various components necessary at each tier. Many of the components, such as restorative justice and advocacy, should be embedded within each tier.

Every new initiative, program, curricula, agenda, activity, and mind-set should align with the LIQUID Model if it is to be implemented successfully in a school. Evidence-based practices must be spearheaded and sustained adequately through the *Leadership* lens: budgets, resources, human capital, staff motivation, systematic supports, vision, and supervision. Educational practices must be *Inclusive*: equitable, equal access, provided in a culturally competent context, examining and challenging implicit bias, and making concerted efforts to improve relationships with people from all backgrounds. All practices must have *Quality controls* in place to ensure implementation fidelity through data obtained by feedback looping. Ineffective practices must be replaced with effective practices. Quality control depends on the strength of leadership to monitor outcomes and revise curriculum factors, implementation factors, and human capital factors. Every practice in a school must be considered in the *Universal* context. How does a practice impact all students? How can educational services have the best outcome for the most students? Do all students have equal access, and do they get what they need when they need it? Universal screening helps target at-risk students quickly so that help starts immediately, leading to better short-term and long-term outcomes. Educational practices must be evaluated through the *Implementation and feedback looping* lens, which requires iterative analysis to engage in continuous improvement of practices. Implementation fidelity is essential to effective teaching and without it, outcome data may be skewed as it assumes that fidelity criteria were observed. Feedback looping provides guidance to school leadership for which quality-control indicators must be addressed. Last, the *Data* never lie. The wrong questions might be asked of the data that can lead to erroneous conclusions, but the data are objective, in and of themselves, as long as the fidelity of standardized testing procedures is observed. Using the preponderance

Table 15.1 Examples of Tiered Components for Academic MTSS and SEB MTSS

	Academic MTSS	Social-Emotional-Behavioral MTSS
Tier 1 Supports	• Evidence-based Tier 1 curriculum implemented with fidelity • Regular benchmark screening, summative and formative assessment • Block scheduling with opportunities for differentiation and enrichment • Support for accomplished teaching as outlined by the National Board for Professional Teaching Standards • Family engagement and outreach • Inclusive school materials and dialogue	• Evidence-based positive behavioral intervention supports • Universal schoolwide and classroom management strategies • Universal social-emotional curriculum implemented • Regular benchmark screening • Advocacy for mandated social-emotional-behavioral curriculum K–12 • School counseling services • Family engagement and outreach • Culturally competent teaching practices • Restorative justice • Access to social services providing basic needs and housing security • Student-centered advocacy, communication, and leadership • Trauma-sensitive instructional care and awareness of adverse childhood experiences (ACEs) • Inclusive school materials and dialogue
Tier 2 Supports	• Extended school year in at-risk communities • Longer school day opportunities for at-risk students • Daily access to evidence-based Tier 2 curriculum implemented with fidelity in scheduled classes of reading/English language arts and math • Tutoring and homework assistance is available to all students requiring academic support on a volunteer (or scheduled) basis • Technological supports with instructional skills practice is used to generalize skills practiced with direction instruction	• Targeted social skills curriculum in scheduled classes (anger management, empathy training, problem solving, etc.) • School counseling services • Restorative justice • School social worker involvement • Check in–check out, pressure passes, short-term accommodations, targeted communication between school and home • Incentive Plans • Referral to community services (i.e., Boys' Town or therapeutic counseling) • Consultation with the school psychologist

	- Students with higher needs in Tier 2 will require active case management to determine whether targeted needs become intensive over time - Progress is monitored monthly and rate of improvement analyzed	- Staff development in Life Space Crisis Intervention (Long, Wood, & Fecser, 2001) - Family–teacher–student conferences and contracts between home and school
Tier 3 Supports	- Teacher coaching and support for coordination of individualized supports - Implementation of academic plans with discrete goals and supports defined which are monitored for progress weekly to bimonthly - Tier 3 intensive academic curriculum implemented with fidelity in scheduled classes in addition to core curriculum classes - Intensive classes should have smaller class sizes than Tier 2 intervention blocks - Technological supports with Tier 3–level instructional skills practice is used to generalize skills practiced with direction instruction - The Academic MTSS team is actively monitoring students for improvement - The most intensive instructional resources are exhausted in documented poor response to instruction - Referral to Multidisciplinary Team for educational eligibility consideration - Individualized Education Plans and protections under Individuals with Disabilities Education Improvement Act (IDEA)	- Teacher coaching and support for coordination of individualized supports, implementation of individualized behavior plans (requiring a high ratio of positive reinforcement and data collection of antecedents, behaviors, and consequences, in addition to frequency, intensity, duration data in response to interventions) - Trauma-informed care, requiring trusting relationships with teachers engaging in repeated rehearsals of replacement behaviors - Restorative justice - Functional behavioral analyses - School counseling services - School social worker involvement supporting treatment at home and school - Referral to the Social-Emotional-Behavior (SEB) MTSS team for active case management of most severe Tier 3 students (potential danger to self and/or others) - The team is actively supporting families in community-based and school-based treatments for students - Students are monitored for improvement at least monthly by the SEB MTSS team or bimonthly SEB MTSS team - Referral to Multidisciplinary Team for educational eligibility consideration - Individualized education programs and protections under IDEA

of evidence to lead and drive better practices, actively analyzed by relevant stakeholders on a regular basis to review and revise, result in better outcomes for all.

Final Words

Public education is at a crossroads. It is preparing some of our children for bright futures while leaving others stranded in the middle of nowhere with little chance of moving forward. Regardless of school, socioeconomic area, or population, individual educators can make or break opportunities for students to succeed in academic rigor, independent living skills, mental and behavioral health, and social responsibility with respect for self and others. Every child should have the opportunity to learn how to be a productive member of society, to be independent, and to be self-sufficient. *Educators must first and foremost make students partners in their learning.* Life is very complicated for children, and many are vulnerable to dangers and have life traumas that are more horrific than any scary movie ever made. Educators must team up with students to inspire their young minds, challenge them to think critically while developing academic excellence, and nurture their ability to make healthy connections with others. When students want to come to school and look forward to that time-honored relationship between teachers and students, educators have excelled at the relationship piece of the learning equation. A master educator once said that there are no attention deficits, only deficiencies in making things interesting or motivating enough for students that they cannot help but to attend and learn. Learning has to be something students are partners in, not just something that is happening to them. Trust plus curiosity equals optimal learning conditions.

Not all children have the organic or environmental capacity to learn or perform at the same rate as typical students. Even so, educators must be able to connect student interests and potential to positive outcomes. Targeted and intensive learning opportunities need to be *more* interesting and motivating to attract the curiosity of the students who have to work harder to succeed. Despite all the other variables that have an impact on student achievement, positive relationships with caring teachers are the magic bonds for students to remain invested in learning when things get difficult, rather than giving up. Since evidence-based practices clearly support positive relationships with educators, educators must feel more supported by administrators and systems in place to make their jobs possible. Educators who do not have the financial security to pay for their own basic needs, those who do not have administrative backing and clear access to structures and functions that support at-risk students, and those who do not know how to effectively respond to and correct student misbehavior are being set up to fail. Positive relationships with students are a clear and obvious job responsibility for educators that should be part of educators' continuous training, performance evaluation rubrics, and valued as much as any other performance indicator.

American education has gotten off track, as deep-pocketed private interests have become more involved in the policy-making process, blurring the distinctions between public and private sectors in education (Lubienski, 2016). In the process, private interests are supplanting public education and student rights; educational access and equity are marginalized (Singh, 2015). "Education policymaking itself is being privatized through a significant shift toward private interests in the making of public policy for public education" (Lubienski, 2016, p. 192). This includes the promotion of implicitly biased, expensive, high-stakes tests that result in big business turning a profit while it simultaneously uses propaganda to turn public opinion against the public's best interests. The use of propaganda to influence public opinion is nothing new (Wind-Cowie, 2014; Exley, 1949), and the unfortunate target of this new campaign for social control (Freeley, 2002) is our students. This destroys the civil right to a free appropriate public education (FAPE) and delivers socially unjust consequences when at-risk students, especially those of color or impacted by poverty, fail.

Big businesses have devised a business plan to prove that public schools are failing by developing tests that large segments of the population will never pass and will be disproportionality punished for not achieving. Minority students, students living in poverty, students with poor language skills, and students in the process of learning English as a second language will be significantly impacted by this test bias disproportionately (Au, 2015; Solórzano, 2008). These test biases only serve to promulgate racism under a so-called antiracism wave of education reform (Au, 2015). Charter schools with little accountability are gobbling up public schools while providing worse outcomes (Chingos & West, 2015) and giving families no choice under the guise of increasing school choice. There also exists a lack of democratic influence within charter school policies, and until these democratic principles exist, justice within charter schools cannot be achieved (Abowitz & Karaba, 2009). Private and charter schools do not have to pass the same tests or "rigor" public schools must endure, and public schools will always fail in comparison until all school types are held to the same standards. All schools that receive public monies should have to meet the same criteria, which should not be left up to the whims of state legislators who are often indebted to big businesses.

Public education currently spends much of its energies on teaching practices to pass tests that are funded by the very interests that wish to destroy it. Hens meet the foxes guarding your house. How did these high-stakes tests take over the goal of public schooling? Marketing and public deception may be at the root of private interest's effectiveness in their big grab for monies dedicated to public education funding, playing on the public's fear (Cooper & Randall, 2008). Savvy local school districts are starting to hire public relations managers to counter the negative publicity bombarding the media largely promoted by a few well-endowed individuals and corporate entities who benefit financially by swaying public opinion against public education. When public opinion is swayed, then hawks can swoop in to institutionalize racism, abuse, and social injustice while maximizing corporate profits. Fortunately, public apathy is not a permanent condition, and a defense of hardworking educators in public schools can be rallied successfully by coordinated efforts of educators in solidarity with parent groups and community leaders, as evidenced by successes in recent educator walkouts nationwide.

Public educators and local communities must quickly figure out how to prepare our children for survival skills, vocational training, and consumer science while providing social-emotional and behavioral regulation skills and relationship building in the technology age. They must also do this while meeting the required accountability standards. Public schools are inherent to the American way of life as we now know it; that every child can learn up because education is at the heart of democratic schooling and social justice. In the words of a prominent social justice advocate and researcher, "none of us created the racial and social injustice that is deeply rooted in U.S. society and none of us can solve these problems by ourselves" (Shriberg, 2016, p. 339). Educators must become intellectual soldiers in the army defending knowledge, research, and evidence-based practices, with the goal of a humane society. *Advocacy is the urgent call to battle for the survival of public education.* The civil right to FAPE is eroding quickly, and with public support from students, families, and communities, educators must step up and organize. Attention current and retired educators and child caregivers: run for political office, help someone run for office, join a policy committee, show up and testify during public comment at public meetings such as State Board of Education meetings, legislative meetings, or meetings of other government entities. Additionally, submit written comments to these meetings, write letters to your representatives, vote, and make donations to candidates that support the value of education. Be a force and speak up at every opportunity. There are many partners who can help you achieve positive things for children, and having socially just, evidence-based practices, such as MTSS, memorialized in education policy and practice, at any level, is an incredible accomplishment.

References

Abowitz, K. K., & Karaba, R. (2009). Charter schooling and democratic justice. *Educational Policy, 24*(3), 534–558.

Au, W. (2015). Meritocracy 2.0: High-stakes, standardized testing as a racial project of neoliberal multiculturalism. *Educational Policy, 30*(1), 39–62.

Bialystok, L., & Kukar, P. (2017). Authenticity and empathy in education. *Theory and Research in Education, 16*(1), 23–39.

Bryk, A. S., Gomez, L. M., Grunow, A., & LeMahieu, P. G. (2016). *Learning to improve: How America's schools can get better at getting better.* Cambridge, MA: Harvard Education Press.

Chingos, M. M., & West, M. R. (2015). The uneven performance of Arizona's charter schools. *Educational Evaluation and Policy Analysis, 37*(1), 120–134.

Cooper, B. S., & Randall, V. (2008). Fear and privatization. *Educational Policy, 22*(1), 204–227.

Creighton, F. P., Doub, G. T., & Scott, V. M. (1999). *Survival skills for healthy families* (2nd ed.). Holly Springs, NC: Family Wellness Associates.

Exley, D. (1949). The role of public opinion in the modern state. *Political Science, 1*(2), 14–19.

Freeley, M. M. (2002). Entrepreneurs of punishment: The legacy of privatization. *Punishment & Society, 4*(3), 321–344.

Grissom, J. A., & Loeb, S. (2011). Triangulating principal effectiveness: How perspectives of parents, teachers, and assistant principals identify the central importance of managerial skills. *American Education Research Journal, 48*(5), 1091–1123.

Long, N. J., Wood, M. M., & Fecser, F. A. (2001). *Life space crisis intervention: Talking with students in conflict* (2nd ed.). Charlottesville, VA: Pro-Ed.

Lubienski, C. (2016). Sector distinctions and the privatization of education policymaking. *Theory and Research in Education, 14*(2), 192–212.

Shriberg, D. (2016). Commentary: School psychologists as advocates for racial justice and social justice: Some proposed steps. *School Psychology Forum, 10*(3), 337–339.

Singh, K. (2015). Safeguarding education as public good and regulating private providers. *Social Change, 45*(2), 308–323.

Solórzano, R. W. (2008). High stakes testing: Issues, implications and remedies for English language learners. *Review of Educational Research, 78*(2), 260–329.

Song, S. Y., & Swearer, S. M. (2016). The cart before the horse: The challenge and promise of restorative justice consultation in schools. *Journal of Educational and Psychological Consultation, 26*(4), 313–324.

Stetler, C. B., Ritchie, J. A., Rycroft-Malone, J., & Charns, M. P. (2014). Leadership for evidence-based practice: Strategic and functional behaviors for institutionalizing EBP. *Worldviews on Evidence-Based Nursing, 11*(4), 219–226.

Wind-Cowie, M. (2014). Political vacuum opens up propaganda possibilities. *Index on Censorship, 43*(1), 74–77.

Chapter 16

Resources and Glossary

Quick Reference Guide and Resources

Program Level

- Healthy Minds, Safe Schools: http://healthymindssafeschools.com
- Center on the Social and Emotional Foundations for Early Learning: http://csefel.vanderbilt.edu
- National Center for Pyramid Model Innovations: https://challengingbehavior.cbcs.usf.edu
- Turning Around Low-Performing Schools: A Guide for State and Local Leaders (U.S. Department of Education, 1998): https://www2.ed.gov/PDFDocs/turning.pdf
- Nine Characteristics of High Performing Schools (Shannon & Bylsma, 2007): www.k12.wa.us/research/pubdocs/NineCharacteristics.pdf
- Models that Can Help Improve Low-Performing Schools (Center for American Progress, 2016): https://cdn.americanprogress.org/wp-content/uploads/2016/03/01075517/NonCharterSchools-report.pdf

Interventions

- Intervention Central: www.interventioncentral.org
- Collaborative for Academic, Social, and Emotional Learning: https://casel.org
- Evidence for ESSA: www.evidenceforessa.org
- Positive Behavioral Interventions and Supports: www.PBIS.org
- Blueprints for Healthy Youth Development: www.blueprintsprograms.com
- The U.S. Substance Abuse and Mental Health Services Administration's National Registry of Evidence-based Programs and Practices: www.nrepp.samhsa.gov (Mental and Substance Abuse Disorders)
- The Department of Education's What Works Clearinghouse: http://ies.ed.gov/ncee/wwc (Education)

Family Engagement

- Triple P-Positive Parenting Program: www.triplep-parenting.com/us/triple-p/
- Systematic Training for Effective Parenting (STEP): www.steppublishers.com
- Strengthening Families Program: www.strengtheningfamiliesprogram.org
- STAR Parenting: http://starparent.com

- Survival Skills for Healthy Families: www.familywellness.com/programs.php
- Promising Practices Network: www.promisingpractices.net

Social Justice Resources

- Teaching Tolerance: www.tolerance.org/classroom-resources (Classroom Resources)
- Facing History and Ourselves: www.facinghistory.org
- National Urban League: https://nul.org
- Native American Rights Fund: www.narf.org/our-work/promotion-human-rights/ (Promote Native American Human Rights)
- Rethinking Schools: www.rethinkingschools.org
- Teaching for Change: Building Social Justice Starting in the Classroom: www.teachingforchange.org
- Global Oneness Project: www.globalonenessproject.org
- GLSEN: www.glsen.org/educate/resources (Educator Resources)
- Human Rights Campaign: www.hrc.org/resources/project-thrive (Project THRIVE)
- Gender Spectrum: www.genderspectrum.org
- Welcoming Schools: www.welcomingschools.org
- Family Acceptance Project: https://familyproject.sfsu.edu
- Anti-Defamation League: www.adl.org

Additional Resources

- National Alliance on Mental Illness: www.nami.org/Find-Support/NAMI-Programs
- National Association of School Psychologists: www.nasponline.org
- American School Counselor Association: www.schoolcounselor.org
- School Social Work Association of America: www.sswaa.org
- National Association of School Resource Officers: https://nasro.org
- The U.S. Department of Justice's CrimeSolutions.gov: www.crimesolutions.gov (Criminal and Juvenile Justice)
- What Works in Reentry: http://whatworks.csgjusticecenter.org (Re-entry)
- California Evidence-Based Clearinghouse for Child Welfare: www.cebc4cw.org (Child Welfare)
- Coalition for Evidence-Based Policy http://coalition4evidence.org (Social Policy)

Glossary

6–13–13–6 benchmark model is a guideline for traditional 38-week academic calendar schools to follow when scheduling their universal screening benchmark windows.

About Me Care-to-Share are one-on-one teacher-student conversations that help build rapport and facilitate a deeper understanding of what the students' experiences are on a daily basis; they are guided by the content encompassed in the About Me Everywhere tool.

About Me Everywhere is a tool for teachers to use to get to know their students; it helps to capture relevant student data without being intrusive and becomes the springboard from which to have unique About Me Care-to-Share student conversations.

Academic MTSS is the framework in which to provide students with layers of academic supports at their instructional level.

Academic MTSS Student Database is the storehouse that archives all data for students who are discussed at MTSS team meetings and is achieved by creating and maintaining a running record of at-risk student history, interventions implemented, school performance, current needs, and recommendations for school success.

Adept MTSS Schools have built capacity over time and have fully functional and sustainable MTSS practices

Alingual is the classification of students who are not proficient in any language.

The Ask is a specific request made from one individual or group to another.

Automatization is the result of processes that have been converted from loose implementation to automatic implementation.

Base funding is the amount of money a state sets aside to cover the basic costs of education.

Benchmarking is conducted at set intervals throughout the year to provide a snapshot of a student's performance.

Braided funding is the weaving of funds from multiple sources and is useful in maximizing impact without relying too heavily on any one funding source.

Brokers are people within an organization who keep people working together, alleviating tension, and moving forward by cultivating relationships, negotiating respectful conflict, and ultimately getting consensus to solve problems.

Case manager model is student-centered and assigns a specific educator to advocate for the students they are assigned to represent.

Case notes are supplemental data that are entered into the MTSS Student Database that are not otherwise captured in one of the predetermined columns.

Categorical funding is reserved for a very specific program or purpose.

Change agents influence innovation and make decisions that align with the central entity.

Connector is someone with high social capital who can put a group in touch with other likeminded individuals or with individuals who have a specific skill set that can benefit an initiative.

Contagion effect refers to a replication of a particular behavior by others, due to proximity or social media exposure.

Controlled chaos is a term borrowed from the biology, engineering, and life sciences fields that recognizes some or whole segments may be disorganized yet can be controlled within given parameters.

Commissive is a manner in which a state policy is written that commits itself to action.

Community-centric in the sense that a broader community influences and promotes student success, not just the immediate family.

Counterintuitive cultures arise when practices in the field are producing results opposite to that which is desired.

Cultural brokering promotes culture as an asset that can be used to positively influence and bridge family and school relationships.

Cultural change is the observable shift toward new standards, attitudes, and behavior.

Data-triangulation chats transpire during grade-level data-triangulation meetings after each benchmark period and are intended to eliminate false positives or negatives, prioritize students and their needs, and empower teachers to assist in the decision-making process for their students.

Decentralized is the transfer of power and decision making from central government to local government.

Dedicated funding is money dedicated for a specific purpose, such as teacher salaries, through a specific funding source, such as specific tax revenues.

Developmental MTSS Schools are on one end of the continuum and require significant technical support and leadership in getting their MTSS processes up, running, and remaining operationalized.

Directive is a manner in which a state policy is written that tells the local education agencies what to do.

Discipline is the training of adherence to codes or behavior and may include punishments to correct noncompliance.

Discretionary grant funding is monies that are awarded through a competitive application process.

Distributed presentation style where the grade-level representatives come to MTSS meetings and present data on the students pertaining to their grade level on behalf of all teachers in that grade level.

Early childhood curriculum standards are the developmental and learning expectations that young children are typically expected to meet within a chronological age bracket.

Early Childhood MTSS is the framework in which to provide young students and families with layers of supports at the student's developmental level.

Early childhood program standards set the quality levels in a variety of domains to ensure specific criteria are maintained on behalf of young children.

Ecosystems are the confluence and interaction of all persons on a campus who influence student growth, development, and experiences.

Education malpractice is the preventable adverse impact on a student through educator negligence or incompetence that goes against evidence-based practices.

Ethnic match occurs when a student's teacher and family both identify with the same ethnic background.

Feedback looping is when the outputs of a reflection or outcome are used as inputs to inform and improve upon the next phase of the cycle.

Fidelity is trust in the accuracy and quality of the overall implementation process.

Formula funding is the dollar amount assigned from the state to each district based on various computed factors.

Gerrymandering is when the geographic boundaries are manipulated to benefit one party over another.

Grade-level representatives are a member of the Social-Emotional-Behavioral (SEB) MTSS team and liaise between the grade-level team and the SEB MTSS team.

Growth model is composed of rich data points that measure student growth, or lack thereof, over time. It is well documented as more effective at determining a student's performance than high stakes tests in high-risk schools.

Human capital includes the competencies, value, and knowledge the professionals on campus bring to the table.

Hybrid Committee Selection Model assigns each teacher to one committee by the administrator based on the individual's strengths and then has him or her volunteer for the other committee(s) that the teacher would like to serve on.

Implementation science deals with the integration, application, and refinement of evidence-based practices in the field.

Implicit bias is the underlying beliefs, stereotypes, and attitudes that unconsciously has an impact on a person's decision making.

Implicit partnership naïveté is the inherent belief educators hold with regard to engaging the families they serve based on their own cultural experiences, expectations, and institutionalized assumptions

Incremental correction systems are flow charts of specific cognitive-behavioral correction opportunities and include when to offer them and under what conditions are used prior to discipline procedures.

Infrastructure is the foundational framework that supports data-based decisions about students on campus.

Intermediate organizations are typically not practitioners and their involvement can either impede or facilitate implementation depending on resources and motivations.

Internal validity as the data collected will be compromised due to teacher error and participant experience.

Intervention graph is the visual representation of scores obtained during progress monitoring data collection cycles.

Intervention log   tracks the date, type, and duration of intervention provided.

Intervention plan   defines the student's area of difficulty and targets a discrete skill for a baseline to enable goal setting.

Iterative   refers to a repeated process that occurs at regular intervals with the purpose of achieving an established goal.

LGBTQ+   are individuals who identify as being lesbian, gay, bisexual, transgender, questioning, or gender diverse along a spectrum of sexuality and gender.

Leadership fidelity checks   are the review of all aspects of the implementation procedures conducted by the administration or a member of the leadership team that occurs on both a random or as-needed basis.

Legitimization   occurs within an organization when an act or process becomes entrenched in its values and norms.

Lever   a bureaucratic layer, person, or organization in which support for change must be sought to help remediate identified barriers to an initiative.

LIQUID Model   is represented by the nonnegotiable variables of Leadership, Inclusiveness, Quality control, Universal, Implementation and feedback, and Data-based decision making to guide teams through all phases of the MTSS process using critical exploration and problem solving.

LIQUID Theory   explains the process, constructs, and intersectionality necessary for successful MTSS implementation and sustainability: Leadership, Inclusiveness, Quality control, Universality, Implementation and feedback looping, and Data-based decision making.

Logic models   can be used as an effectiveness framework to ensure inputs are leading to desired outputs in the short and long term.

Lynchpins   hold various elements of complicated structures in place to keep students from sliding off into an abyss of school failure.

Master schedule   is the calendar and timetable to support the hourly, daily, weekly, monthly, and annual activities on a campus and is essential for successful program implementation.

Mental health transition team   often includes school-based mental health professionals as well as any other professionals required by the school district or state and assists to put supports in place for students who transfer back to campus from a residential treatment facility.

MTSS   is a socially just approach to providing equitable access and support to all students in the educational setting.

MTSS case managers   are responsible for researching and documenting student history, collecting data from multiple sources, presenting data at meetings, communicating changes to student instructional interventions to relevant stakeholders, and getting feedback from students and teachers on efficacy of interventions.

MTSS chairs   communicate MTSS meeting dates, record meeting discussions, lead meetings, problem solve MTSS functions and processes, and liaise with stakeholder groups.

MTSS Evaluation Frequency and Intensity Framework outlines that some practices must be evaluated universally, or on a regular basis, while others must be evaluated on a targeted basis, such as during benchmark windows; and others will require intensive, in-depth, and thorough investigation, such as through an annual reporting of the program.

MTSS extension opportunities are programming options or incentives for students outside the traditional school offerings.

MTSS grade-level representatives are teachers who have been designated to liaise between their grade-level teams and the MTSS team, supporting active problem solving in both communities.

MTSS meeting logs are the official dated documentation of the MTSS Student Portfolios and case notes discussed at MTSS Team Meetings and are updated during or after each meeting.

MTSS Student Portfolios are composed of the artifacts to present to the MTSS team when making decisions about a student and help support the MTSS Student Database.

Neo-institutional theory is a sociopolitical lens in which to view how organizations interact and how they impact society.

Outside evaluator is an impartial person hired to collect data and report on the program's progress toward its stated goals and may include information about resource utilization, efficiency, effectiveness, and fiscal allocations.

Overcorrection is the explicit repeated practice of a desired behavior.

Peer coaching is a valuable tool to reinforce sound instructional practices from one teacher to another.

Phase I Prioritization is a basic sorting and ranking of data stored in the SEB universal screening warehouse of students who scored high for (1) externalized and (2) internalized behaviors.

Phase II Prioritization takes place at grade-level data-triangulation meetings to further refine which students from the initial sorting and ranking will need additional supports and what those supports may look like.

Physical capital includes the tangible tools necessary to implement an MTSS program and includes materials needed to execute the research-based interventions as well as the computerized assessment tools necessary for benchmarking and progress monitoring.

Positive class culture is a learning environment based on trust in which the students are encouraged and empowered to make and learn from mistakes.

Progress monitoring is conducted at regular intervals, such as weekly, to build into the overall portfolio of student progress in response to the interventions provided.

Protective factors are conditions that positively contribute to student well-being and include factors such as having their basic needs met as well as having resilience skills, strong social connections, and social-emotional skills.

Rate of improvement is the student's actual rate of improvement and is contrasted against his or her goal rate of improvement to make decisions about the adequacy of progress.

Reentry plan is the specific plan devised by the mental health transition team to support the student who transitions back to campus from a residential treatment facility.

Reliability is the consistency of the implementation and delivery of the intervention procedures as a treatment each time the classes meet.

Resource allocation is part of the school's overall school improvement plan linked to fiscal management and is a puzzle to be assembled by administrators in school settings.

Responsive adaptability is the ability to quickly and seamlessly adjust to ever-changing environmental demands.

Restorative justice is a strengths-based approach to student behavior in which the student is an active participant in changing their own behavior through a series of cognitive-behavioral techniques.

Role is a function assumed by a particular person; it is duty- or skill-specific, not title-specific.

School-centric is when the narrative is framed around how parents can help schools to promote student education.

School counselors provide academic, personal, social, and career support to students.

School psychologists are uniquely trained individuals on a school campus that provide mental and behavioral supports to students, assist teams with intervention planning, and help school administration implement evidence-based policies and programs.

Smart teams are composed of individuals who contribute equally to the task at hand, are adept at reading the complex emotional states of others, and have a greater number of female team members than male members (Woolley, Chabris, Pentland, Hashmini, & Malone, 2010).

Social-emotional regulation is the ability to control and negotiate emotions, thoughts, and behaviors effectively and efficiently.

Social-Emotional-Behavioral MTSS is the framework in which to provide students with layers of social-emotional and behavioral supports according to their individual risk and need levels.

Social-Emotional-Behavioral MTSS Student Database includes student name, identification number, grade, classroom teacher, adverse childhood experiences, scores on SEB benchmark screeners, academic benchmark scores, medical diagnoses and medication (if any), interventions implemented, intervention outcomes, and dated case notes.

Social-Emotional-Behavioral MTSS Team is composed of highly trained individuals tasked with school safety, student behavioral health, and mental well-being of students in a school setting.

Social justice occurs when all children, from all different backgrounds, regardless of socioeconomic background or demographic characteristics, are valued in a school community and have access to a relevant education.

Specialists are often teachers on special assignment and are one of the most adaptable resources on campus, fulfilling any role or function that is required to support administrators looking to accomplish miscellaneous responsibilities for students on campus.

Stakeholder networks "are based on a common understanding and extend beyond a single stakeholder group, which can lead to greater impact in times of need" (Dockweiler, 2018, p. 26).

Strategic opportunism is a term borrowed from the business world that simply means the leader is able to adhere to the long-term vision, for example, higher student achievement, while remaining flexible enough in the short-term to take advantage of opportunities that arise to support and help meet the long-term vision, for example, implementing a model of support consisting of multiple tiers.

Student-led informational conferences are a powerful evidence-based method to encourage students to take responsibility for their own learning and require self-reflection, identification of strengths and needs, goal setting, self-monitoring, organizational practice, and communication skills.

Student-Centered Academic Sessions help students and families be collaborators in the learning process, be viewed as an active partner and asset, and can start conversations at home about empowering students to achieve academic goals.

Student-centric is a learning environment in which the student remains at the core of all decision making and the adults surround that student in a circle of collaborative partnership

Tactical Advocacy Steps take place on the front end of advocacy planning and include identifying the desired initiative, identifying the necessary level of advocacy, identifying the barriers, identifying the levers and strategies to eliminate barriers, and beginning coalition building.

Teacher efficacy is a teacher's perceived level of ability to impact student learning through his or her instruction, data analysis, motivation, and organization.

Three-Pronged Motivation Approach consists of including students in the data collection and analysis process, increasing student buy-in through teacher motivation, and incentivizing achievement at all levels.

Teacher–student relationships fuel the efforts of students, who can persist despite challenges and are resilient in times of adversity, with the right level of support.

Threat assessment team most often includes the school psychologist, school counselor, school social worker, and school nurse who are trained to conduct an assessment of whether a student is an immediate threat to him- or herself and/or others.

Three As of awareness, access, and action are all necessary components of inserting the school psychologist's perspective into a school and community's ecosystem.

Transitional MTSS Schools are beginning to master some of the foundational components of the MTSS model and are growing beyond a Developmental school.

Trauma-informed care is an organizational framework that can be used to guide responsiveness to various types of trauma.

Triangulating data across multiple sources helps teams validate a student's need for intervention and provides insight into what type of support best meets the student's need.

Unfunded mandates are statutory requirements or regulations imposed without funds provided to carry out the directive.

Unicorns are mythological creatures with unique talents and characteristics who can make an extraordinary impact.

Unintended consequences are outcomes that are realized without purposefully working toward them.

Universal screening is administered to all students to determine their current level of performance in any given domain.

Validity is when the data collected can be used meaningfully to create inferences and make decisions about the students from the scores collected.

The Why is the individual's purpose or motivations behind his or her actions.

References

Center for American Progress. (2016). *Models that can help improve low-performing schools*. Retrieved from https://cdn.americanprogress.org/wpcontent/uploads/2016/03/01075517/NonCharterSchools-report.pdf

Shannon, G. S., & Bylsma, P. (2007). *Nine characteristics of high-performing schools*. Retrieved from Washington State Office of Superintendent of Public Instruction website: www.k12.wa.us/research/pubdocs/NineCharacteristics.pdf

U.S. Department of Education. (1998). *Turning around low-performing schools: A guide for state and local leaders*. Retrieved from https://www2.ed.gov/PDFDocs/turning.pdf

Index

Note: Page numbers in *italic* refers to figure page numbers

6-13-13-6 benchmark model 242

About Me Everywhere 242
academic MTSS documentation 119–121
academic MTSS student database 103, 121–122
academic MTSS student portfolios 120
academic MTSS team 97–98; academic MTSS chair 101–107; classroom teachers 98–99; meeting etiquette 112–115; MTSS grade-level representative 100–101; school counselors 108–109; school psychologists 109–111; special education teachers 111–112; specialists 107–108
Academic Parent–Teacher Teams 185
access 57
accountability standards 201
adept MTSS schools 97, 101
administrative accountability 289
administrative leadership 6
adult behavior 37
adverse childhood experiences (ACEs) 153, 196
advocacy 258–267, 298; advocate early 262–263
AIMSweb Plus 58, 59, 61
alingual 141
antiracism wave of education reform 297
assessment tools 56–59
attention school psychologists 142–146
attention specialists 146–148
automatization 118–119

bad-hair moment 63
barrier identification 260
base funding 265
basic informal communication skills (BICS) 141
behavioral and mental health prevention 208–212
behavioral interventions 122
behavior intervention plans (BIPs) 226
benchmarking 32
Body of Liberties 48
Bolman, L. G. 8, 271
braided funding 264
brokers 249–250
Bronfenbrenner, U. 179
budgeting 80–81
Burnout Syndrome 118

caregiver factors 154
case manager model 99
case notes 103
cause-and-effect processes 13
change agents 216–217
charter schools 297
child refugees 156
civil rights 4
classroom teachers 98–99, 147
cognitive academic language proficiency (CALP) 141
cognitive-behavioral strategies 195
collaborative problem solving 38–39
Come-If-We-Call schools 175
Common Core State Standards 47
common sense 162
communicator 102
community-centric views 177
Community Health Investment, Modernization, and Excellence Act 162
computerized intervention programs 67
computer programs 66
computer time 66
contagion effect 208

Index 311

controlled chaos 54
CORE Phonics Survey 70
corporal punishment 47
corporate interest campaigns 4
Costner, Kevin 79
counterintuitive cultures 15–16
critical thinking skills 195
cultural brokering 177
cultural change 28
cultural competence 11
CVC (consonant–vowel–consonant) patterns 87

data-based decision making 37–38, 61–64, 289
data-triangulation chats 243
Deal, T. E. 8, 271
decentralized 164
dedicated funding 265
developmental MTSS schools 97
differentiated MTSS block scheduling 83–88
discipline 133
discretionary grant funding 264
distributed presentation style 98
documentation 144
do-it-yourself (DIY) benchmarking 58
Dual Capacity Framework 183

early childhood curriculum standards 164
early childhood MTSS structure 166–168
early childhood program standards 164
early childhood recommendations 152–169; federal law 161–163; funding 163–164; inclusion 158–160; six opportunities 157–166; standards 164–165; state and district policies 160–161; unions 165–166
early education opportunities 155
ecosystem 14
education field, realities 47–49
education malpractice 47
education policymaking 296
educator value 50–53
effective leadership 19
English-language learners 1, 34, 67
environmental trauma 127
ethnic match 177
evaluation tools 254–256
Every Student Succeeds Act (ESSA) 16, 83, 162, 265
evidence-based curriculum 117

FAIR (Fair, Accurate, Inclusive, and Respectful) Education Act 139
Fair Labor Standards Act 173, 174

family center 187–191
Family Educational Rights and Privacy Act 103
family engagement 172–191; family center and wellness opportunities 187–191; increase engagement, opportunities 180–183; *versus* "parental" engagement 177; school and student realities 173–175; shifting perspectives 175–176; student-centered academic sessions 185–186
family–teacher factors 182
family wellness opportunities 187–191
feedback looping 13, 30, 249–256, 288–289
fidelity 56, 58, 83, 253
Field of Dreams 79
fiscal resources, allocating 53–56
Five Core Propositions 55
fluency measures 129
formula funding 264
free appropriate public education (FAPE) 297
functional multi-tiered support 28
funding streams 263–265

Gender Support Plan 139
Gerrymandering 173
Glaser, B. G. 9
grade-level team meetings 88–89
grounded theory research 9
growth model 63

Hailee's Law 204
hard knowledge 38
Harvest Music Festival 2
Head Start Early Learning Outcomes framework 167
Health Insurance and Portability and Accountability Act (HIPPA) 236
Healthy Minds, Safe Schools 1, 239–240, 242, 243, 246
Hexagon Tool rubric 251
high-level skill 15
high-risk schools 89
high-stakes tests 289
human capital 29, 81
human capital support 35–37
hybrid committee selection process 96

implementation science 6
implicit bias 137, 138
implicit partnership naïveté 175
incentives 64
inclusiveness 30, 287
incremental correction systems 214
Industrial Revolution 173
infrastructure 79–80

institutional isomorphism 31
intermediate organizations 160
internal validity 84
intervention graph 121
intervention group 128–129
intervention log 121
intervention plan 121
iterative process 251

key members, program evaluation 251
kindergarten 154
Kingdon, J. W. 268
knee-jerk policy reactions 202

leadership 30, 286–287
Leadership, Inclusivity, Quality control, Universality, Implementation and feedback looping, and Data-based decision making (LIQUID) 2, 9
Leadership, Inclusivity, Quality control, Universality, Implementation and feedback looping, and Data-based decision making (LIQUID) model 9, *10*, 12, 18, 19, 28, 29–31, 34, 52, 177, 239, 256, 293
leadership commitment 42
leadership fidelity checks 33
legitimate educational interest 103
legitimization 103
Le Peletier, M. 133–134
leverage 261
LGBTQ+ 138, 139, 160
liaison 107
Lister, Joseph 29
Lord of the Flies 271
lower-risk schools 168
low socioeconomic schools 39

Maslow, A. 180
master schedule 82–83
medicaid and insurance 291
mental health providers 212, 236
mental health transition team 210
MTSS extension opportunities 89–90
MTSS meeting logs 126
multiple tiers of support appraisal 31–34
multi-tiered systems of support (MTSS) 6–8; administrator has decided that intervention blocks cannot be scheduled and that interventions should be taught within the classrooms 282; behavioral supports are too complicated to implement systematically 280; chair 98, 101–107; common barriers to implementation 269–284; comparing practices 17–19; counterintuitive cultures 15–16; data-based decision making 13; in elementary schools 5; evaluation frequency and intensity 251–254; foundations for 4–25; grade-level representative 98, 100–101; high-needs students are frequently absent or tardy for classes 280–281; implementation and feedback looping 13; inclusiveness 11; interventions are not being documented adequately 275; interventions are not being implemented with fidelity 274–275; leadership 10–11; meaningful change and law 16–17; organizational framing 8; our local education agency prefers identification for specific learning disabilities based on cognitive-achievement discrepancy model 283; parents or guardians do not want interventions 279–280; perception and value 19–20; planning and implementation timetable 90–92; principal has left the school, will any of the MTSS infrastructure that was created last 284; process 21–24; quality control 11–12; school does not engage in universal benchmarking 276–277; school does not have a principal who actively leads MTSS on campus 271–272; school does not have a principal who is on board with supporting MTSS 269–270; school does not have sufficient funding in terms of personnel and resources 276; school has teachers who are resistant to MTSS Despite training efforts 273–274; school lacks research-based curriculum or interventions 272–273; school psychologist does not honor teachers' intervention implementation or documentation 278–279; school staff perceives MTSS as a function of special education eligibility outcome 275–276; and special education intersection 133–135; students 14–15; teachers are overwhelmed, cannot take on new responsibilities 277–278; team development mirror exercise 41–42; theory 8–9; tier 1 instructional practices are not as effective as they should be and getting tier 3 supports 281–282; universality 12–13

National Association for the Education of Young Children 164
National Association of School Psychologists 109

National Board for Professional Teaching Standards 87
National Implementation Research Network 215
neo-institutional theory 31
nonsuicidal self-injury 145

Open-Door schools 175
Open House events 184
organizational framing 8
organizational psychology principles 2
outside evaluator 252
overcorrection 61
overcrowded classrooms 49
overspending meeting time 105

parent–child interactions 189
Patient Protection Affordable Care Act of 2010 203
peer coaching 253
Perry Preschool Program 154
Phase II Prioritization 243
Phase I Prioritization 243
physical capital 81
policy making 258–267
positive behavioral instructional supports (PBIS) 123
positive behavioral interventions 239
positive class culture 87
potential barriers, mental health 217
PREPaRE training curriculum 207
preventative student structures 201
proactive classroom management 226
problem-solving process 56, 106
program evaluation 249–256
progress monitoring 32
protective factors 135
public education 4, 5, 296
Public Law 197 202

qualitative teacher progress reports 129
quality control 30, 287–288

rate of improvement 32
red flags 205–208
reentry plan 210
reflection journaling 24–25
Reggio Emilia approach 154
relationship skills 209
reliability 83
research-based interventions 64–70
response to intervention (RTI) 7, 53–54
responsive adaptability 103
restorative justice 214
Road Trip to Learning 179

Safe2Tell program 205, 233
SafeVoice under Senate Bill 80 205
school-based mental health providers 239
school-centric views 177
school counselors 108–109
"school knows best" perspective 178
school psychologists 109–111, 142, 143
School Risk Assessment Survey (SRAS) 39, *40*
school safety 194–221
SEB MTSS benchmark screenings 231
SEB MTSS documentation 122–125
SEB MTSS student database 238
SEB MTSS student database structure 125–126
SEB MTSS team 226
SEB MTSS team meeting decision making 126–130
second-language acquisition factors 127
Semmelweis, Ignaz 29
Senate Bill 504 204
Shinn, M. R. 6
Skinner, B. F. 130
smart teams 28
social-emotional-behavioral learning 162
social-emotional-behavioral (SEB) MTSS 1, 6, 7, 33, 34, 68, 195, 225–246, 292; data-triangulation meetings 243–244; essential SEB MTSS team functions 236–237; interventions and progress monitoring 244–245; iterative phases 245–246; school administrators 233; school counselors 233–234; school nurse 235; school psychologists 234–235; SEB instruction and intervention 227–229; SEB MTSS meetings 237–239; SEB MTSS team members 232–233; social workers and licensed service providers 235–236; universal screening cycles 242–243
social-emotional learning (SEL) experiences 134
social-emotional learning (SEL) skills 195
social-emotional regulation 135
social implicit cognition 137
social justice 1, 5, 135
social perspectives 50–53
soft knowledge 38
special education eligibility 132–148; attention school psychologists 142–146; attention specialists 146–148; special considerations 137–142
special education teachers 111–112
specialists 107–108
stakeholder networks 259

strategic opportunism 41
strategic resource allocation 81
student-centered academic sessions (SCASs) 185–186
student-centric learning environment 178
Student Data Feedback Request Form 179, 180
student problems 129
student well-being 194–221; behavioral and mental health policies 199–205; trauma and emotional response 196–199
summer school 89, 90
systemic transformation 177

tactical advocacy steps 260
talented individual practitioners 2
teacher effectiveness 43
teacher efficacy 123
teacher motivation and compensation 290
teacher–student relationships 153
TeachStrong coalition partners 47
team processes 130
threat assessment team 210
Three As 143
three-pronged motivation approach 63
Three-Pronged Motivation Approach 64

tier 1, core curriculum 67
tier 3 supports 119
transitional MTSS schools 101
trauma-informed care 196
Trevor Project 139
triage model 145
triangulation, data sources 65, 238
troubleshooting guide 269–284

underfunding remedial supports 164
unfunded mandates 263
unicorns 142
unintended consequences 86, 198, 250
universal benchmarking 61
universality 30, 288
universal screening 28, 32
universal screening cycles 242–243

validity 83

well-run MTSS 130
whole school 243
Wilson Elementary School 68

Zeitgeist 4
zero-tolerance policies 218